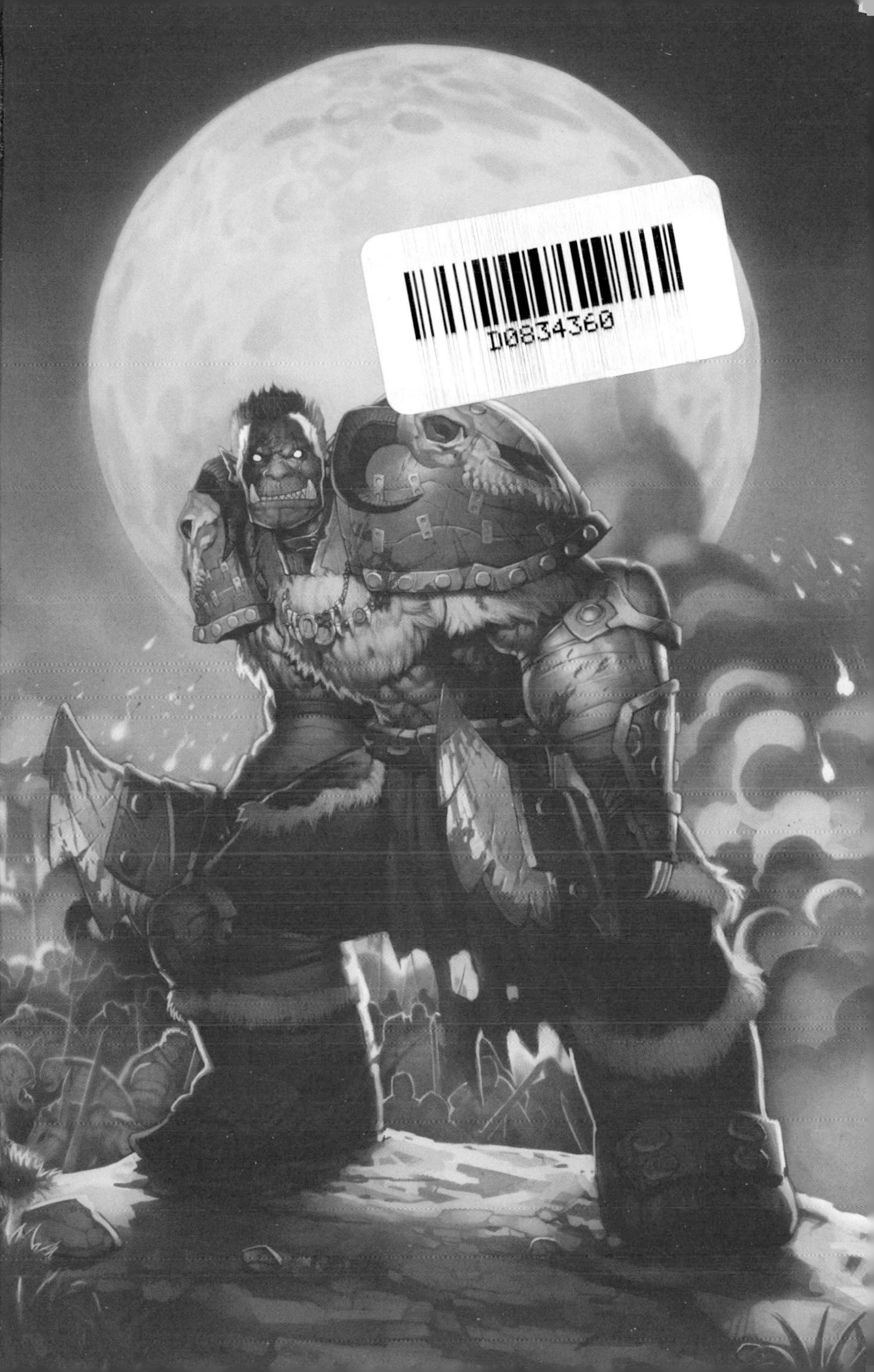

Warcraft Legends Vol. 1

Original Series Editors - Tim Beedle and Troy Lewter
Contributing Editors - Rob Tokar, Luis Reyes and Hyun Joo Kim
Original Associate Editor - Shannon Walters
Original Managing Editor - Vy Nguyen
Original Senior Designer - Louis Csontos
Original Graphic Designer - James Lee
Contributing Editor - Hyun Joo Kim
Layout and Lettering - Michael Paolilli and Lucas Rivera
Creative Consultant - Michael Paolilli
Cover Artist - UDON with Saejin Oh

BLIZZARD ENTERTAINMENT

Senior Vice President, Story & Franchise Development - Chris Metzen
Director, Story and Creative Development - James Waugh
Lead Editor, Publishing - Robert Simpson
Senior Editor - Cate Gary
Producer - Jeffrey Wong
Story Consultation and Development - Micky Neilson
Art Director - Glenn Rane
Vice President, Global Consumer Products - Matt Beecher
Senior Manager, Global Licensing - Byron Parnell
Additional Development - Ben Brode, Sean Copeland, Samwise Didier, Evelyn Fredericksen, Justin Parker, Charlotte Racioppo, Bob Richardson, Sean Wang

BLIZZARD ENTERTAINMENT

gear.blizzard.com

This book contains material originally published by TOKYOPOP Inc.

First Blizzard Entertainment printing: November 2016

ISBN: 978-0-9897001-4-6

10 9 8 7 6 5 4 3 2 1

Printed in China

WarCraft®

LEGENDS™

VOLUME ONE

BLIZZARD
ENTERTAINMENT

WARCRAFT

LEGENDS

VOLUME ONE

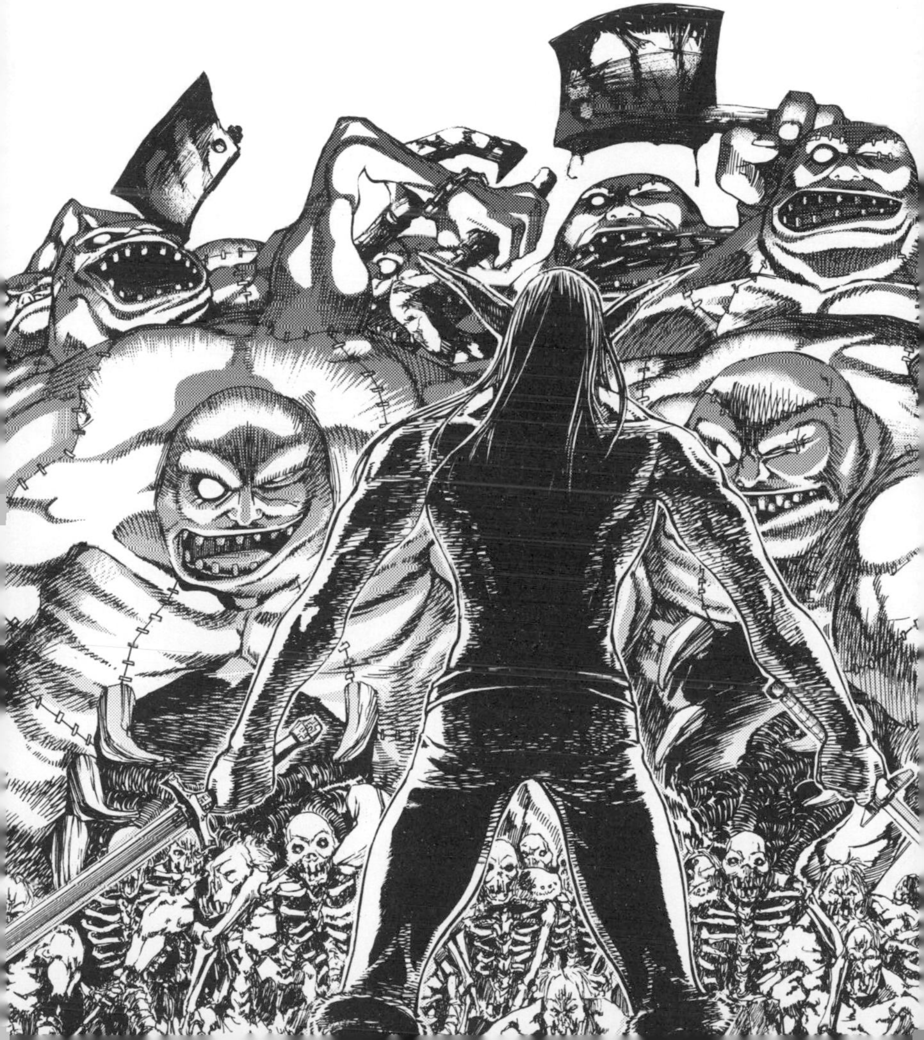

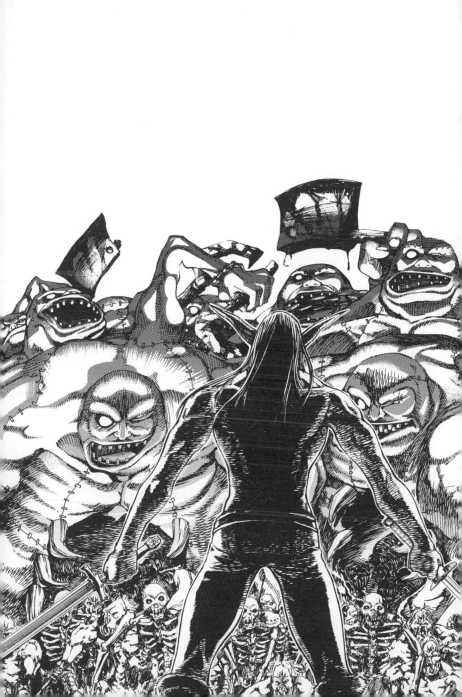

WARCRAFT

LEGENDS

VOLUME ONE

FALLEN

WRITTEN BY RICHARD A. KNAAK

ART BY JAE-HWAN KIM

EDITOR: TIM BEEDLE
CONTRIBUTING EDITOR: HYUN JOO KIM
ASSOCIATE EDITOR: SHANNON WATTERS
LETTERER: MICHAEL PAOLILLI

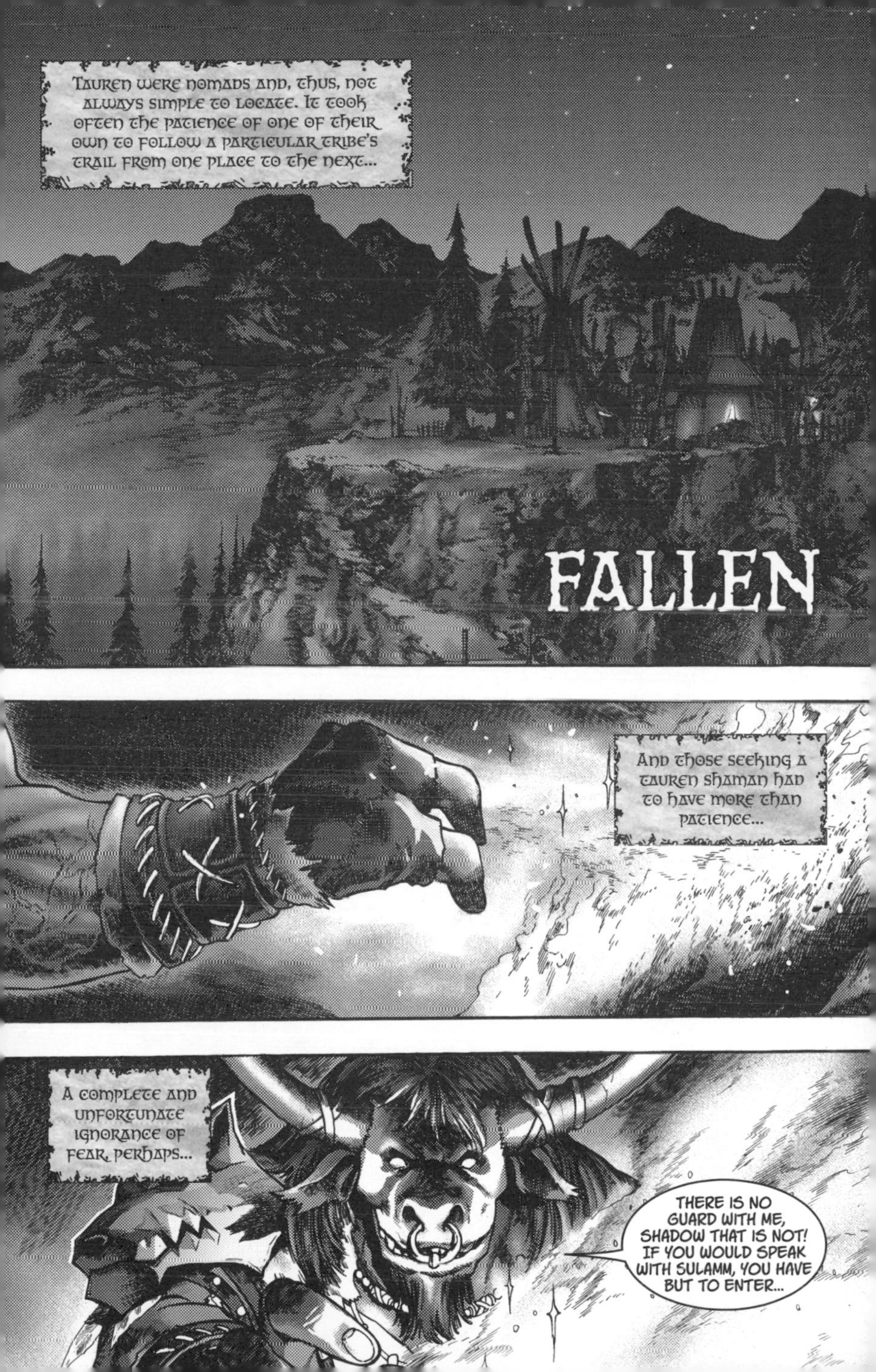
Tauren were nomads and, thus, not always simple to locate. It took often the patience of one of their own to follow a particular tribe's trail from one place to the next...
FALLEN
And those seeking a tauren shaman had to have more than patience...
A complete and unfortunate ignorance of fear, perhaps...
THERE IS NO GUARD WITH ME, SHADOW THAT IS NOT! IF YOU WOULD SPEAK WITH SULAMM, YOU HAVE BUT TO ENTER...

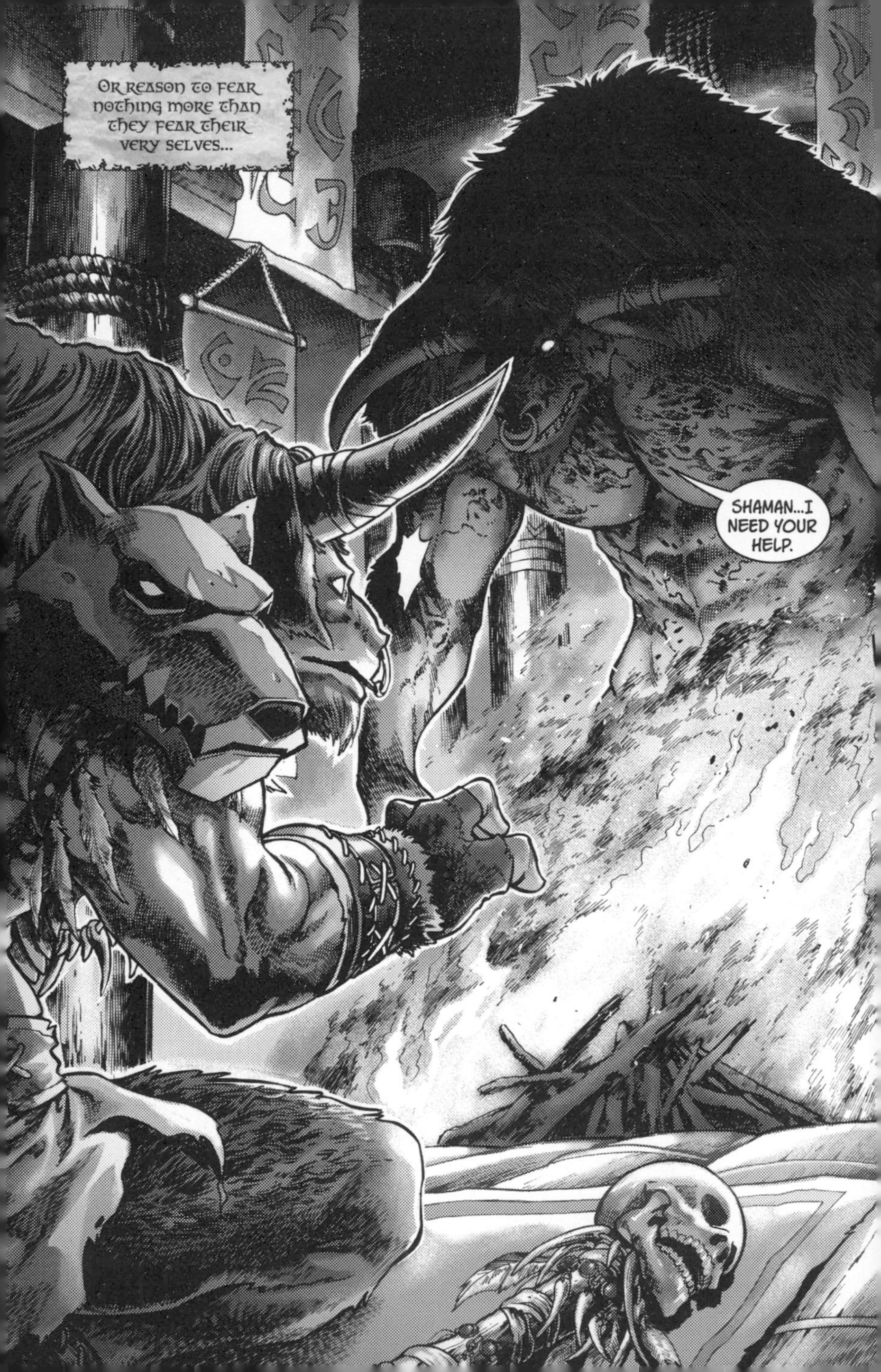
OR REASON TO FEAR NOTHING MORE THAN THEY FEAR THEIR VERY SELVES...
SHAMAN...I NEED YOUR HELP.

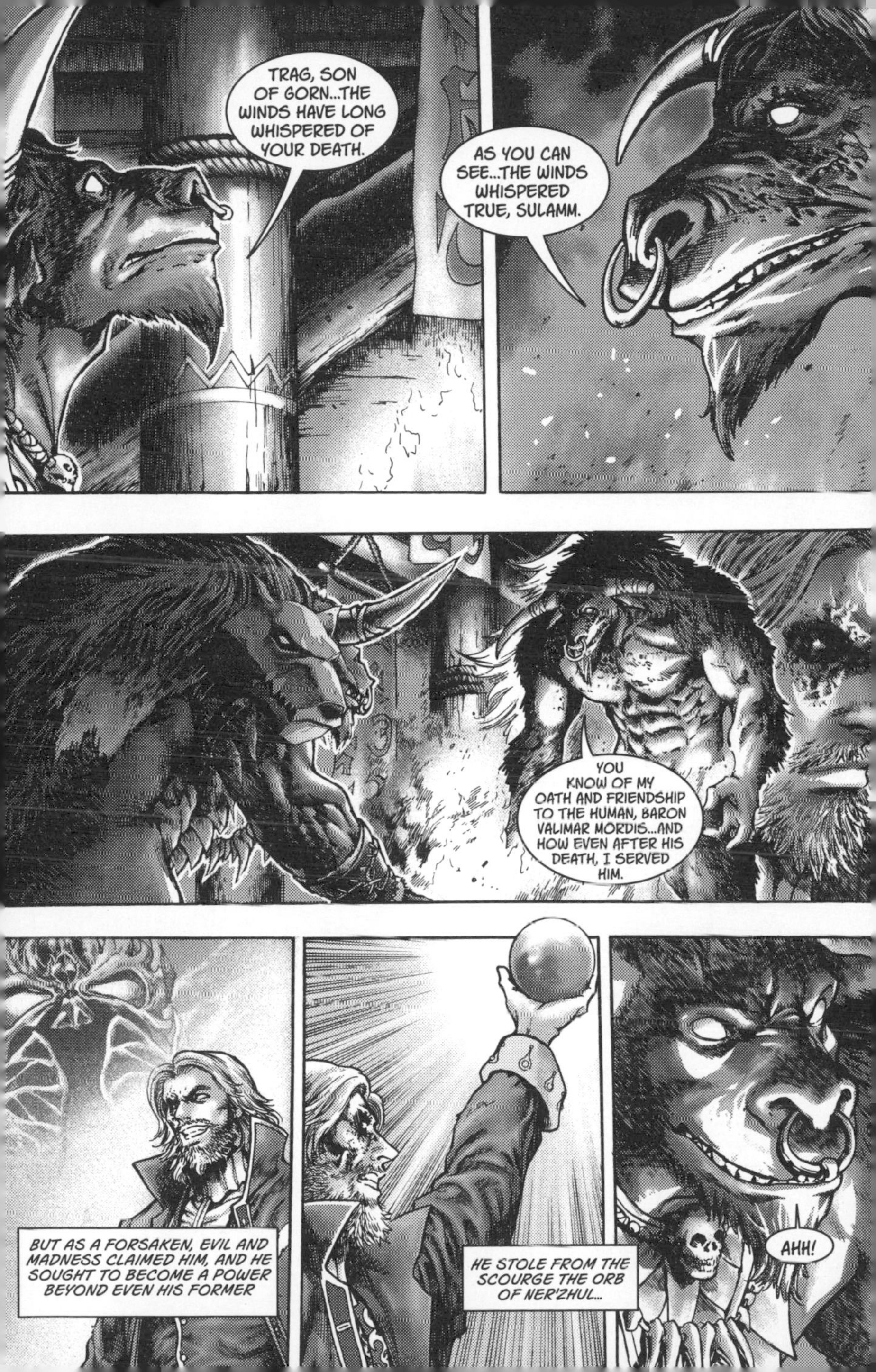
TRAG, SON OF GORN...THE WINDS HAVE LONG WHISPERED OF YOUR DEATH.
AS YOU CAN SEE...THE WINDS WHISPERED TRUE, SULAMM.
YOU KNOW OF MY OATH AND FRIENDSHIP TO THE HUMAN, BARON VALIMAR MORDIS...AND HOW EVEN AFTER HIS DEATH, I SERVED HIM.
BUT AS A FORSAKEN, EVIL AND MADNESS CLAIMED HIM, AND HE SOUGHT TO BECOME A POWER BEYOND EVEN HIS FORMER
HE STOLE FROM THE SCOURGE THE ORB OF NER'ZHUL...
AHH!

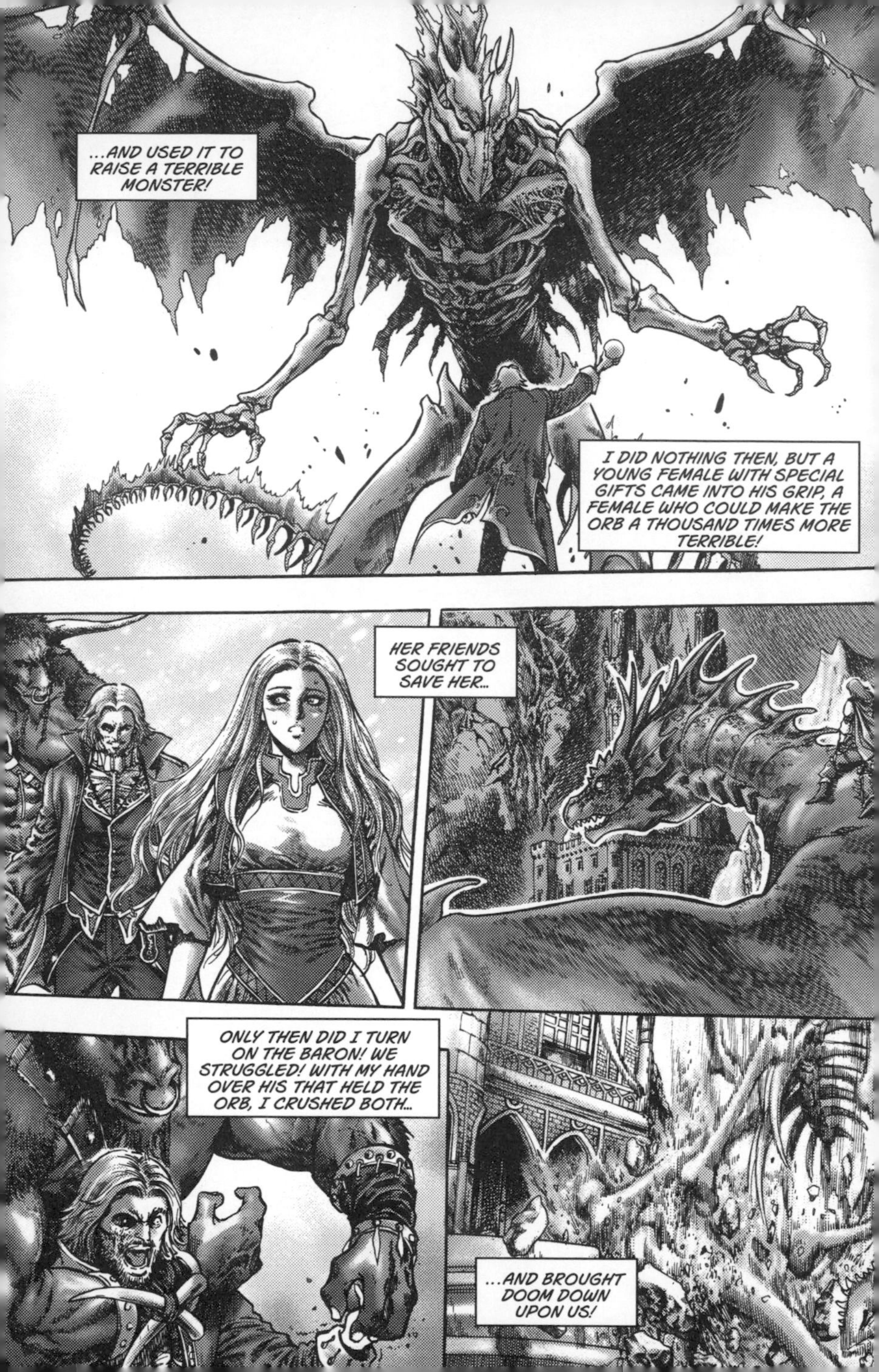
...AND USED IT TO RAISE A TERRIBLE MONSTER!
I DID NOTHING THEN, BUT A YOUNG FEMALE WITH SPECIAL GIFTS CAME INTO HIS GRIP, A FEMALE WHO COULD MAKE THE ORB A THOUSAND TIMES MORE TERRIBLE!
HER FRIENDS SOUGHT TO SAVE HER...
ONLY THEN DID I TURN ON THE BARON! WE STRUGGLED! WITH MY HAND OVER HIS THAT HELD THE ORB, I CRUSHED BOTH...
...AND BROUGHT DOOM DOWN UPON US!

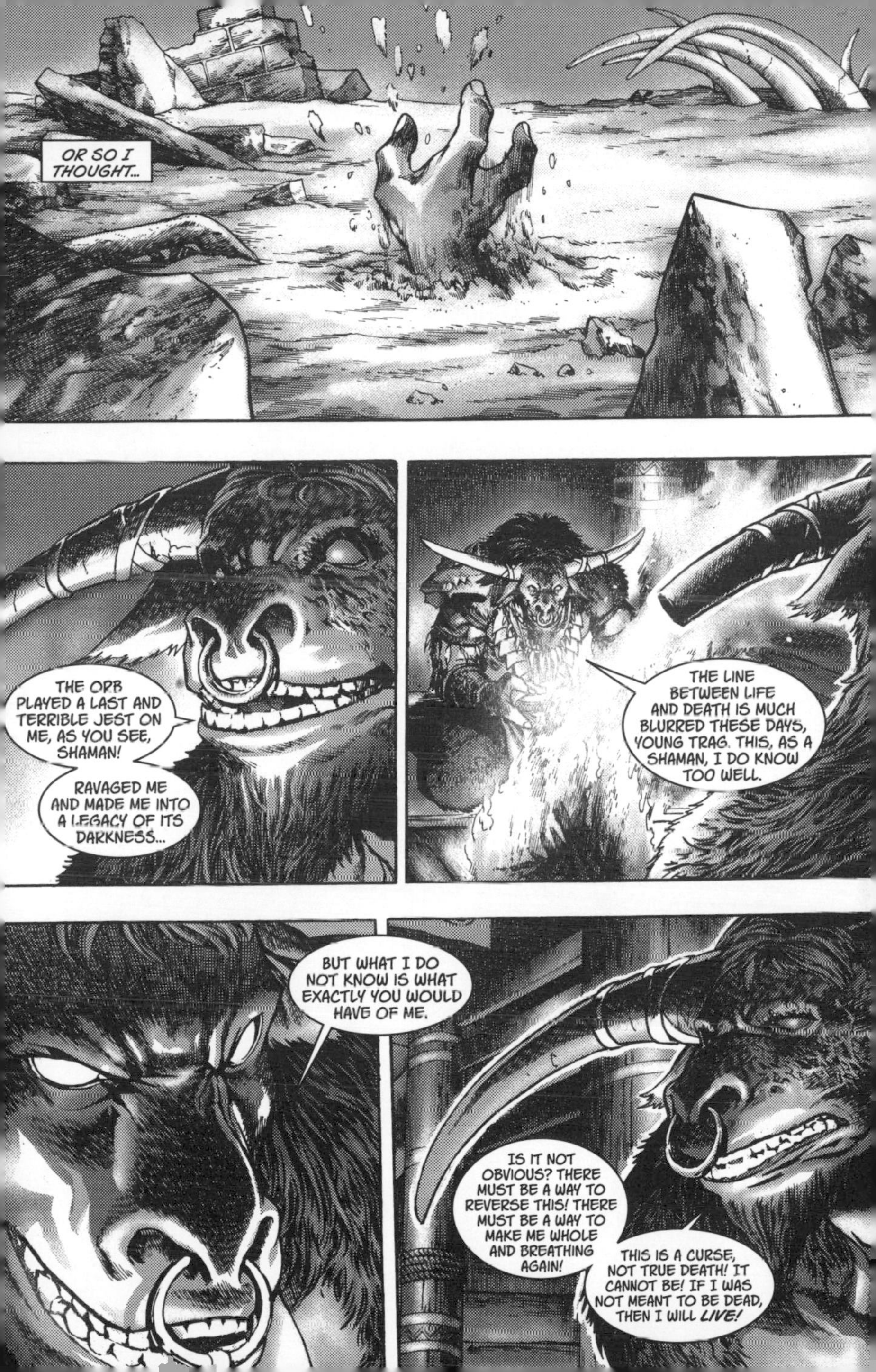
OR SO I THOUGHT...
THE ORB PLAYED A LAST AND TERRIBLE JEST ON ME, AS YOU SEE, SHAMAN!
RAVAGED ME AND MADE ME INTO A LEGACY OF ITS DARKNESS...
THE LINE BETWEEN LIFE AND DEATH IS MUCH BLURRED THESE DAYS, YOUNG TRAG. THIS, AS A SHAMAN, I DO KNOW TOO WELL.
BUT WHAT I DO NOT KNOW IS WHAT EXACTLY YOU WOULD HAVE OF ME.
IS IT NOT OBVIOUS? THERE MUST BE A WAY TO REVERSE THIS! THERE MUST BE A WAY TO MAKE ME WHOLE AND BREATHING AGAIN!
THIS IS A CURSE, NOT TRUE DEATH! IT CANNOT BE! IF I WAS NOT MEANT TO BE DEAD, THEN I WILL *LIVE!*

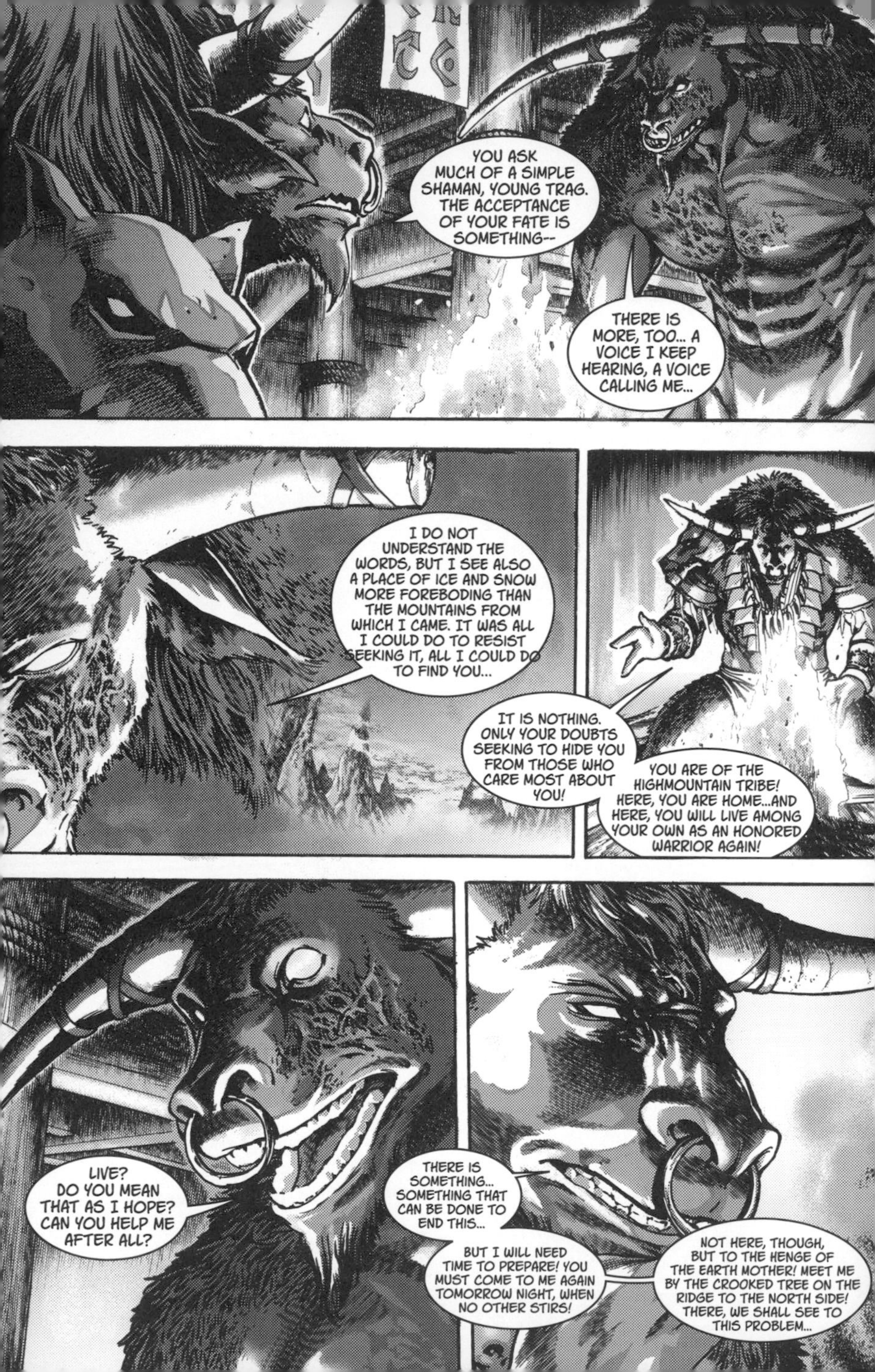
YOU ASK MUCH OF A SIMPLE SHAMAN, YOUNG TRAG. THE ACCEPTANCE OF YOUR FATE IS SOMETHING--
THERE IS MORE, TOO... A VOICE I KEEP HEARING, A VOICE CALLING ME...
I DO NOT UNDERSTAND THE WORDS, BUT I SEE ALSO A PLACE OF ICE AND SNOW MORE FOREBODING THAN THE MOUNTAINS FROM WHICH I CAME. IT WAS ALL I COULD DO TO RESIST SEEKING IT, ALL I COULD DO TO FIND YOU...
IT IS NOTHING. ONLY YOUR DOUBTS SEEKING TO HIDE YOU FROM THOSE WHO CARE MOST ABOUT YOU!
YOU ARE OF THE HIGHMOUNTAIN TRIBE! HERE, YOU ARE HOME...AND HERE, YOU WILL LIVE AMONG YOUR OWN AS AN HONORED WARRIOR AGAIN!
LIVE? DO YOU MEAN THAT AS I HOPE? CAN YOU HELP ME AFTER ALL?
THERE IS SOMETHING... SOMETHING THAT CAN BE DONE TO END THIS...
BUT I WILL NEED TIME TO PREPARE! YOU MUST COME TO ME AGAIN TOMORROW NIGHT, WHEN NO OTHER STIRS!
NOT HERE, THOUGH, BUT TO THE HENGE OF THE EARTH MOTHER! MEET ME BY THE CROOKED TREE ON THE RIDGE TO THE NORTH SIDE! THERE, WE SHALL SEE TO THIS PROBLEM...

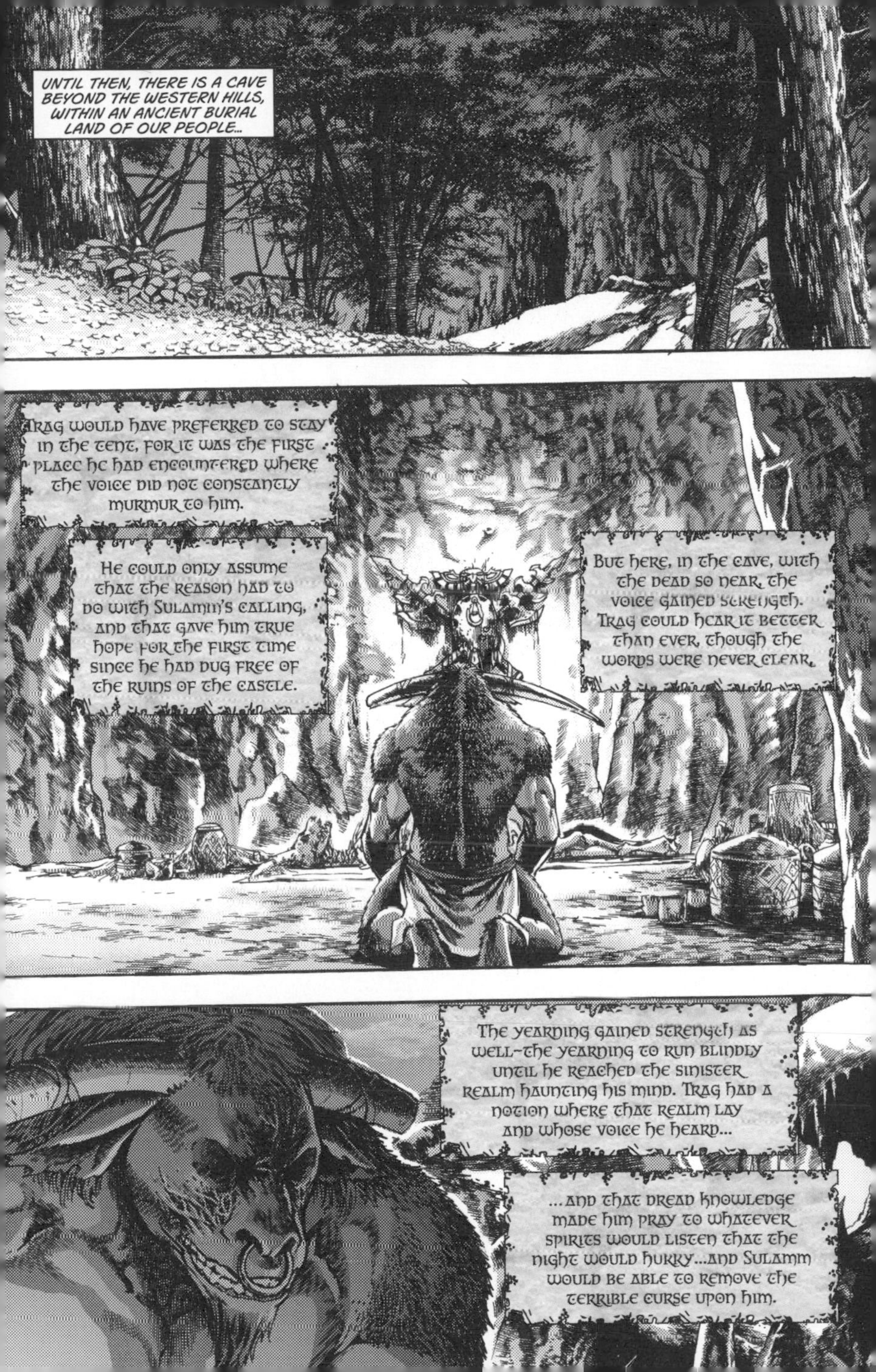
UNTIL THEN, THERE IS A CAVE BEYOND THE WESTERN HILLS, WITHIN AN ANCIENT BURIAL LAND OF OUR PEOPLE...
Trag would have preferred to stay in the tent, for it was the first place he had encountered where the voice did not constantly murmur to him.
He could only assume that the reason had to do with Sulamin's calling, and that gave him true hope for the first time since he had dug free of the ruins of the castle.
But here, in the cave, with the dead so near, the voice gained strength. Trag could hear it better than ever, though the words were never clear.
The yearning gained strength as well—the yearning to run blindly until he reached the sinister realm haunting his mind. Trag had a notion where that realm lay and whose voice he heard...
...and that dread knowledge made him pray to whatever spirits would listen that the night would hurry...and Sulamm would be able to remove the terrible curse upon him.

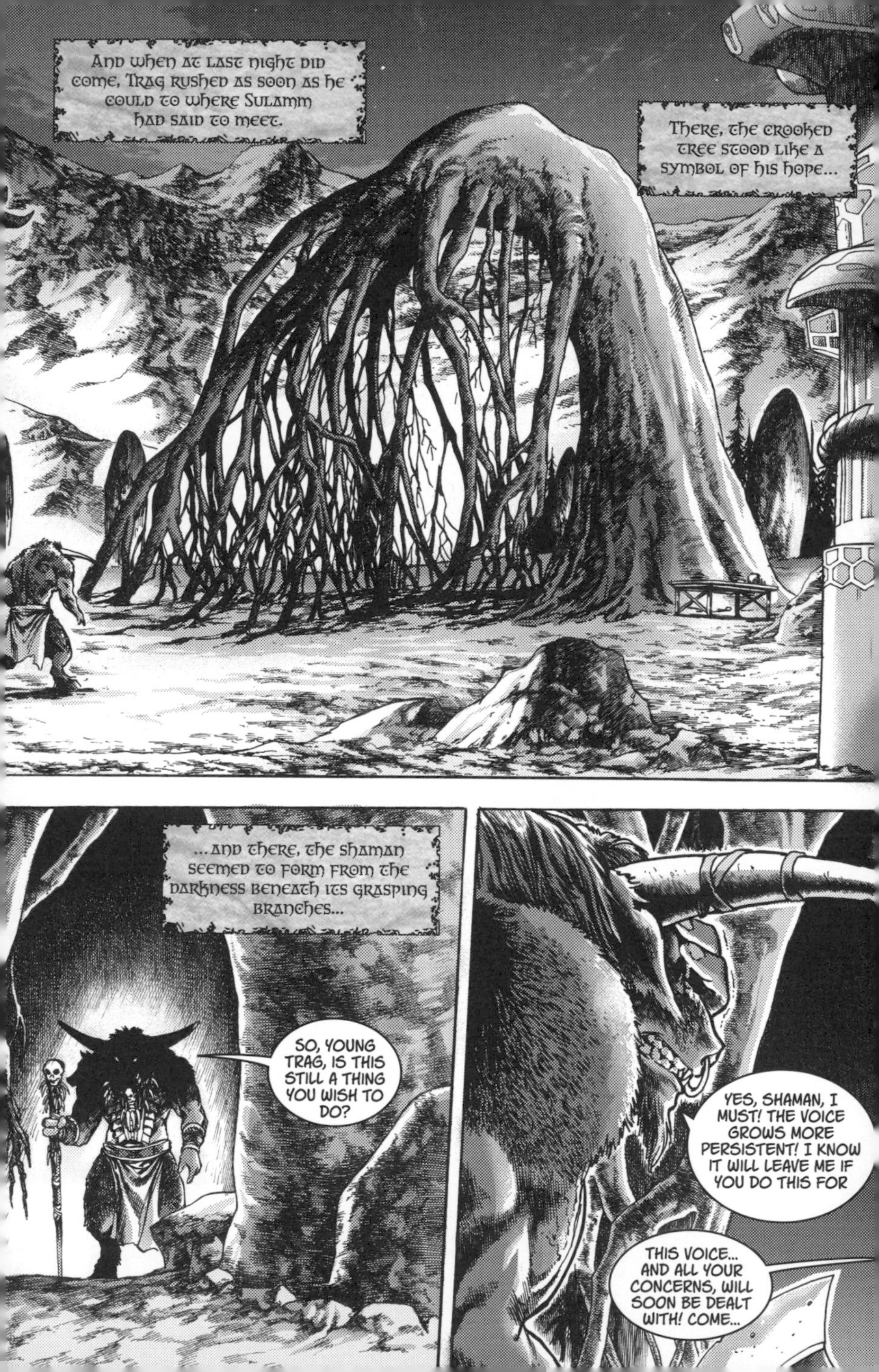
And when at last night did come, Trag rushed as soon as he could to where Sulamm had said to meet.
There, the crooked tree stood like a symbol of his hope...
...and there, the shaman seemed to form from the darkness beneath its grasping branches...
SO, YOUNG TRAG, IS THIS STILL A THING YOU WISH TO DO?
YES, SHAMAN, I MUST! THE VOICE GROWS MORE PERSISTENT! I KNOW IT WILL LEAVE ME IF YOU DO THIS FOR
THIS VOICE... AND ALL YOUR CONCERNS, WILL SOON BE DEALT WITH! COME...

WHAT'S THIS?

YOU MUST KNEEL IN THE MIDDLE OF THIS PATTERN WITH YOUR EYES SHUT. I WILL SIT BEYOND YOUR HEAD.

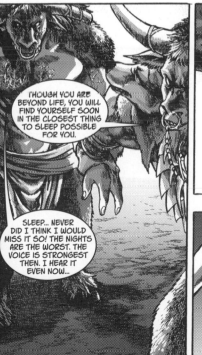

THOUGH YOU ARE BEYOND LIFE, YOU WILL FIND YOURSELF SOON IN THE CLOSEST THING TO SLEEP POSSIBLE FOR YOU.

SLEEP... NEVER DID I THINK I WOULD MISS IT SO! THE NIGHTS ARE THE WORST. THE VOICE IS STRONGEST THEN. I HEAR IT EVEN NOW...

BE AT EASE... I WILL SOON END YOUR SUFFERING...

TO LIVE AGAIN...

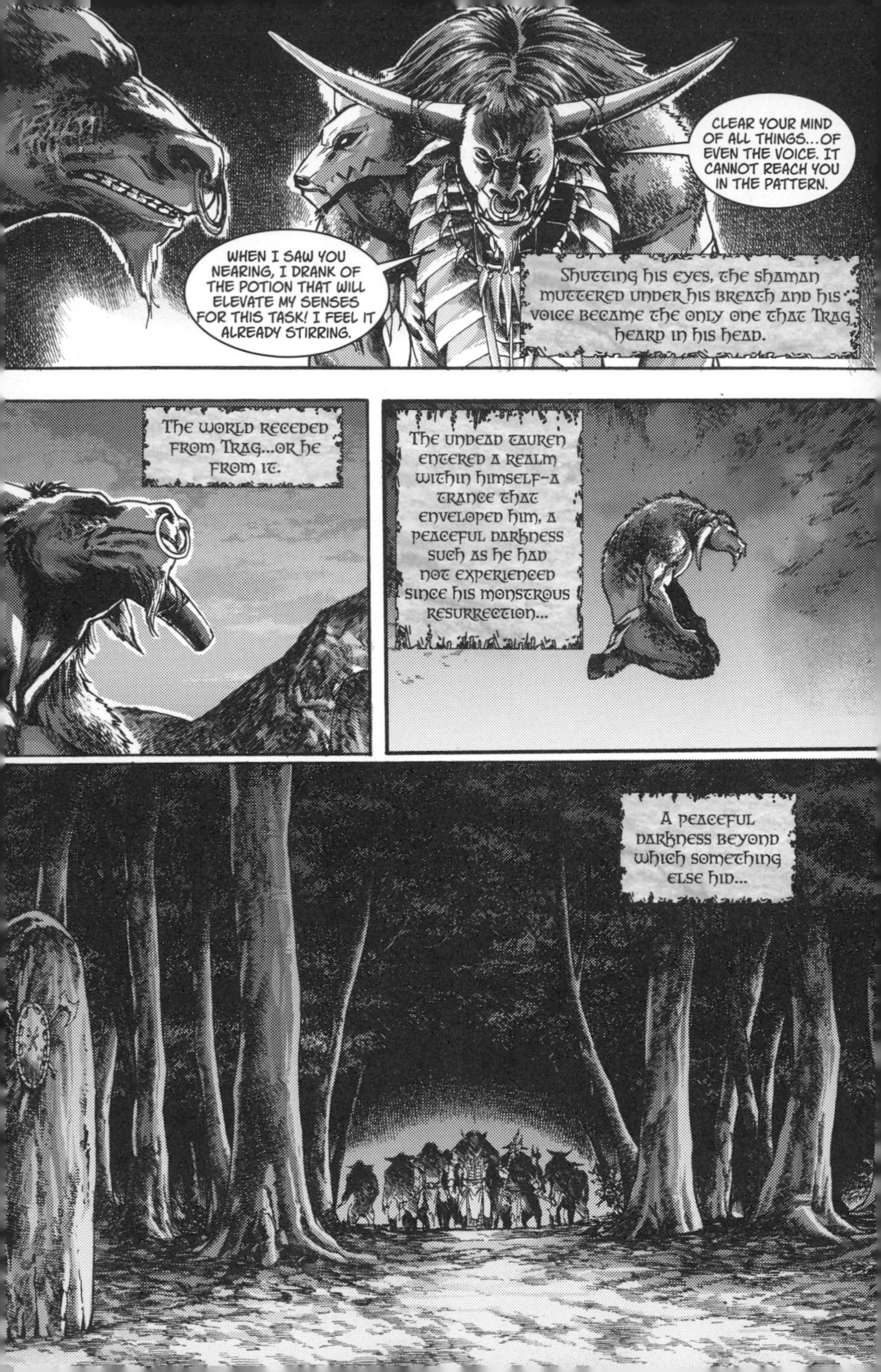
WHEN I SAW YOU NEARING, I DRANK OF THE POTION THAT WILL ELEVATE MY SENSES FOR THIS TASK! I FEEL IT ALREADY STIRRING.
CLEAR YOUR MIND OF ALL THINGS...OF EVEN THE VOICE. IT CANNOT REACH YOU IN THE PATTERN.
Shutting his eyes, the shaman muttered under his breath and his voice became the only one that Trag heard in his head.
The world receded from Trag...or he from it.
The undead tauren entered a realm within himself—a trance that enveloped him, a peaceful darkness such as he had not experienced since his monstrous resurrection...
A peaceful darkness beyond which something else hid...

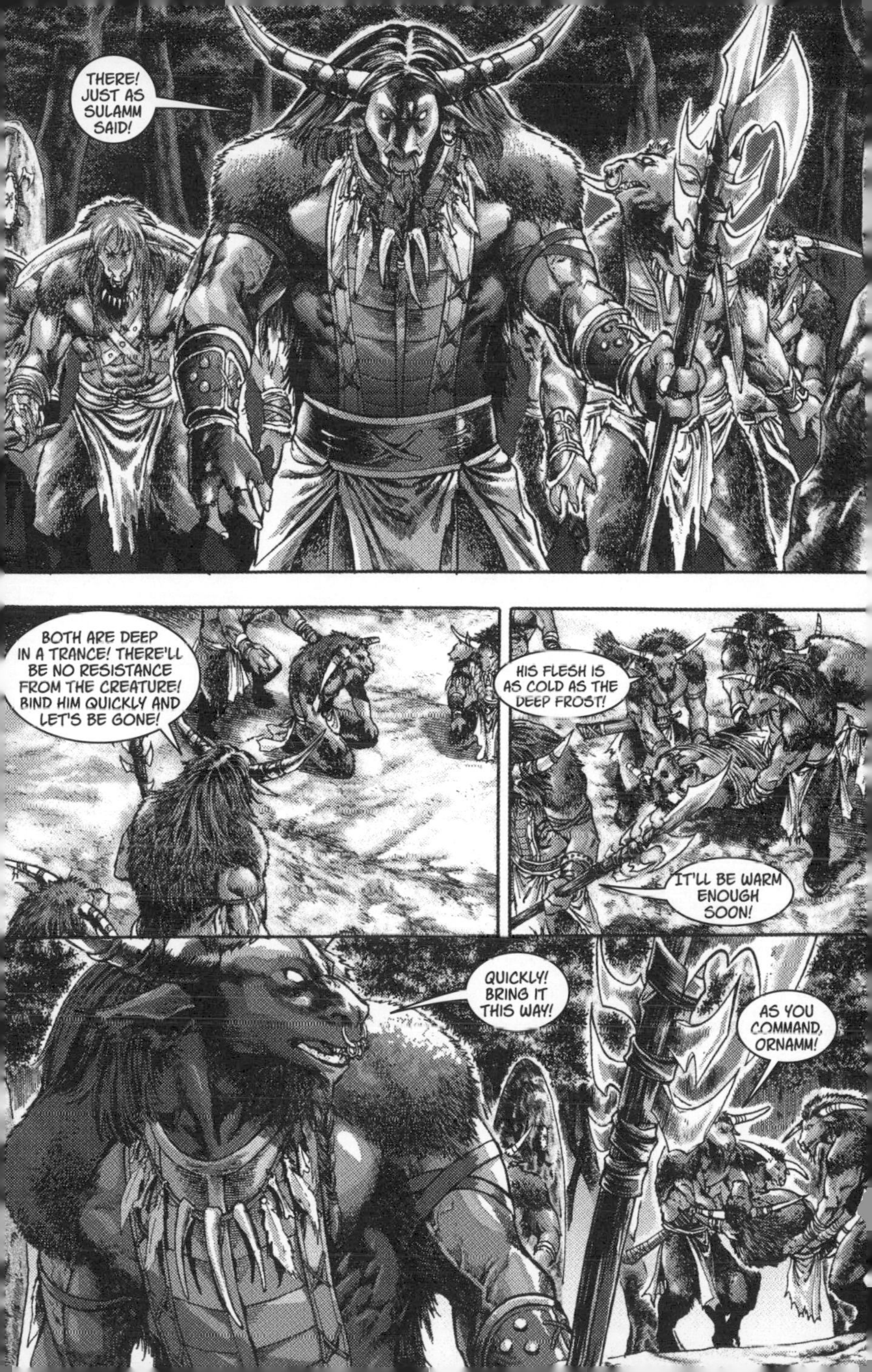
THERE! JUST AS SULAMM SAID!
BOTH ARE DEEP IN A TRANCE! THERE'LL BE NO RESISTANCE FROM THE CREATURE! BIND HIM QUICKLY AND LET'S BE GONE!
HIS FLESH IS AS COLD AS THE DEEP FROST!
IT'LL BE WARM ENOUGH SOON!
QUICKLY! BRING IT THIS WAY!
AS YOU COMMAND, ORNAMM!

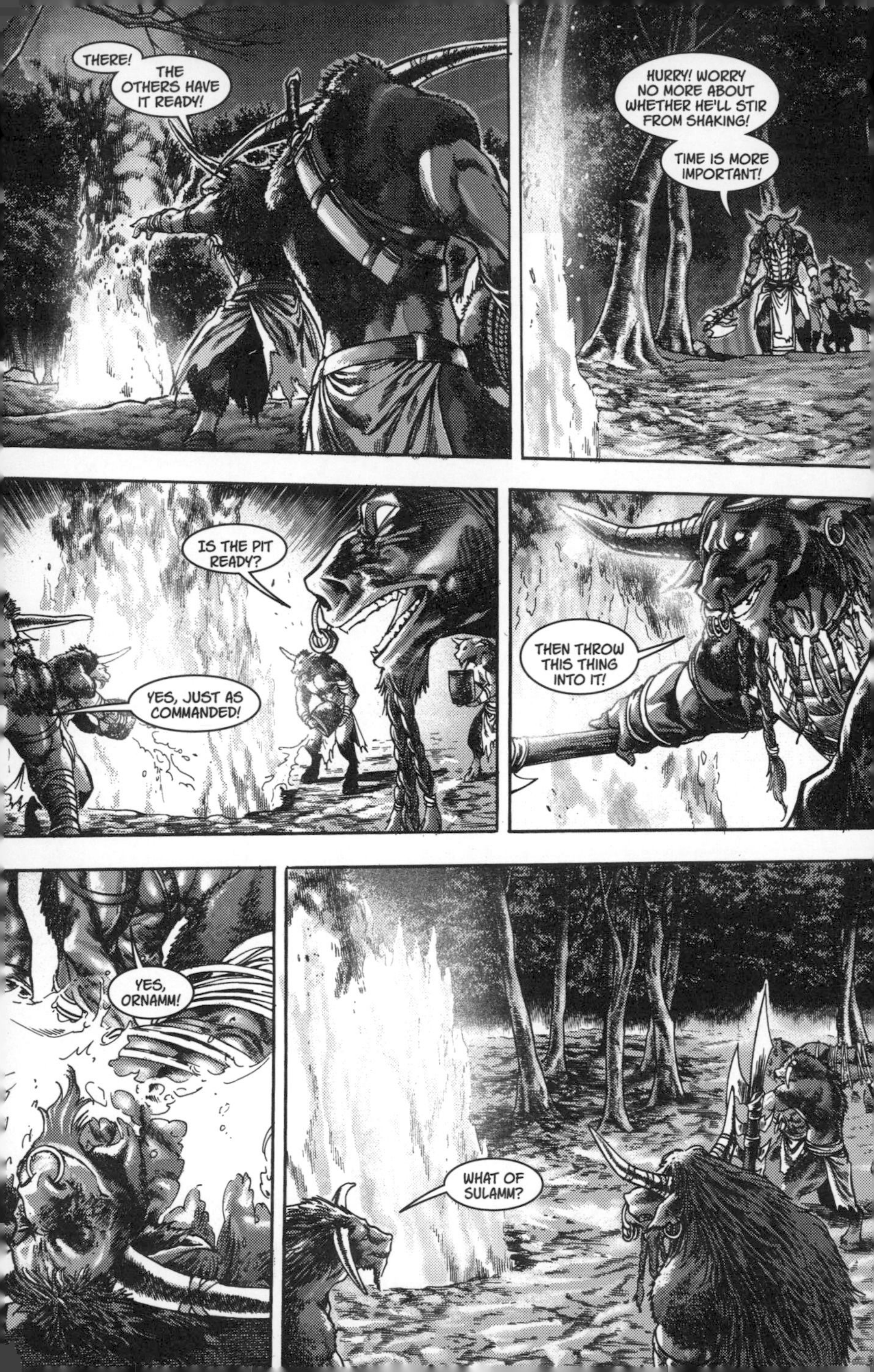
THERE!
THE OTHERS HAVE IT READY!
HURRY! WORRY NO MORE ABOUT WHETHER HE'LL STIR FROM SHAKING!
TIME IS MORE IMPORTANT!
IS THE PIT READY?
YES, JUST AS COMMANDED!
THEN THROW THIS THING INTO IT!
YES, ORNAMM!
WHAT OF SULAMM?

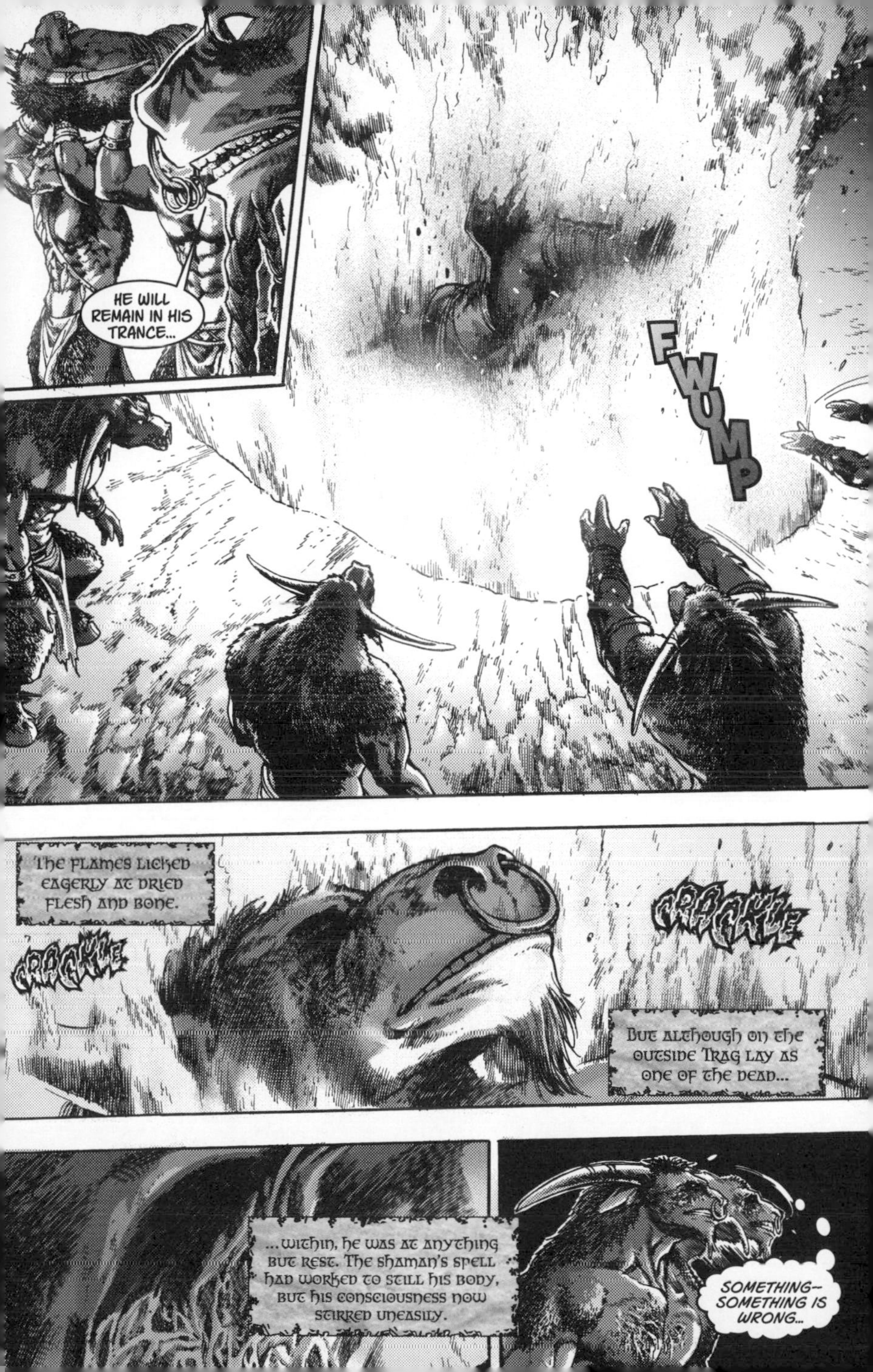
HE WILL REMAIN IN HIS TRANCE...
FWUMP
The flames licked eagerly at dried flesh and bone.
CRACKLE
CRACKLE
But although on the outside Trag lay as one of the dead...
...within, he was at anything but rest. The shaman's spell had worked to still his body, but his consciousness now stirred uneasily.
SOMETHING— SOMETHING IS WRONG...

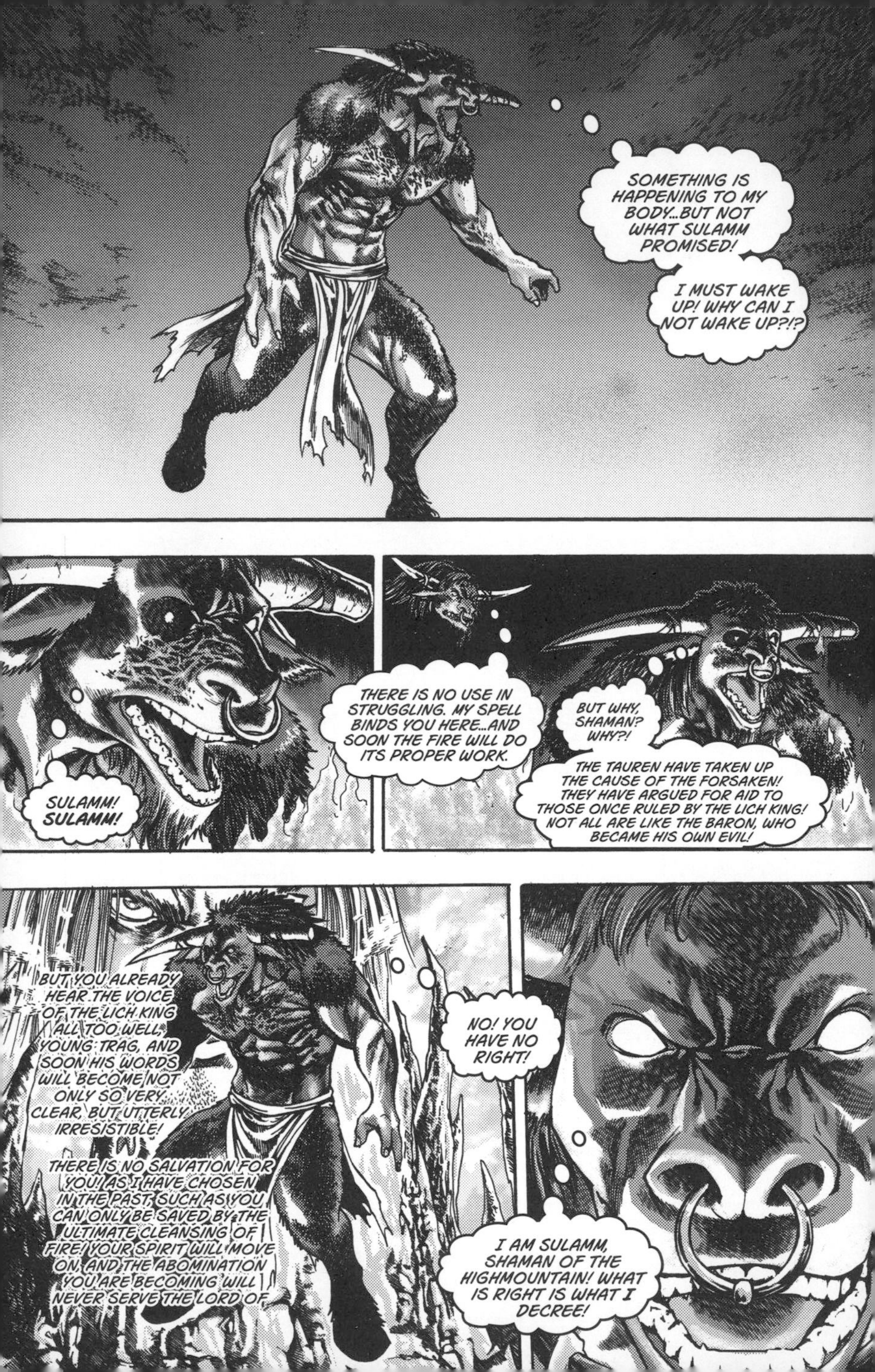
SOMETHING IS HAPPENING TO MY BODY...BUT NOT WHAT SULAMM PROMISED!
I MUST WAKE UP! WHY CAN I NOT WAKE UP?!?
SULAMM! SULAMM!
THERE IS NO USE IN STRUGGLING. MY SPELL BINDS YOU HERE...AND SOON THE FIRE WILL DO ITS PROPER WORK.
BUT WHY, SHAMAN? WHY?!
THE TAUREN HAVE TAKEN UP THE CAUSE OF THE FORSAKEN! THEY HAVE ARGUED FOR AID TO THOSE ONCE RULED BY THE LICH KING! NOT ALL ARE LIKE THE BARON, WHO BECAME HIS OWN EVIL!
BUT YOU ALREADY HEAR THE VOICE OF THE LICH KING ALL TOO WELL, YOUNG TRAG, AND SOON HIS WORDS WILL BECOME NOT ONLY SO VERY CLEAR, BUT UTTERLY IRRESISTIBLE!
THERE IS NO SALVATION FOR YOU! AS I HAVE CHOSEN IN THE PAST, SUCH AS YOU CAN ONLY BE SAVED BY THE ULTIMATE CLEANSING OF FIRE! YOUR SPIRIT WILL MOVE ON, AND THE ABOMINATION YOU ARE BECOMING WILL NEVER SERVE THE LORD OF
NO! YOU HAVE NO RIGHT!
I AM SULAMM, SHAMAN OF THE HIGHMOUNTAIN! WHAT IS RIGHT IS WHAT I DECREE!

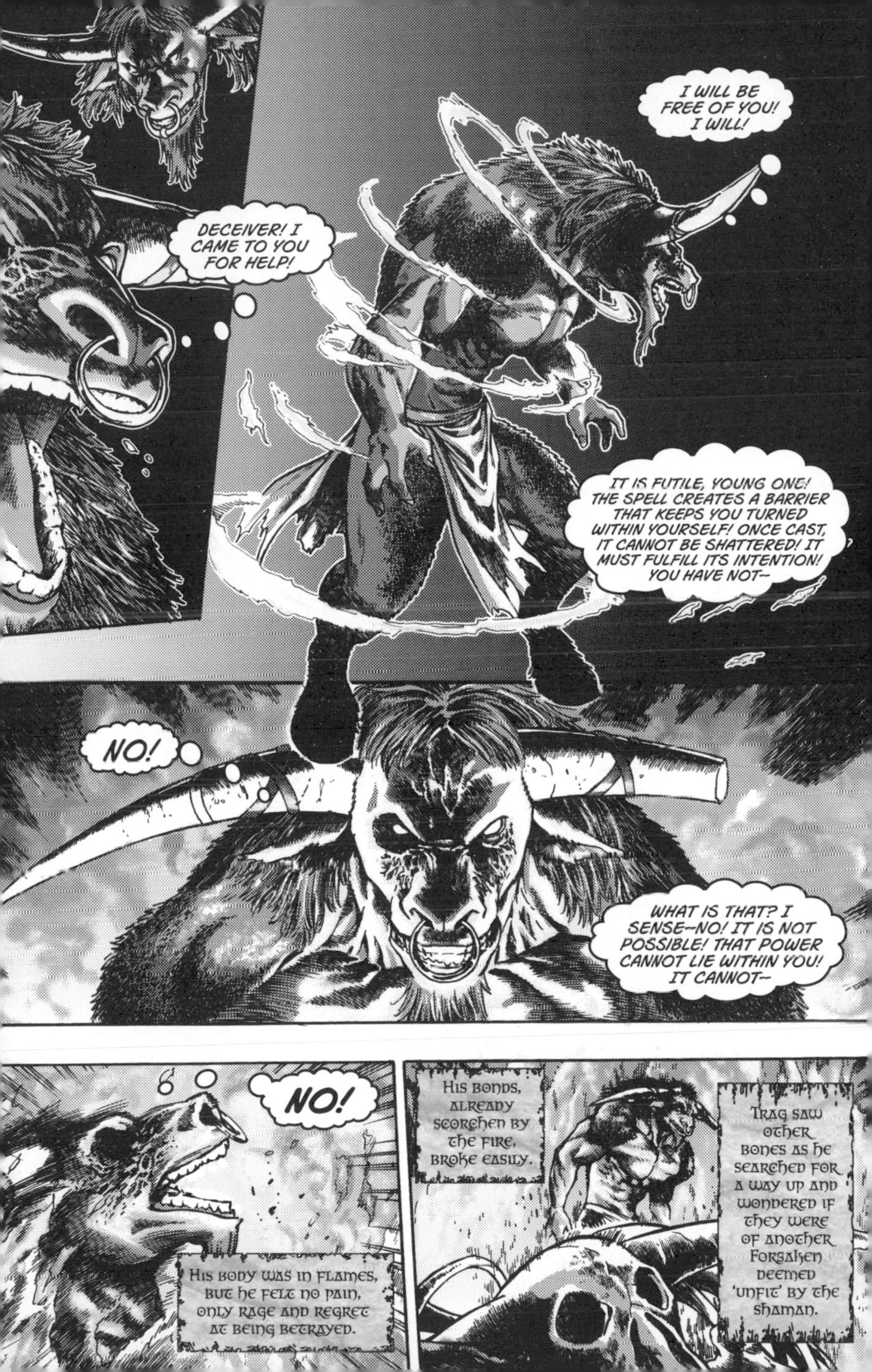
DECEIVER! I CAME TO YOU FOR HELP!
I WILL BE FREE OF YOU! I WILL!
IT IS FUTILE, YOUNG ONE! THE SPELL CREATES A BARRIER THAT KEEPS YOU TURNED WITHIN YOURSELF! ONCE CAST, IT CANNOT BE SHATTERED! IT MUST FULFILL ITS INTENTION! YOU HAVE NOT--
NO!
WHAT IS THAT? I SENSE--NO! IT IS NOT POSSIBLE! THAT POWER CANNOT LIE WITHIN YOU! IT CANNOT--
NO!
His body was in flames, but he felt no pain, only rage and regret at being betrayed.
His bonds, already scorched by the fire, broke easily.
Trag saw other bones as he searched for a way up and wondered if they were of another Forsaken deemed 'unfit' by the shaman.

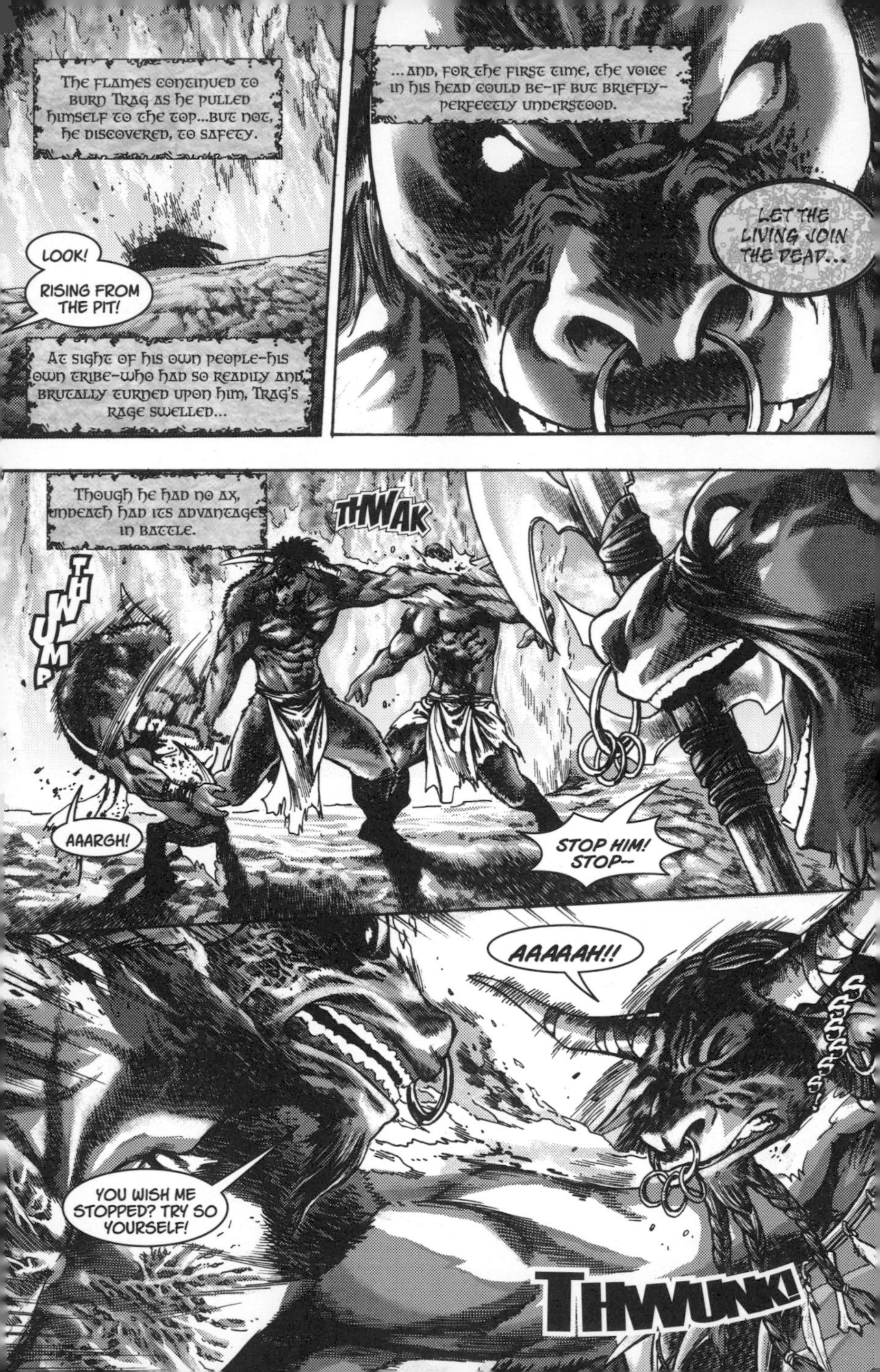

The flames continued to burn Trag as he pulled himself to the top...but not, he discovered, to safety.
LOOK!
RISING FROM THE PIT!
At sight of his own people–his own tribe–who had so readily and brutally turned upon him, Trag's rage swelled...
...and, for the first time, the voice in his head could be–if but briefly–perfectly understood.
LET THE LIVING JOIN THE DEAD...
Though he had no ax, undeath had its advantages in battle.
THWAK
THWUMP
AAARGH!
STOP HIM! STOP--
AAAAAH!!
YOU WISH ME STOPPED? TRY SO YOURSELF!
THWUNK!

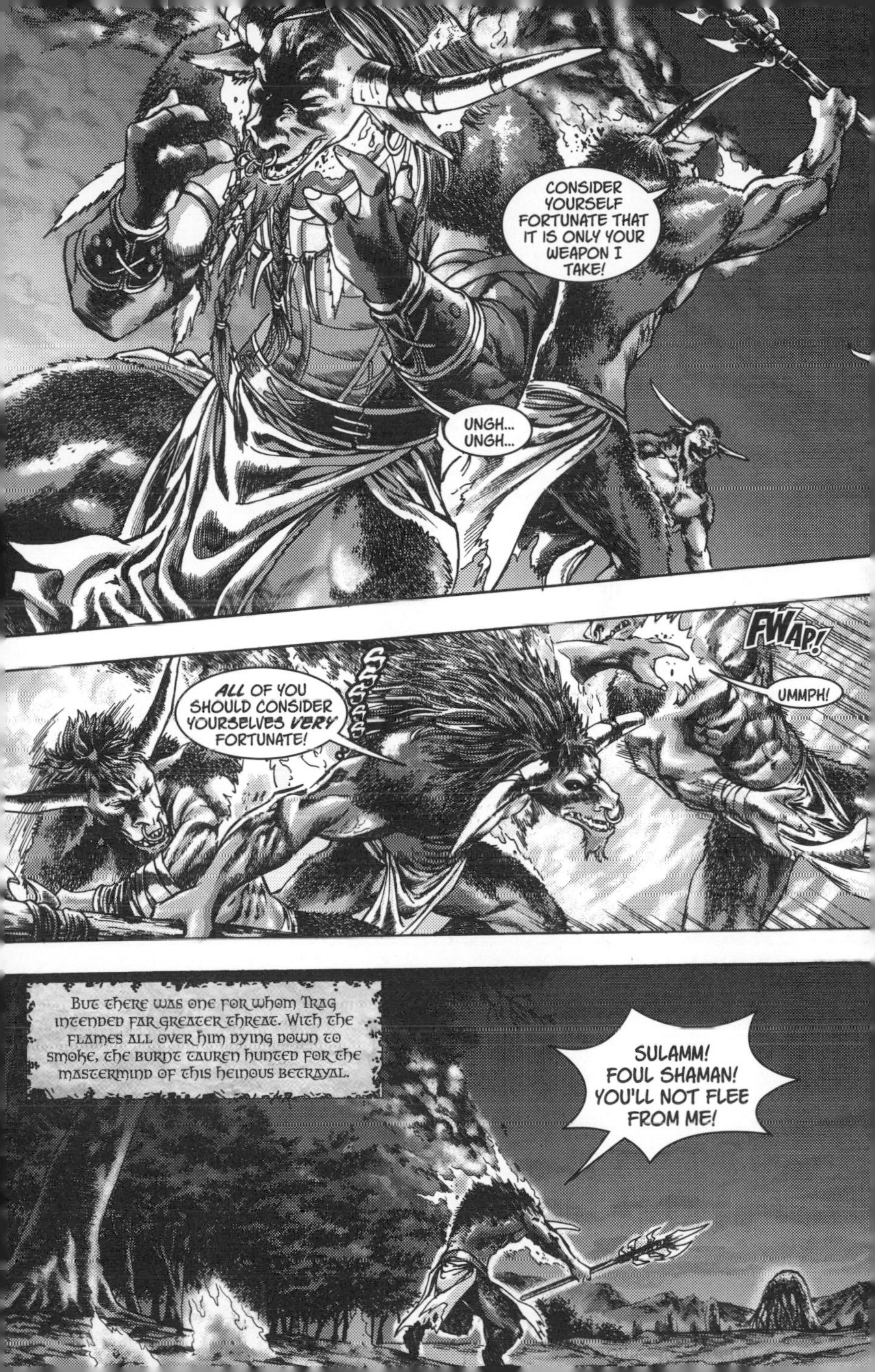
CONSIDER YOURSELF FORTUNATE THAT IT IS ONLY YOUR WEAPON I TAKE!
UNGH... UNGH...
ALL OF YOU SHOULD CONSIDER YOURSELVES VERY FORTUNATE!
FWAP!
UMMPH!
But there was one for whom Trag intended far greater threat. With the flames all over him dying down to smoke, the burnt tauren hunted for the mastermind of this heinous betrayal.
SULAMM! FOUL SHAMAN! YOU'LL NOT FLEE FROM ME!

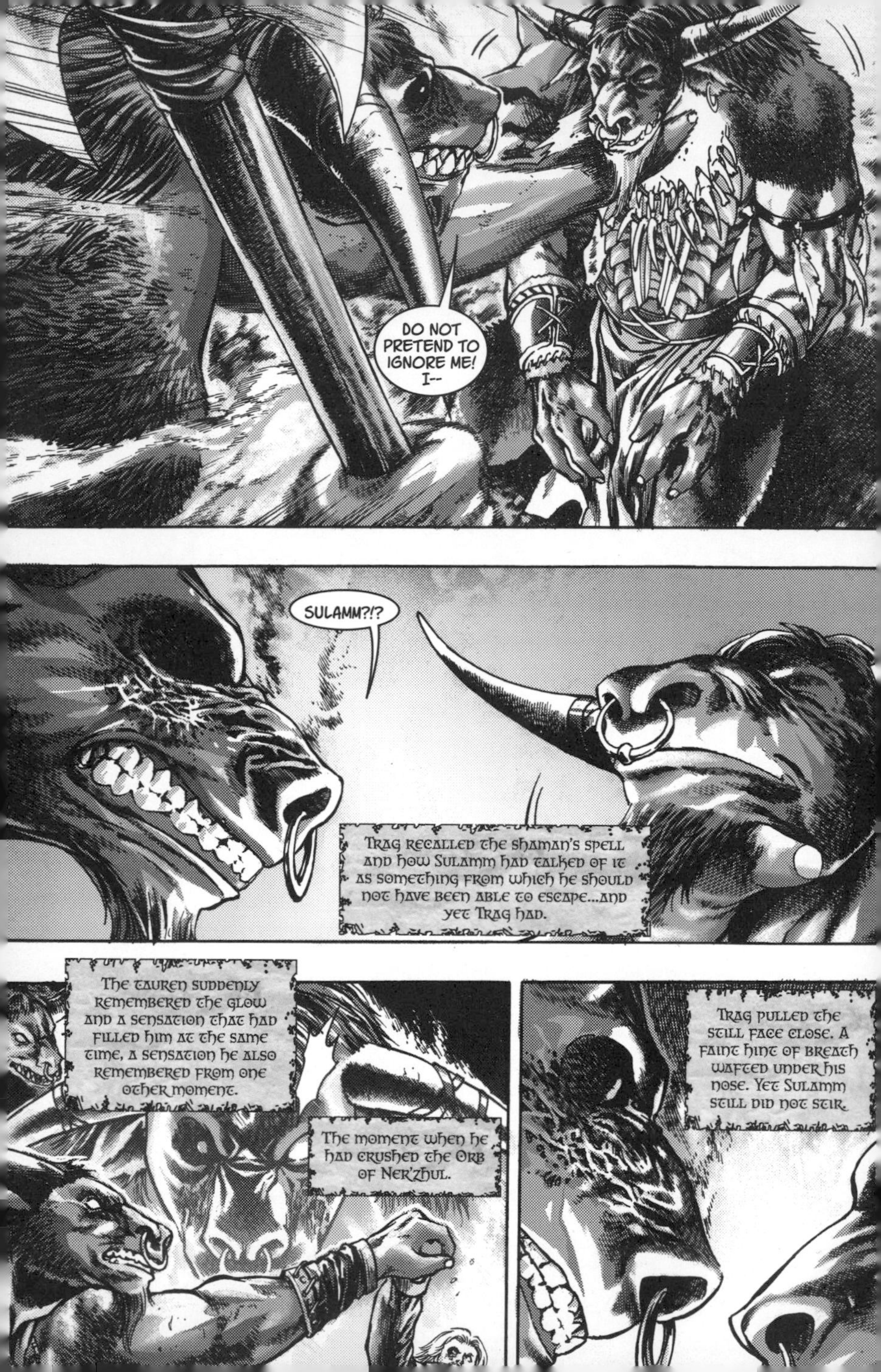
DO NOT PRETEND TO IGNORE ME! I--
SULAMM?!?
Trag recalled the shaman's spell and how Sulamm had talked of it as something from which he should not have been able to escape...and yet Trag had.
The tauren suddenly remembered the glow and a sensation that had filled him at the same time, a sensation he also remembered from one other moment.
The moment when he had crushed the Orb of Ner'zhul.
Trag pulled the still face close. A faint hint of breath wafted under his nose. Yet Sulamm still did not stir.

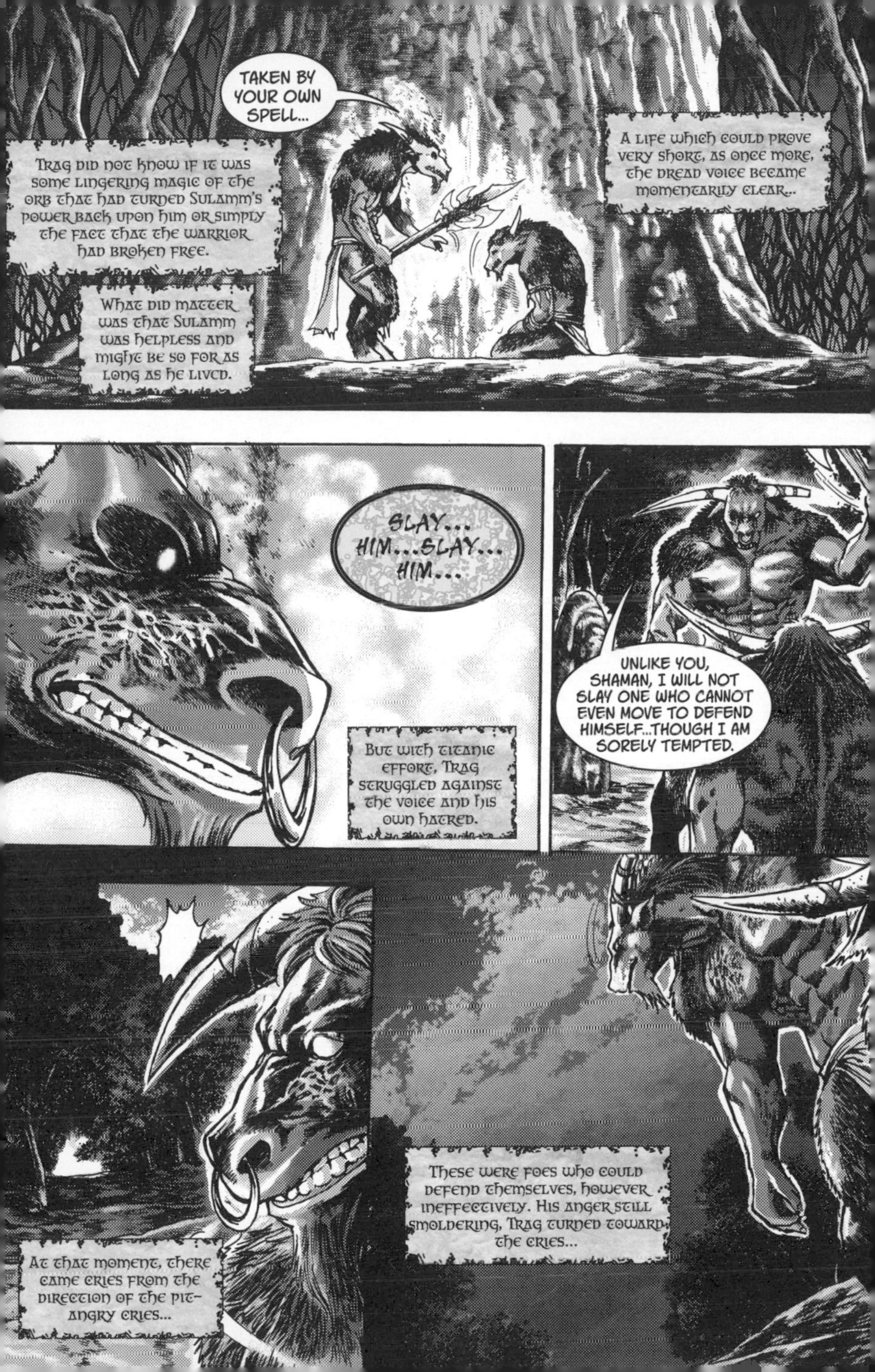
Trag did not know if it was some lingering magic of the orb that had turned Sulamm's power back upon him or simply the fact that the warrior had broken free.
TAKEN BY YOUR OWN SPELL...
What did matter was that Sulamm was helpless and might be so for as long as he lived.
A life which could prove very short, as once more, the dread voice became momentarily clear...
SLAY... HIM...SLAY... HIM...
But with titanic effort, Trag struggled against the voice and his own hatred.
UNLIKE YOU, SHAMAN, I WILL NOT SLAY ONE WHO CANNOT EVEN MOVE TO DEFEND HIMSELF...THOUGH I AM SORELY TEMPTED.
At that moment, there came cries from the direction of the pit-angry cries...
These were foes who could defend themselves, however ineffectively. His anger still smoldering, Trag turned toward the cries...

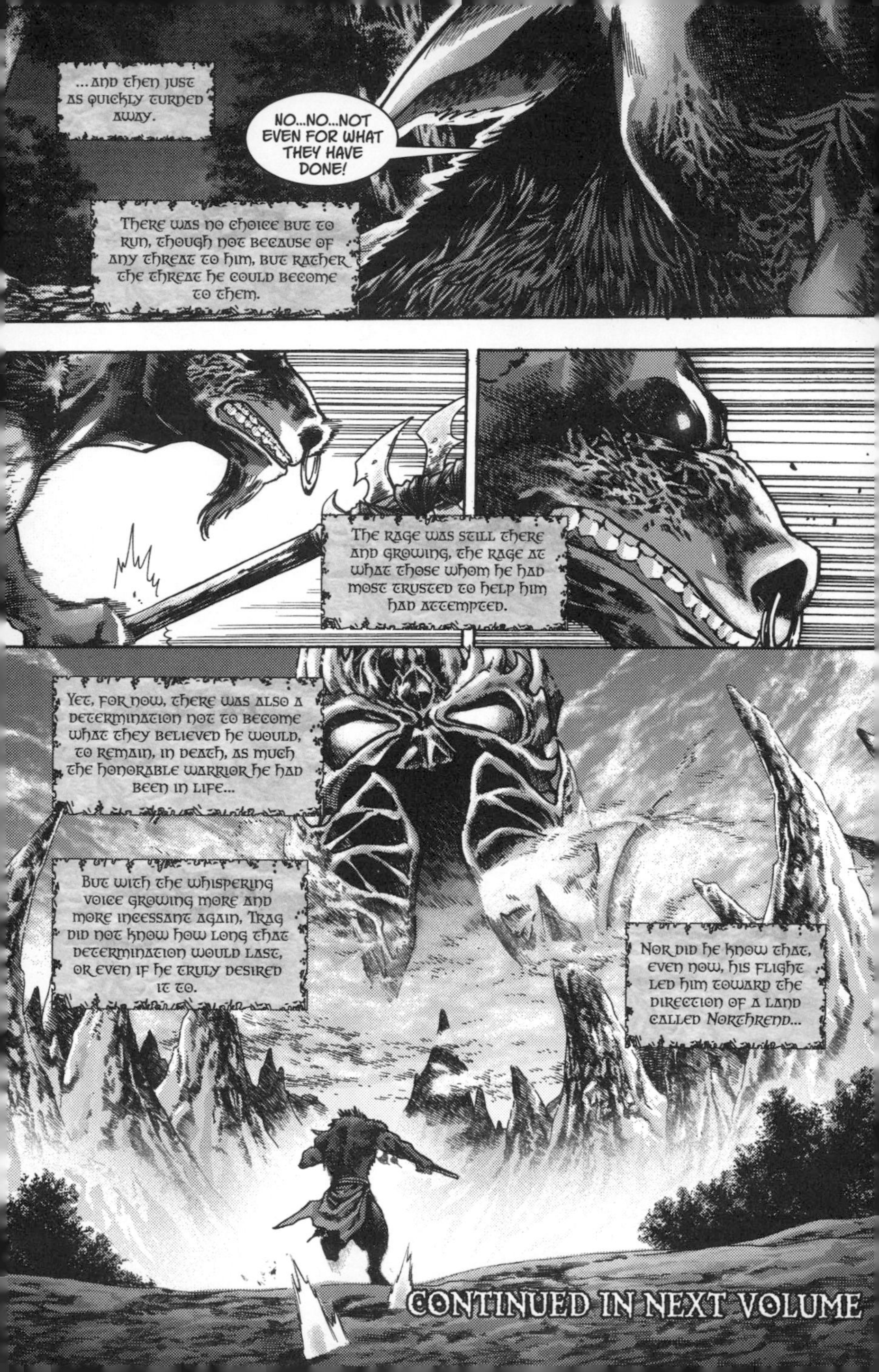
...AND THEN JUST AS QUICKLY TURNED AWAY.
NO...NO...NOT EVEN FOR WHAT THEY HAVE DONE!
THERE WAS NO CHOICE BUT TO RUN, THOUGH NOT BECAUSE OF ANY THREAT TO HIM, BUT RATHER THE THREAT HE COULD BECOME TO THEM.
THE RAGE WAS STILL THERE AND GROWING, THE RAGE AT WHAT THOSE WHOM HE HAD MOST TRUSTED TO HELP HIM HAD ATTEMPTED.
YET, FOR NOW, THERE WAS ALSO A DETERMINATION NOT TO BECOME WHAT THEY BELIEVED HE WOULD, TO REMAIN, IN DEATH, AS MUCH THE HONORABLE WARRIOR HE HAD BEEN IN LIFE...
BUT WITH THE WHISPERING VOICE GROWING MORE AND MORE INCESSANT AGAIN, TRAG DID NOT KNOW HOW LONG THAT DETERMINATION WOULD LAST, OR EVEN IF HE TRULY DESIRED IT TO.
NOR DID HE KNOW THAT, EVEN NOW, HIS FLIGHT LED HIM TOWARD THE DIRECTION OF A LAND CALLED NORTHREND...
CONTINUED IN NEXT VOLUME

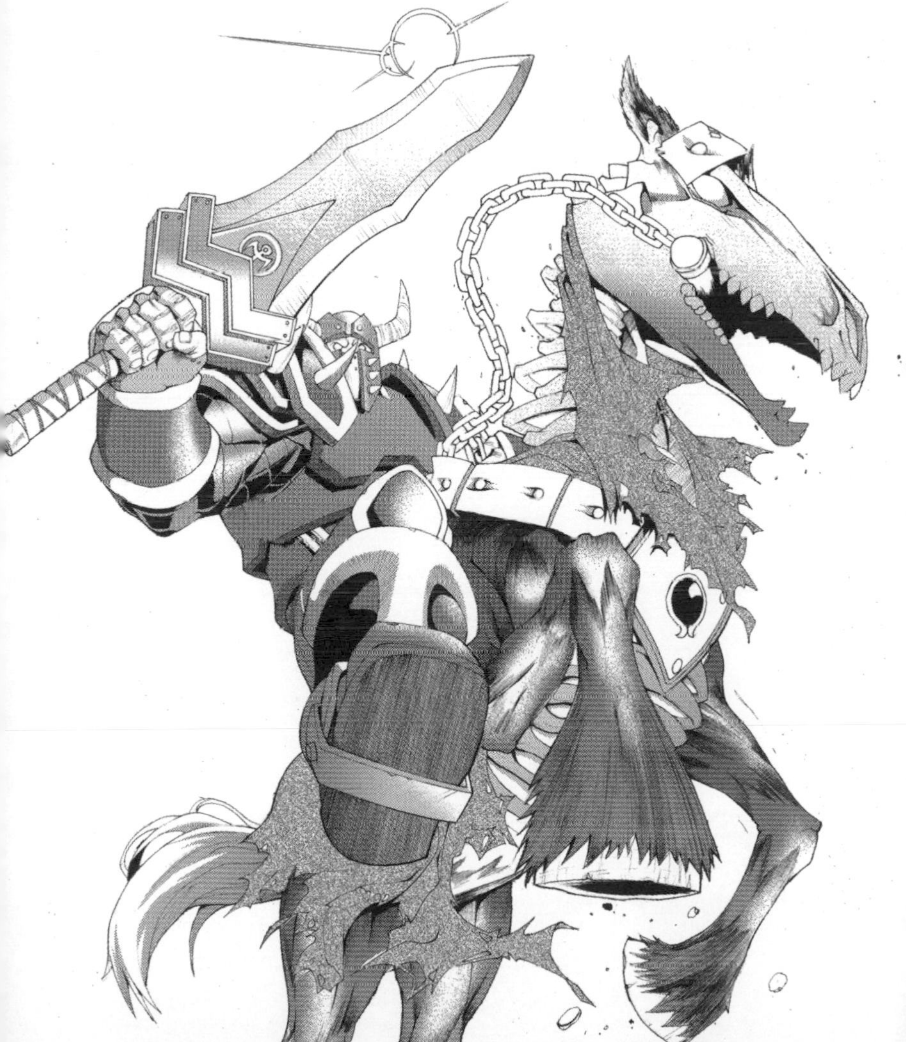

WARCRAFT®

LEGENDS™

VOLUME ONE

THE JOURNEY

STORY BY TROY LEWTER & MIKE WELLMAN
WRITTEN BY TROY LEWTER

PENCILS BY MI-YOUNG NO
BACKGROUNDS BY MI-JUNG KANG
INKS BY MI-YOUNG NO & MI-JUNG KANG
TONES BY HYUN-HONG YOOK & SOON-SHIK HONG

EDITOR: TROY LEWTER
CONTRIBUTING EDITOR: HYUN JOO KIM
ASSOCIATE EDITOR: SHANNON WATTERS
LETTERER: MICHAEL PAOLILLI

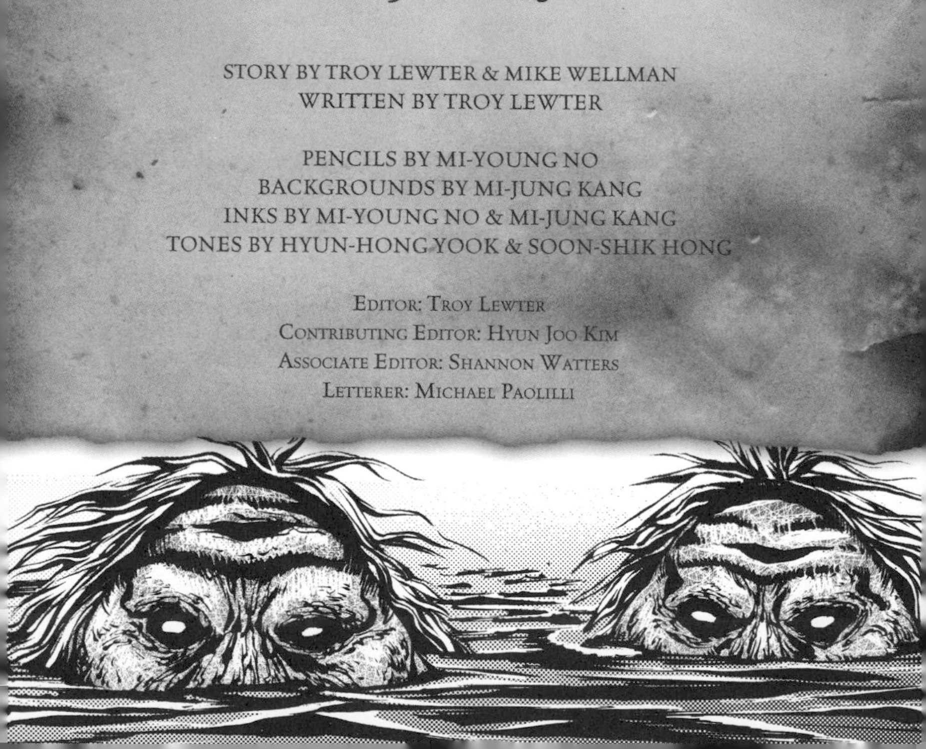

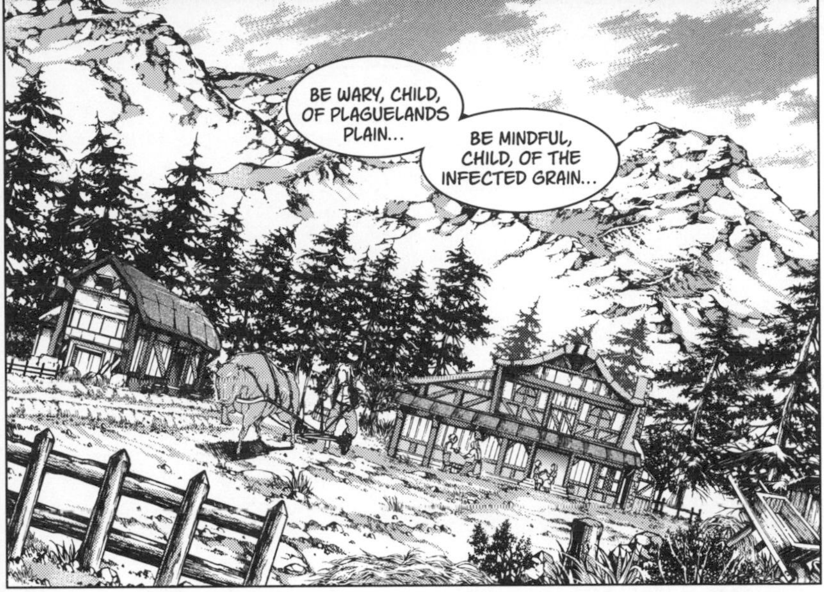
BE WARY, CHILD, OF PLAGUELANDS PLAIN...
BE MINDFUL, CHILD, OF THE INFECTED GRAIN...

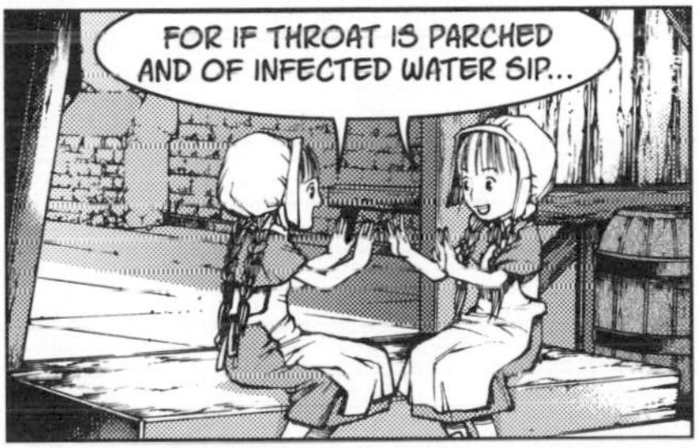
FOR IF THROAT IS PARCHED AND OF INFECTED WATER SIP...

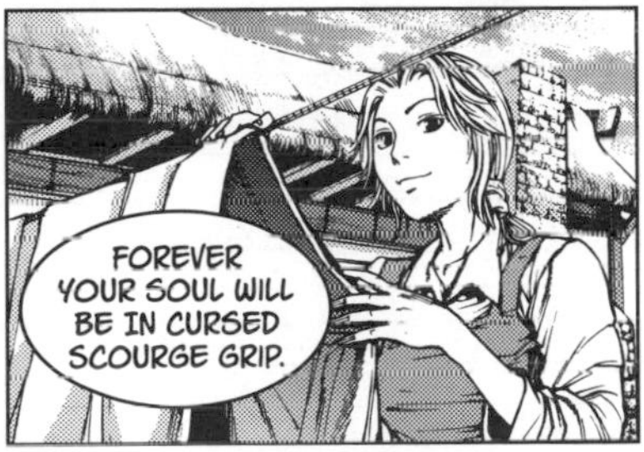
FOREVER YOUR SOUL WILL BE IN CURSED SCOURGE GRIP.

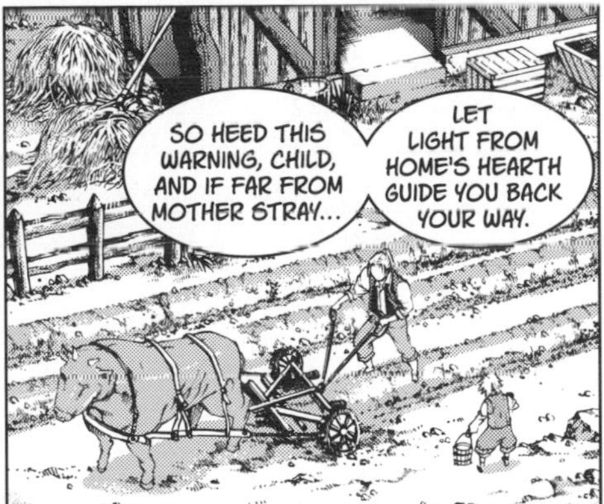
SO HEED THIS WARNING, CHILD, AND IF FAR FROM MOTHER STRAY...
LET LIGHT FROM HOME'S HEARTH GUIDE YOU BACK YOUR WAY.

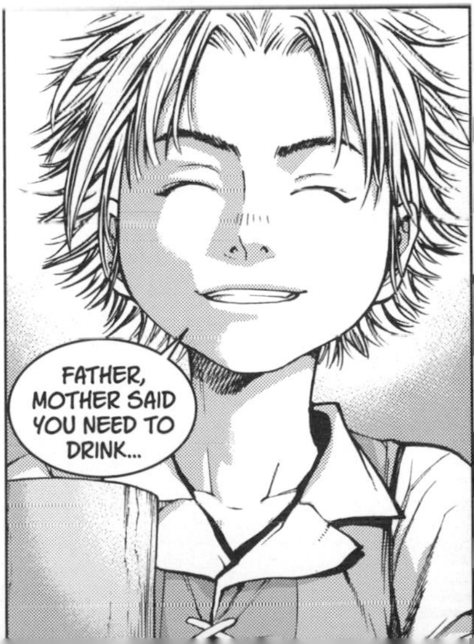
FATHER, MOTHER SAID YOU NEED TO DRINK...

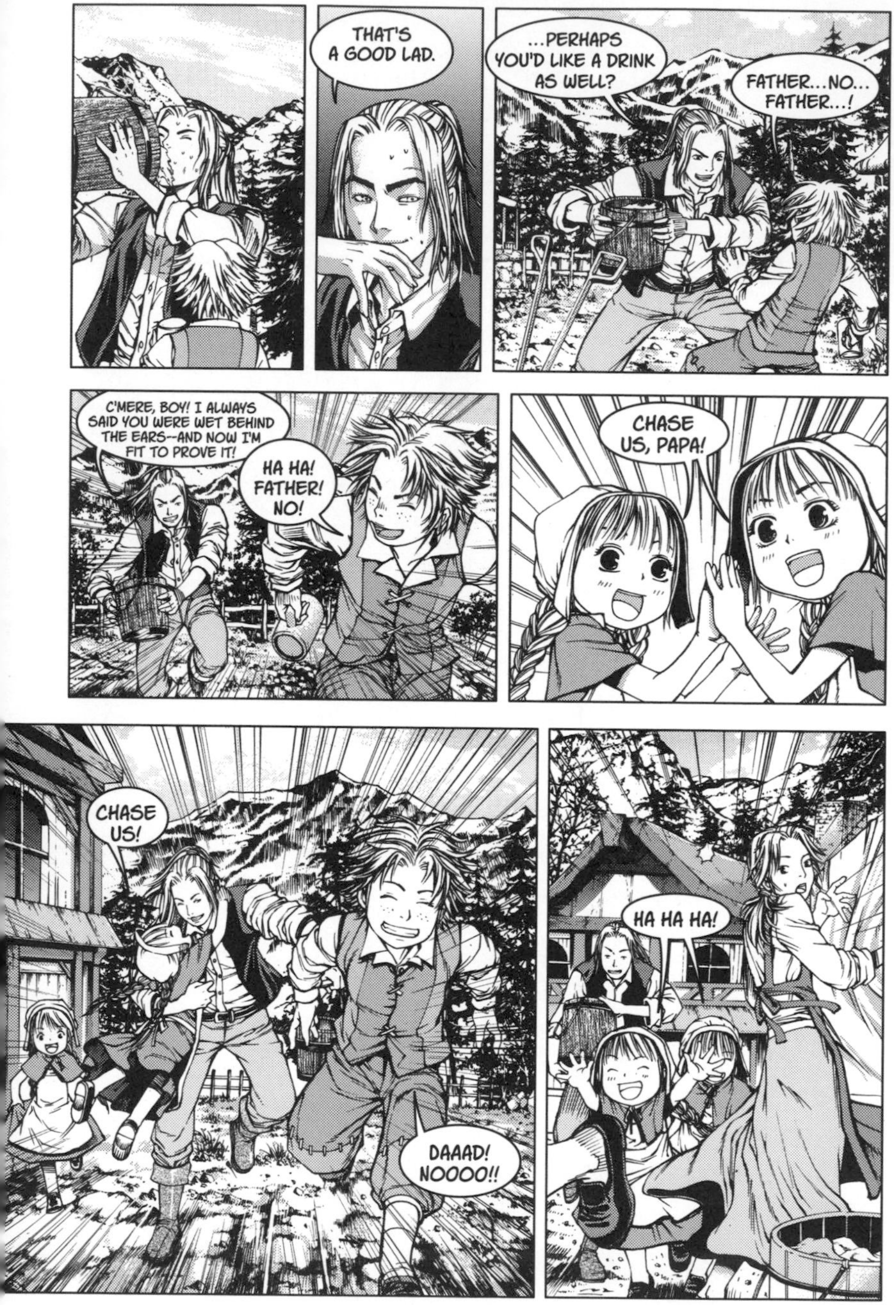
THAT'S A GOOD LAD.
...PERHAPS YOU'D LIKE A DRINK AS WELL?
FATHER...NO... FATHER...!
C'MERE, BOY! I ALWAYS SAID YOU WERE WET BEHIND THE EARS--AND NOW I'M FIT TO PROVE IT!
HA HA! FATHER! NO!
CHASE US, PAPA!
CHASE US!
DAAAD! NOOOO!!
HA HA HA!

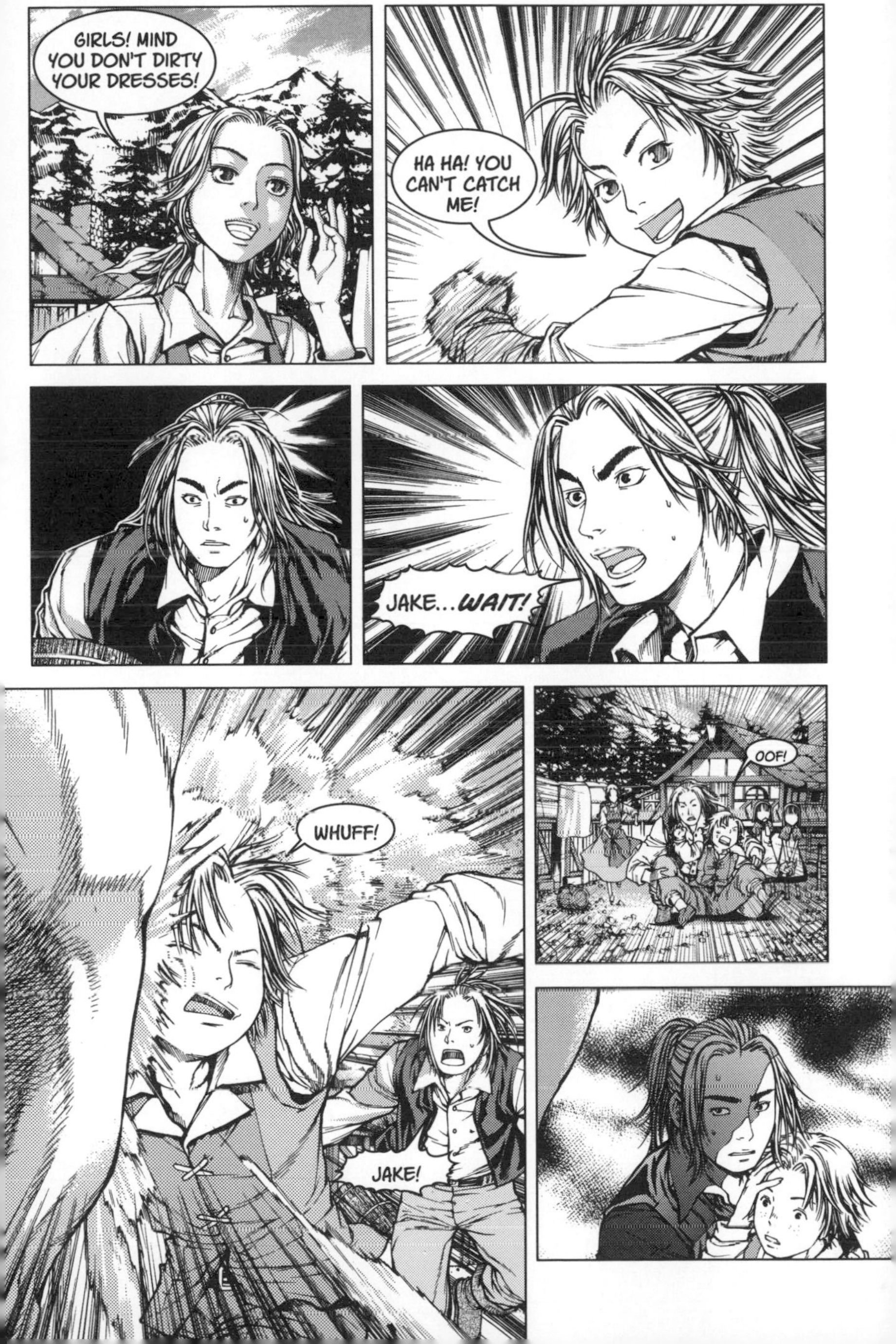
GIRLS! MIND YOU DON'T DIRTY YOUR DRESSES!
HA HA! YOU CAN'T CATCH ME!
JAKE...WAIT!
WHUFF!
JAKE!
OOF!

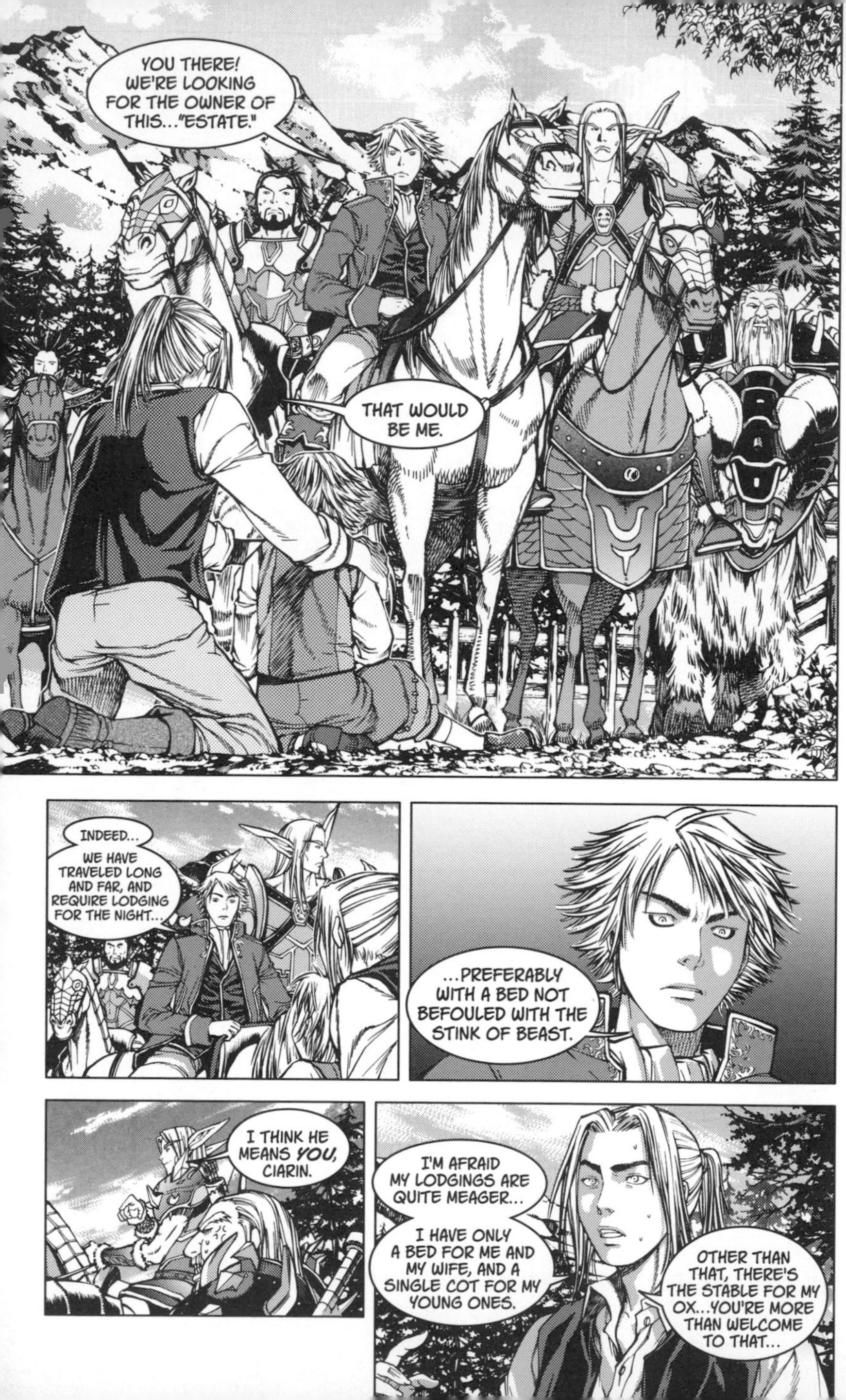
YOU THERE! WE'RE LOOKING FOR THE OWNER OF THIS..."ESTATE."
THAT WOULD BE ME.
INDEED...
WE HAVE TRAVELED LONG AND FAR, AND REQUIRE LODGING FOR THE NIGHT...
...PREFERABLY WITH A BED NOT BEFOULED WITH THE STINK OF BEAST.
I THINK HE MEANS *YOU,* CIARIN.
I'M AFRAID MY LODGINGS ARE QUITE MEAGER...
I HAVE ONLY A BED FOR ME AND MY WIFE, AND A SINGLE COT FOR MY YOUNG ONES.
OTHER THAN THAT, THERE'S THE STABLE FOR MY OX...YOU'RE MORE THAN WELCOME TO THAT...

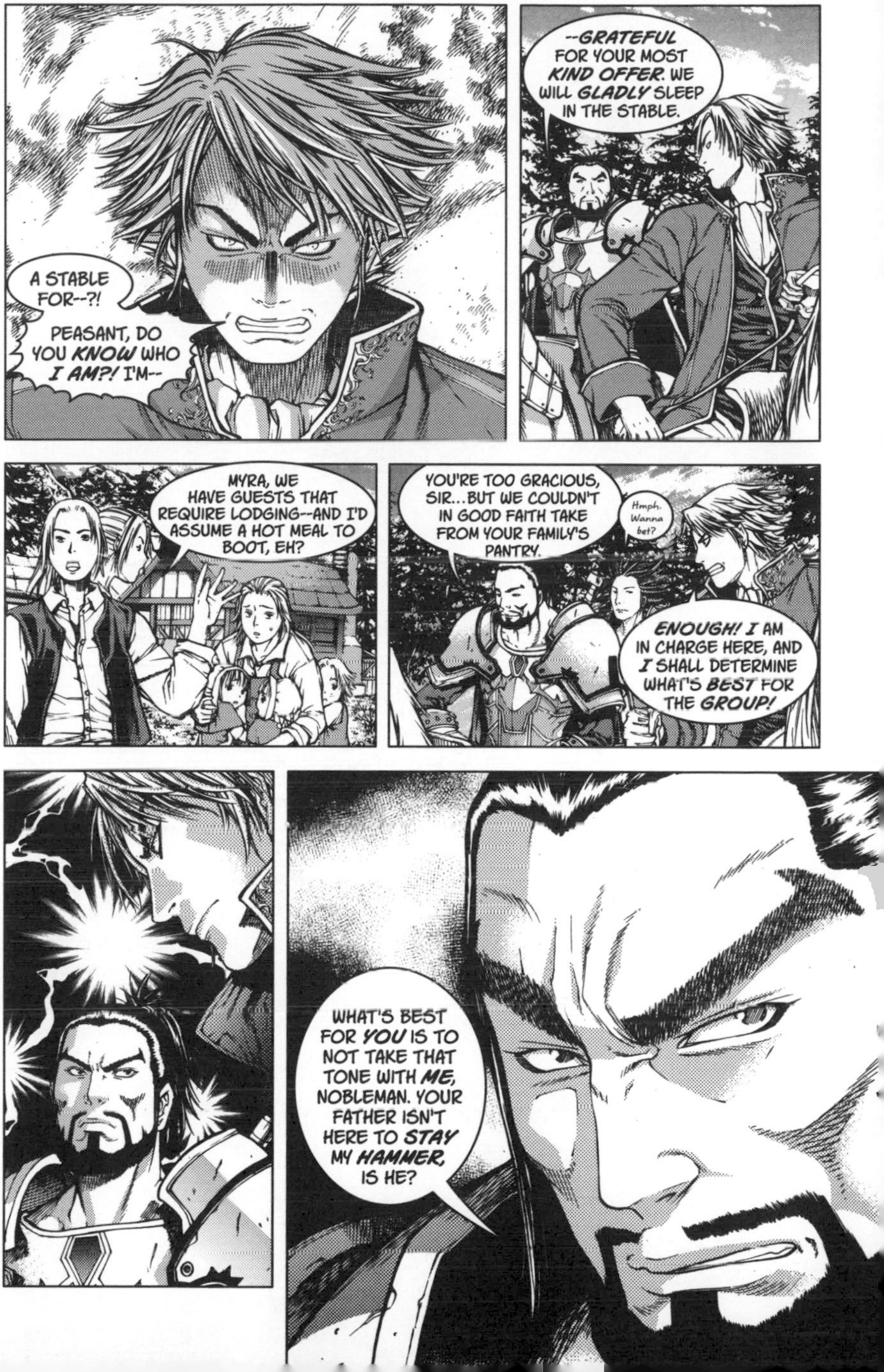
A STABLE FOR--?!
PEASANT, DO YOU KNOW WHO I AM?! I'M--
--GRATEFUL FOR YOUR MOST KIND OFFER. WE WILL GLADLY SLEEP IN THE STABLE.
MYRA, WE HAVE GUESTS THAT REQUIRE LODGING--AND I'D ASSUME A HOT MEAL TO BOOT, EH?
YOU'RE TOO GRACIOUS, SIR...BUT WE COULDN'T IN GOOD FAITH TAKE FROM YOUR FAMILY'S PANTRY.
Hmph. Wanna bet?
ENOUGH! I AM IN CHARGE HERE, AND I SHALL DETERMINE WHAT'S BEST FOR THE GROUP!
WHAT'S BEST FOR YOU IS TO NOT TAKE THAT TONE WITH ME, NOBLEMAN. YOUR FATHER ISN'T HERE TO STAY MY HAMMER, IS HE?

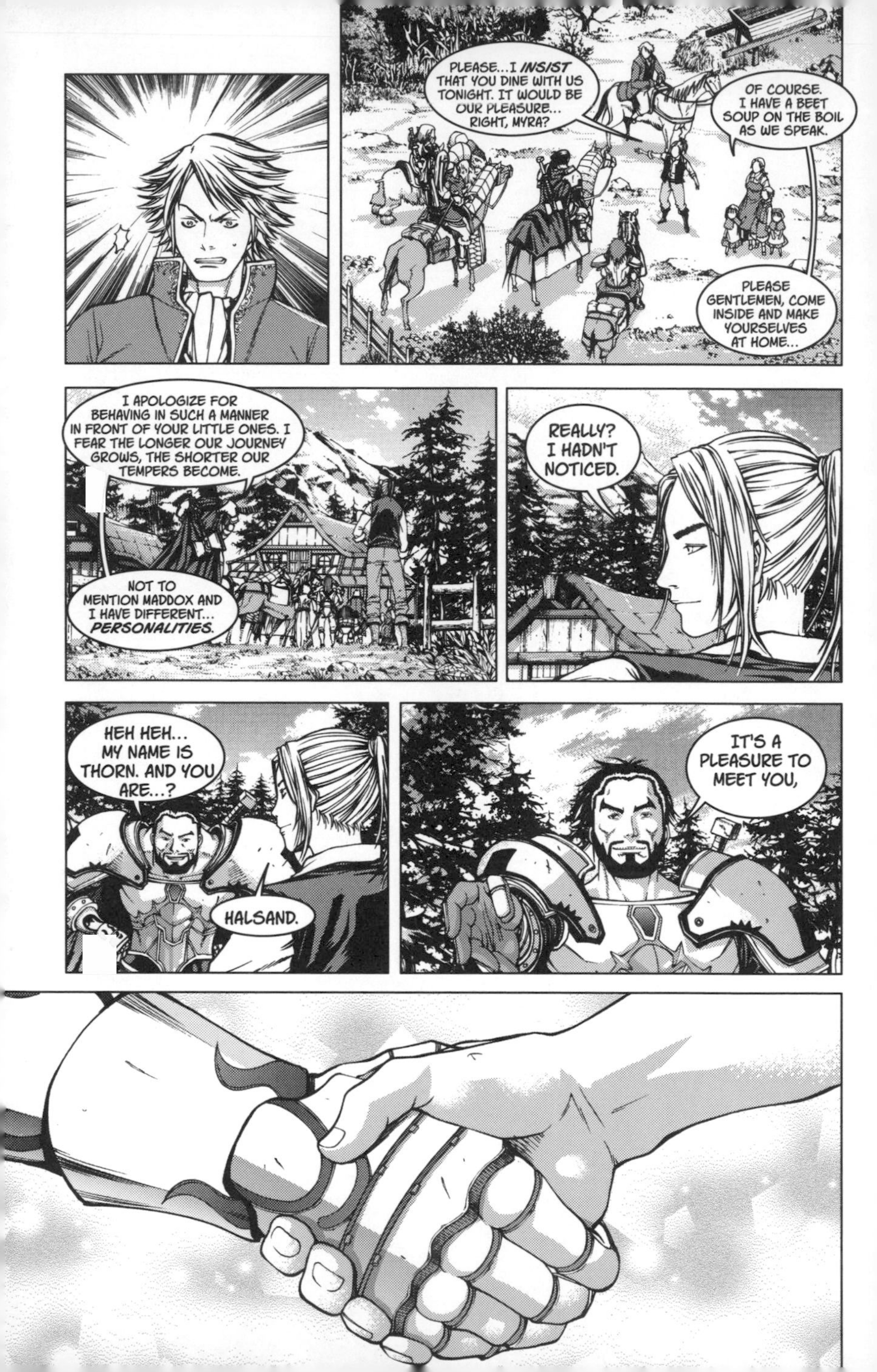
PLEASE...I *INSIST* THAT YOU DINE WITH US TONIGHT. IT WOULD BE OUR PLEASURE... RIGHT, MYRA?
OF COURSE. I HAVE A BEET SOUP ON THE BOIL AS WE SPEAK.
PLEASE GENTLEMEN, COME INSIDE AND MAKE YOURSELVES AT HOME...
I APOLOGIZE FOR BEHAVING IN SUCH A MANNER IN FRONT OF YOUR LITTLE ONES. I FEAR THE LONGER OUR JOURNEY GROWS, THE SHORTER OUR TEMPERS BECOME.
NOT TO MENTION MADDOX AND I HAVE DIFFERENT... ***PERSONALITIES***.
REALLY? I HADN'T NOTICED.
HEH HEH... MY NAME IS THORN. AND YOU ARE...?
HALSAND.
IT'S A PLEASURE TO MEET YOU,

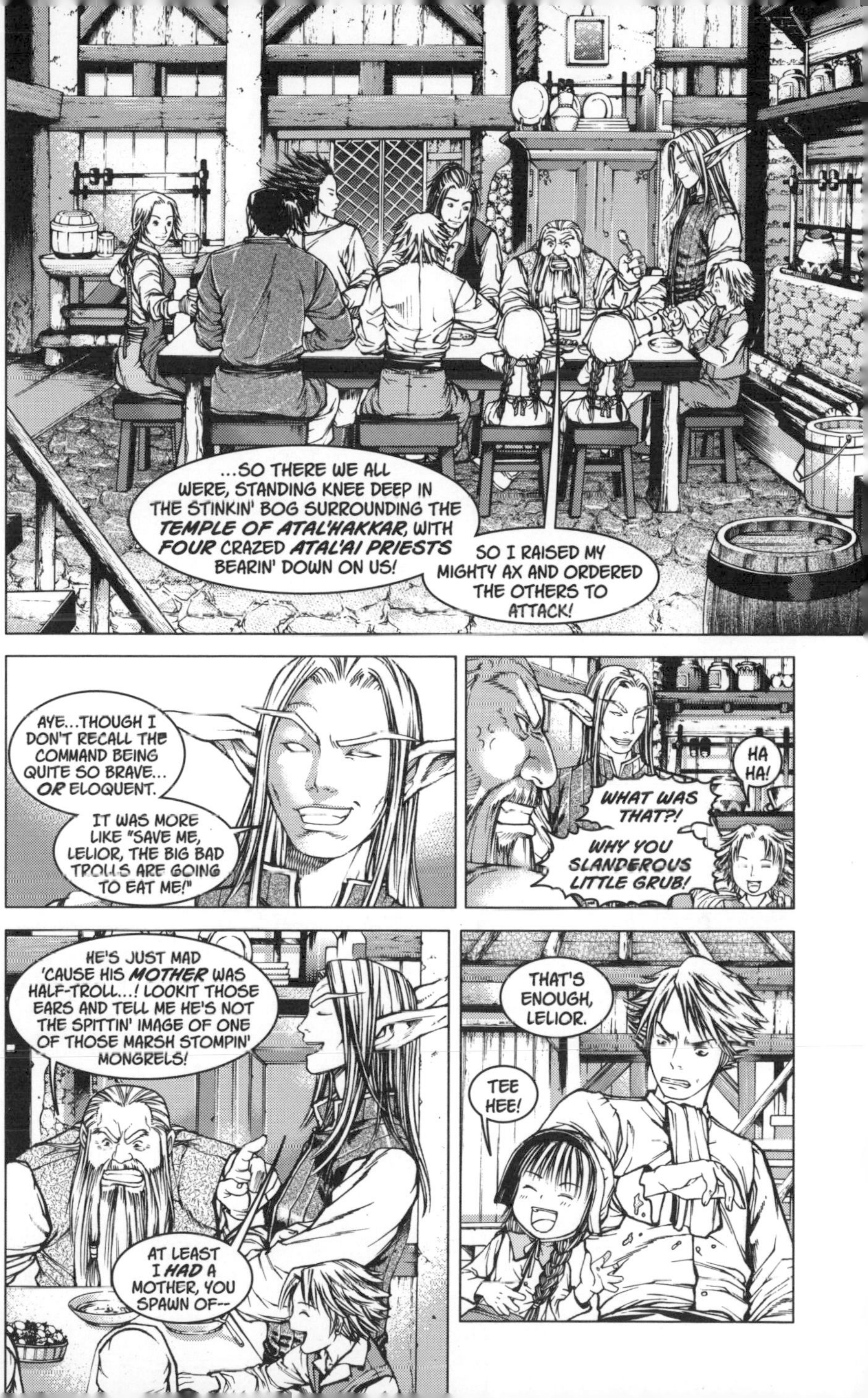
...SO THERE WE ALL WERE, STANDING KNEE DEEP IN THE STINKIN' BOG SURROUNDING THE TEMPLE OF ATAL'HAKKAR, WITH FOUR CRAZED ATAL'AI PRIESTS BEARIN' DOWN ON US!
SO I RAISED MY MIGHTY AX AND ORDERED THE OTHERS TO ATTACK!
AYE...THOUGH I DON'T RECALL THE COMMAND BEING QUITE SO BRAVE... OR ELOQUENT.
IT WAS MORE LIKE "SAVE ME, LELIOR, THE BIG BAD TROLLS ARE GOING TO EAT ME!"
HA HA!
WHAT WAS THAT?!
WHY YOU SLANDEROUS LITTLE GRUB!
HE'S JUST MAD 'CAUSE HIS MOTHER WAS HALF-TROLL...! LOOKIT THOSE EARS AND TELL ME HE'S NOT THE SPITTIN' IMAGE OF ONE OF THOSE MARSH STOMPIN' MONGRELS!
AT LEAST I HAD A MOTHER, YOU SPAWN OF--
THAT'S ENOUGH, LELIOR.
TEE HEE!

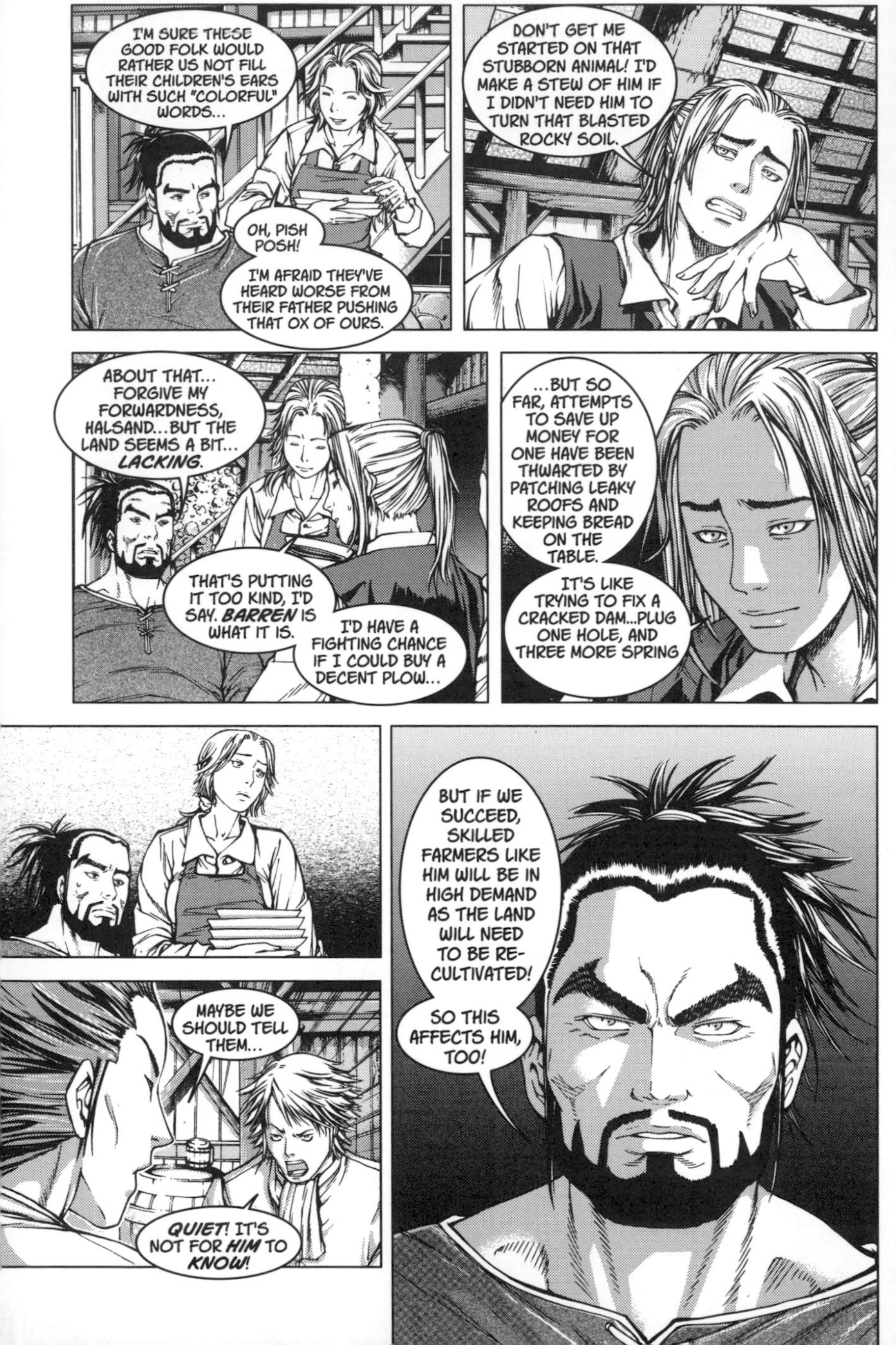
I'M SURE THESE GOOD FOLK WOULD RATHER US NOT FILL THEIR CHILDREN'S EARS WITH SUCH "COLORFUL" WORDS...
OH, PISH POSH!
I'M AFRAID THEY'VE HEARD WORSE FROM THEIR FATHER PUSHING THAT OX OF OURS.
DON'T GET ME STARTED ON THAT STUBBORN ANIMAL! I'D MAKE A STEW OF HIM IF I DIDN'T NEED HIM TO TURN THAT BLASTED ROCKY SOIL.
ABOUT THAT... FORGIVE MY FORWARDNESS, HALSAND...BUT THE LAND SEEMS A BIT... ***LACKING***.
THAT'S PUTTING IT TOO KIND, I'D SAY. ***BARREN*** IS WHAT IT IS.
I'D HAVE A FIGHTING CHANCE IF I COULD BUY A DECENT PLOW...
...BUT SO FAR, ATTEMPTS TO SAVE UP MONEY FOR ONE HAVE BEEN THWARTED BY PATCHING LEAKY ROOFS AND KEEPING BREAD ON THE TABLE.
IT'S LIKE TRYING TO FIX A CRACKED DAM...PLUG ONE HOLE, AND THREE MORE SPRING
MAYBE WE SHOULD TELL THEM...
QUIET! IT'S NOT FOR ***HIM*** TO ***KNOW***!
BUT IF WE SUCCEED, SKILLED FARMERS LIKE HIM WILL BE IN HIGH DEMAND AS THE LAND WILL NEED TO BE RE-CULTIVATED!
SO THIS AFFECTS HIM, TOO!

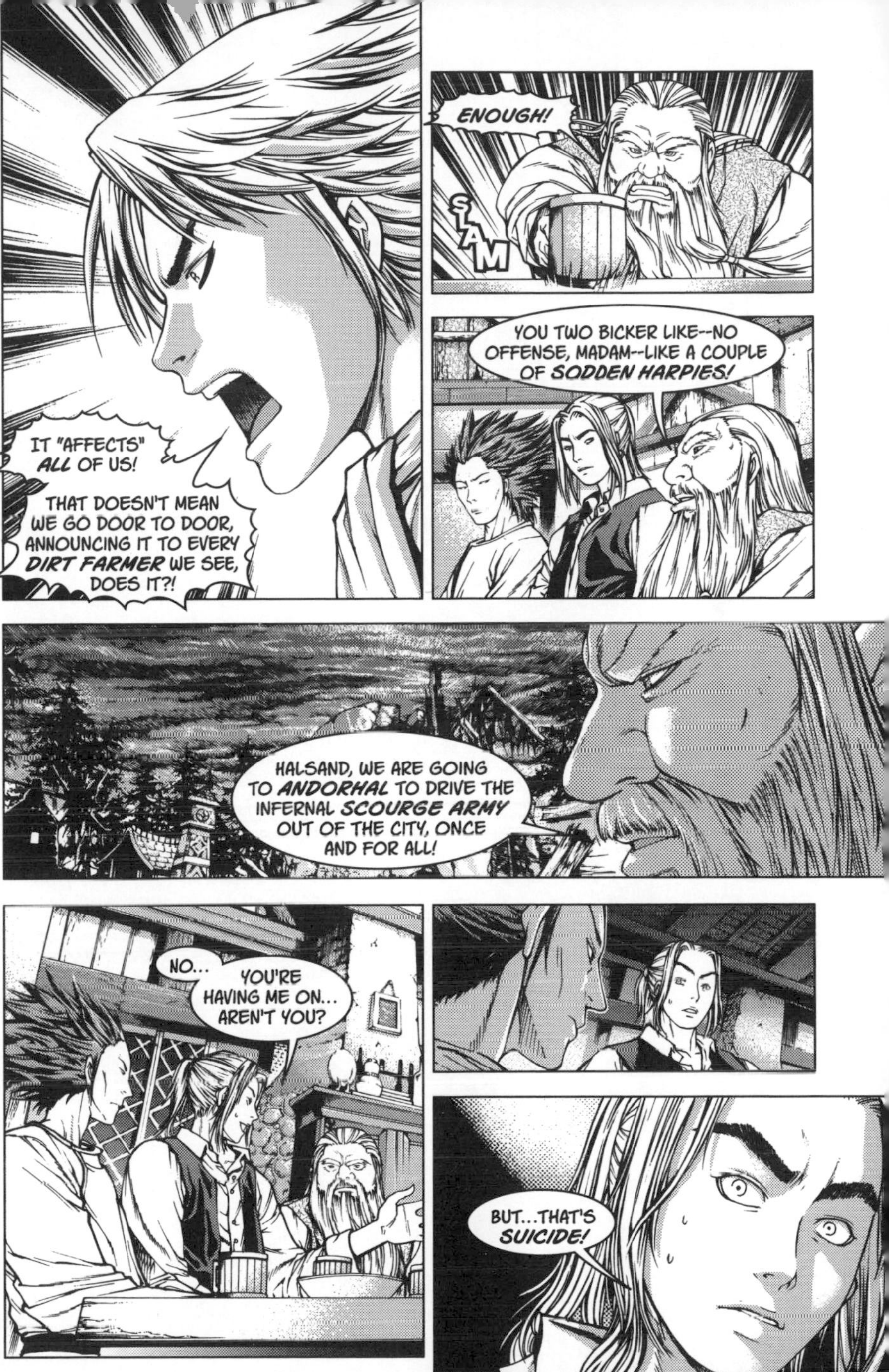
IT "AFFECTS" ALL OF US!
THAT DOESN'T MEAN WE GO DOOR TO DOOR, ANNOUNCING IT TO EVERY DIRT FARMER WE SEE, DOES IT?!
ENOUGH!
SLAM
YOU TWO BICKER LIKE--NO OFFENSE, MADAM--LIKE A COUPLE OF SODDEN HARPIES!
HALSAND, WE ARE GOING TO ANDORHAL TO DRIVE THE INFERNAL SCOURGE ARMY OUT OF THE CITY, ONCE AND FOR ALL!
NO...
YOU'RE HAVING ME ON... AREN'T YOU?
BUT...THAT'S SUICIDE!

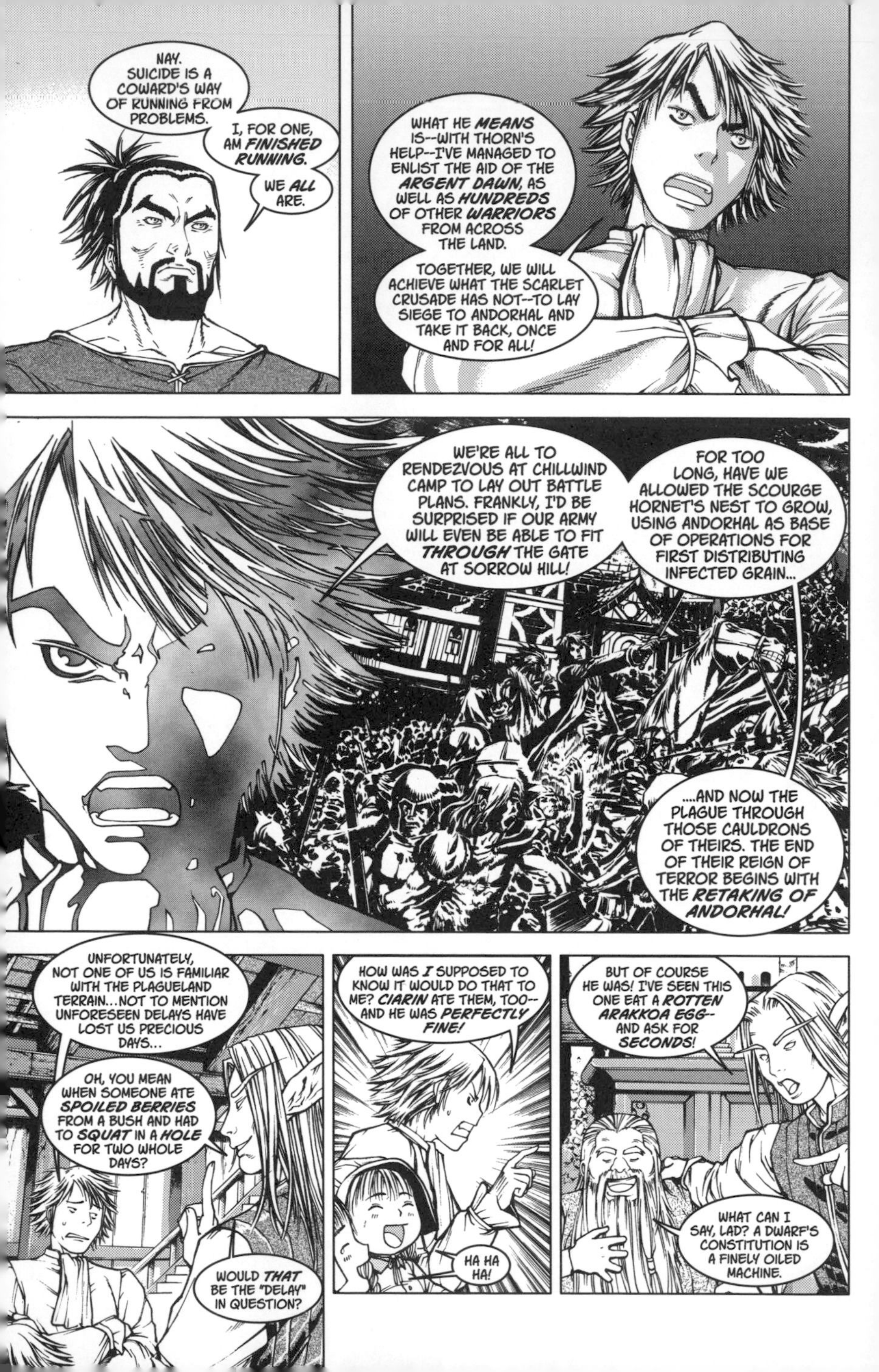
NAY. SUICIDE IS A COWARD'S WAY OF RUNNING FROM PROBLEMS.
I, FOR ONE, AM FINISHED RUNNING.
WE ALL ARE.
WHAT HE MEANS IS--WITH THORN'S HELP--I'VE MANAGED TO ENLIST THE AID OF THE ARGENT DAWN, AS WELL AS HUNDREDS OF OTHER WARRIORS FROM ACROSS THE LAND.
TOGETHER, WE WILL ACHIEVE WHAT THE SCARLET CRUSADE HAS NOT--TO LAY SIEGE TO ANDORHAL AND TAKE IT BACK, ONCE AND FOR ALL!
WE'RE ALL TO RENDEZVOUS AT CHILLWIND CAMP TO LAY OUT BATTLE PLANS. FRANKLY, I'D BE SURPRISED IF OUR ARMY WILL EVEN BE ABLE TO FIT THROUGH THE GATE AT SORROW HILL!
FOR TOO LONG, HAVE WE ALLOWED THE SCOURGE HORNET'S NEST TO GROW, USING ANDORHAL AS BASE OF OPERATIONS FOR FIRST DISTRIBUTING INFECTED GRAIN...
....AND NOW THE PLAGUE THROUGH THOSE CAULDRONS OF THEIRS. THE END OF THEIR REIGN OF TERROR BEGINS WITH THE RETAKING OF ANDORHAL!
UNFORTUNATELY, NOT ONE OF US IS FAMILIAR WITH THE PLAGUELAND TERRAIN...NOT TO MENTION UNFORESEEN DELAYS HAVE LOST US PRECIOUS DAYS...
OH, YOU MEAN WHEN SOMEONE ATE SPOILED BERRIES FROM A BUSH AND HAD TO SQUAT IN A HOLE FOR TWO WHOLE DAYS?
WOULD THAT BE THE "DELAY" IN QUESTION?
HOW WAS I SUPPOSED TO KNOW IT WOULD DO THAT TO ME? CIARIN ATE THEM, TOO--AND HE WAS PERFECTLY FINE!
HA HA HA!
BUT OF COURSE HE WAS! I'VE SEEN THIS ONE EAT A ROTTEN ARAKKOA EGG--AND ASK FOR SECONDS!
WHAT CAN I SAY, LAD? A DWARF'S CONSTITUTION IS A FINELY OILED MACHINE.

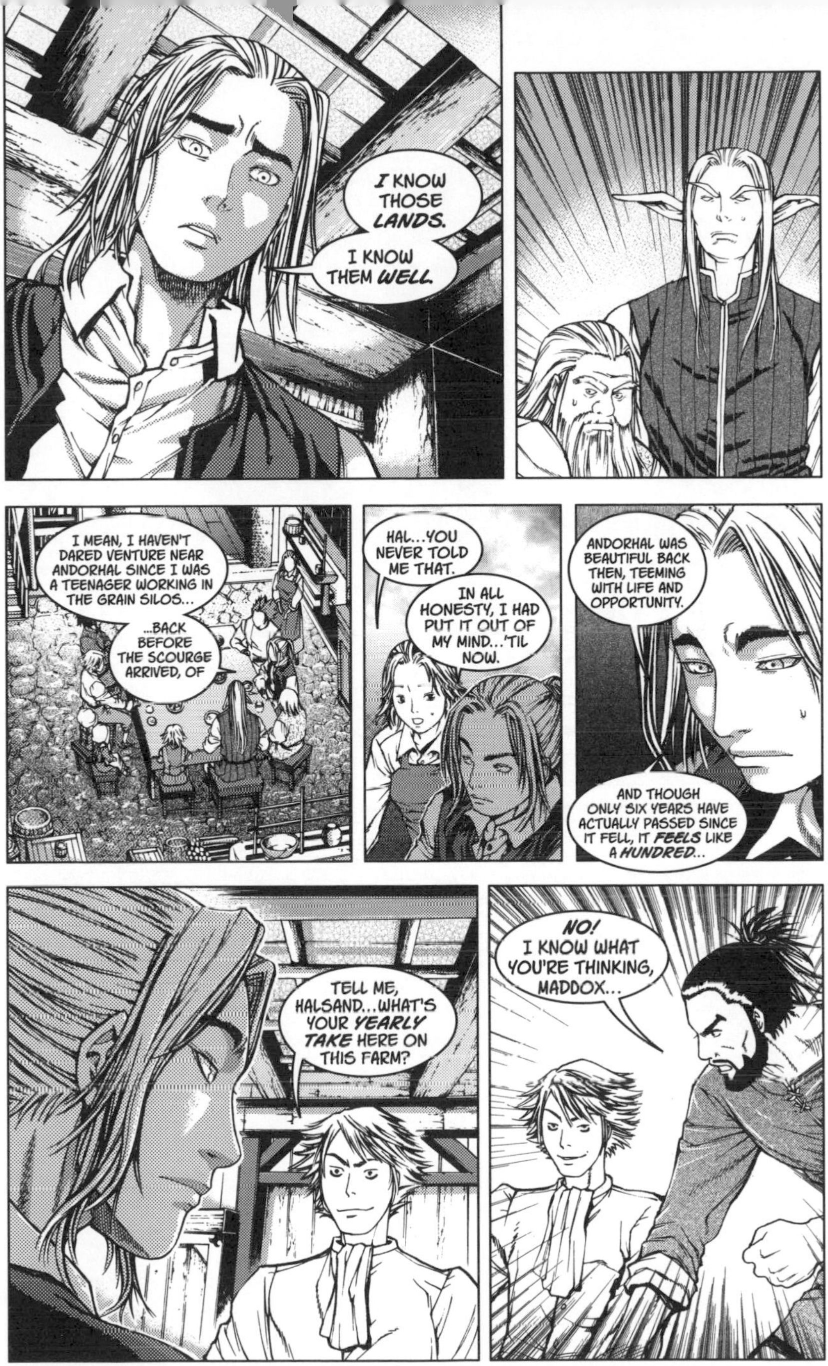
I KNOW THOSE LANDS.
I KNOW THEM WELL.
I MEAN, I HAVEN'T DARED VENTURE NEAR ANDORHAL SINCE I WAS A TEENAGER WORKING IN THE GRAIN SILOS...
...BACK BEFORE THE SCOURGE ARRIVED, OF
HAL...YOU NEVER TOLD ME THAT.
IN ALL HONESTY, I HAD PUT IT OUT OF MY MIND...'TIL NOW.
ANDORHAL WAS BEAUTIFUL BACK THEN, TEEMING WITH LIFE AND OPPORTUNITY.
AND THOUGH ONLY SIX YEARS HAVE ACTUALLY PASSED SINCE IT FELL, IT FEELS LIKE A HUNDRED...
TELL ME, HALSAND...WHAT'S YOUR YEARLY TAKE HERE ON THIS FARM?
NO! I KNOW WHAT YOU'RE THINKING, MADDOX...

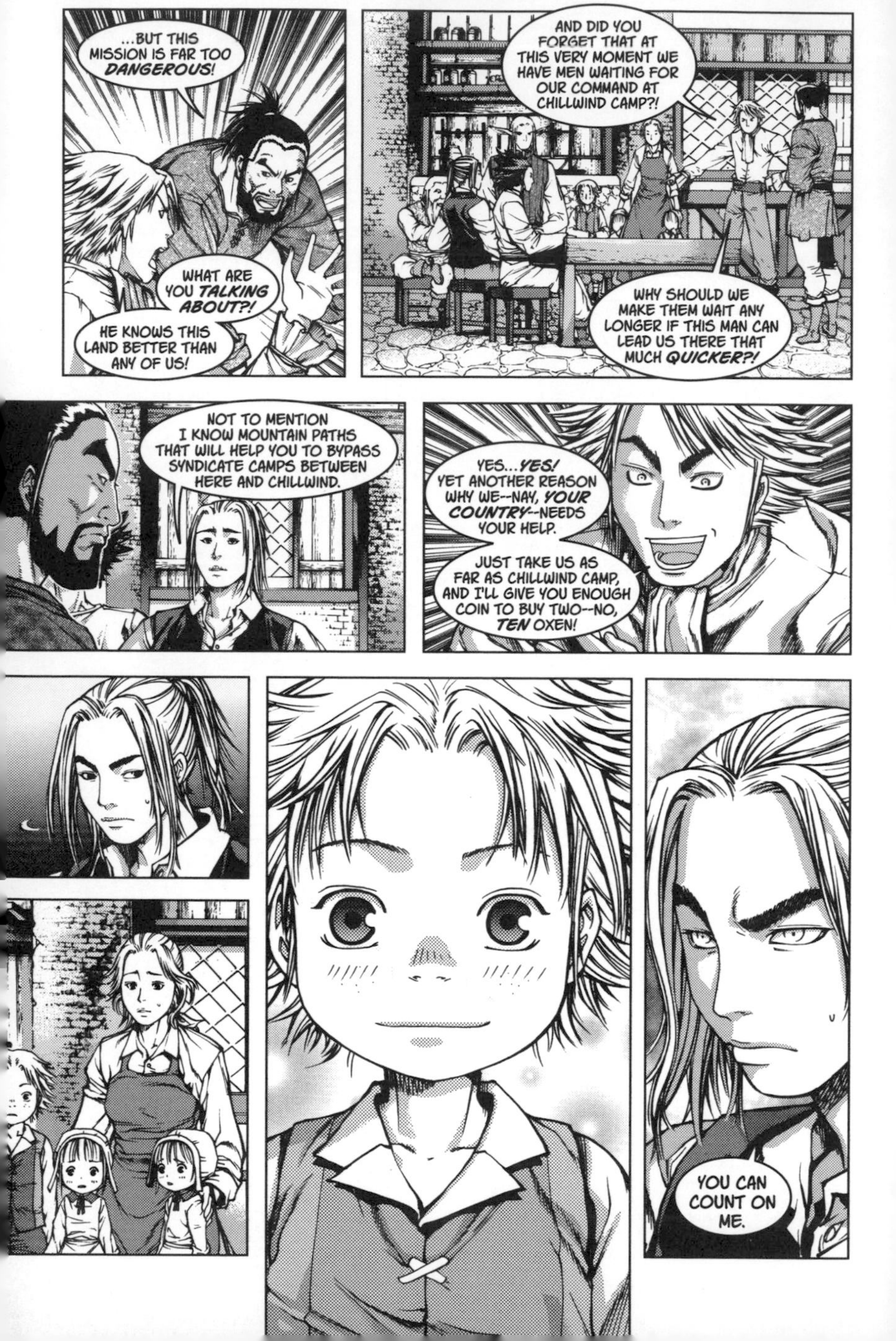
...BUT THIS MISSION IS FAR TOO DANGEROUS!
WHAT ARE YOU TALKING ABOUT?!
HE KNOWS THIS LAND BETTER THAN ANY OF US!
AND DID YOU FORGET THAT AT THIS VERY MOMENT WE HAVE MEN WAITING FOR OUR COMMAND AT CHILLWIND CAMP?!
WHY SHOULD WE MAKE THEM WAIT ANY LONGER IF THIS MAN CAN LEAD US THERE THAT MUCH QUICKER?!
NOT TO MENTION I KNOW MOUNTAIN PATHS THAT WILL HELP YOU TO BYPASS SYNDICATE CAMPS BETWEEN HERE AND CHILLWIND.
YES...YES! YET ANOTHER REASON WHY WE--NAY, YOUR COUNTRY--NEEDS YOUR HELP.
JUST TAKE US AS FAR AS CHILLWIND CAMP, AND I'LL GIVE YOU ENOUGH COIN TO BUY TWO--NO, TEN OXEN!
YOU CAN COUNT ON ME.

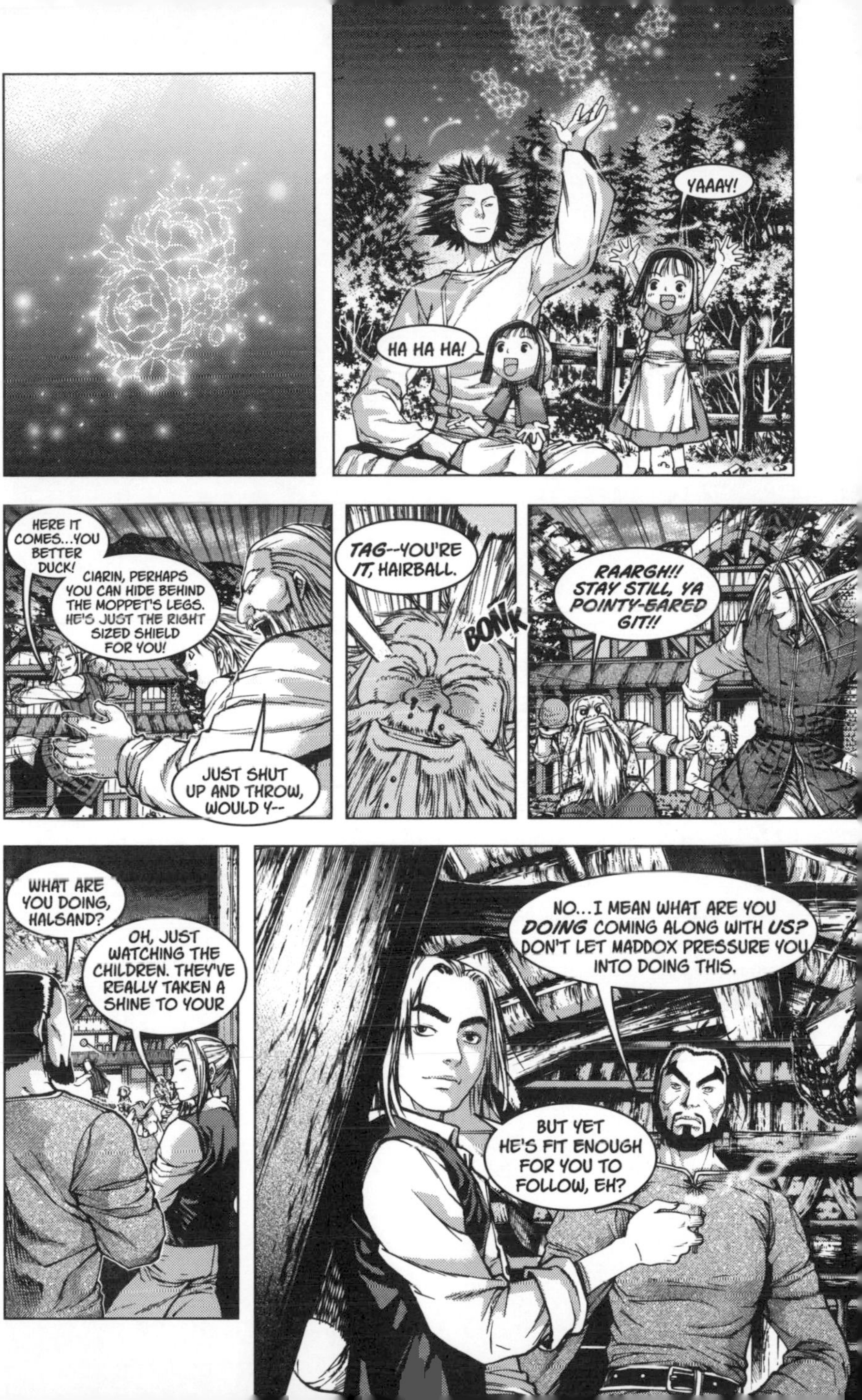
YAAAY!
HA HA HA!
HERE IT COMES...YOU BETTER DUCK!
CIARIN, PERHAPS YOU CAN HIDE BEHIND THE MOPPET'S LEGS. HE'S JUST THE RIGHT SIZED SHIELD FOR YOU!
JUST SHUT UP AND THROW, WOULD Y--
TAG--YOU'RE IT, HAIRBALL.
BONK
RAARGH!! STAY STILL, YA POINTY-EARED GIT!!
WHAT ARE YOU DOING, HALSAND?
OH, JUST WATCHING THE CHILDREN. THEY'VE REALLY TAKEN A SHINE TO YOUR
NO...I MEAN WHAT ARE YOU DOING COMING ALONG WITH US? DON'T LET MADDOX PRESSURE YOU INTO DOING THIS.
BUT YET HE'S FIT ENOUGH FOR YOU TO FOLLOW, EH?

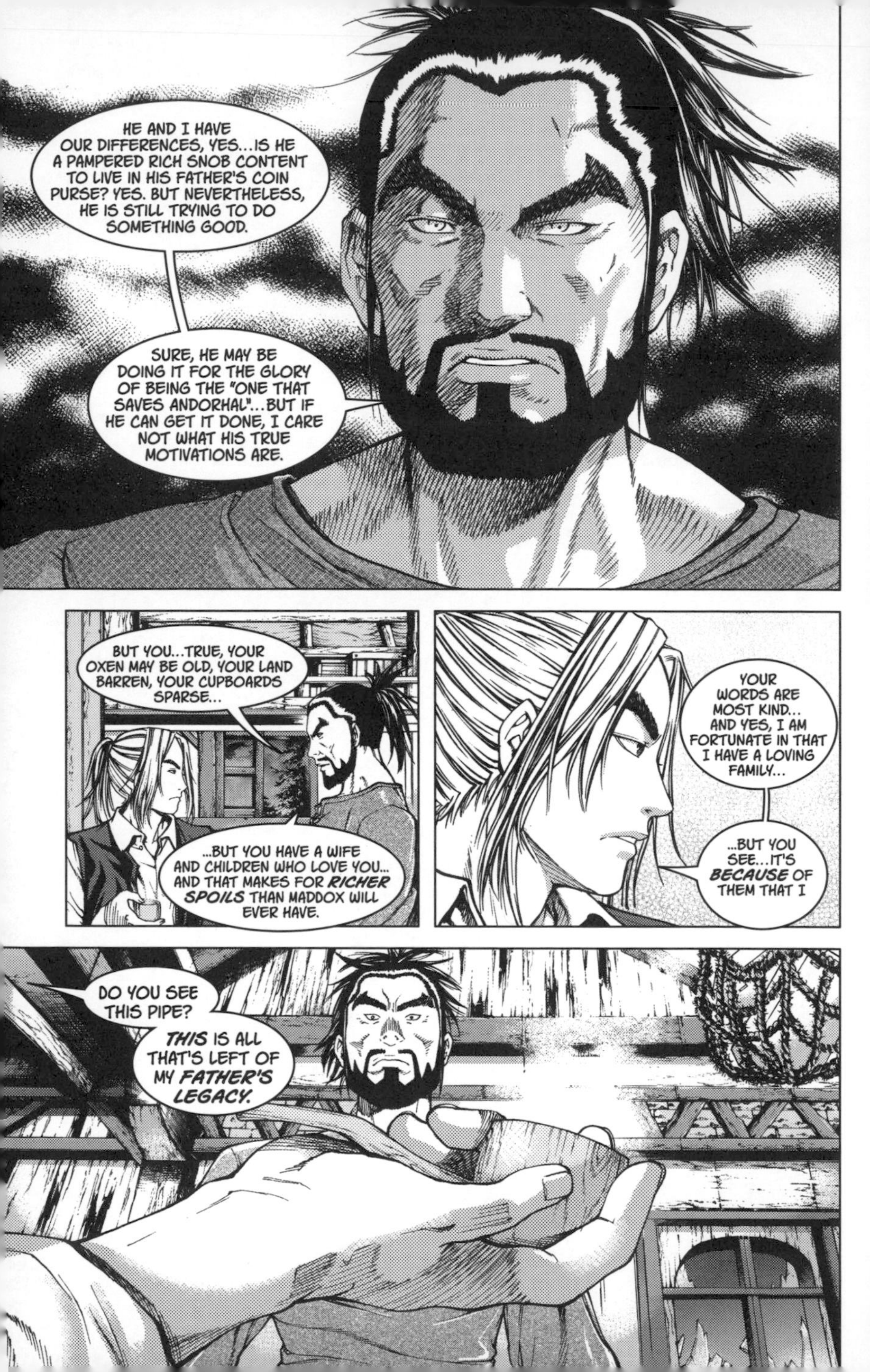
HE AND I HAVE OUR DIFFERENCES, YES...IS HE A PAMPERED RICH SNOB CONTENT TO LIVE IN HIS FATHER'S COIN PURSE? YES. BUT NEVERTHELESS, HE IS STILL TRYING TO DO SOMETHING GOOD.
SURE, HE MAY BE DOING IT FOR THE GLORY OF BEING THE "ONE THAT SAVES ANDORHAL"...BUT IF HE CAN GET IT DONE, I CARE NOT WHAT HIS TRUE MOTIVATIONS ARE.
BUT YOU...TRUE, YOUR OXEN MAY BE OLD, YOUR LAND BARREN, YOUR CUPBOARDS SPARSE...
...BUT YOU HAVE A WIFE AND CHILDREN WHO LOVE YOU... AND THAT MAKES FOR *RICHER SPOILS* THAN MADDOX WILL EVER HAVE.
YOUR WORDS ARE MOST KIND... AND YES, I AM FORTUNATE IN THAT I HAVE A LOVING FAMILY...
...BUT YOU SEE...IT'S *BECAUSE* OF THEM THAT I
DO YOU SEE THIS PIPE?
THIS IS ALL THAT'S LEFT OF MY *FATHER'S LEGACY.*

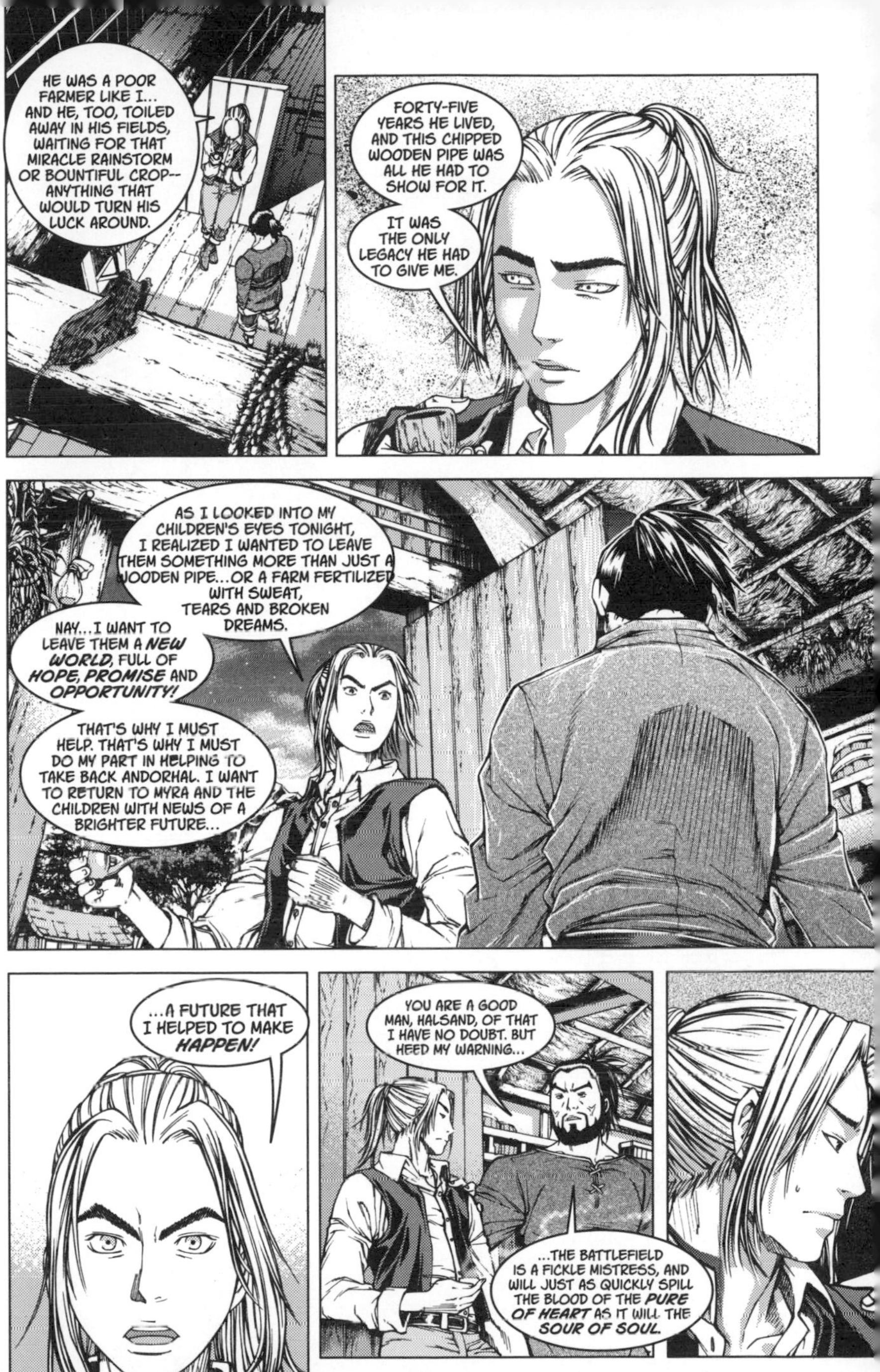
HE WAS A POOR FARMER LIKE I... AND HE, TOO, TOILED AWAY IN HIS FIELDS, WAITING FOR THAT MIRACLE RAINSTORM OR BOUNTIFUL CROP-- ANYTHING THAT WOULD TURN HIS LUCK AROUND.
FORTY-FIVE YEARS HE LIVED, AND THIS CHIPPED WOODEN PIPE WAS ALL HE HAD TO SHOW FOR IT.
IT WAS THE ONLY LEGACY HE HAD TO GIVE ME.
AS I LOOKED INTO MY CHILDREN'S EYES TONIGHT, I REALIZED I WANTED TO LEAVE THEM SOMETHING MORE THAN JUST A WOODEN PIPE...OR A FARM FERTILIZED WITH SWEAT, TEARS AND BROKEN DREAMS.
NAY...I WANT TO LEAVE THEM A *NEW WORLD*, FULL OF *HOPE, PROMISE* AND *OPPORTUNITY!*
THAT'S WHY I MUST HELP. THAT'S WHY I MUST DO MY PART IN HELPING TO TAKE BACK ANDORHAL. I WANT TO RETURN TO MYRA AND THE CHILDREN WITH NEWS OF A BRIGHTER FUTURE...
...A FUTURE THAT I HELPED TO MAKE *HAPPEN!*
YOU ARE A GOOD MAN, HALSAND, OF THAT I HAVE NO DOUBT. BUT HEED MY WARNING...
...THE BATTLEFIELD IS A FICKLE MISTRESS, AND WILL JUST AS QUICKLY SPILL THE BLOOD OF THE *PURE OF HEART* AS IT WILL THE *SOUR OF SOUL.*

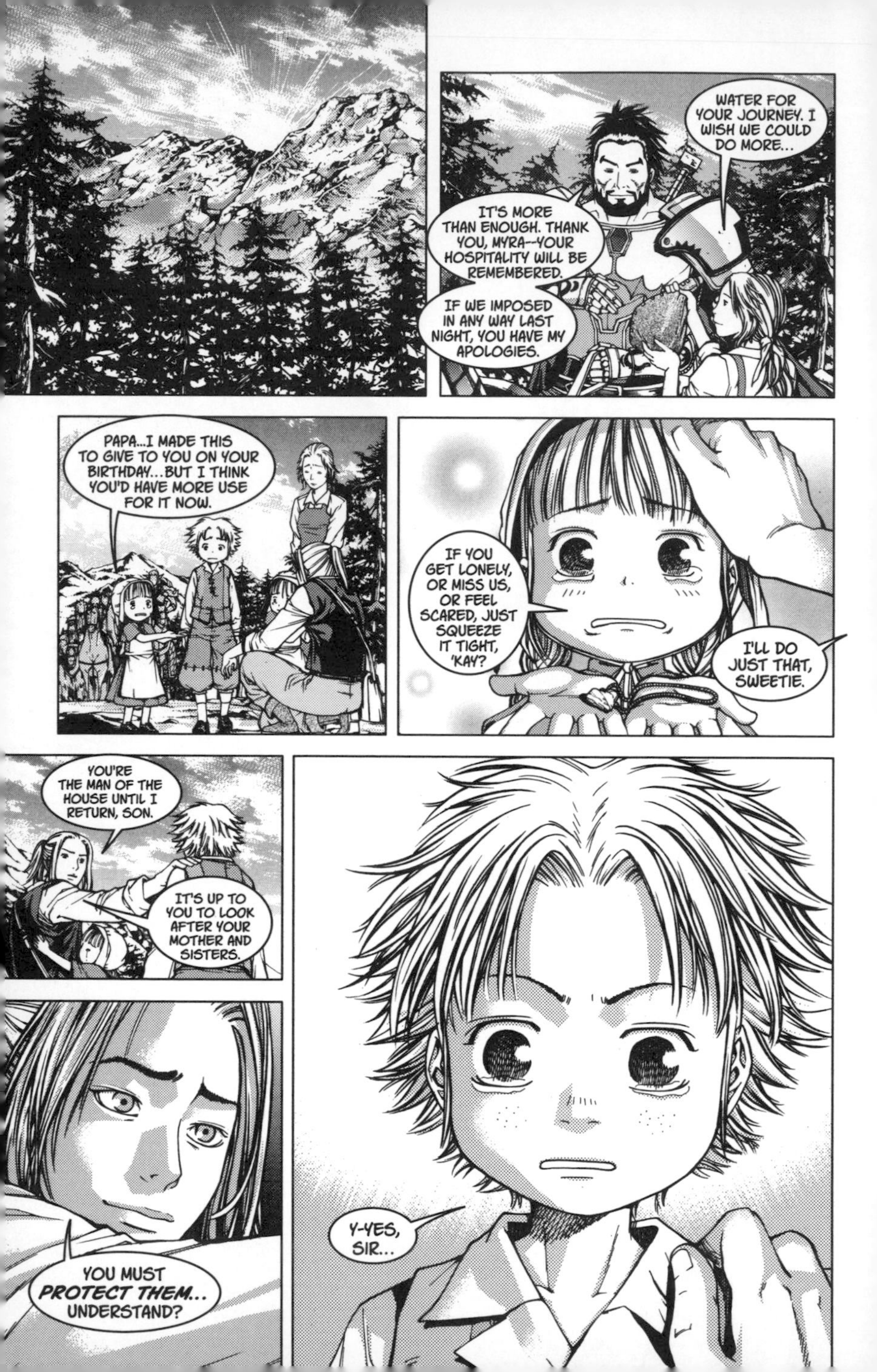
WATER FOR YOUR JOURNEY. I WISH WE COULD DO MORE...
IT'S MORE THAN ENOUGH. THANK YOU, MYRA--YOUR HOSPITALITY WILL BE REMEMBERED.
IF WE IMPOSED IN ANY WAY LAST NIGHT, YOU HAVE MY APOLOGIES.
PAPA...I MADE THIS TO GIVE TO YOU ON YOUR BIRTHDAY...BUT I THINK YOU'D HAVE MORE USE FOR IT NOW.
IF YOU GET LONELY, OR MISS US, OR FEEL SCARED, JUST SQUEEZE IT TIGHT, 'KAY?
I'LL DO JUST THAT, SWEETIE.
YOU'RE THE MAN OF THE HOUSE UNTIL I RETURN, SON.
IT'S UP TO YOU TO LOOK AFTER YOUR MOTHER AND SISTERS.
YOU MUST *PROTECT THEM...* UNDERSTAND?
Y-YES, SIR...

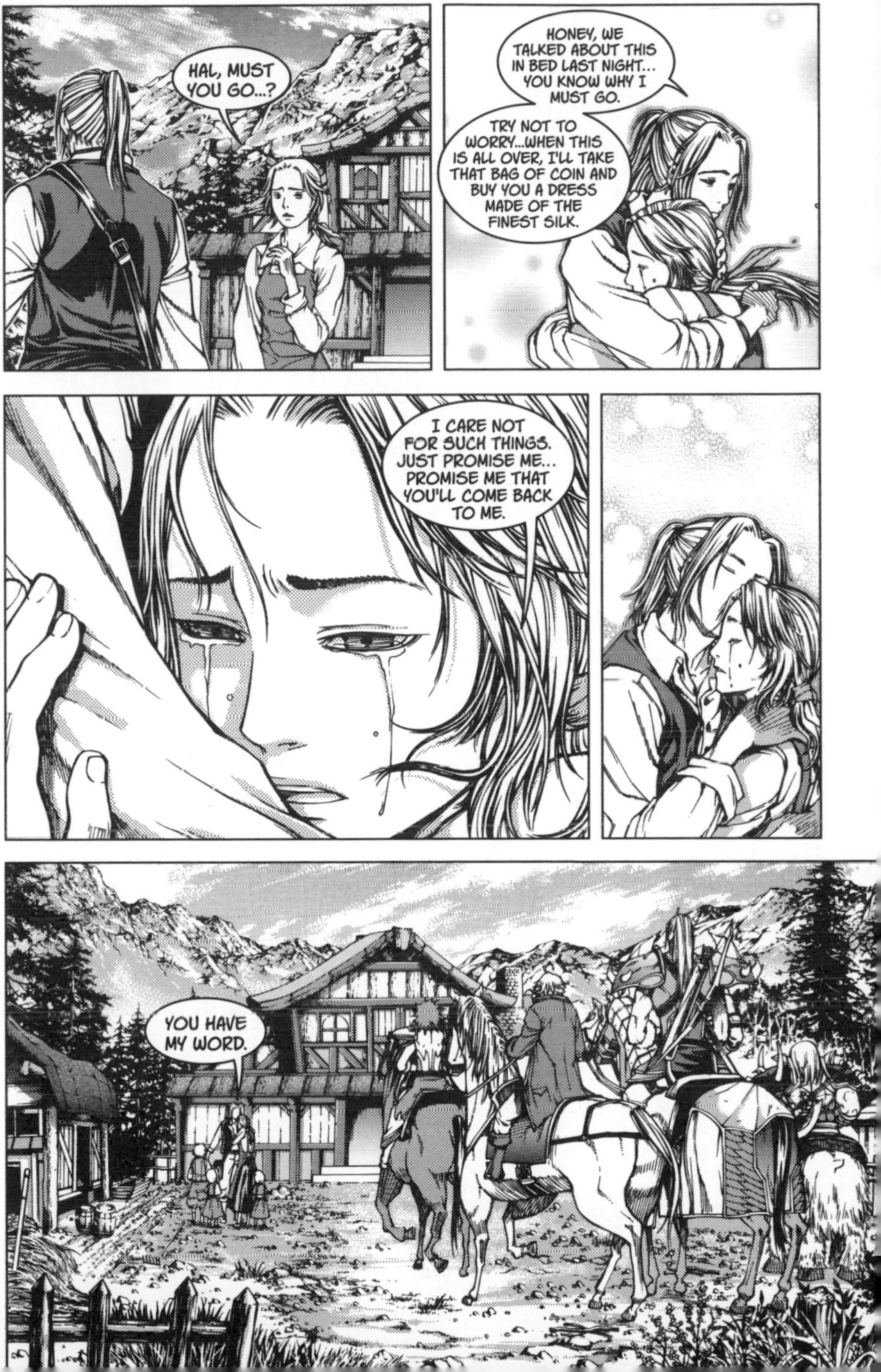
HAL, MUST YOU GO...?
HONEY, WE TALKED ABOUT THIS IN BED LAST NIGHT... YOU KNOW WHY I MUST GO.
TRY NOT TO WORRY...WHEN THIS IS ALL OVER, I'LL TAKE THAT BAG OF COIN AND BUY YOU A DRESS MADE OF THE FINEST SILK.
I CARE NOT FOR SUCH THINGS. JUST PROMISE ME... PROMISE ME THAT YOU'LL COME BACK TO ME.
YOU HAVE MY WORD.

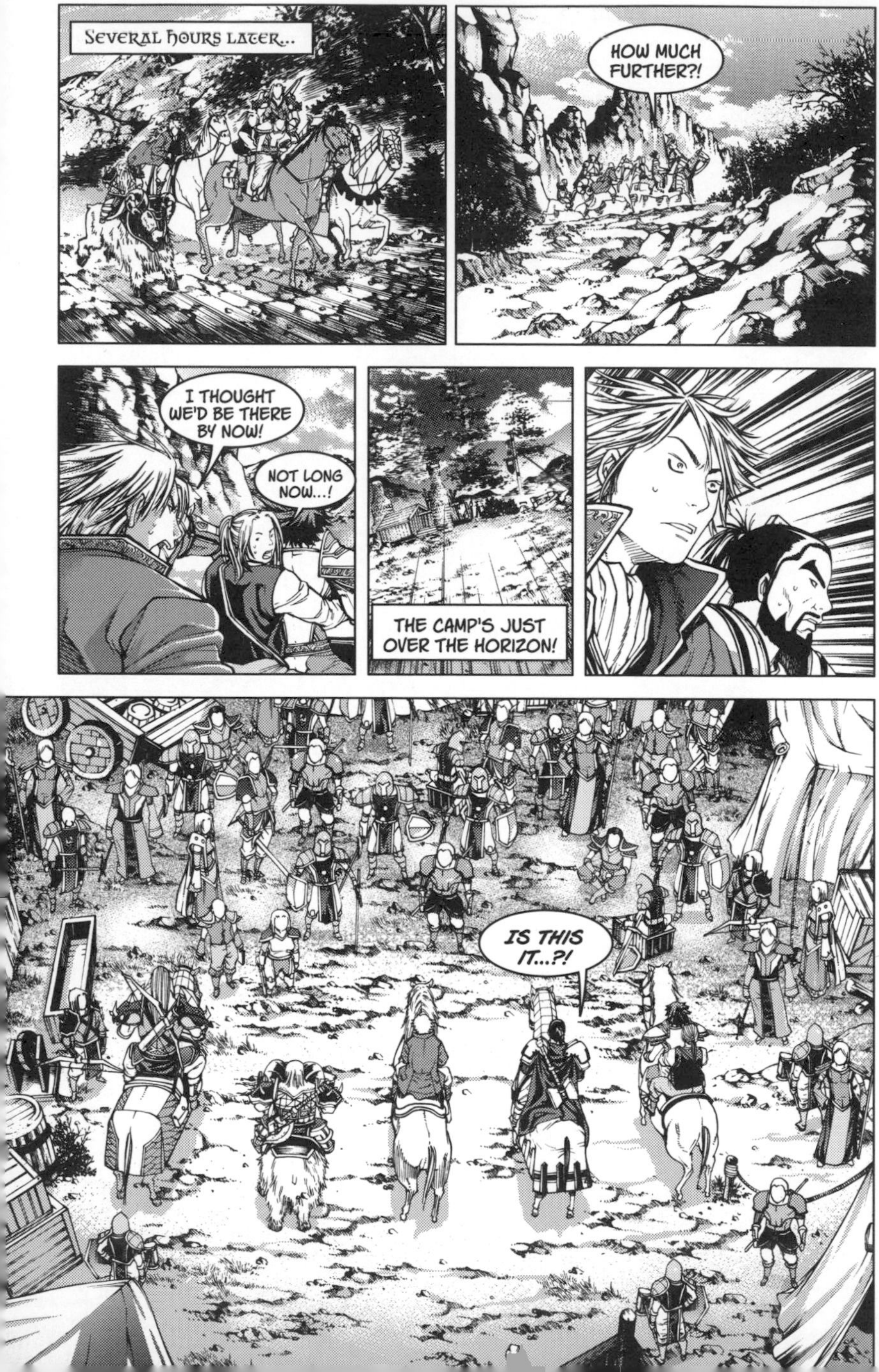
Several hours later...
HOW MUCH FURTHER?!
I THOUGHT WE'D BE THERE BY NOW!
NOT LONG NOW...!
THE CAMP'S JUST OVER THE HORIZON!
IS THIS IT...?!

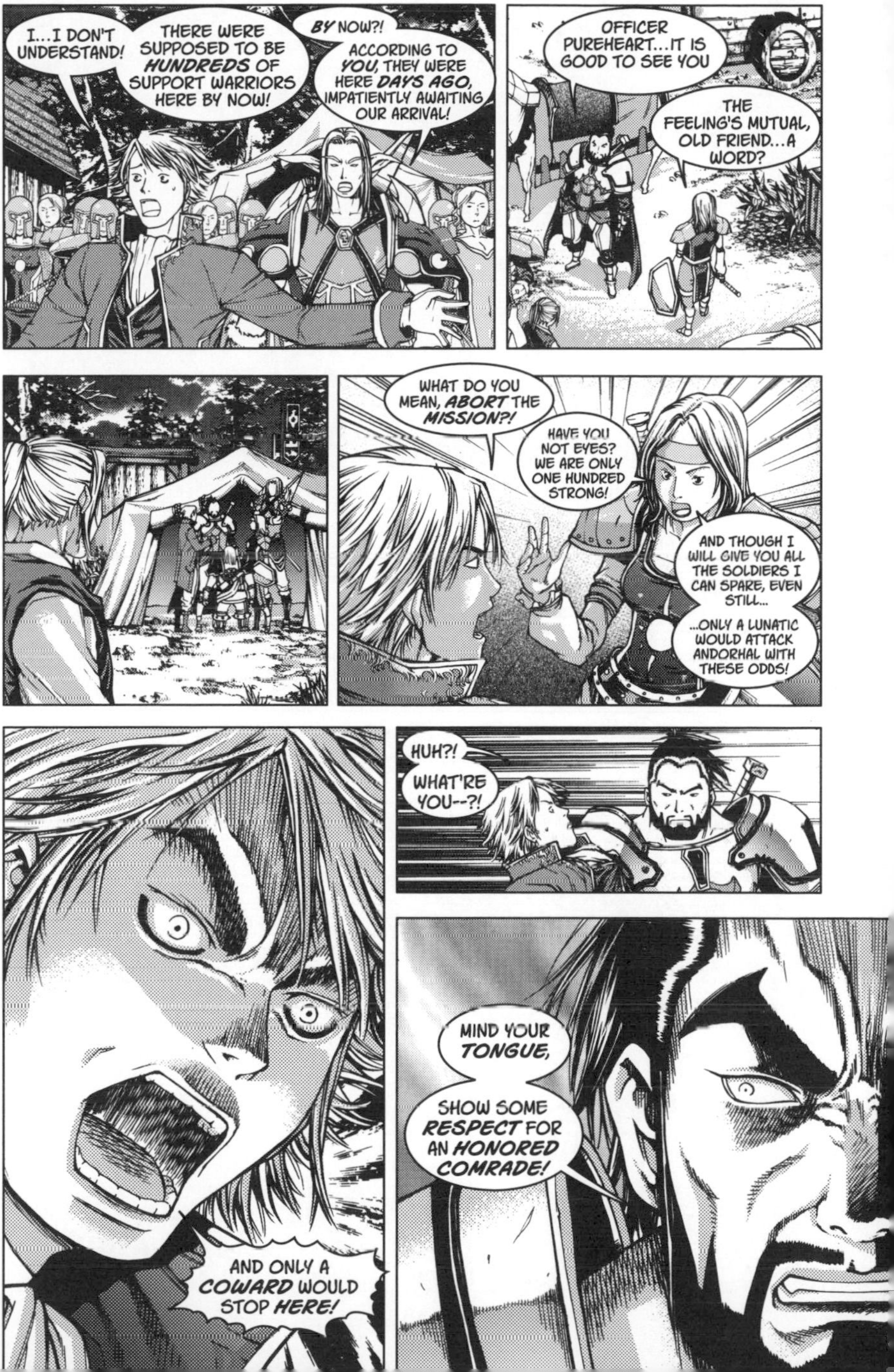
I...I DON'T UNDERSTAND!
THERE WERE SUPPOSED TO BE HUNDREDS OF SUPPORT WARRIORS HERE BY NOW!
BY NOW?!
ACCORDING TO YOU, THEY WERE HERE DAYS AGO, IMPATIENTLY AWAITING OUR ARRIVAL!
OFFICER PUREHEART...IT IS GOOD TO SEE YOU
THE FEELING'S MUTUAL, OLD FRIEND...A WORD?
WHAT DO YOU MEAN, ABORT THE MISSION?!
HAVE YOU NOT EYES? WE ARE ONLY ONE HUNDRED STRONG!
AND THOUGH I WILL GIVE YOU ALL THE SOLDIERS I CAN SPARE, EVEN STILL...
...ONLY A LUNATIC WOULD ATTACK ANDORHAL WITH THESE ODDS!
AND ONLY A COWARD WOULD STOP HERE!
HUH?!
WHAT'RE YOU--?!
MIND YOUR TONGUE,
SHOW SOME RESPECT FOR AN HONORED COMRADE!

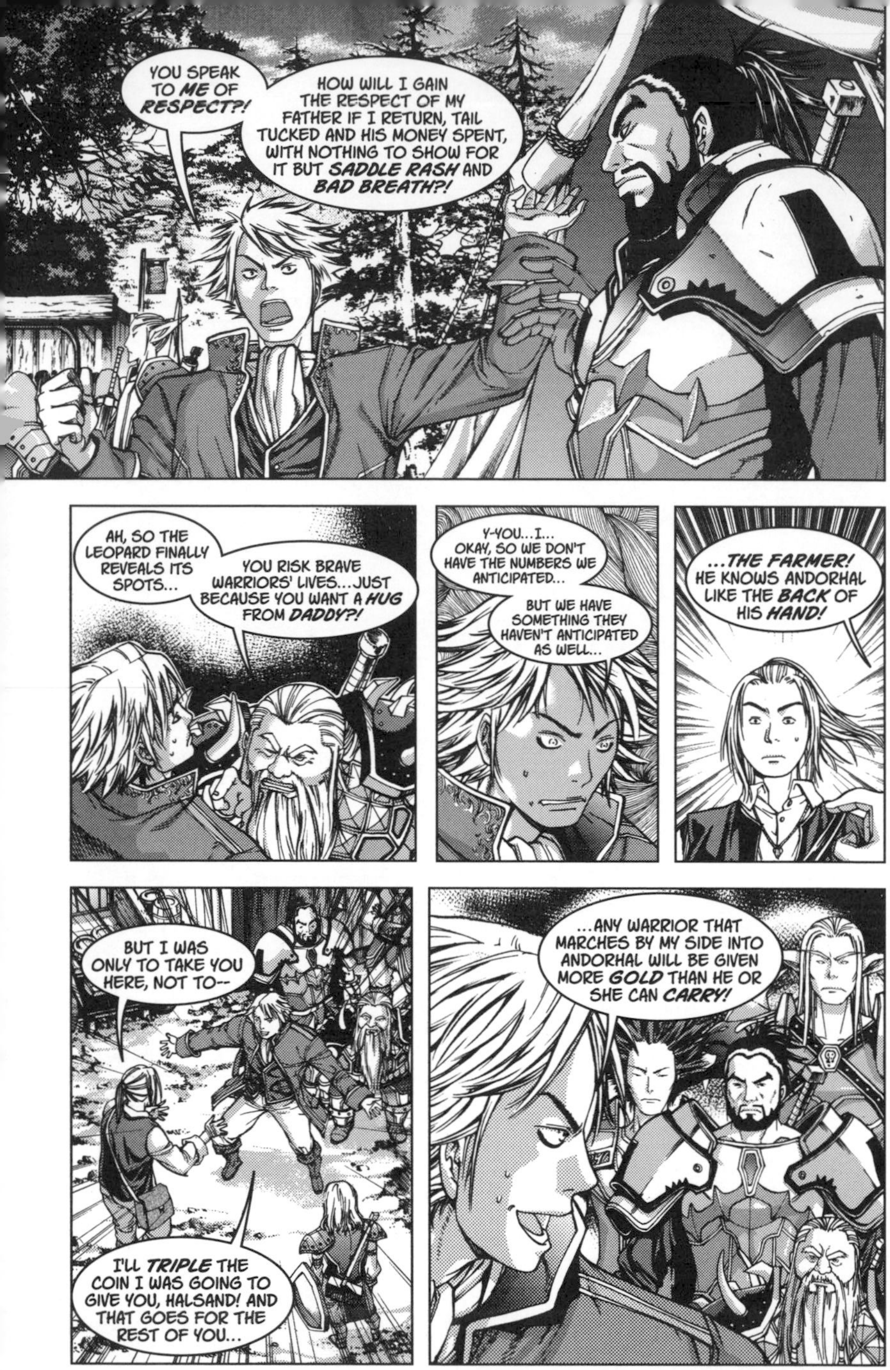
YOU SPEAK TO *ME* OF *RESPECT?!*
HOW WILL I GAIN THE RESPECT OF MY FATHER IF I RETURN, TAIL TUCKED AND HIS MONEY SPENT, WITH NOTHING TO SHOW FOR IT BUT ***SADDLE RASH*** AND ***BAD BREATH?!***
AH, SO THE LEOPARD FINALLY REVEALS ITS SPOTS...
YOU RISK BRAVE WARRIORS' LIVES...JUST BECAUSE YOU WANT A ***HUG*** FROM ***DADDY?!***
Y-YOU...I... OKAY, SO WE DON'T HAVE THE NUMBERS WE ANTICIPATED...
BUT WE HAVE SOMETHING THEY HAVEN'T ANTICIPATED AS WELL...
...***THE FARMER!*** HE KNOWS ANDORHAL LIKE THE ***BACK*** OF HIS ***HAND!***
BUT I WAS ONLY TO TAKE YOU HERE, NOT TO--
I'LL ***TRIPLE*** THE COIN I WAS GOING TO GIVE YOU, HALSAND! AND THAT GOES FOR THE REST OF YOU...
...ANY WARRIOR THAT MARCHES BY MY SIDE INTO ANDORHAL WILL BE GIVEN MORE ***GOLD*** THAN HE OR SHE CAN ***CARRY!***

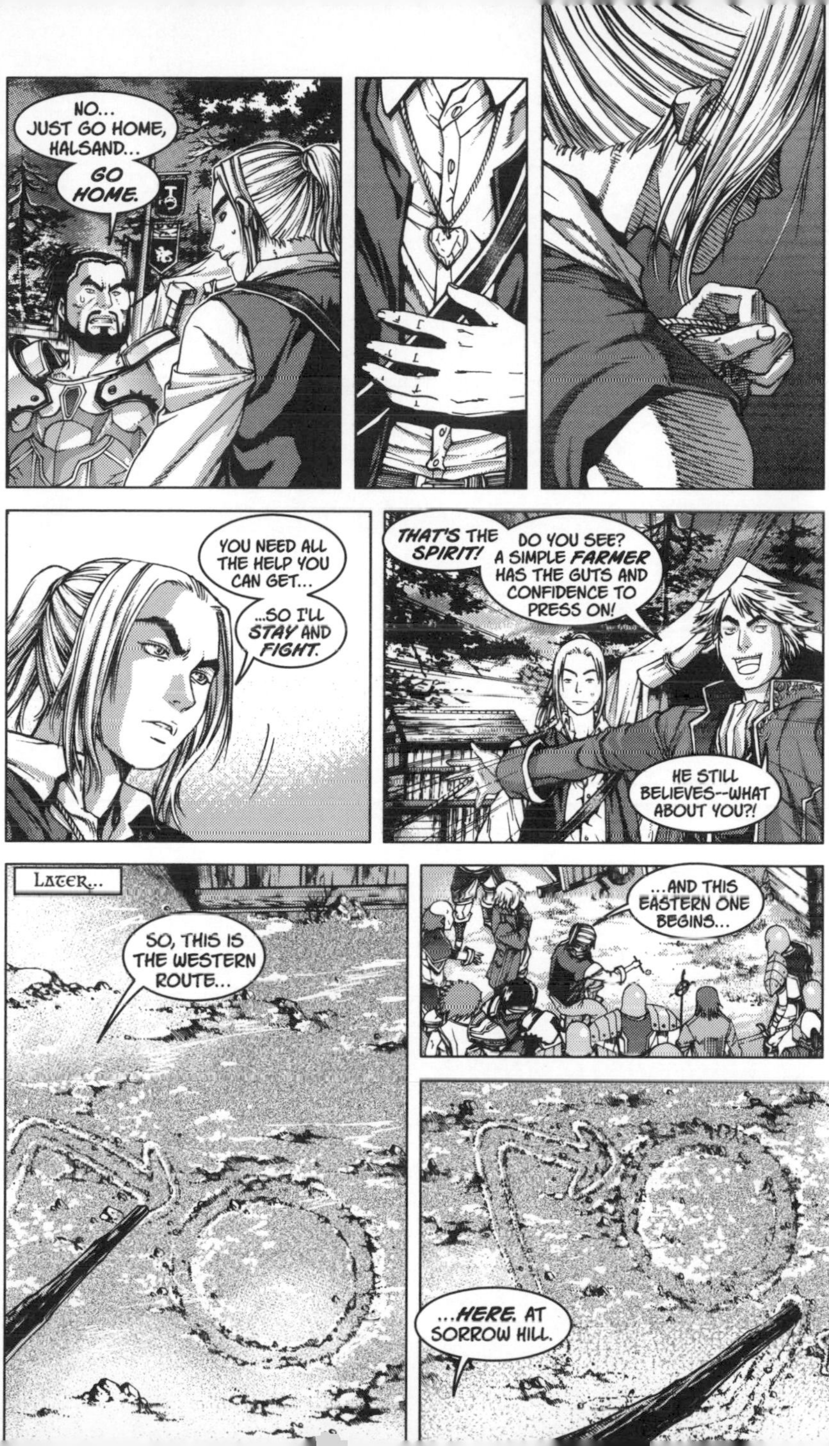
NO... JUST GO HOME, HALSAND...
GO HOME.
YOU NEED ALL THE HELP YOU CAN GET...
...SO I'LL STAY AND FIGHT.
THAT'S THE SPIRIT!
DO YOU SEE? A SIMPLE FARMER HAS THE GUTS AND CONFIDENCE TO PRESS ON!
HE STILL BELIEVES--WHAT ABOUT YOU?!
LATER...
SO, THIS IS THE WESTERN ROUTE...
...AND THIS EASTERN ONE BEGINS...
...HERE. AT SORROW HILL.

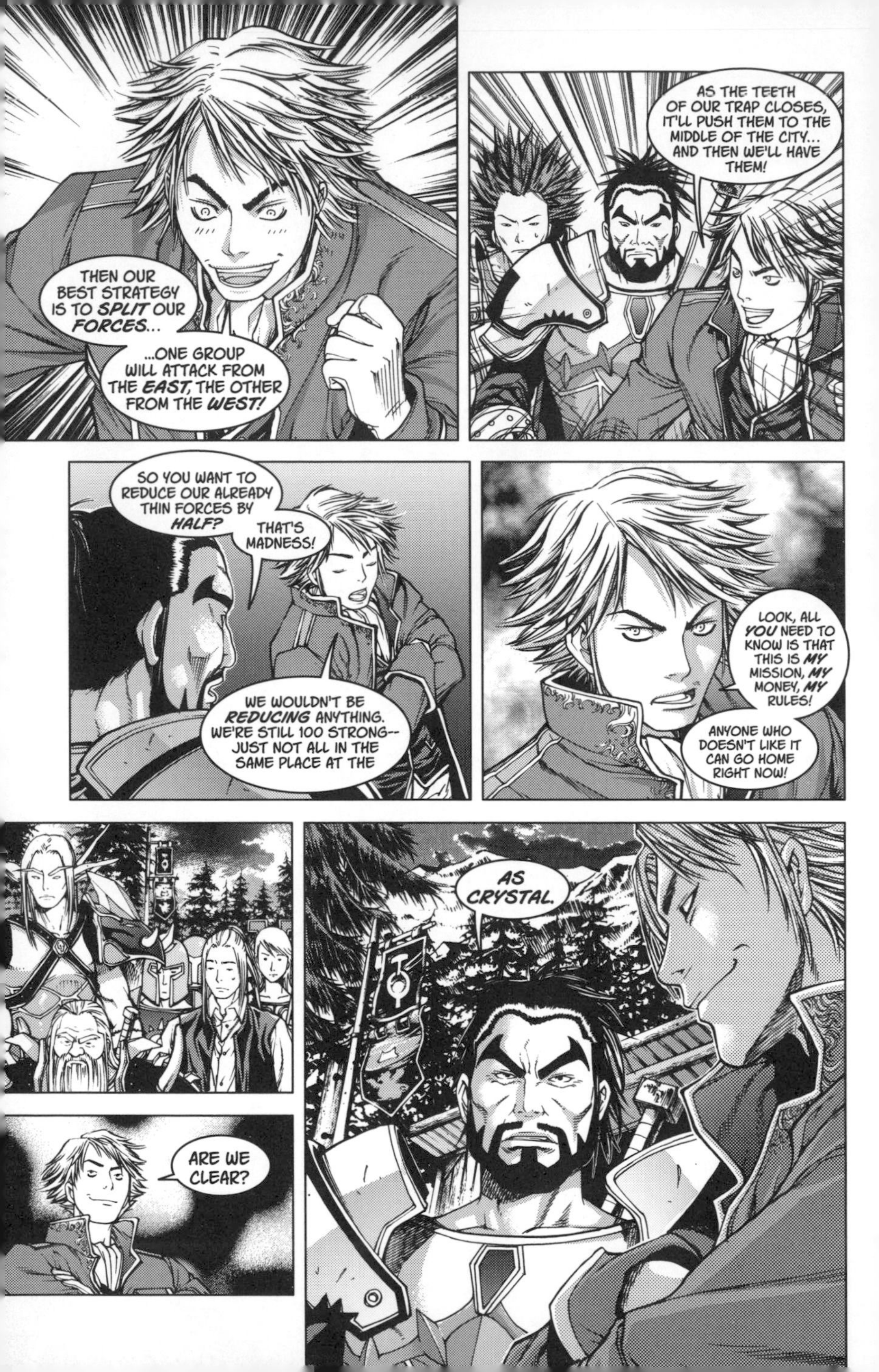

THEN OUR BEST STRATEGY IS TO SPLIT OUR FORCES...
...ONE GROUP WILL ATTACK FROM THE EAST, THE OTHER FROM THE WEST!
AS THE TEETH OF OUR TRAP CLOSES, IT'LL PUSH THEM TO THE MIDDLE OF THE CITY... AND THEN WE'LL HAVE THEM!
SO YOU WANT TO REDUCE OUR ALREADY THIN FORCES BY HALF?
THAT'S MADNESS!
WE WOULDN'T BE REDUCING ANYTHING. WE'RE STILL 100 STRONG-- JUST NOT ALL IN THE SAME PLACE AT THE
LOOK, ALL YOU NEED TO KNOW IS THAT THIS IS MY MISSION, MY MONEY, MY RULES!
ANYONE WHO DOESN'T LIKE IT CAN GO HOME RIGHT NOW!
ARE WE CLEAR?
AS CRYSTAL.

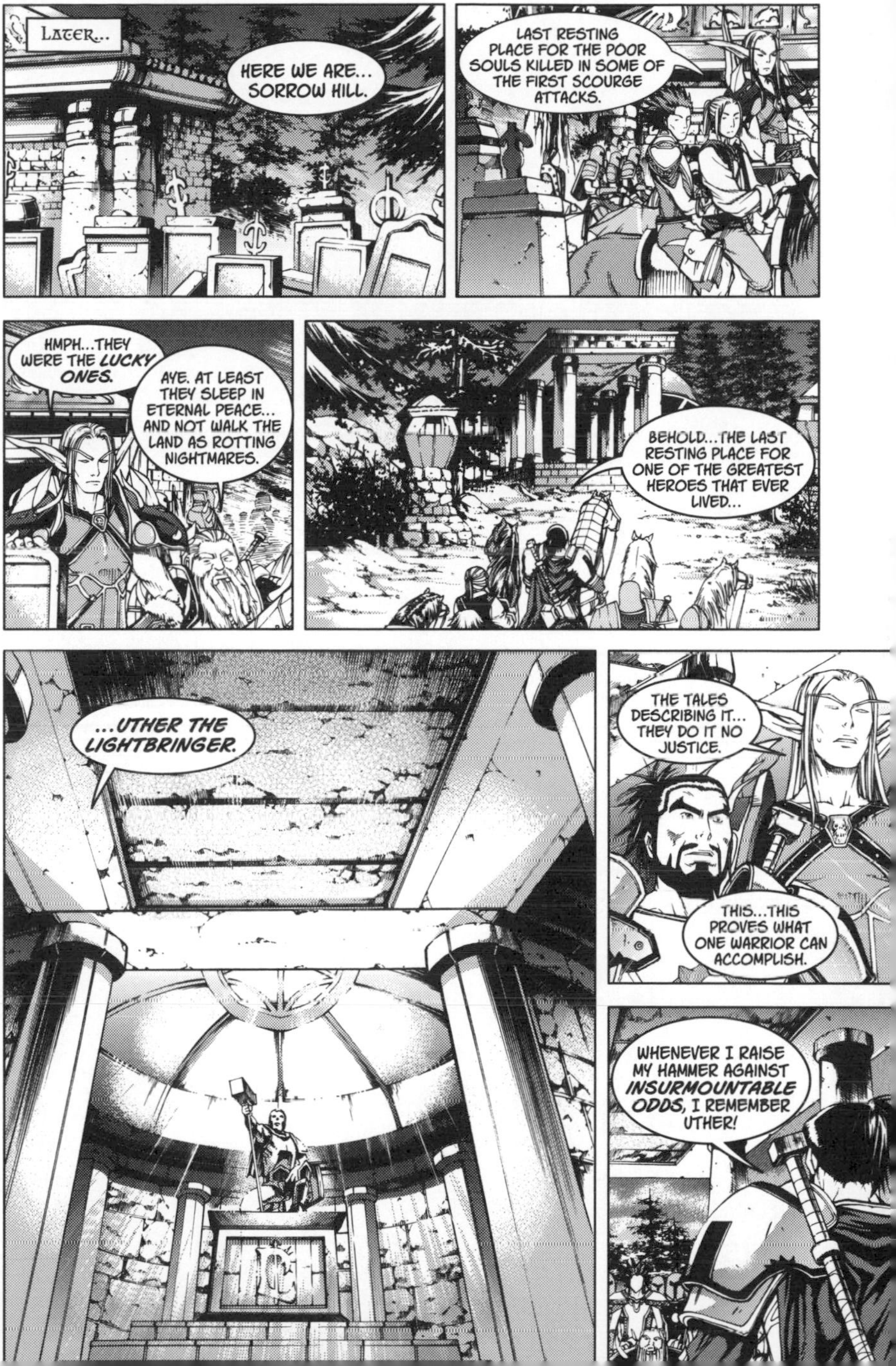
LATER...
HERE WE ARE... SORROW HILL.
LAST RESTING PLACE FOR THE POOR SOULS KILLED IN SOME OF THE FIRST SCOURGE ATTACKS.
HMPH...THEY WERE THE *LUCKY ONES.*
AYE. AT LEAST THEY SLEEP IN ETERNAL PEACE... AND NOT WALK THE LAND AS ROTTING NIGHTMARES.
BEHOLD...THE LAST RESTING PLACE FOR ONE OF THE GREATEST HEROES THAT EVER LIVED...
...UTHER THE LIGHTBRINGER.
THE TALES DESCRIBING IT... THEY DO IT NO JUSTICE.
THIS...THIS PROVES WHAT ONE WARRIOR CAN ACCOMPLISH.
WHENEVER I RAISE MY HAMMER AGAINST *INSURMOUNTABLE ODDS*, I REMEMBER UTHER!

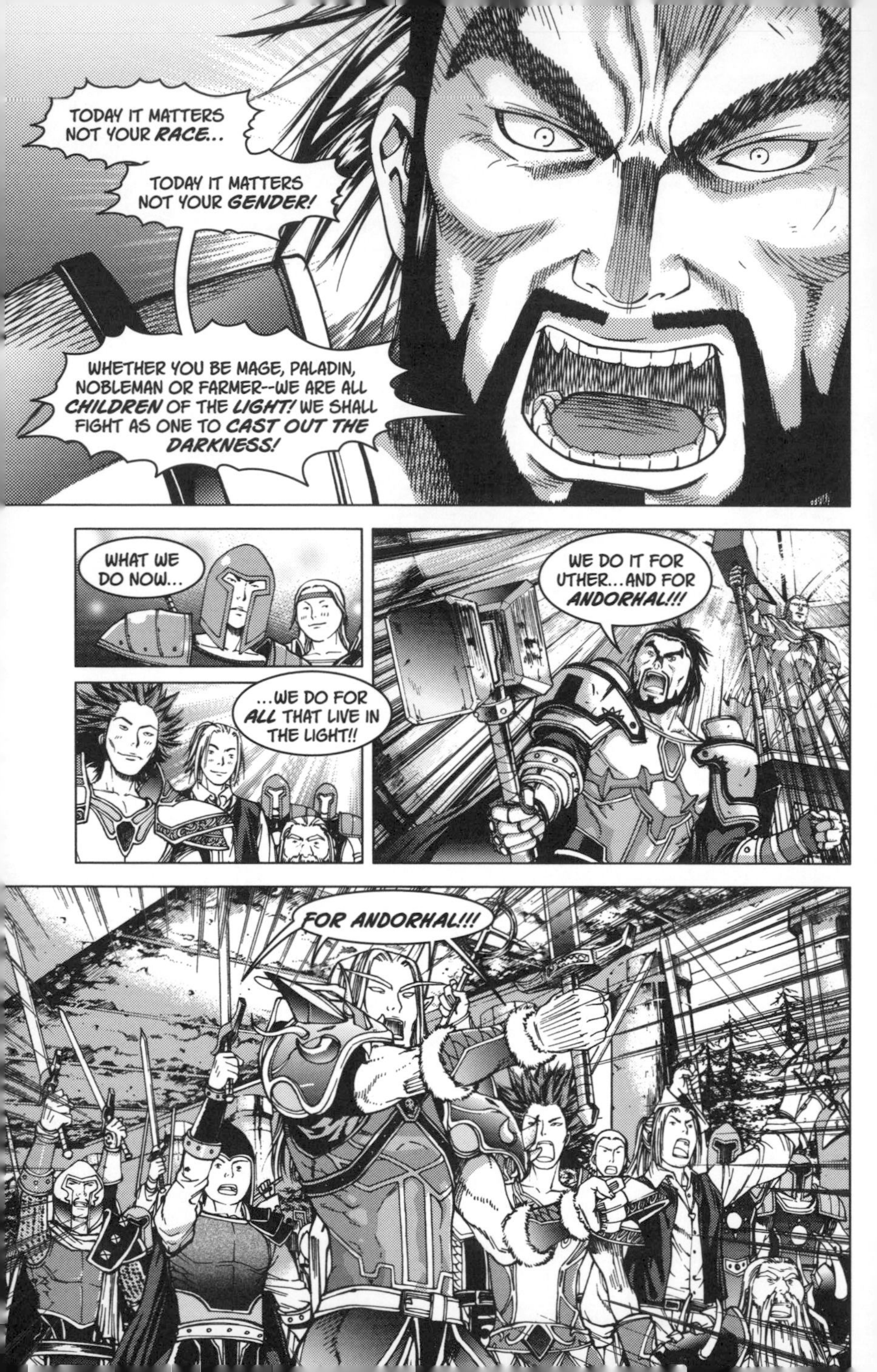
TODAY IT MATTERS NOT YOUR RACE...
TODAY IT MATTERS NOT YOUR GENDER!
WHETHER YOU BE MAGE, PALADIN, NOBLEMAN OR FARMER--WE ARE ALL CHILDREN OF THE LIGHT! WE SHALL FIGHT AS ONE TO CAST OUT THE DARKNESS!
WHAT WE DO NOW...
...WE DO FOR ALL THAT LIVE IN THE LIGHT!!
WE DO IT FOR UTHER...AND FOR ANDORHAL!!!
FOR ANDORHAL!!!

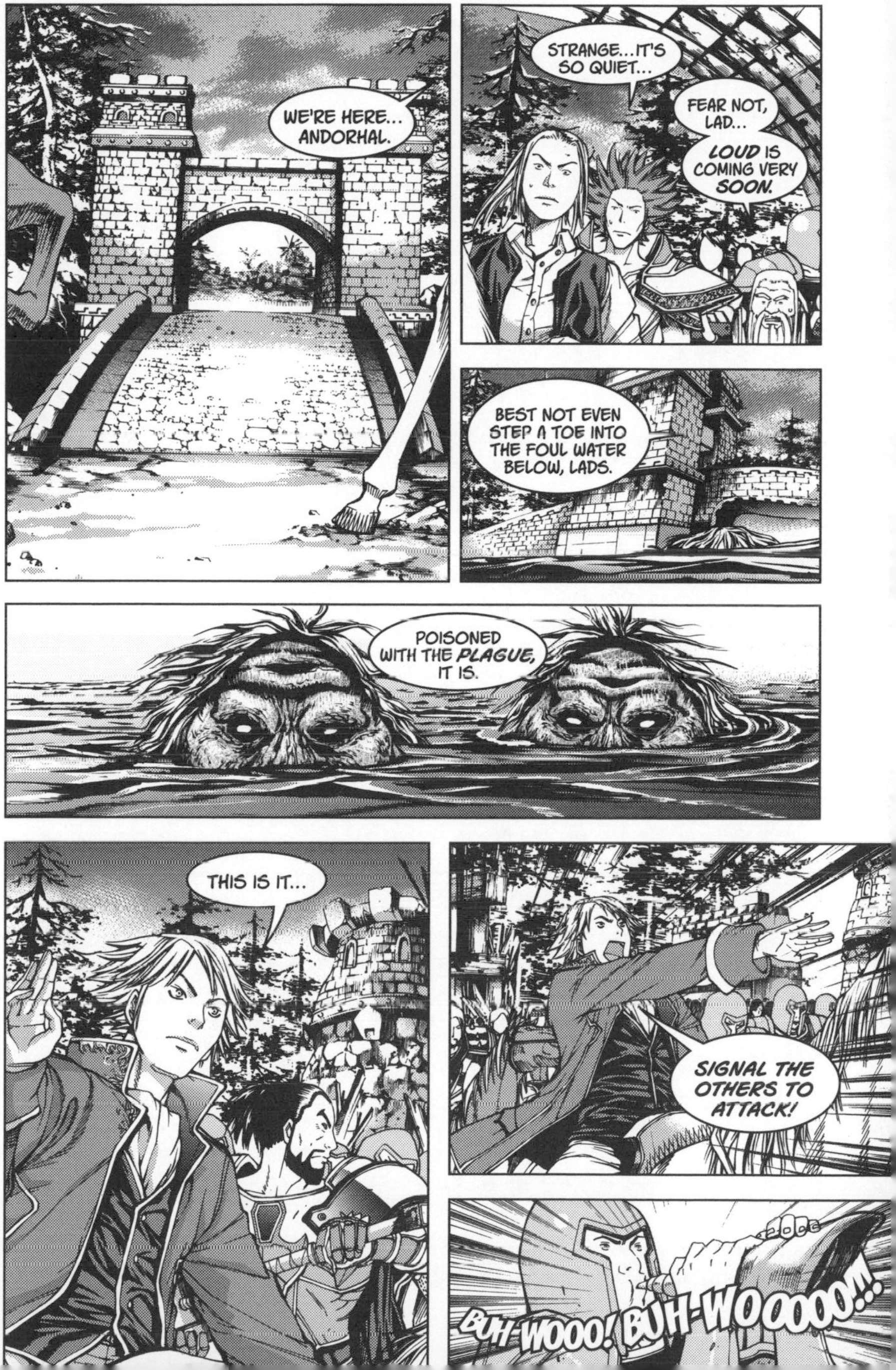
WE'RE HERE... ANDORHAL.
STRANGE...IT'S SO QUIET...
FEAR NOT, LAD...
LOUD IS COMING VERY *SOON.*
BEST NOT EVEN STEP A TOE INTO THE FOUL WATER BELOW, LADS.
POISONED WITH THE *PLAGUE,* IT IS.
THIS IS IT...
SIGNAL THE OTHERS TO ATTACK!
BUH-WOOO! BUH-WOOOOO!!..

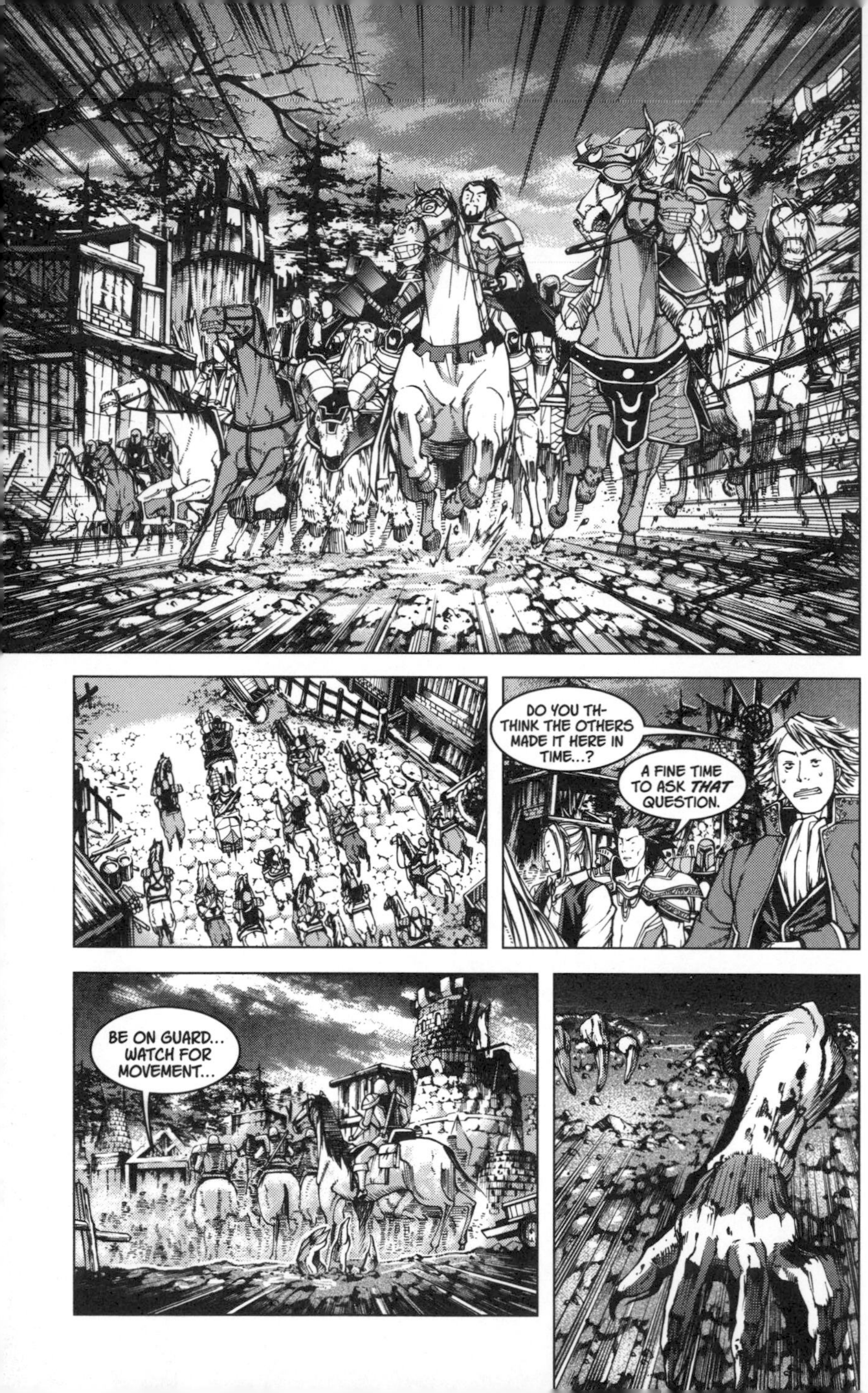
DO YOU TH-THINK THE OTHERS MADE IT HERE IN TIME...?
A FINE TIME TO ASK *THAT* QUESTION.
BE ON GUARD... WATCH FOR MOVEMENT...

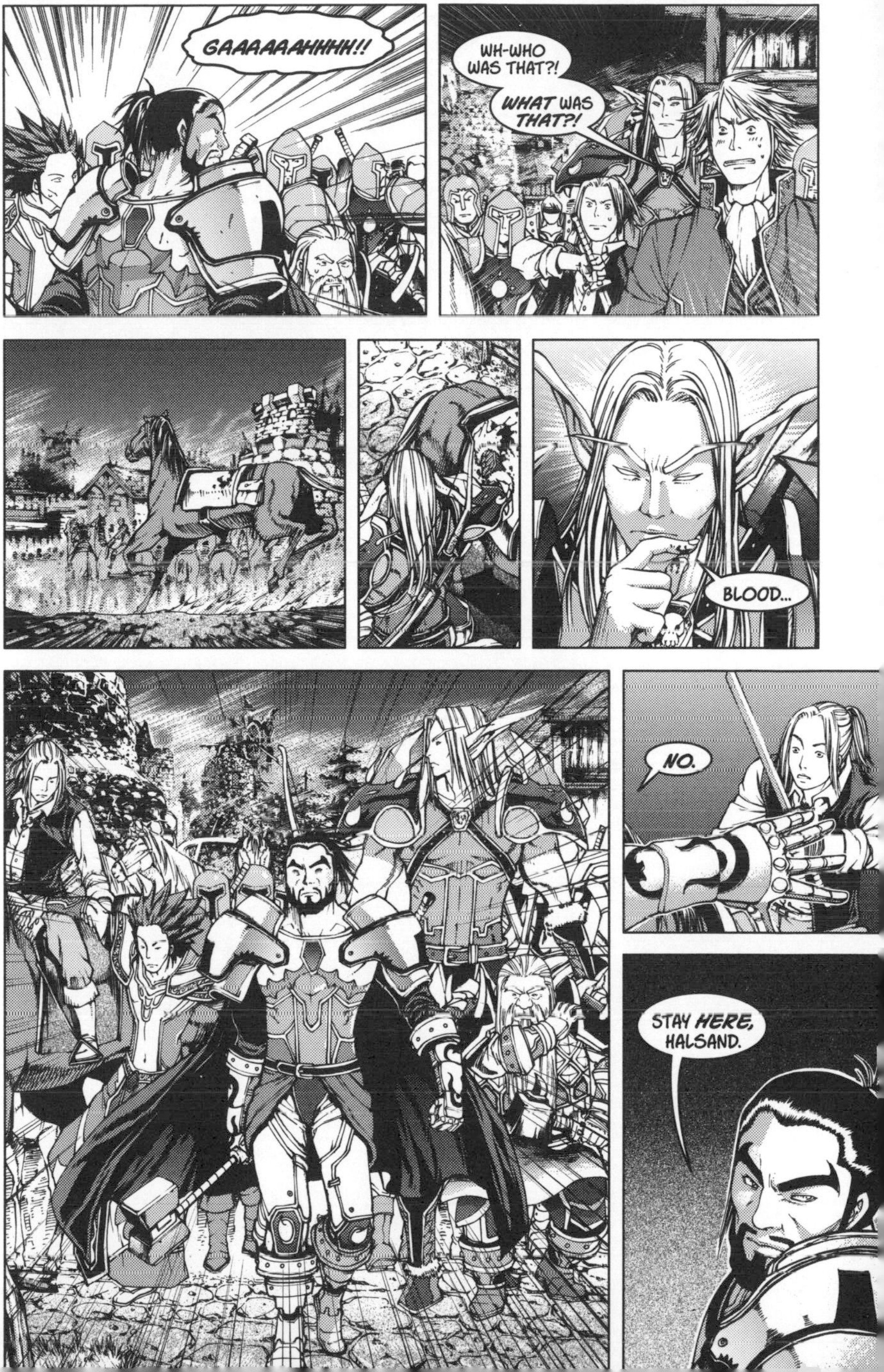
GAAAAAAHHHH!!
WH-WHO WAS THAT?!
WHAT WAS THAT?!
BLOOD...
NO.
STAY HERE, HALSAND.

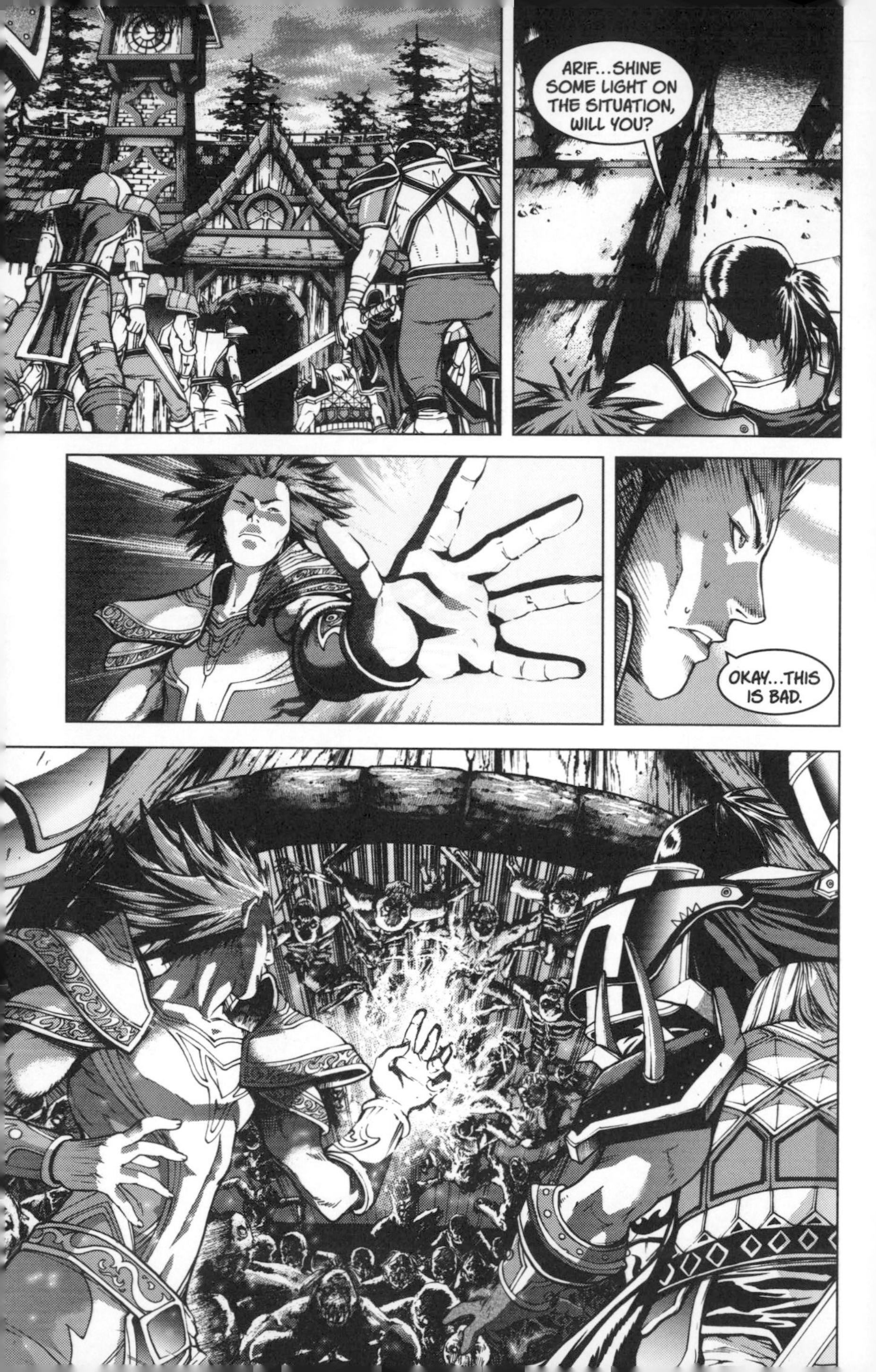
ARIF...SHINE SOME LIGHT ON THE SITUATION, WILL YOU?
OKAY...THIS IS BAD.

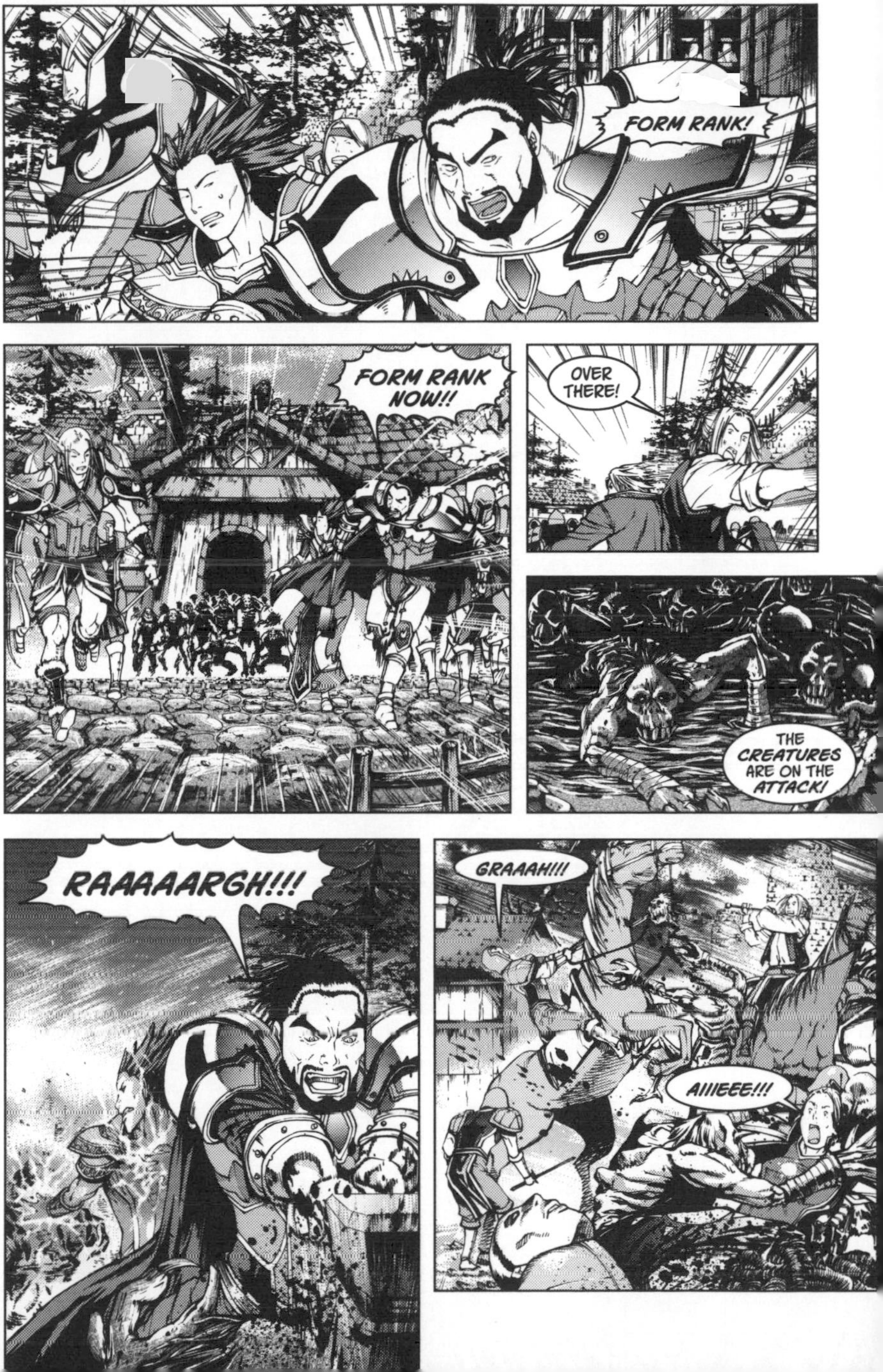
FORM RANK!
FORM RANK NOW!!
OVER THERE!
THE CREATURES ARE ON THE ATTACK!
RAAAAARGH!!!
GRAAAH!!!
AIIIEEE!!!

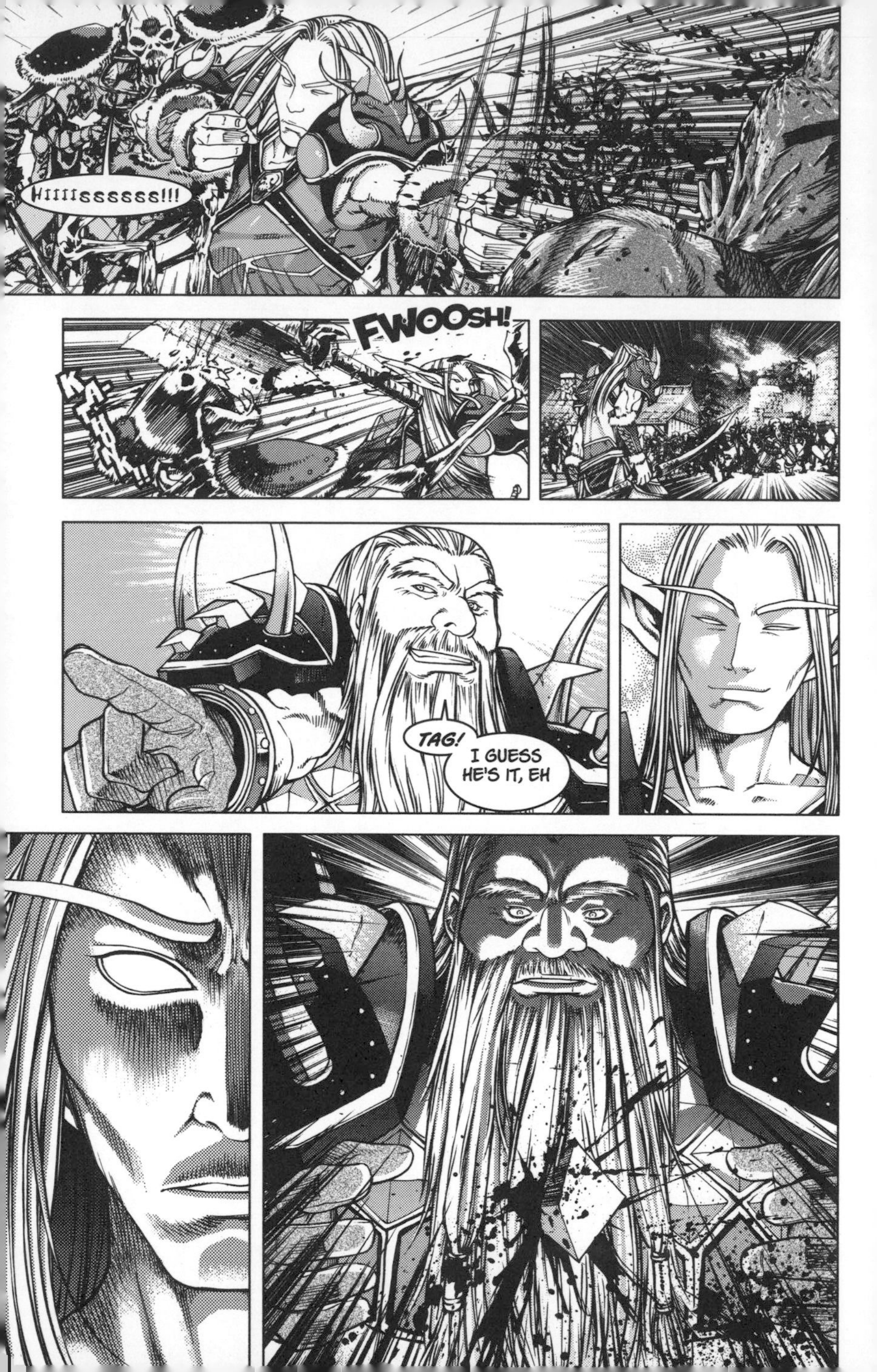
HIIIISSSSSS!!!
FWOOSH!
KA-THUNK!!
TAG!
I GUESS HE'S IT, EH

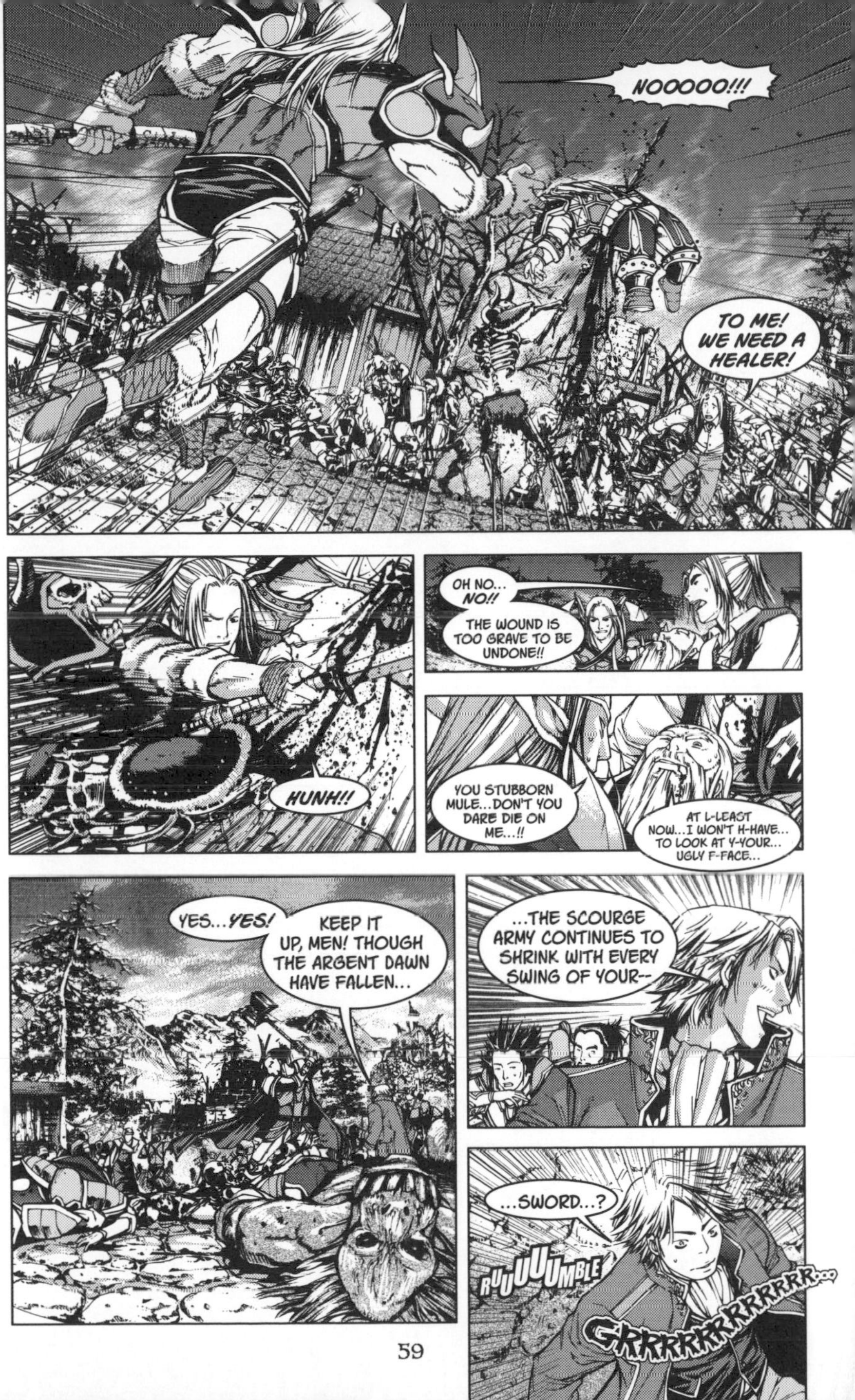
NOOOOO!!!
TO ME! WE NEED A HEALER!
HUNH!!
OH NO... NO!!
THE WOUND IS TOO GRAVE TO BE UNDONE!!
YOU STUBBORN MULE...DON'T YOU DARE DIE ON ME...!!
AT L-LEAST NOW...I WON'T H-HAVE... TO LOOK AT Y-YOUR... UGLY F-FACE...
YES...YES!
KEEP IT UP, MEN! THOUGH THE ARGENT DAWN HAVE FALLEN...
...THE SCOURGE ARMY CONTINUES TO SHRINK WITH EVERY SWING OF YOUR--
...SWORD...?
RUUUUUMBLE
GRRRRRRRRRRRRR...

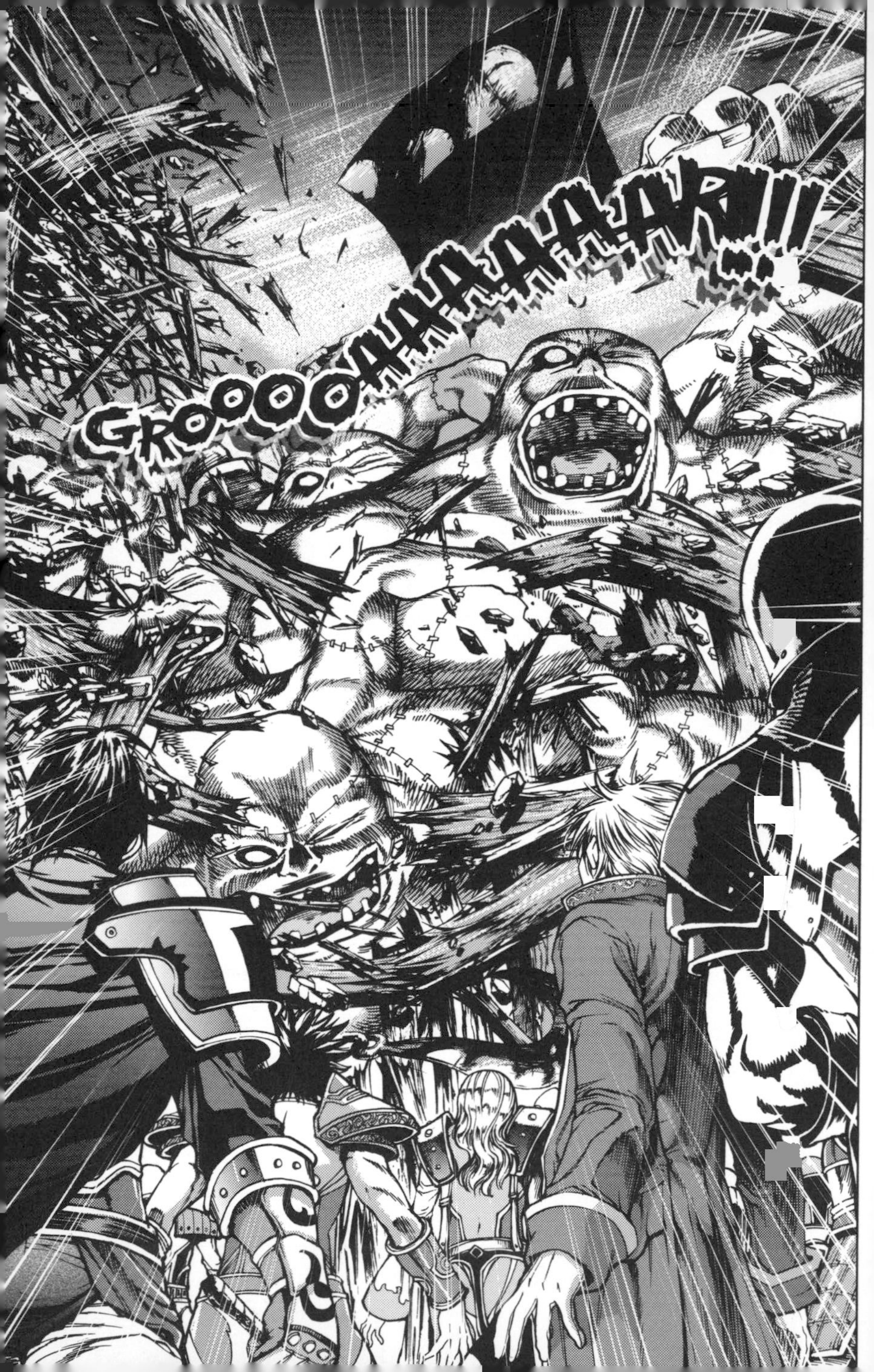
GROOOOOAAAAAAAAR!!!

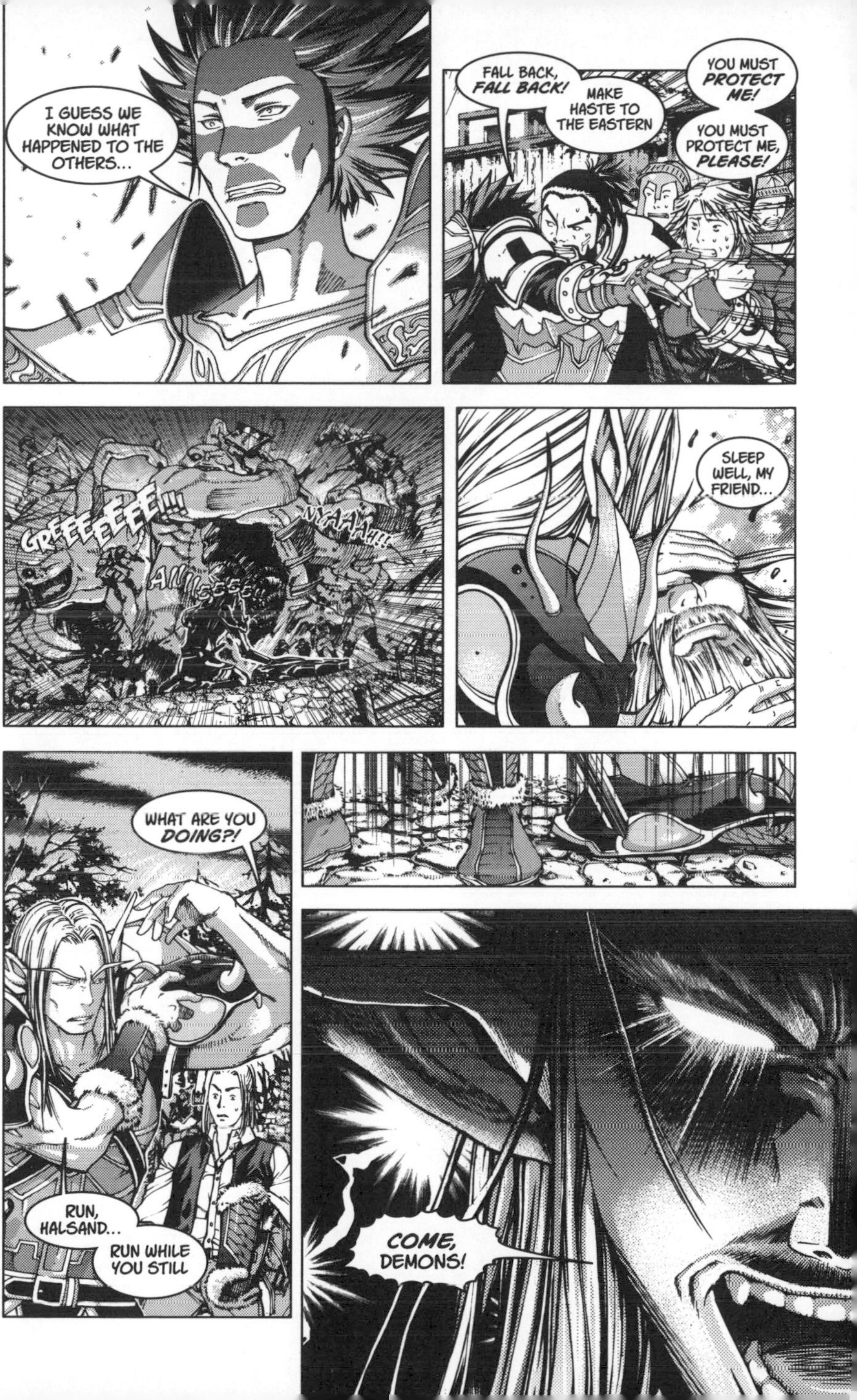
I GUESS WE KNOW WHAT HAPPENED TO THE OTHERS...
FALL BACK, *FALL BACK!*
MAKE HASTE TO THE EASTERN
YOU MUST *PROTECT ME!*
YOU MUST PROTECT ME, *PLEASE!*
GREEEEEEE!!!
NYAAAA!!!
SLEEP WELL, MY FRIEND...
WHAT ARE YOU *DOING?!*
RUN, HALSAND...
RUN WHILE YOU STILL
COME, DEMONS!

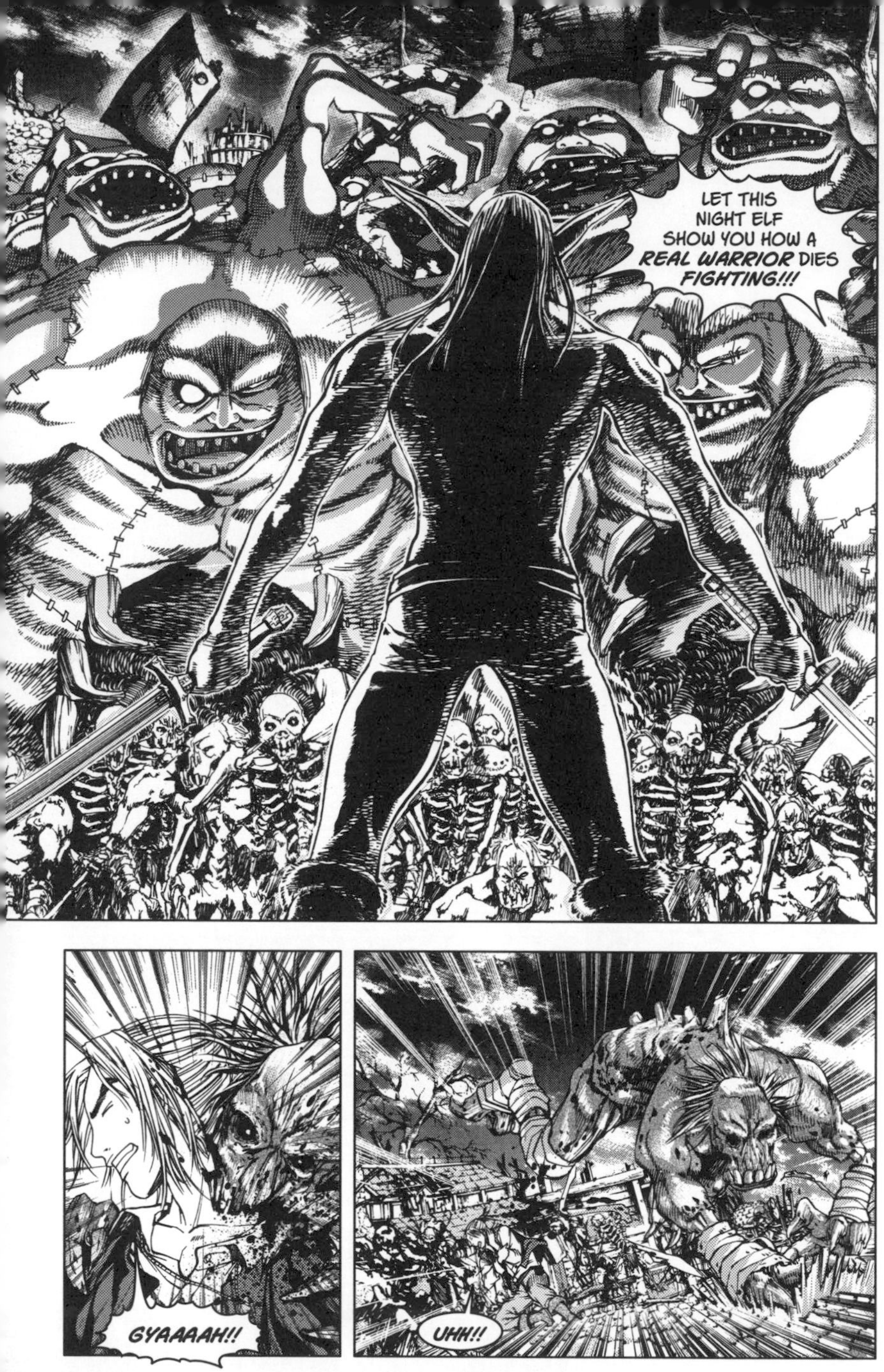
LET THIS NIGHT ELF SHOW YOU HOW A REAL WARRIOR DIES FIGHTING!!!
GYAAAAH!!
UHH!!

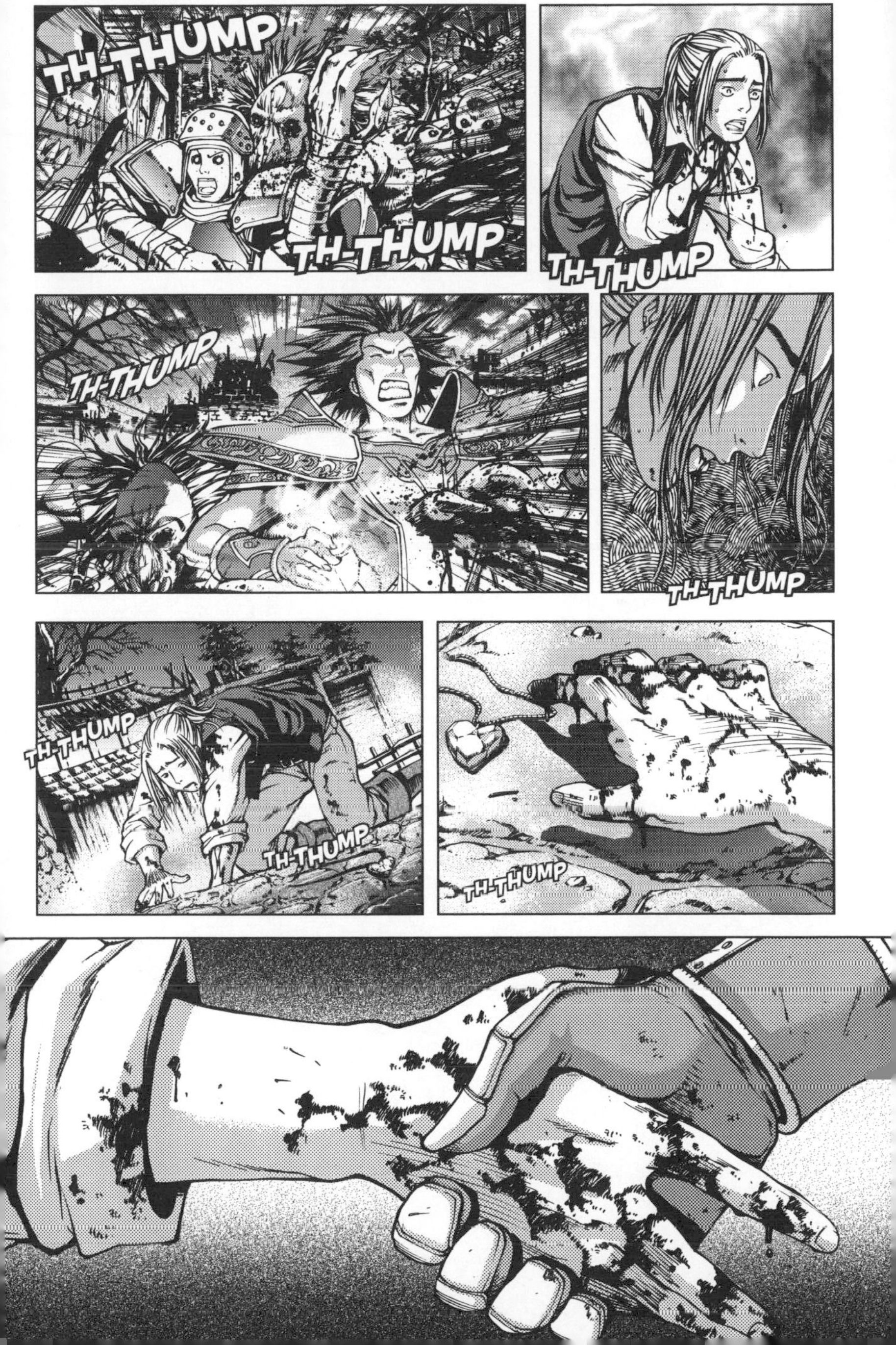
TH-THUMP
TH-THUMP
TH-THUMP
TH-THUMP
TH-THUMP
TH-THUMP
TH-THUMP
TH-THUMP

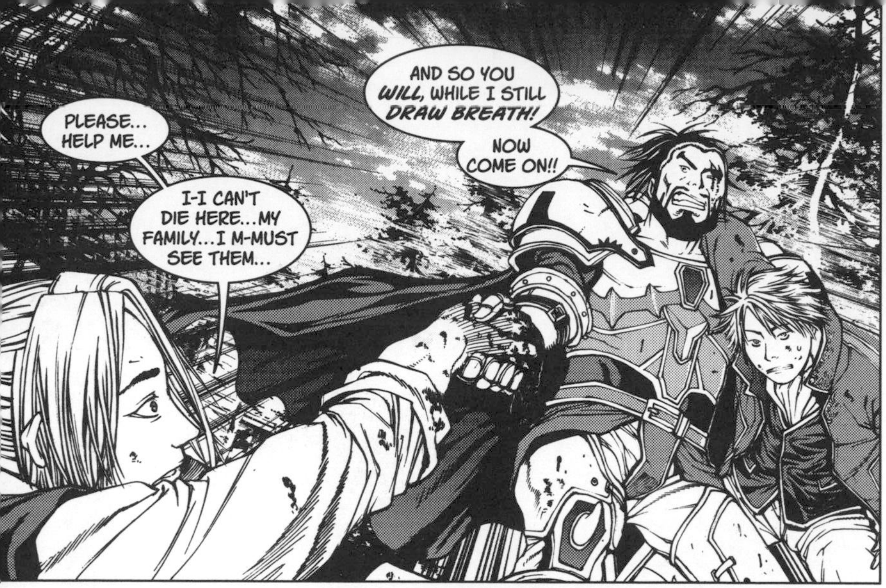
PLEASE... HELP ME...
I-I CAN'T DIE HERE...MY FAMILY...I M-MUST SEE THEM...
AND SO YOU *WILL*, WHILE I STILL *DRAW BREATH!*
NOW COME ON!!

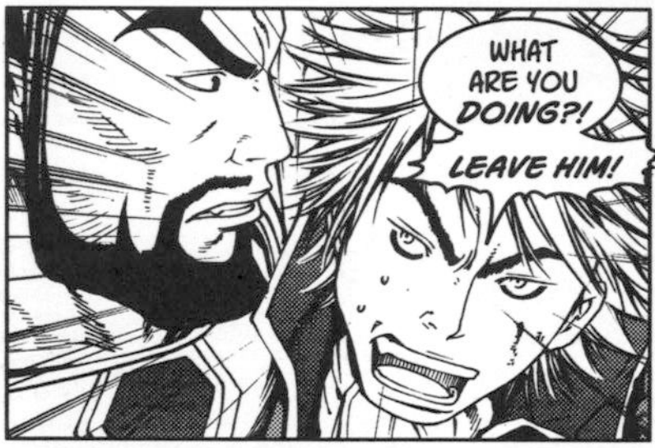
WHAT ARE YOU *DOING?!*
LEAVE HIM!

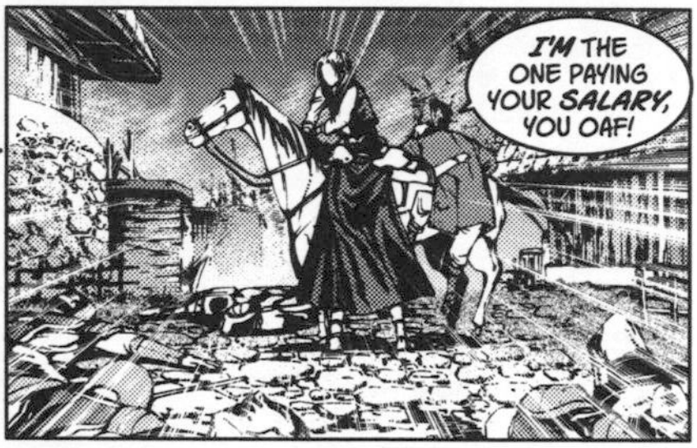
I'M THE ONE PAYING YOUR *SALARY*, YOU OAF!

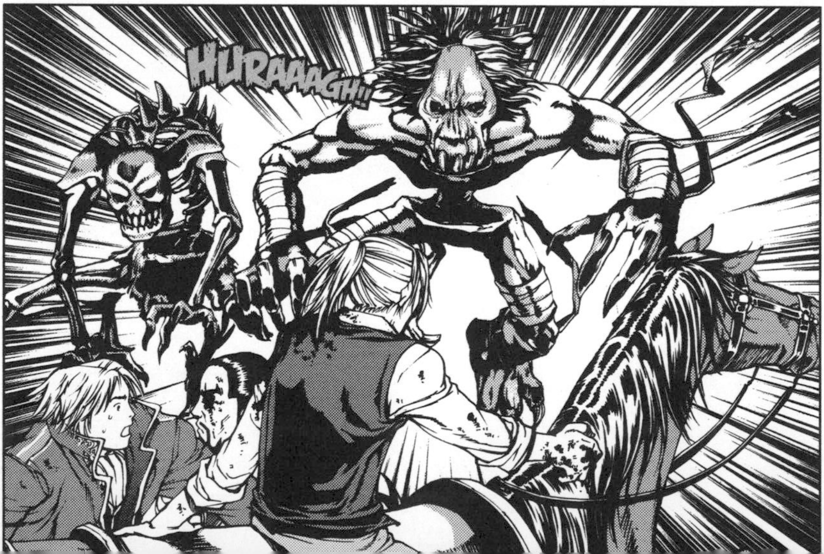
HURAAAGH!!

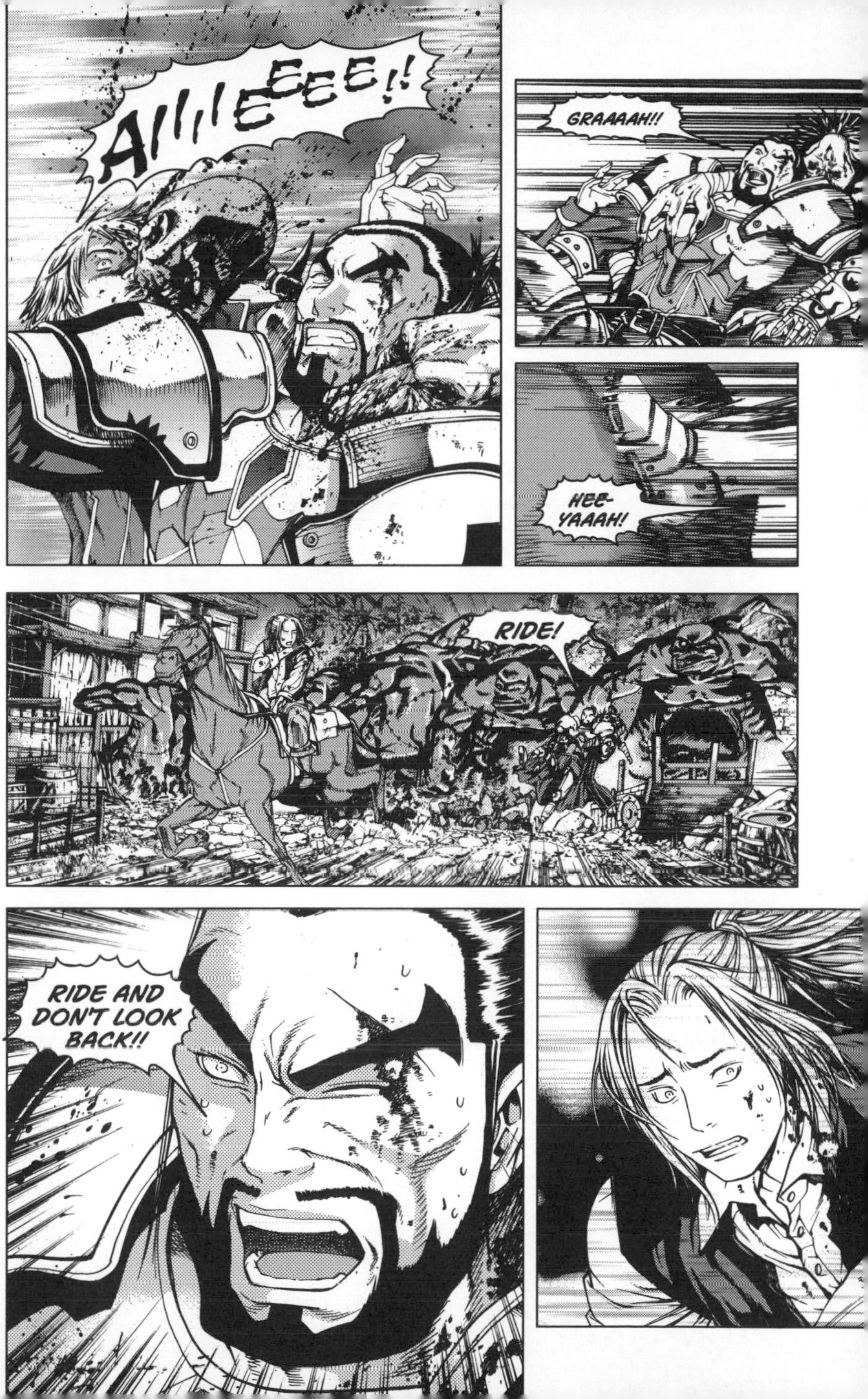
AIIIEEEEE!!
GRAAAAH!!
HEE-YAAAH!
RIDE!
RIDE AND DON'T LOOK BACK!!

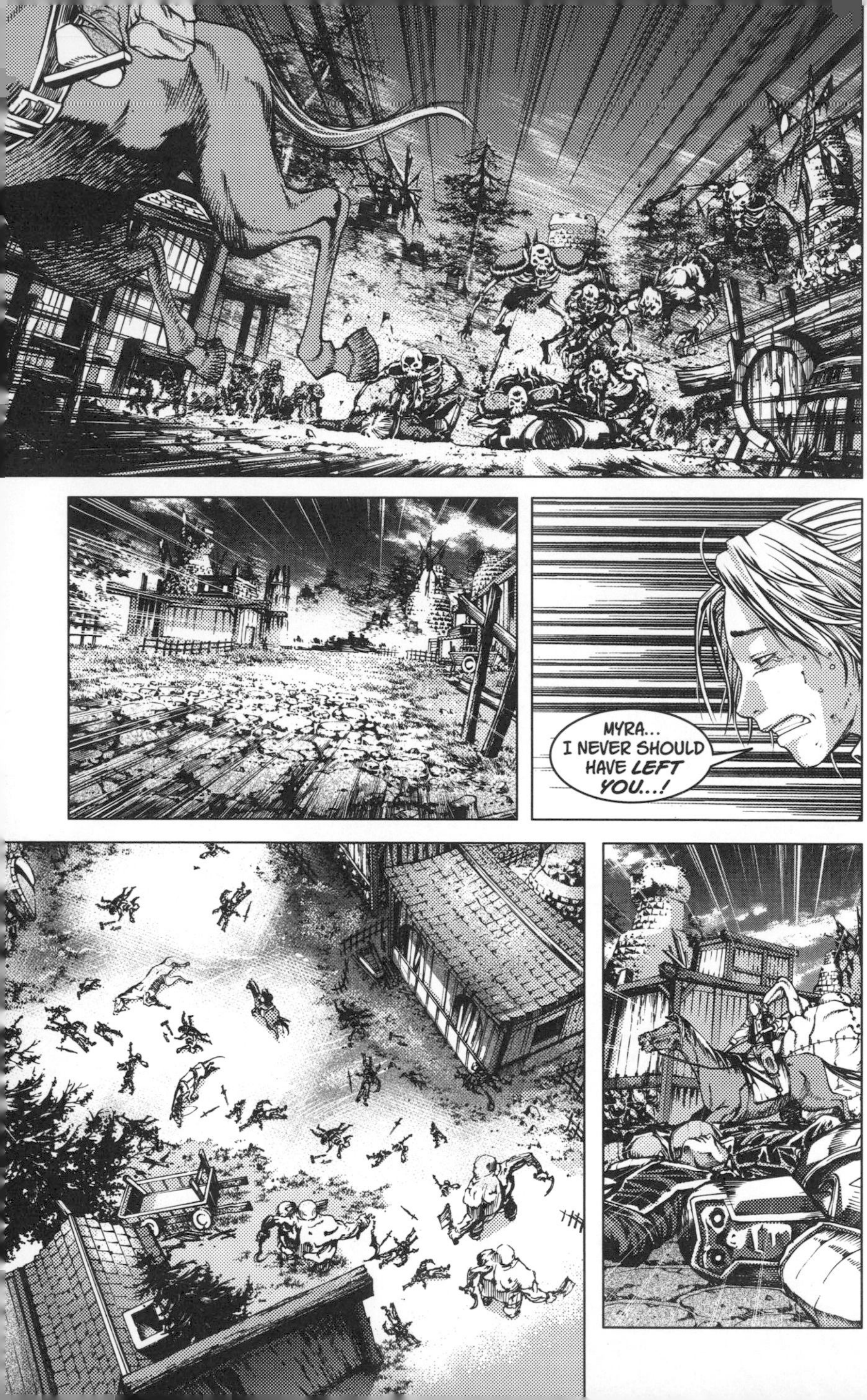
MYRA... I NEVER SHOULD HAVE *LEFT YOU*...!

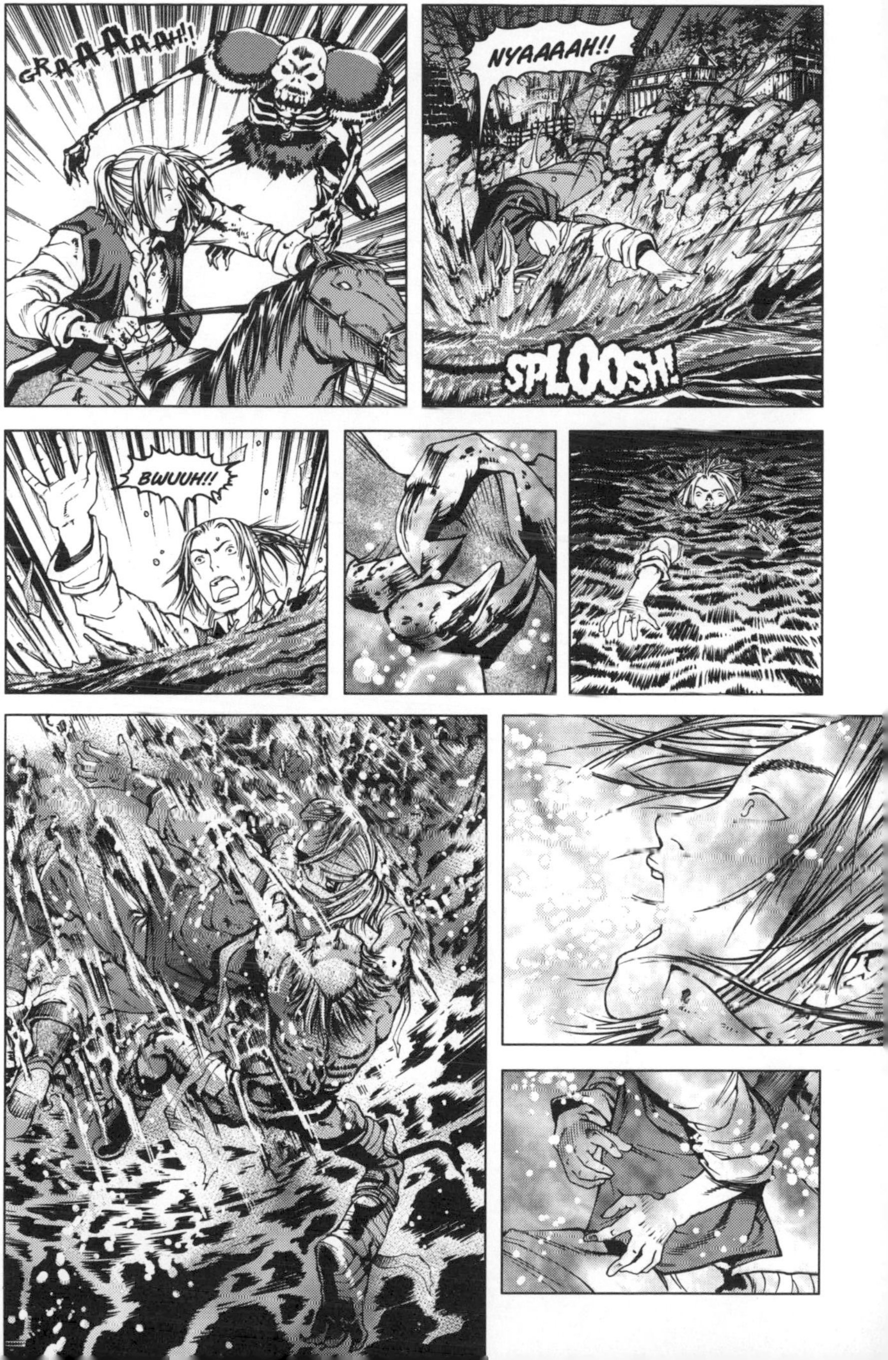
GRAAAAAH!!
NYAAAAH!!
SPLOOSH!
BWUUH!!

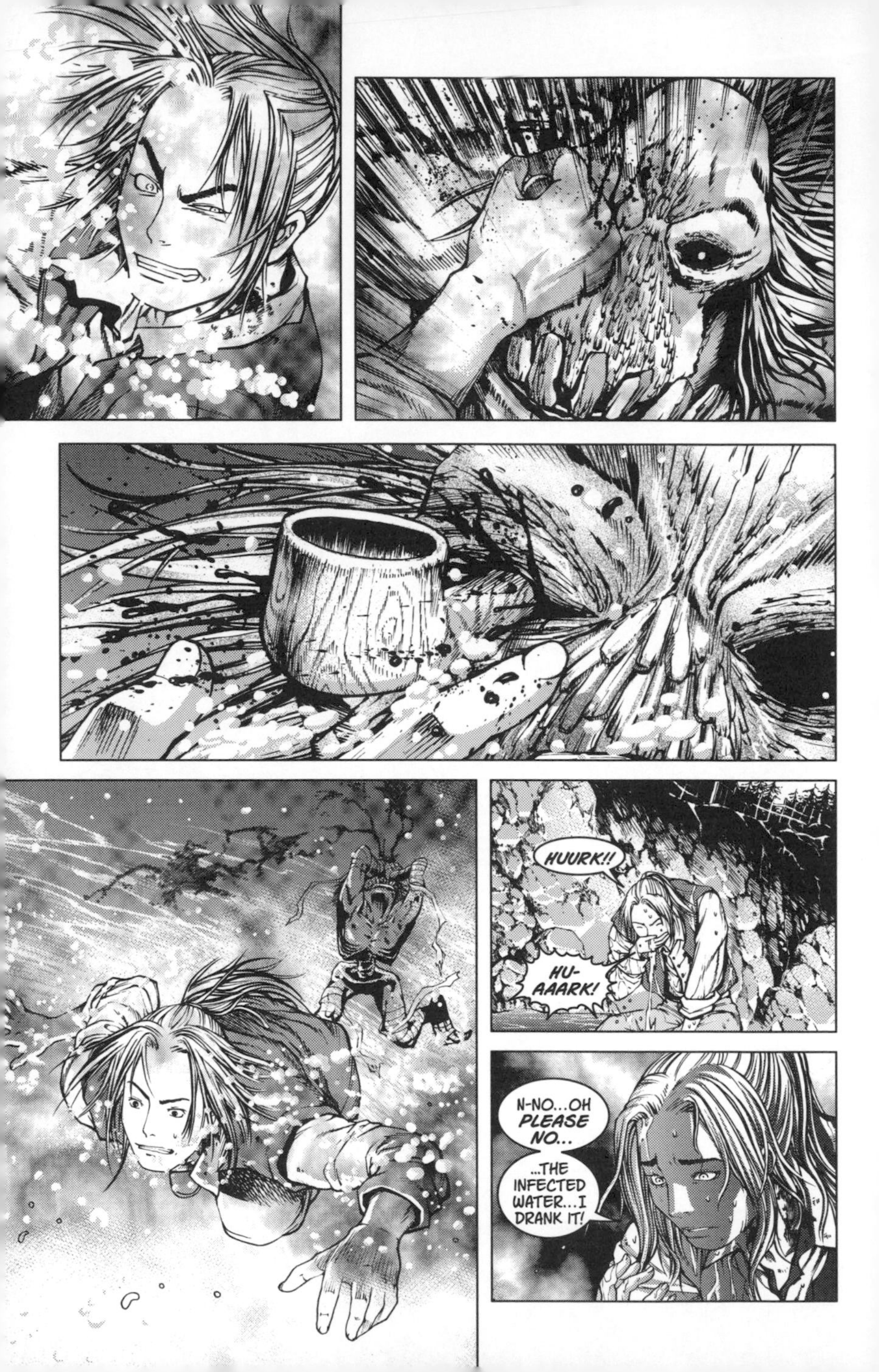
HUURK!!
HU-AAARK!
N-NO...OH PLEASE NO...
...THE INFECTED WATER...I DRANK IT!

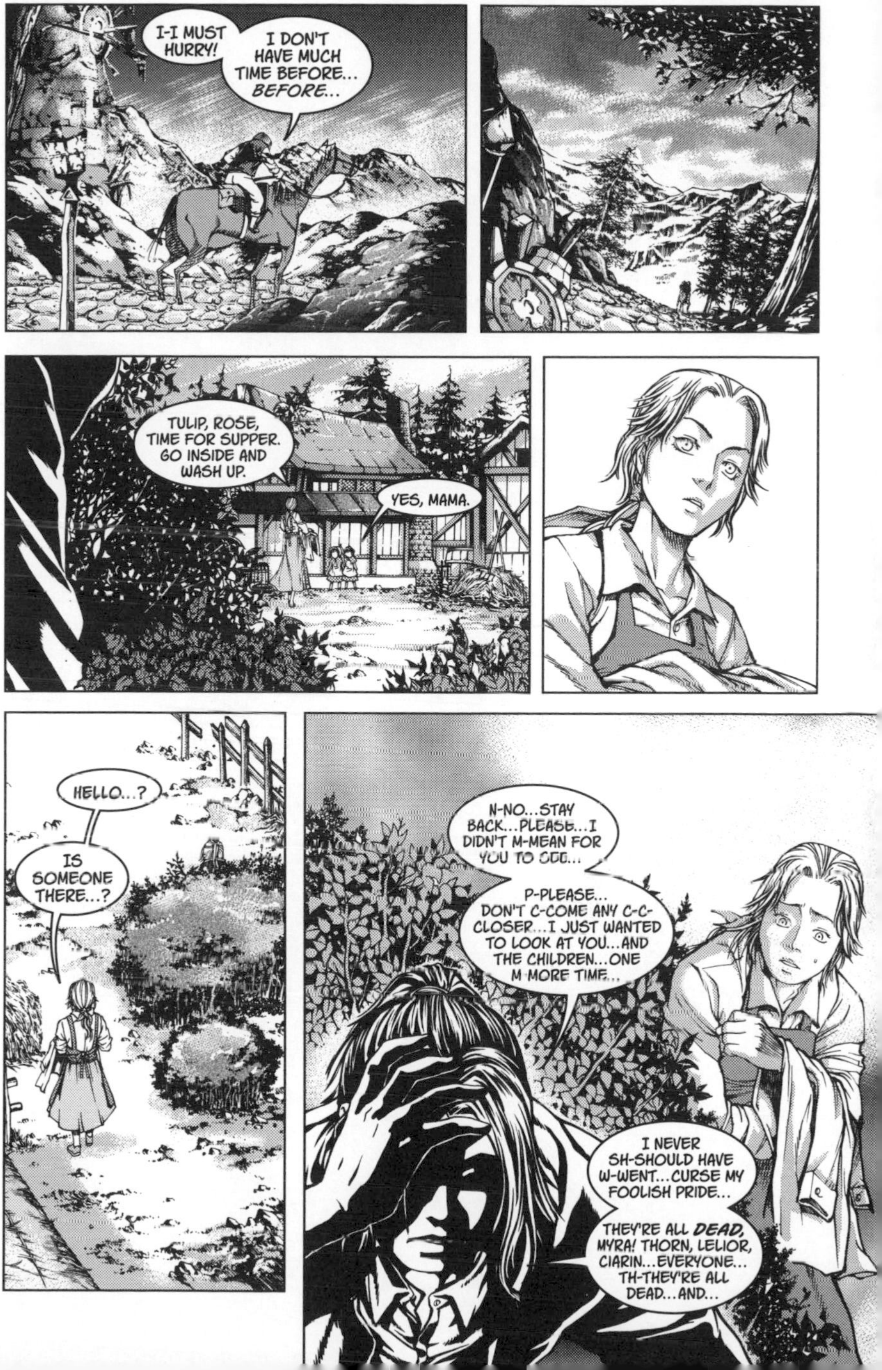
I-I MUST HURRY!
I DON'T HAVE MUCH TIME BEFORE... *BEFORE...*
TULIP, ROSE, TIME FOR SUPPER. GO INSIDE AND WASH UP.
YES, MAMA.
HELLO...?
IS SOMEONE THERE...?
N-NO...STAY BACK...PLEASE...I DIDN'T M-MEAN FOR YOU TO SEE...
P-PLEASE... DON'T C-COME ANY C-C-CLOSER...I JUST WANTED TO LOOK AT YOU...AND THE CHILDREN...ONE M-MORE TIME...
I NEVER SH-SHOULD HAVE W-WENT...CURSE MY FOOLISH PRIDE...
THEY'RE ALL ***DEAD,*** MYRA! THORN, LELIOR, CIARIN...EVERYONE... TH-THEY'RE ALL DEAD...AND...

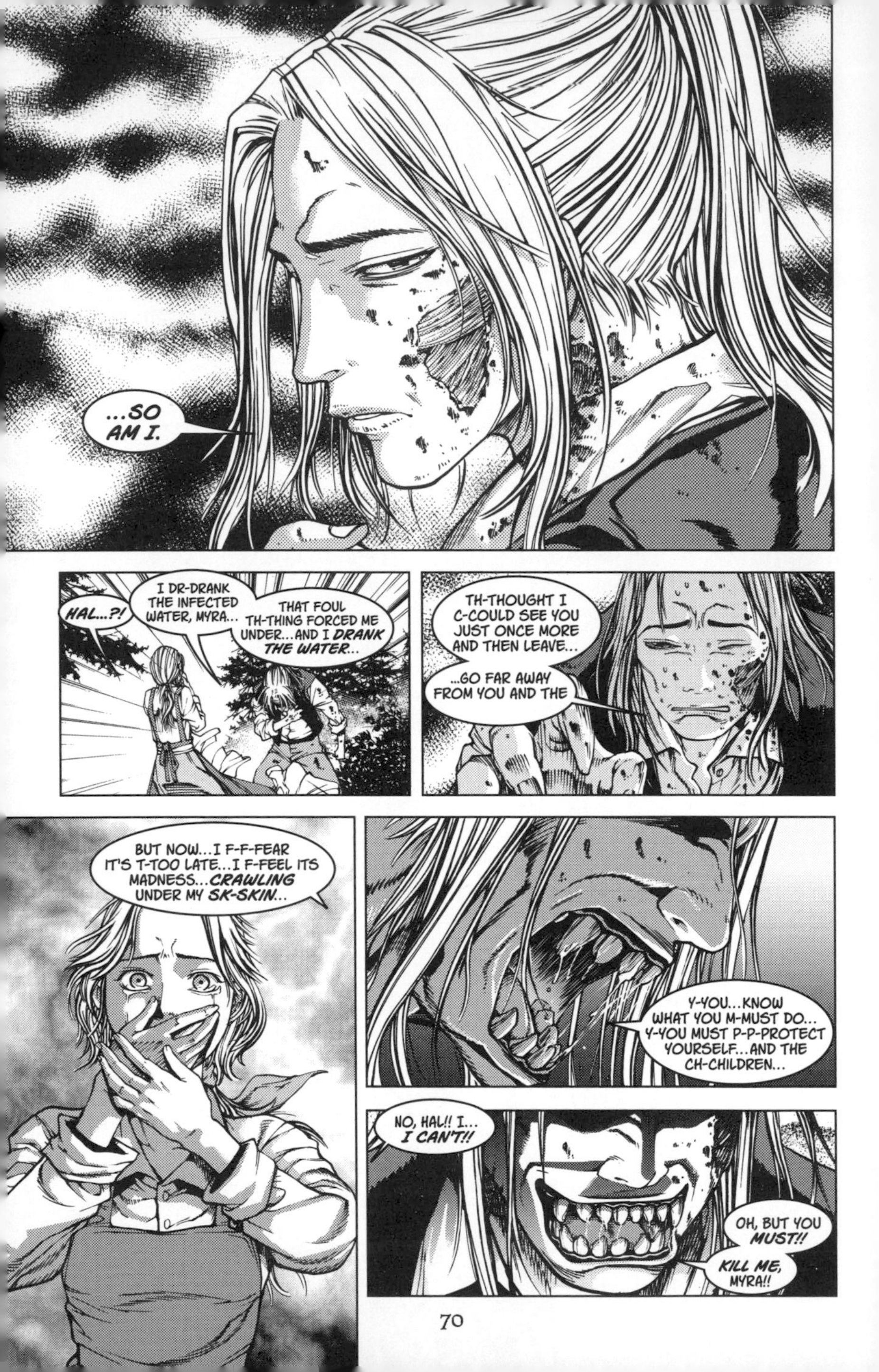
...SO AM I.
HAL...?!
I DR-DRANK THE INFECTED WATER, MYRA...
THAT FOUL TH-THING FORCED ME UNDER...AND I DRANK THE WATER...
TH-THOUGHT I C-COULD SEE YOU JUST ONCE MORE AND THEN LEAVE...
...GO FAR AWAY FROM YOU AND THE
BUT NOW...I F-F-FEAR IT'S T-TOO LATE...I F-FEEL ITS MADNESS...CRAWLING UNDER MY SK-SKIN...
Y-YOU...KNOW WHAT YOU M-MUST DO... Y-YOU MUST P-P-PROTECT YOURSELF...AND THE CH-CHILDREN...
NO, HAL!! I... I CAN'T!!
OH, BUT YOU MUST!!
KILL ME, MYRA!!

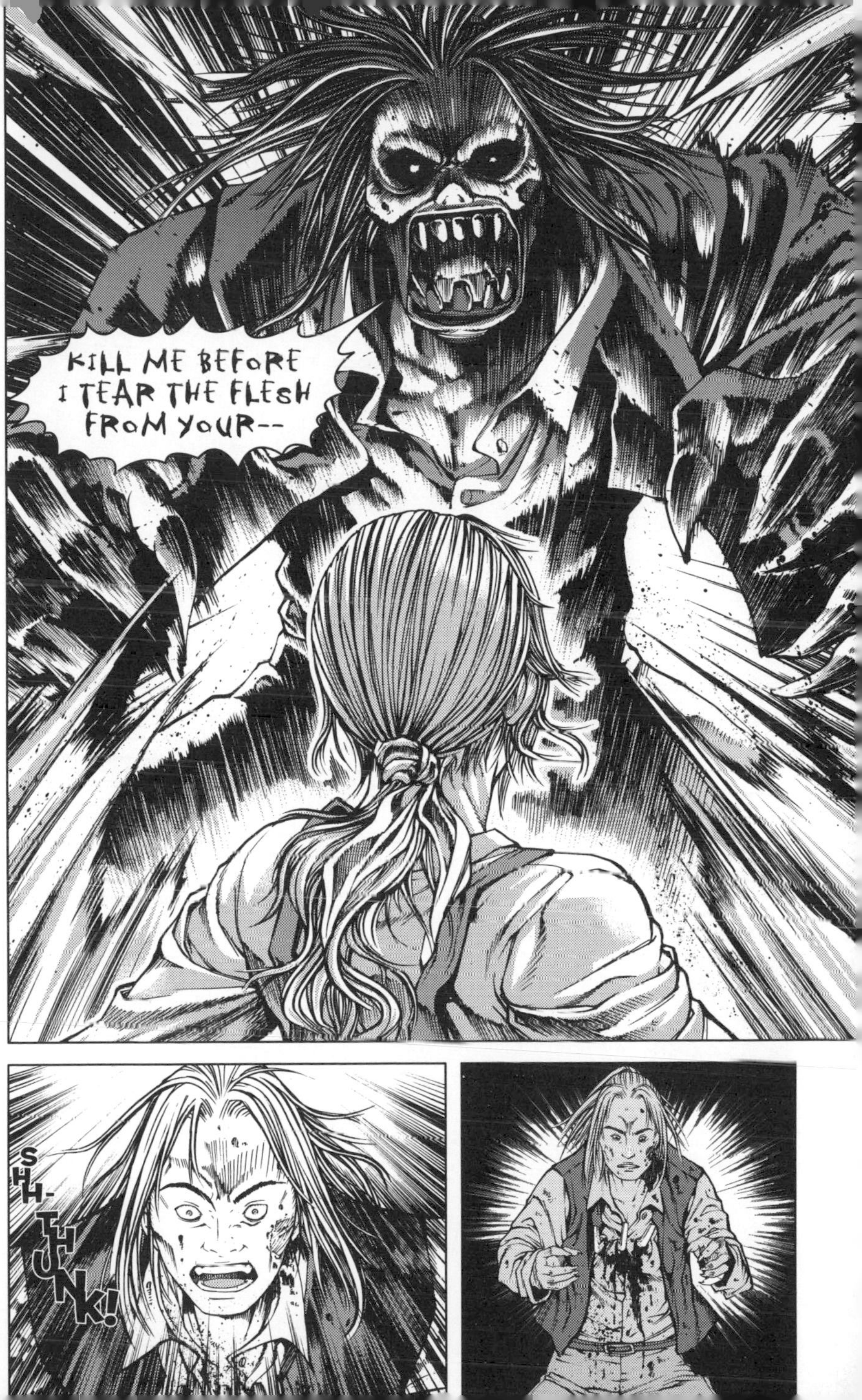
KILL ME BEFORE I TEAR THE FLESH FROM YOUR--
SHH-THUNK!

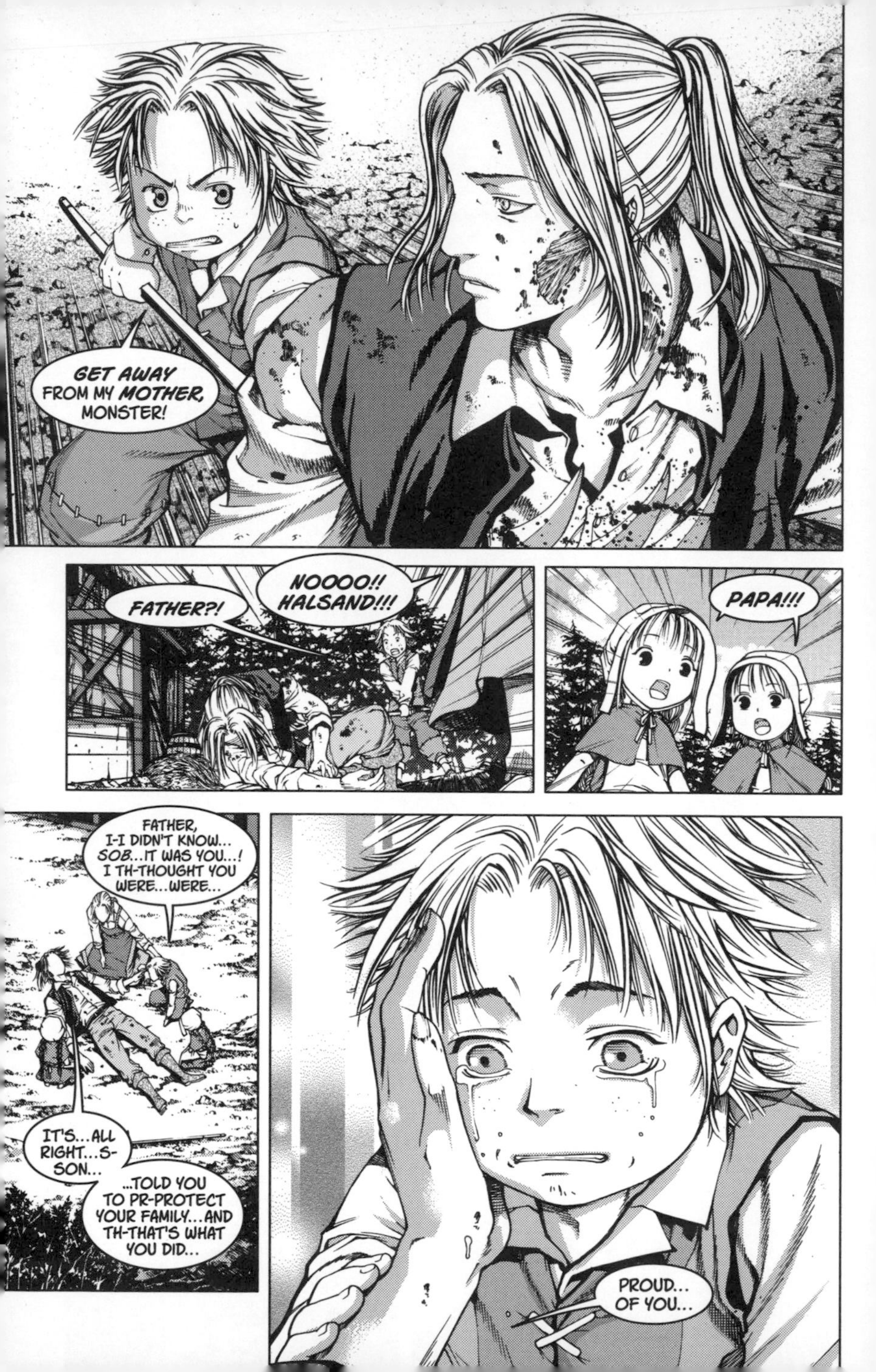
GET AWAY FROM MY MOTHER, MONSTER!
FATHER?!
NOOOO!! HALSAND!!!
PAPA!!!
FATHER, I-I DIDN'T KNOW... SOB...IT WAS YOU...! I TH-THOUGHT YOU WERE...WERE...
IT'S...ALL RIGHT...S-SON...
...TOLD YOU TO PR-PROTECT YOUR FAMILY...AND TH-THAT'S WHAT YOU DID...
PROUD... OF YOU...

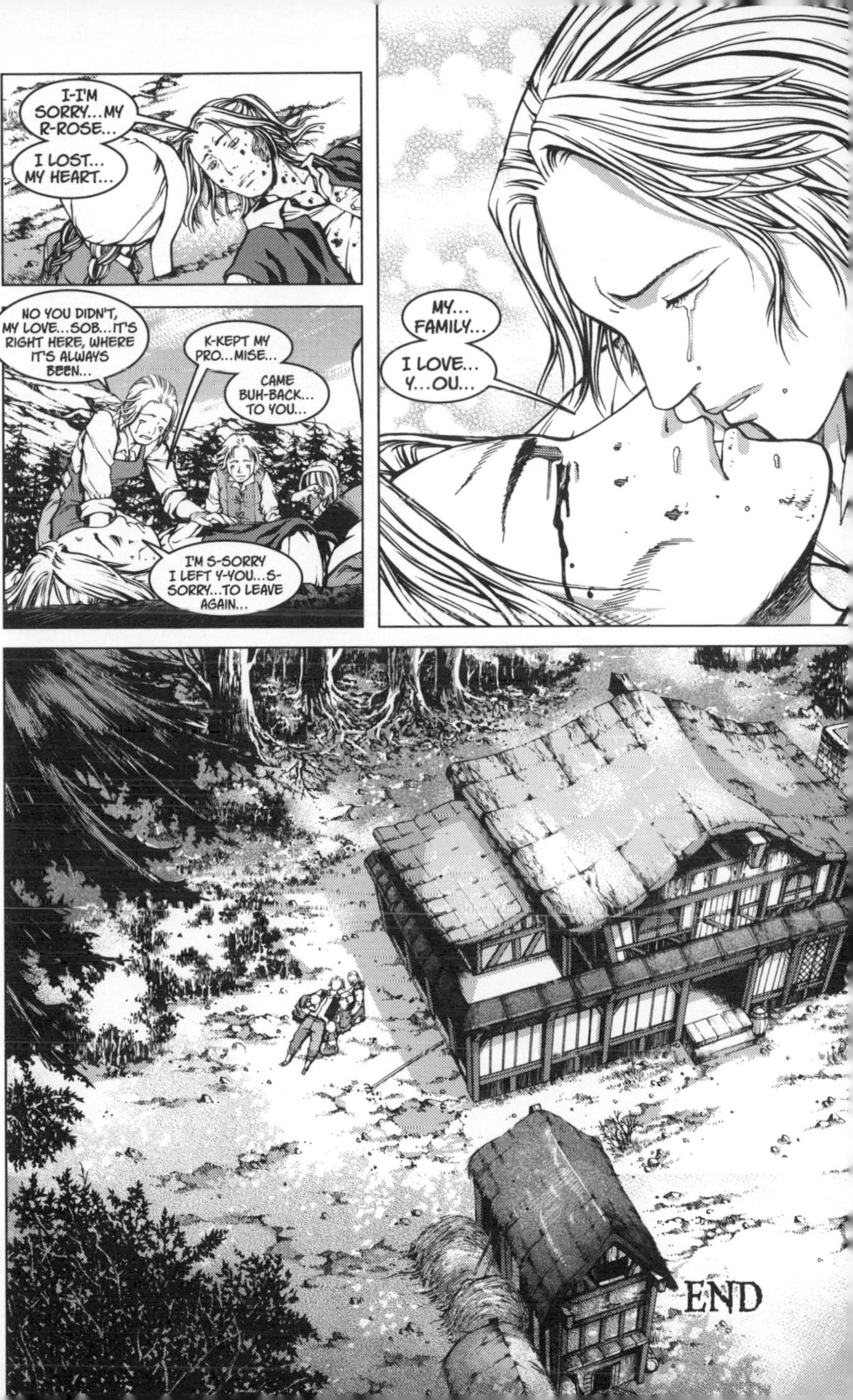
I-I'M SORRY...MY R-ROSE...
I LOST... MY HEART...
NO YOU DIDN'T, MY LOVE...SOB...IT'S RIGHT HERE, WHERE IT'S ALWAYS BEEN...
K-KEPT MY PRO...MISE...
CAME BUH-BACK... TO YOU...
I'M S-SORRY I LEFT Y-YOU...S-SORRY...TO LEAVE AGAIN...
MY... FAMILY...
I LOVE... Y...OU...
END

LEGENDS
VOLUME ONE

HOW TO WIN FRIENDS

WRITTEN BY DAN JOLLEY

PENCILS BY CARLOS OLIVARES
INKS & TONES BY CARLOS OLIVARES, MARC RUEDA
& JANINA GORRISSEIN

EDITOR: TROY LEWTER
ASSOCIATE EDITOR: SHANNON WATTERS
LETTERER: LUCAS RIVERA

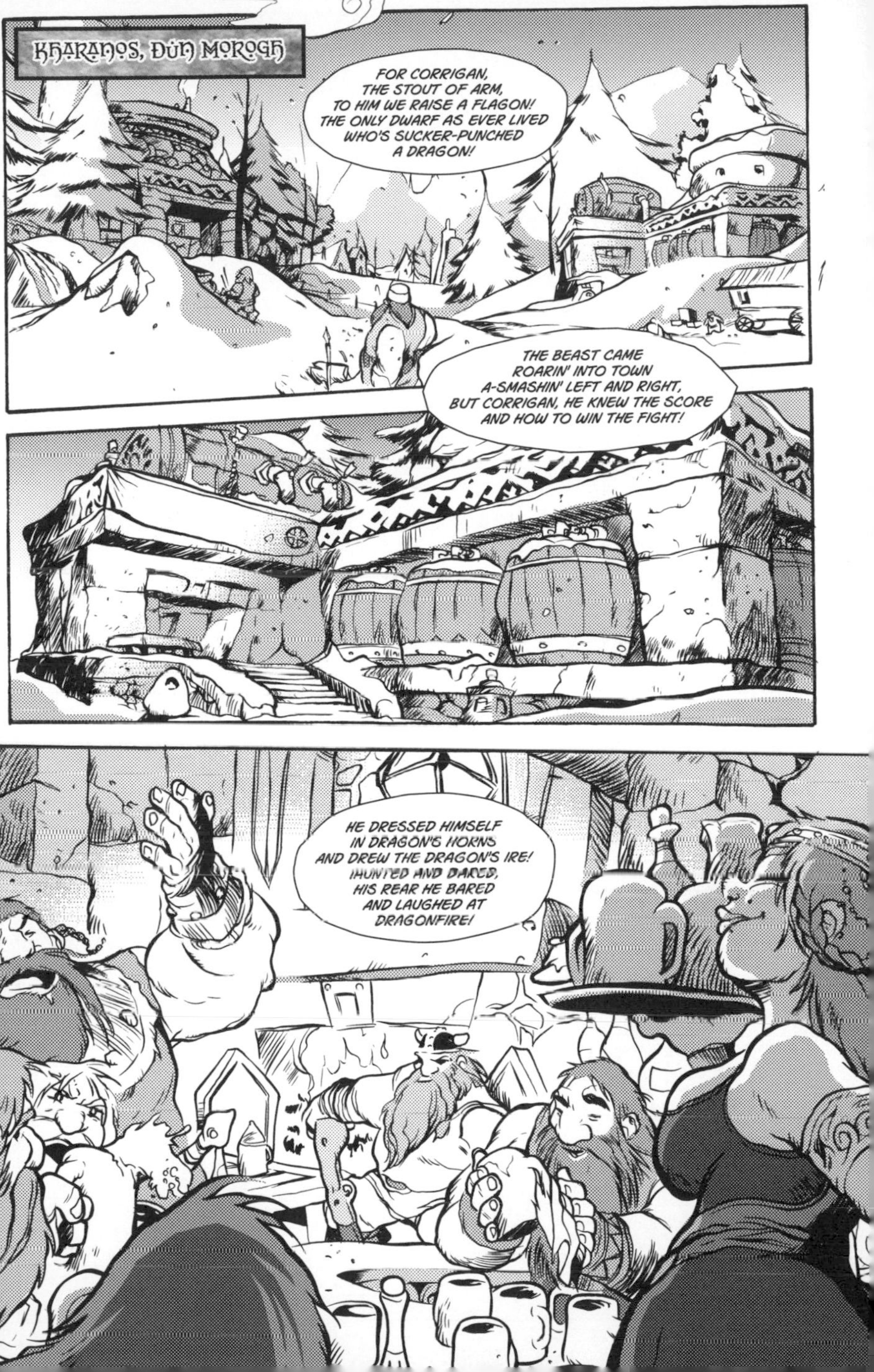

KHARANOS, DUN MOROGH
FOR CORRIGAN, THE STOUT OF ARM, TO HIM WE RAISE A FLAGON! THE ONLY DWARF AS EVER LIVED WHO'S SUCKER-PUNCHED A DRAGON!
THE BEAST CAME ROARIN' INTO TOWN A-SMASHIN' LEFT AND RIGHT, BUT CORRIGAN, HE KNEW THE SCORE AND HOW TO WIN THE FIGHT!
HE DRESSED HIMSELF IN DRAGON'S HORNS AND DREW THE DRAGON'S IRE! TAUNTED AND DARED, HIS REAR HE BARED AND LAUGHED AT DRAGONFIRE!

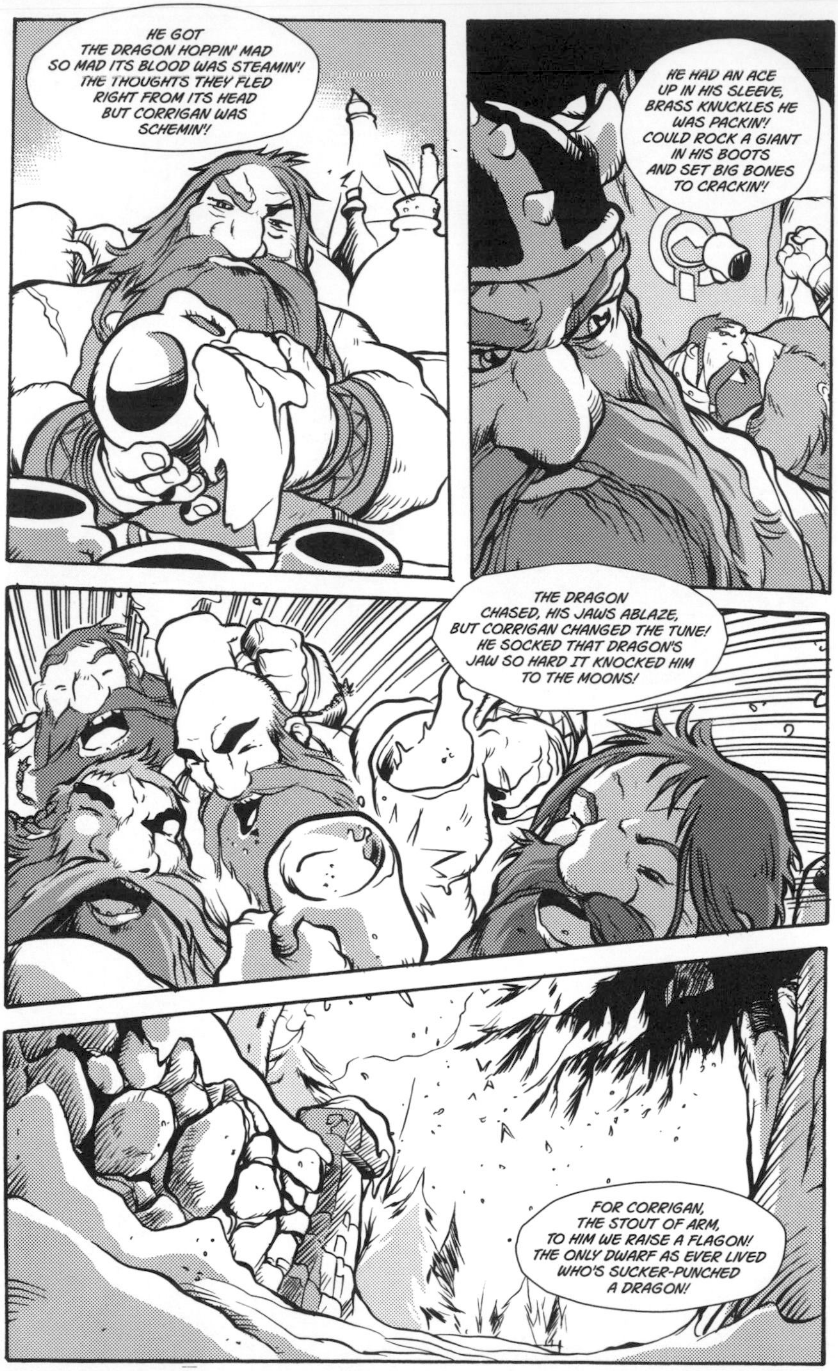
HE GOT THE DRAGON HOPPIN' MAD SO MAD ITS BLOOD WAS STEAMIN'! THE THOUGHTS THEY FLED RIGHT FROM ITS HEAD BUT CORRIGAN WAS SCHEMIN'!
HE HAD AN ACE UP IN HIS SLEEVE, BRASS KNUCKLES HE WAS PACKIN'! COULD ROCK A GIANT IN HIS BOOTS AND SET BIG BONES TO CRACKIN'!
THE DRAGON CHASED, HIS JAWS ABLAZE, BUT CORRIGAN CHANGED THE TUNE! HE SOCKED THAT DRAGON'S JAW SO HARD IT KNOCKED HIM TO THE MOONS!
FOR CORRIGAN, THE STOUT OF ARM, TO HIM WE RAISE A FLAGON! THE ONLY DWARF AS EVER LIVED WHO'S SUCKER-PUNCHED A DRAGON!

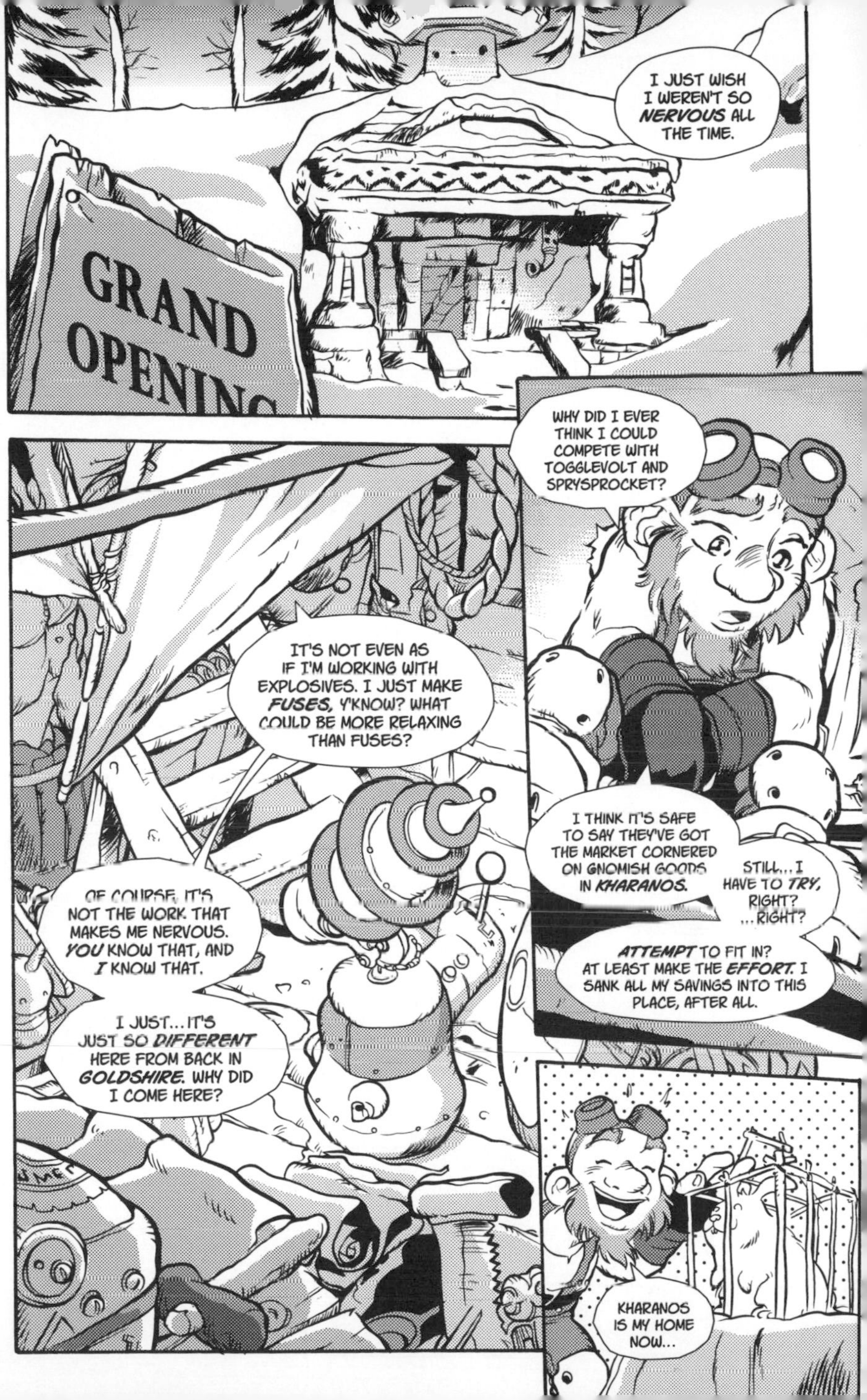
I JUST WISH I WEREN'T SO *NERVOUS* ALL THE TIME.
GRAND OPENING
IT'S NOT EVEN AS IF I'M WORKING WITH EXPLOSIVES. I JUST MAKE *FUSES,* Y'KNOW? WHAT COULD BE MORE RELAXING THAN FUSES?
OF COURSE, IT'S NOT THE WORK THAT MAKES ME NERVOUS. *YOU* KNOW THAT, AND *I* KNOW THAT.
I JUST... IT'S JUST SO *DIFFERENT* HERE FROM BACK IN *GOLDSHIRE*. WHY DID I COME HERE?
WHY DID I EVER THINK I COULD COMPETE WITH TOGGLEVOLT AND SPRYSPROCKET?
I THINK IT'S SAFE TO SAY THEY'VE GOT THE MARKET CORNERED ON GNOMISH GOODS IN *KHARANOS*.
STILL... I HAVE TO *TRY,* RIGHT? ...RIGHT?
ATTEMPT TO FIT IN? AT LEAST MAKE THE *EFFORT.* I SANK ALL MY SAVINGS INTO THIS PLACE, AFTER ALL.
KHARANOS IS MY HOME NOW...

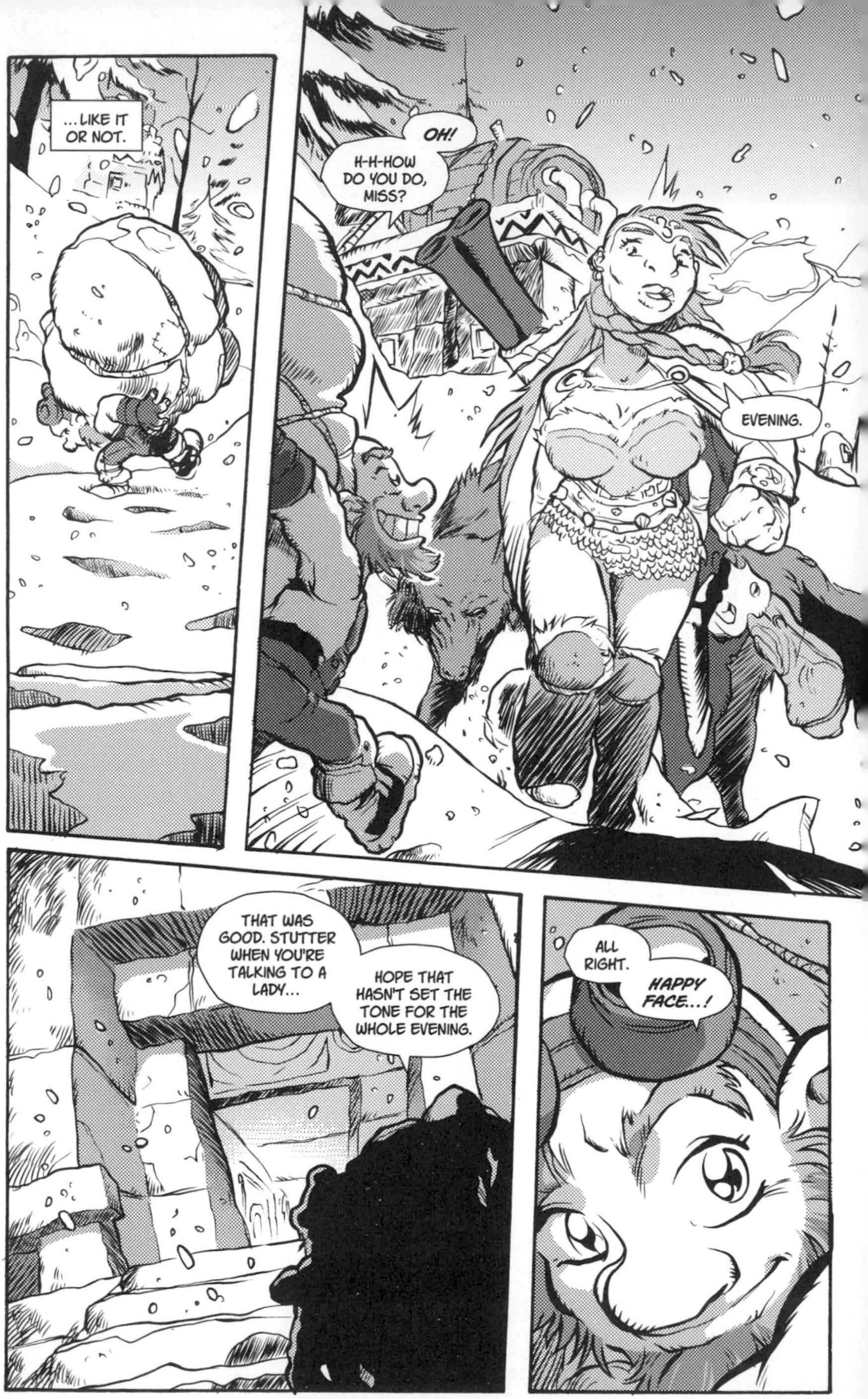
...LIKE IT OR NOT.
OH!
H-H-HOW DO YOU DO, MISS?
EVENING.
THAT WAS GOOD. STUTTER WHEN YOU'RE TALKING TO A LADY...
HOPE THAT HASN'T SET THE TONE FOR THE WHOLE EVENING.
ALL RIGHT.
HAPPY FACE...!

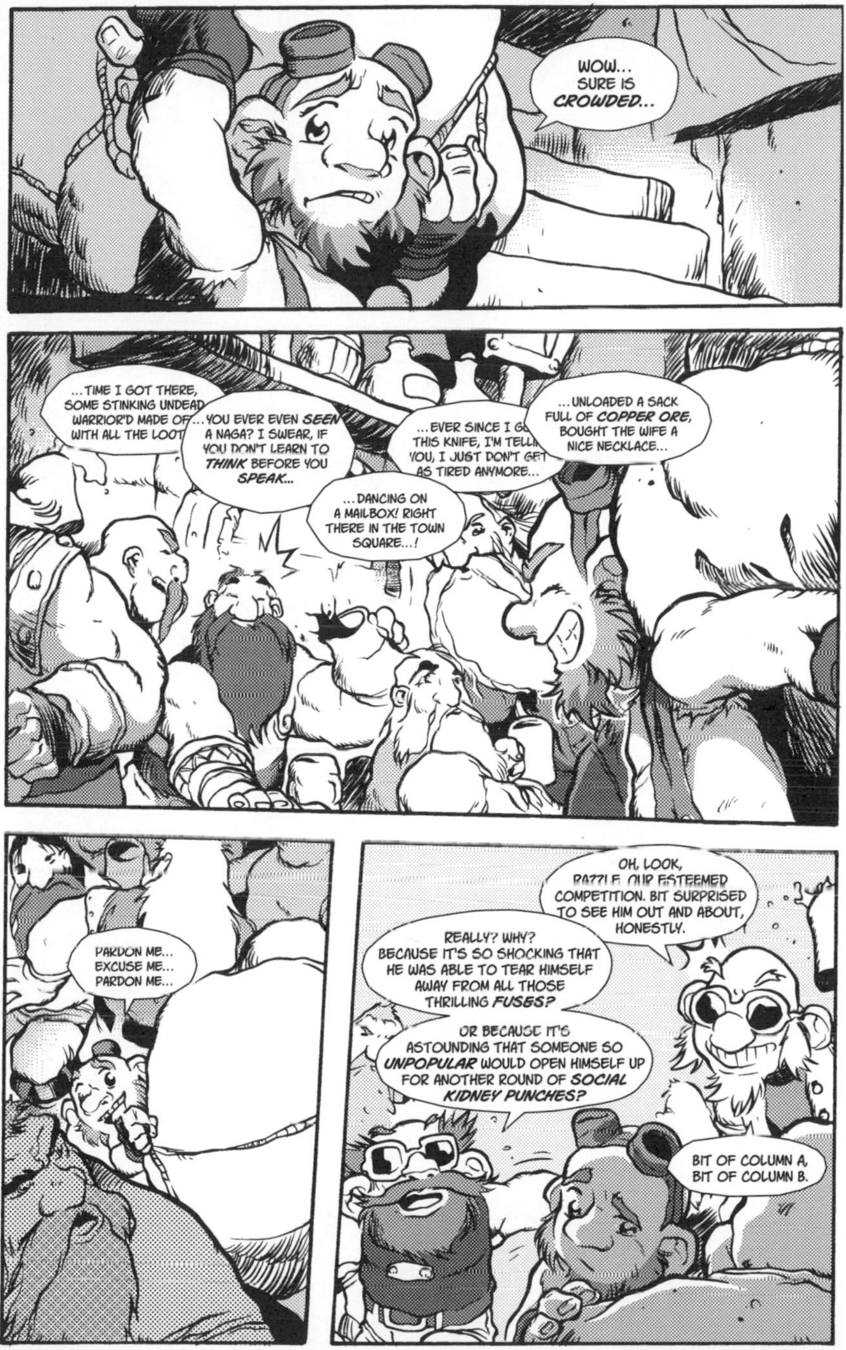

WOW... SURE IS *CROWDED...*
...TIME I GOT THERE, SOME STINKING UNDEAD WARRIOR'D MADE OF WITH ALL THE LOOT
...YOU EVER EVEN *SEEN* A NAGA? I SWEAR, IF YOU DON'T LEARN TO *THINK* BEFORE YOU *SPEAK...*
...EVER SINCE I GOT THIS KNIFE, I'M TELLIN' YOU, I JUST DON'T GET AS TIRED ANYMORE...
...UNLOADED A SACK FULL OF *COPPER ORE*, BOUGHT THE WIFE A NICE NECKLACE...
...DANCING ON A MAILBOX! RIGHT THERE IN THE TOWN SQUARE...!
PARDON ME... EXCUSE ME... PARDON ME...
OH, LOOK, RAZZLE, OUR ESTEEMED COMPETITION. BIT SURPRISED TO SEE HIM OUT AND ABOUT, HONESTLY.
REALLY? WHY? BECAUSE IT'S SO SHOCKING THAT HE WAS ABLE TO TEAR HIMSELF AWAY FROM ALL THOSE THRILLING *FUSES?*
OR BECAUSE IT'S ASTOUNDING THAT SOMEONE SO *UNPOPULAR* WOULD OPEN HIMSELF UP FOR ANOTHER ROUND OF *SOCIAL KIDNEY PUNCHES?*
BIT OF COLUMN A, BIT OF COLUMN B.

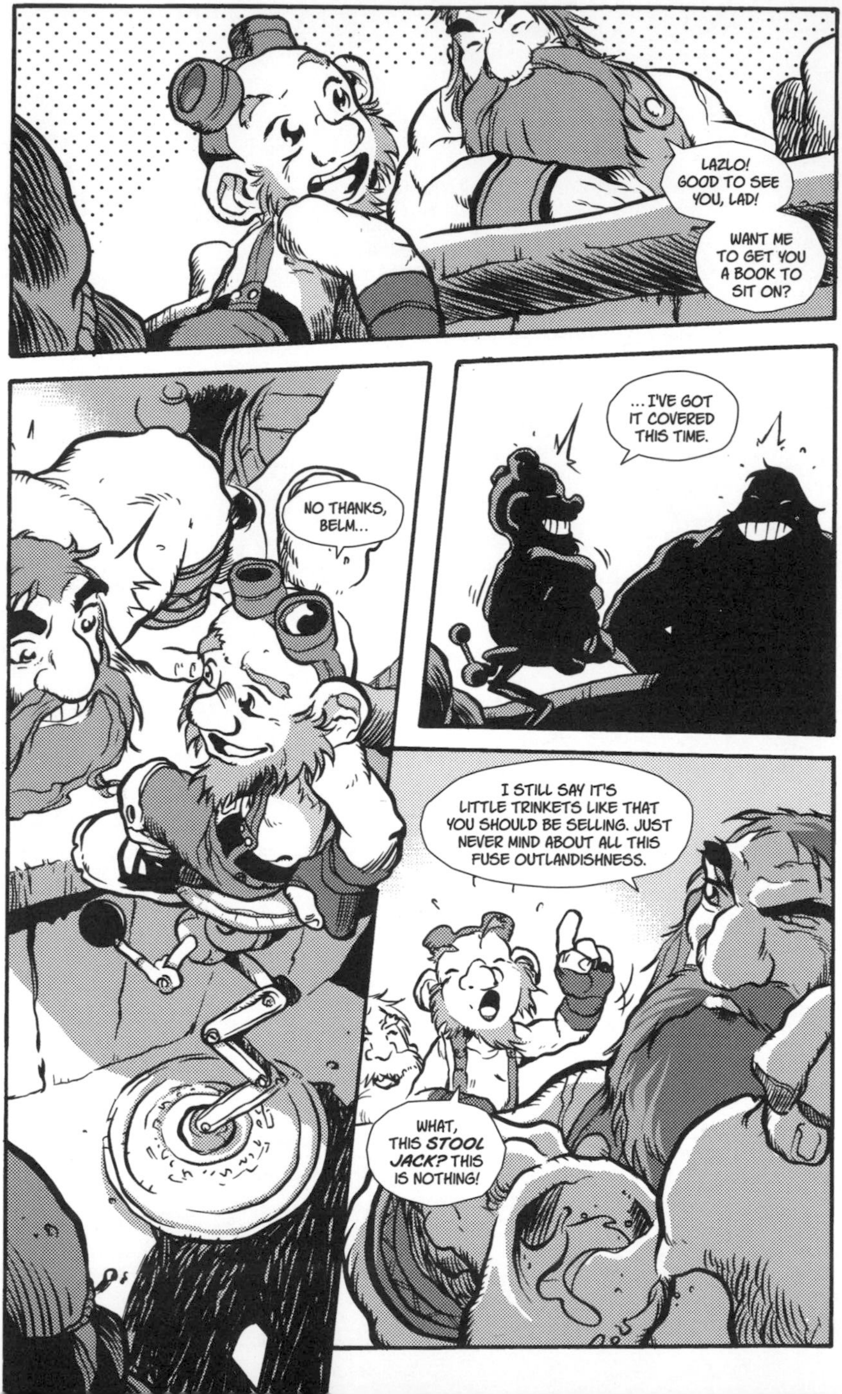
LAZLO! GOOD TO SEE YOU, LAD!
WANT ME TO GET YOU A BOOK TO SIT ON?
NO THANKS, BELM...
...I'VE GOT IT COVERED THIS TIME.
I STILL SAY IT'S LITTLE TRINKETS LIKE THAT YOU SHOULD BE SELLING. JUST NEVER MIND ABOUT ALL THIS FUSE OUTLANDISHNESS.
WHAT, THIS *STOOL JACK?* THIS IS NOTHING!

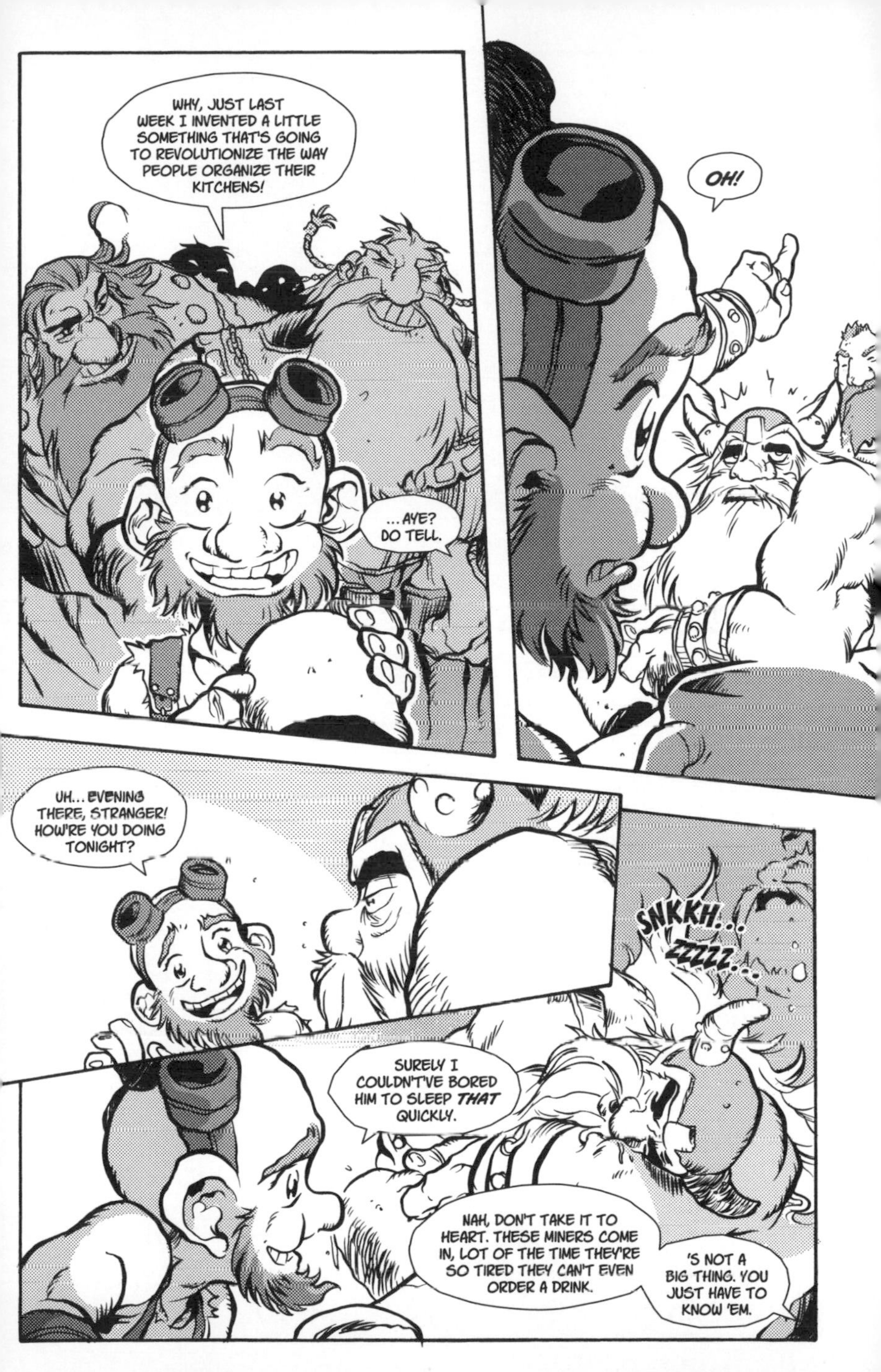

WHY, JUST LAST WEEK I INVENTED A LITTLE SOMETHING THAT'S GOING TO REVOLUTIONIZE THE WAY PEOPLE ORGANIZE THEIR KITCHENS!
...AYE? DO TELL.
OH!
UH... EVENING THERE, STRANGER! HOW'RE YOU DOING TONIGHT?
SNKKH...
ZZZZZ...
SURELY I COULDN'T'VE BORED HIM TO SLEEP *THAT* QUICKLY.
NAH, DON'T TAKE IT TO HEART. THESE MINERS COME IN, LOT OF THE TIME THEY'RE SO TIRED THEY CAN'T EVEN ORDER A DRINK.
'S NOT A BIG THING. YOU JUST HAVE TO KNOW 'EM.

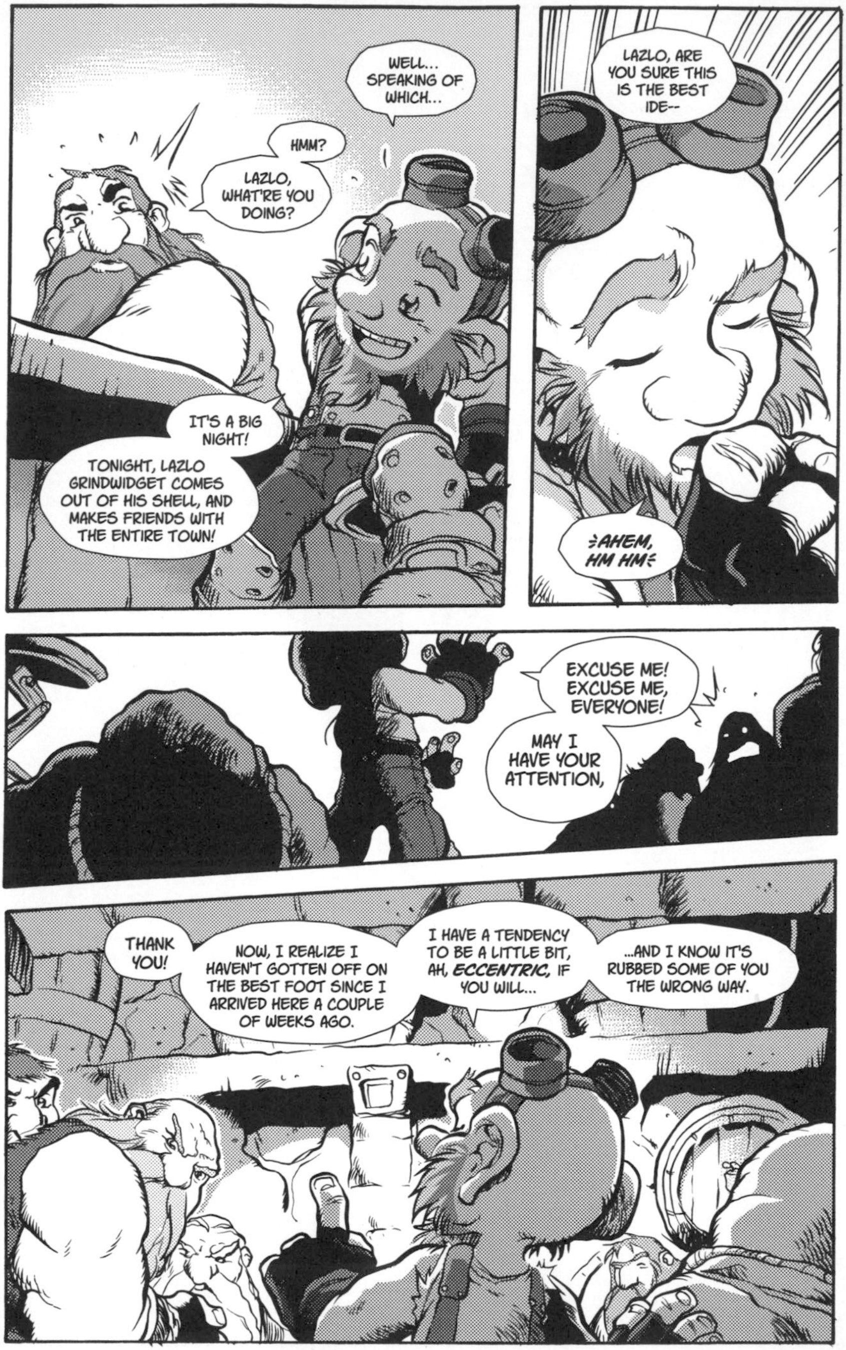
WELL... SPEAKING OF WHICH...
HMM?
LAZLO, WHAT'RE YOU DOING?
IT'S A BIG NIGHT!
TONIGHT, LAZLO GRINDWIDGET COMES OUT OF HIS SHELL, AND MAKES FRIENDS WITH THE ENTIRE TOWN!
LAZLO, ARE YOU SURE THIS IS THE BEST IDE--
AHEM, HM HM
EXCUSE ME! EXCUSE ME, EVERYONE!
MAY I HAVE YOUR ATTENTION,
THANK YOU!
NOW, I REALIZE I HAVEN'T GOTTEN OFF ON THE BEST FOOT SINCE I ARRIVED HERE A COUPLE OF WEEKS AGO.
I HAVE A TENDENCY TO BE A LITTLE BIT, AH, ECCENTRIC, IF YOU WILL...
...AND I KNOW IT'S RUBBED SOME OF YOU THE WRONG WAY.

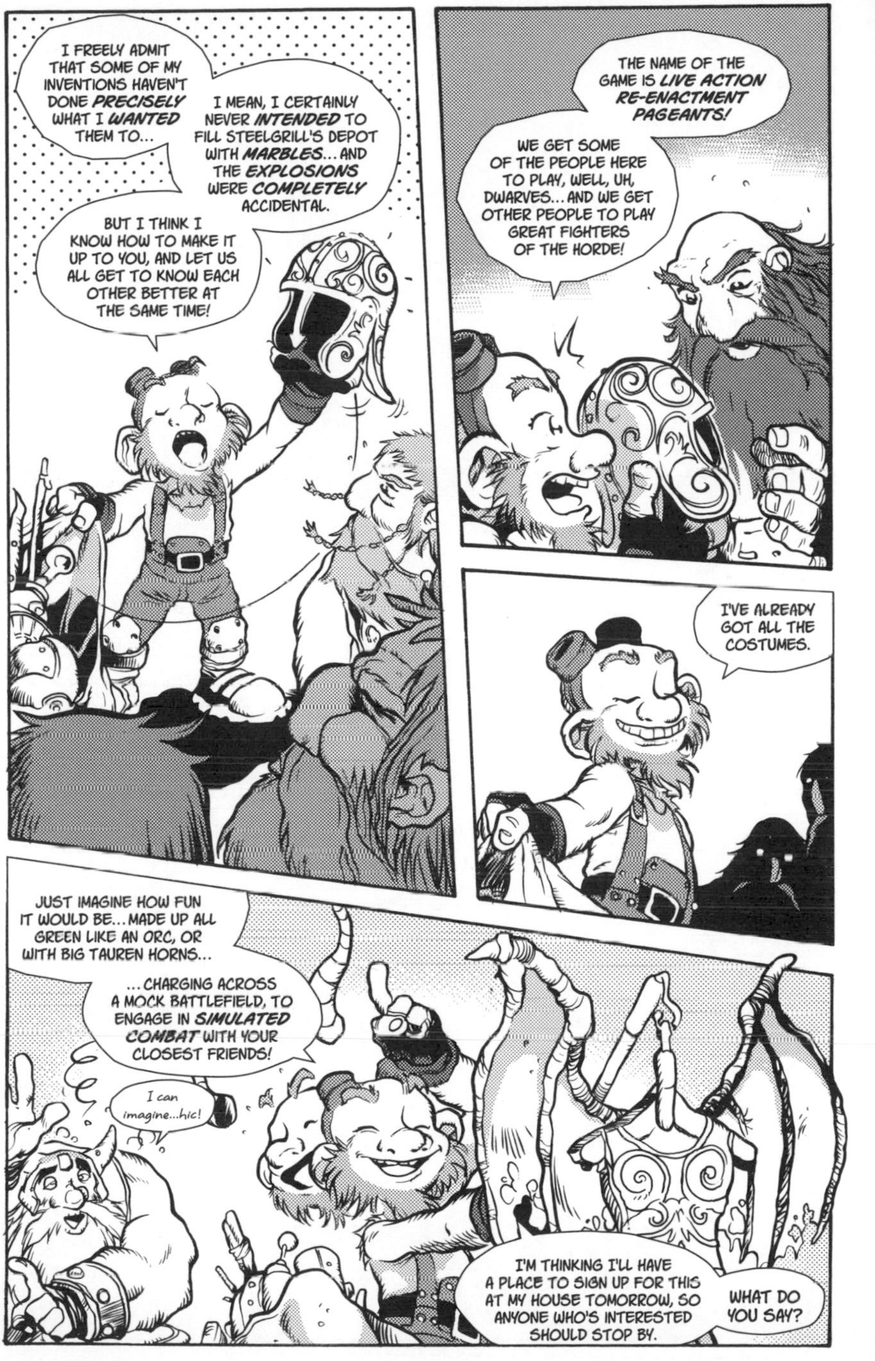

I FREELY ADMIT THAT SOME OF MY INVENTIONS HAVEN'T DONE *PRECISELY* WHAT I *WANTED* THEM TO...
I MEAN, I CERTAINLY NEVER *INTENDED* TO FILL STEELGRILL'S DEPOT WITH *MARBLES*... AND THE *EXPLOSIONS* WERE *COMPLETELY* ACCIDENTAL.
BUT I THINK I KNOW HOW TO MAKE IT UP TO YOU, AND LET US ALL GET TO KNOW EACH OTHER BETTER AT THE SAME TIME!
THE NAME OF THE GAME IS *LIVE ACTION RE-ENACTMENT PAGEANTS!*
WE GET SOME OF THE PEOPLE HERE TO PLAY, WELL, UH, DWARVES... AND WE GET OTHER PEOPLE TO PLAY GREAT FIGHTERS OF THE HORDE!
I'VE ALREADY GOT ALL THE COSTUMES.
JUST IMAGINE HOW FUN IT WOULD BE... MADE UP ALL GREEN LIKE AN ORC, OR WITH BIG TAUREN HORNS...
...CHARGING ACROSS A MOCK BATTLEFIELD, TO ENGAGE IN *SIMULATED COMBAT* WITH YOUR CLOSEST FRIENDS!
I can imagine...hic!
I'M THINKING I'LL HAVE A PLACE TO SIGN UP FOR THIS AT MY HOUSE TOMORROW, SO ANYONE WHO'S INTERESTED SHOULD STOP BY.
WHAT DO YOU SAY?

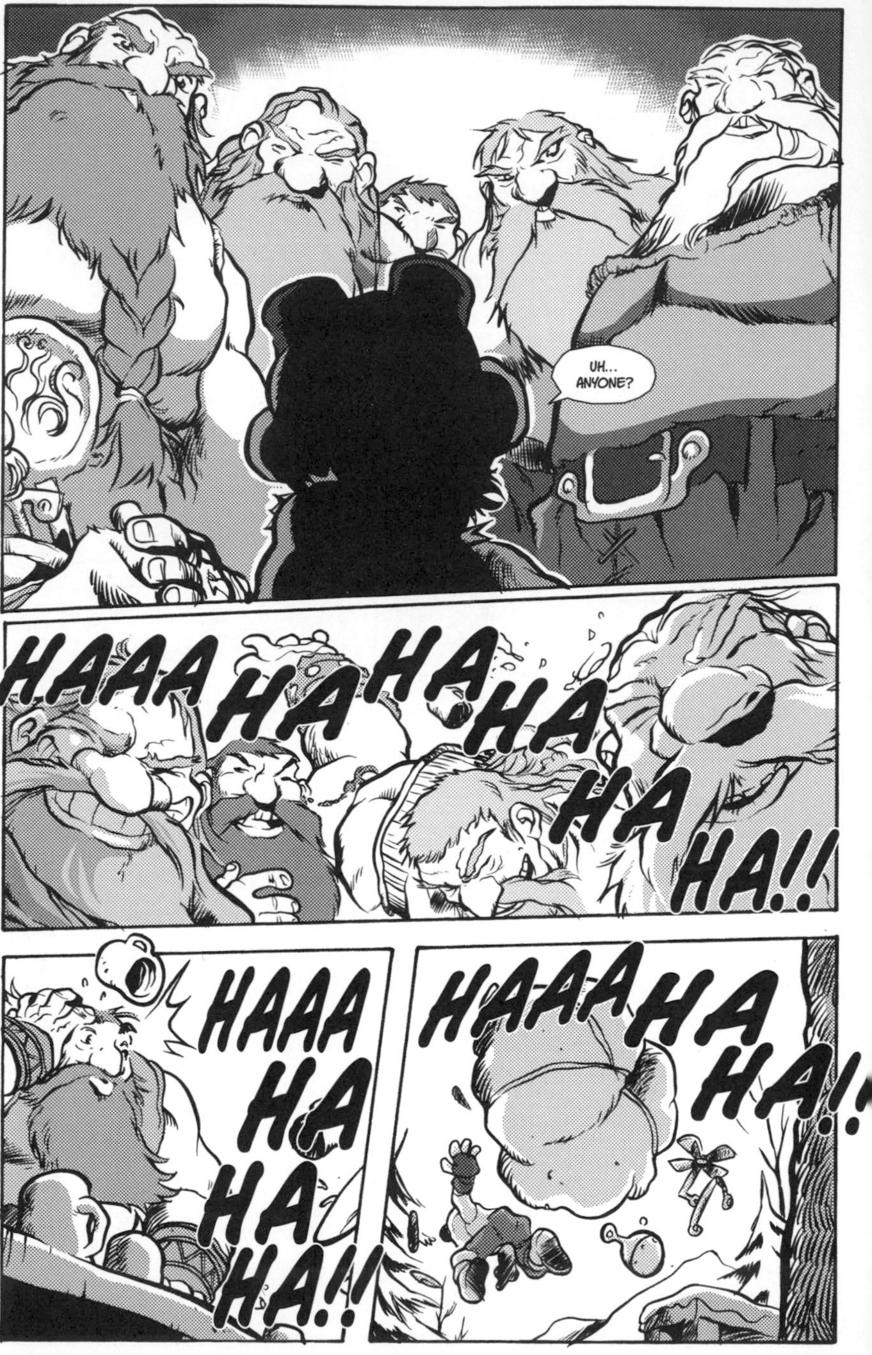
UH... ANYONE?
HAAAHAHAHAHAHAHA!!
HAAAHAHAHAHA!!
HAAAAHAHAHA!!

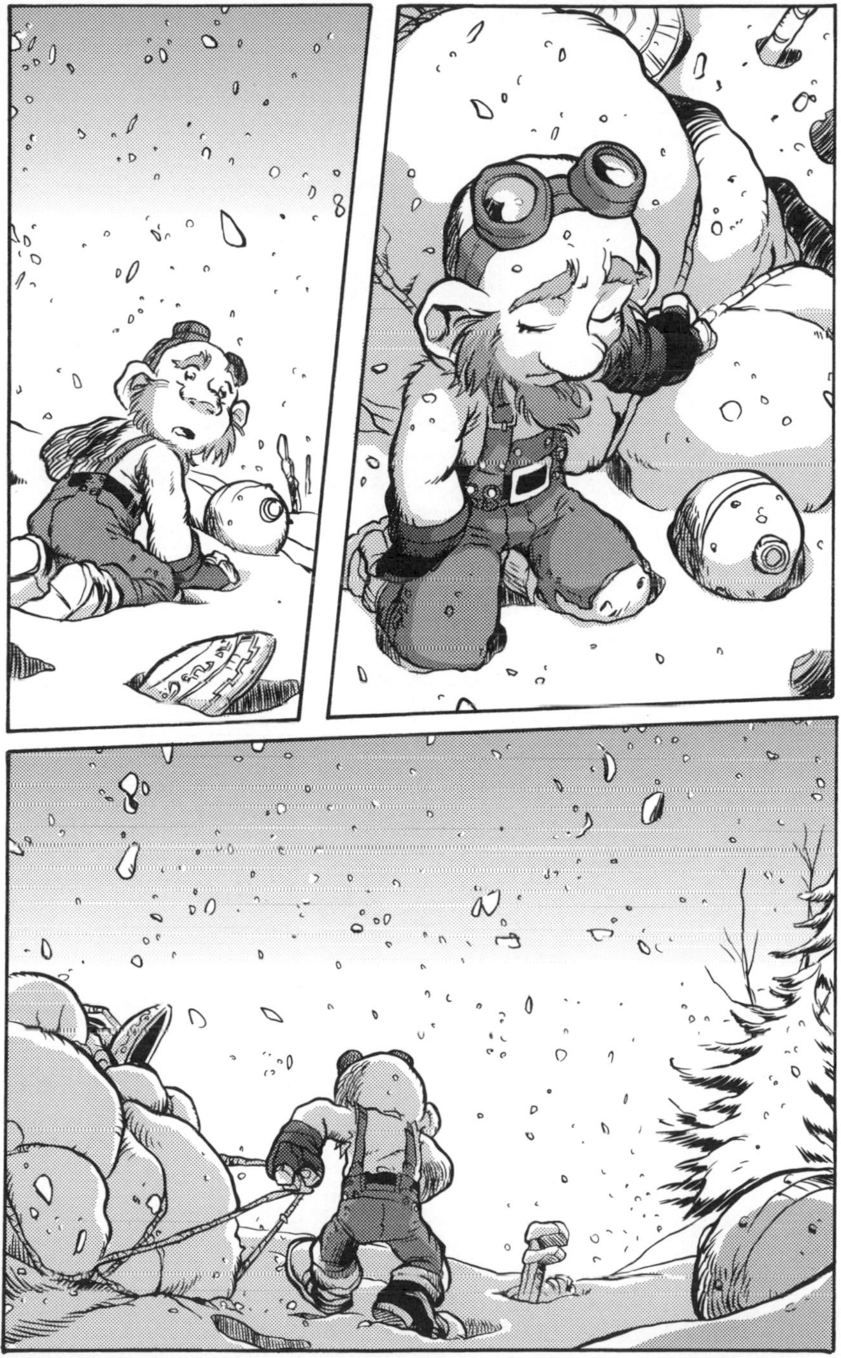

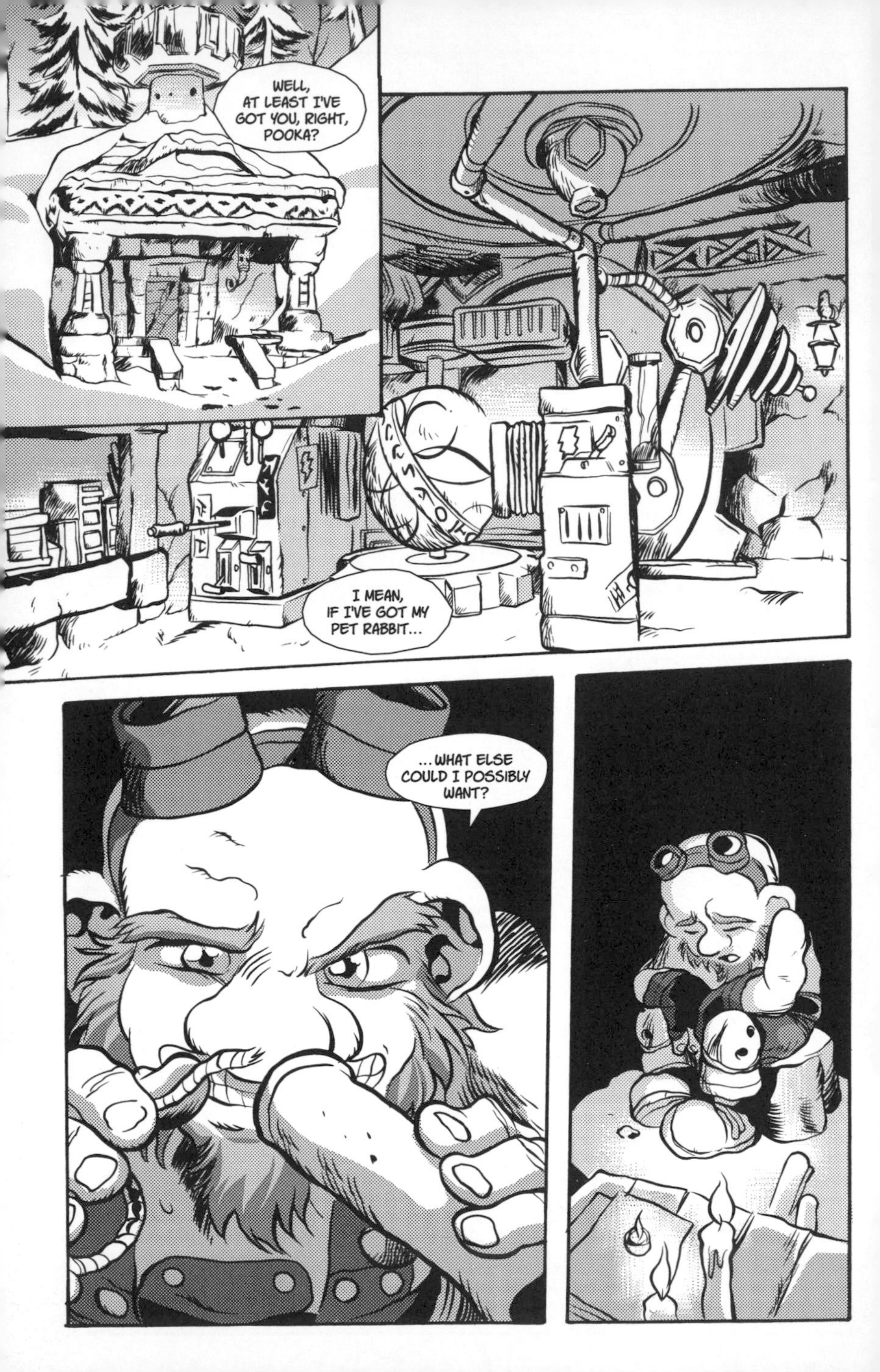
WELL, AT LEAST I'VE GOT YOU, RIGHT, POOKA?
I MEAN, IF I'VE GOT MY PET RABBIT...
...WHAT ELSE COULD I POSSIBLY WANT?

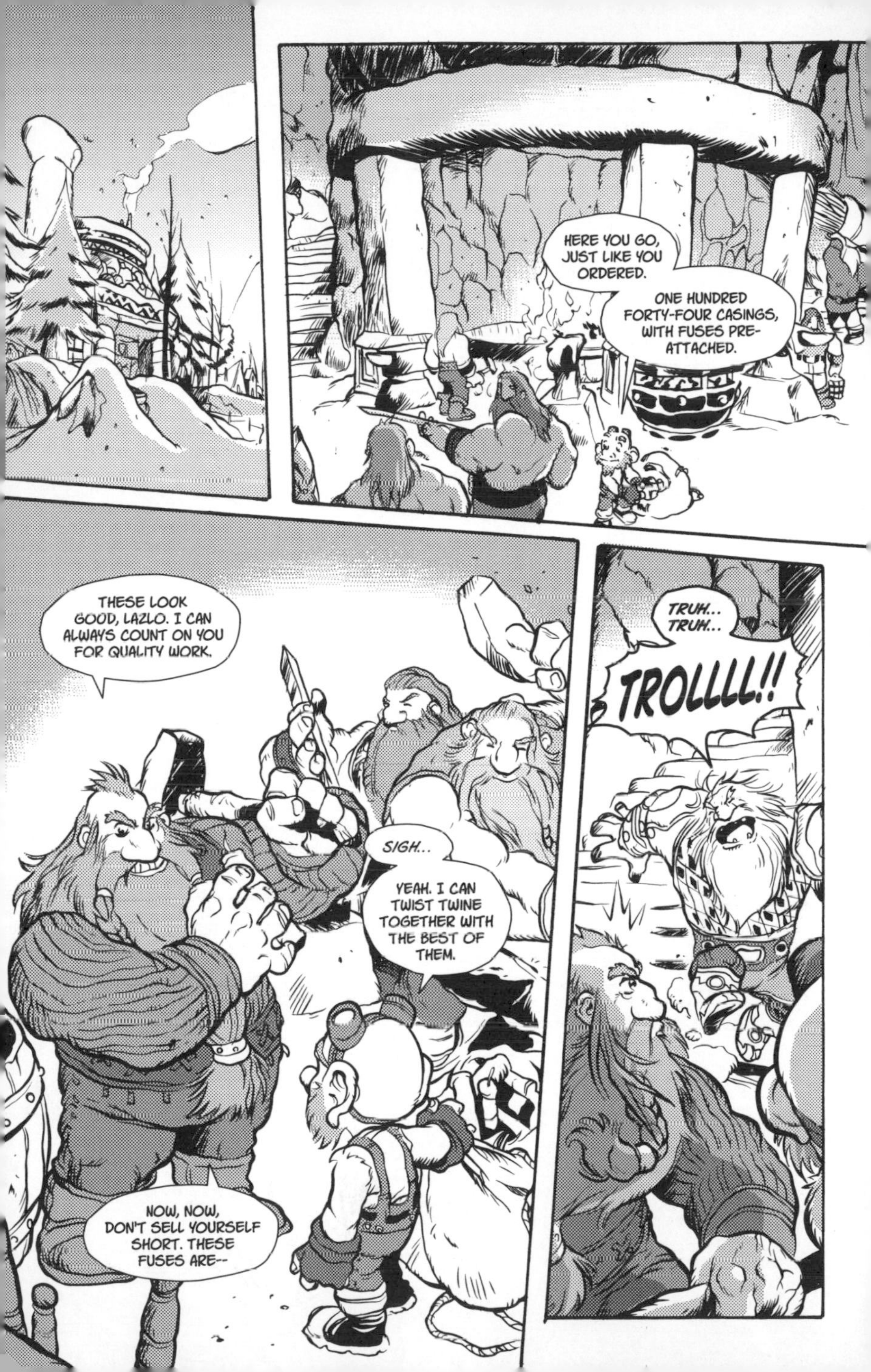
HERE YOU GO, JUST LIKE YOU ORDERED.
ONE HUNDRED FORTY-FOUR CASINGS, WITH FUSES PRE-ATTACHED.
THESE LOOK GOOD, LAZLO. I CAN ALWAYS COUNT ON YOU FOR QUALITY WORK.
SIGH...
YEAH. I CAN TWIST TWINE TOGETHER WITH THE BEST OF THEM.
NOW, NOW, DON'T SELL YOURSELF SHORT. THESE FUSES ARE--
TRUH... TRUH...
TROLLLL!!

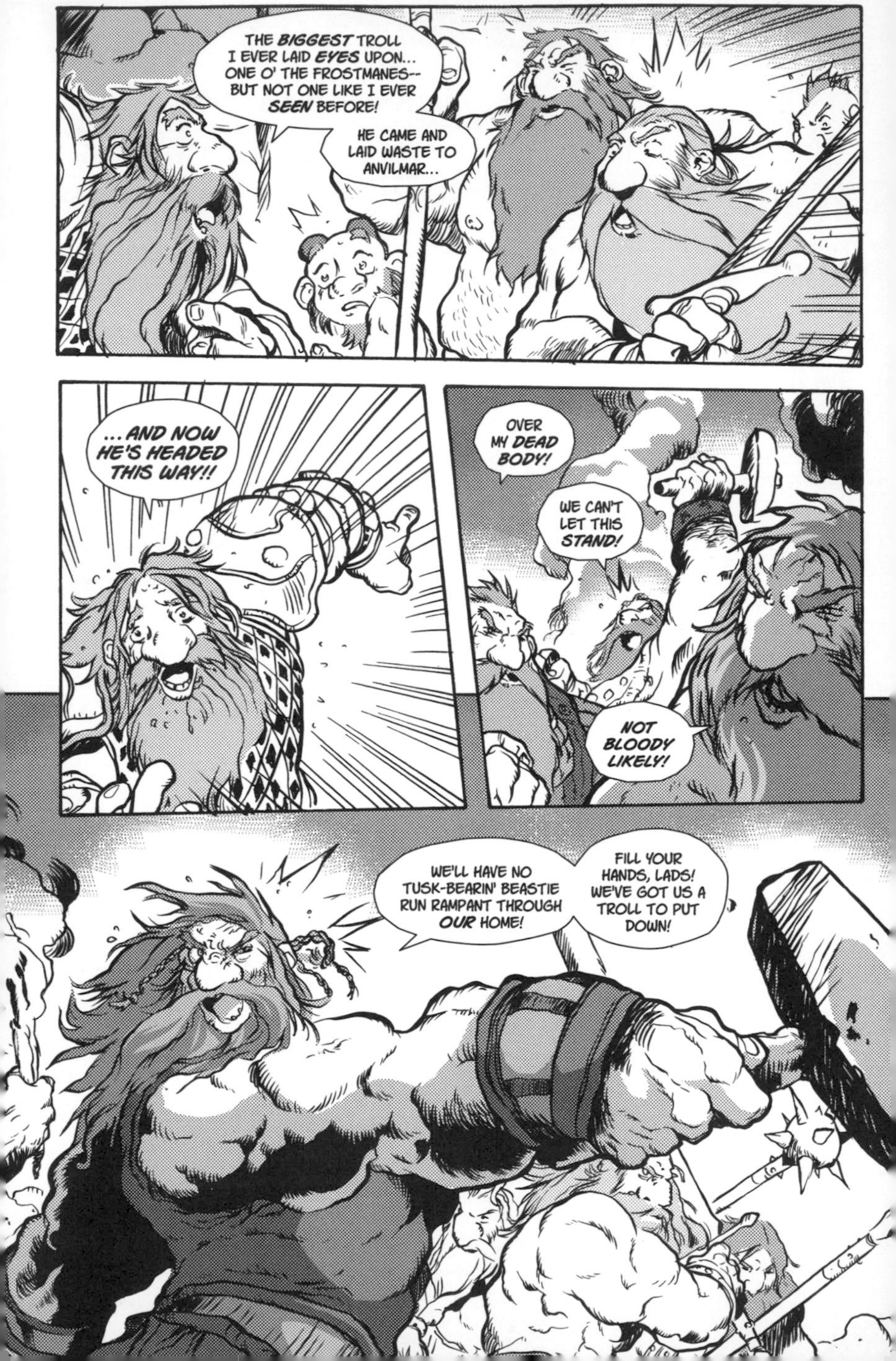
THE *BIGGEST* TROLL I EVER LAID *EYES* UPON... ONE O' THE FROSTMANES-- BUT NOT ONE LIKE I EVER *SEEN* BEFORE!
HE CAME AND LAID WASTE TO ANVILMAR...
...AND NOW HE'S HEADED THIS WAY!!
OVER MY *DEAD* BODY!
WE CAN'T LET THIS *STAND!*
NOT BLOODY LIKELY!
WE'LL HAVE NO TUSK-BEARIN' BEASTIE RUN RAMPANT THROUGH *OUR* HOME!
FILL YOUR HANDS, LADS! WE'VE GOT US A TROLL TO PUT DOWN!

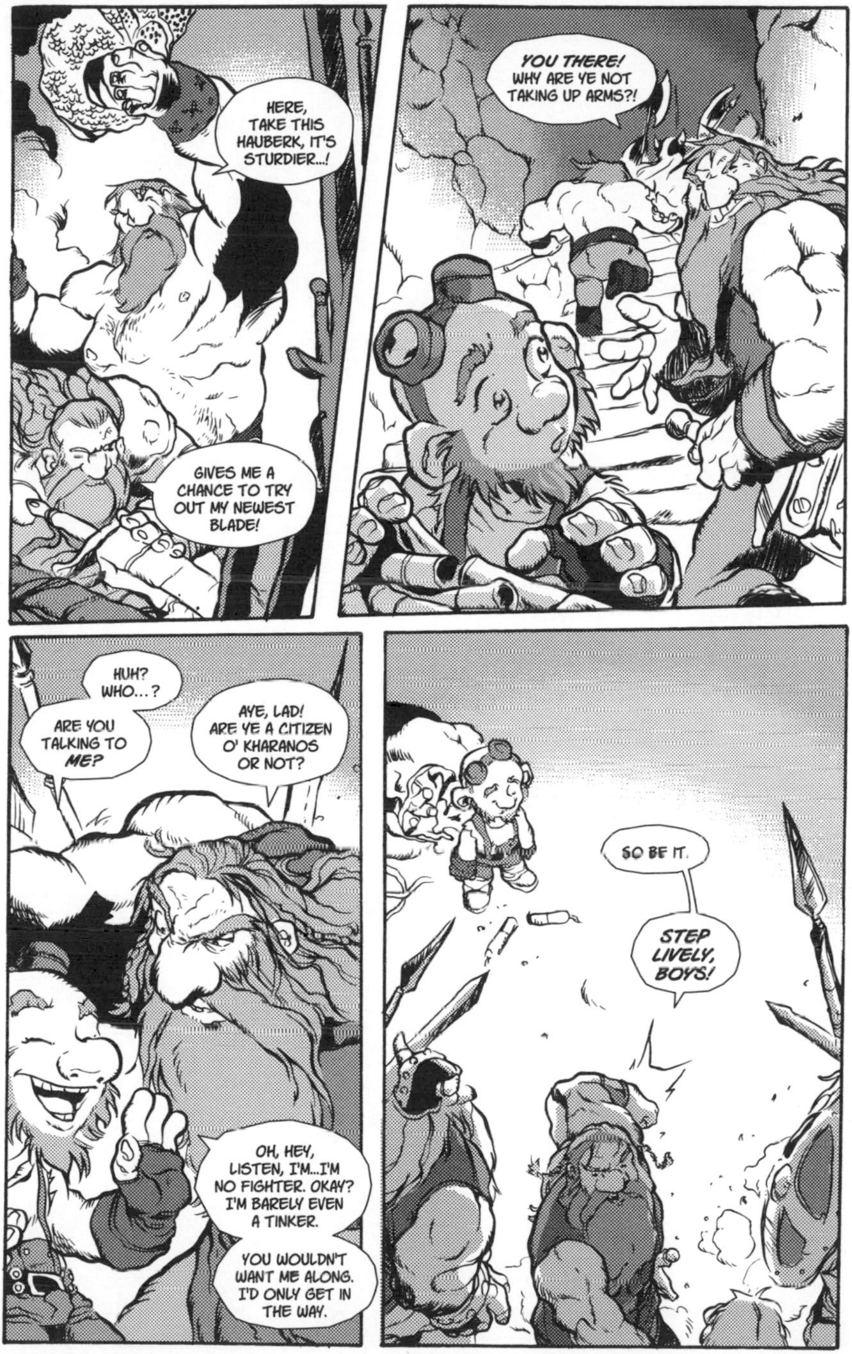
HERE, TAKE THIS HAUBERK, IT'S STURDIER...!
GIVES ME A CHANCE TO TRY OUT MY NEWEST BLADE!
YOU THERE! WHY ARE YE NOT TAKING UP ARMS?!
HUH? WHO...?
ARE YOU TALKING TO ME?
AYE, LAD! ARE YE A CITIZEN O' KHARANOS OR NOT?
OH, HEY, LISTEN, I'M...I'M NO FIGHTER. OKAY? I'M BARELY EVEN A TINKER.
YOU WOULDN'T WANT ME ALONG. I'D ONLY GET IN THE WAY.
SO BE IT.
STEP LIVELY, BOYS!

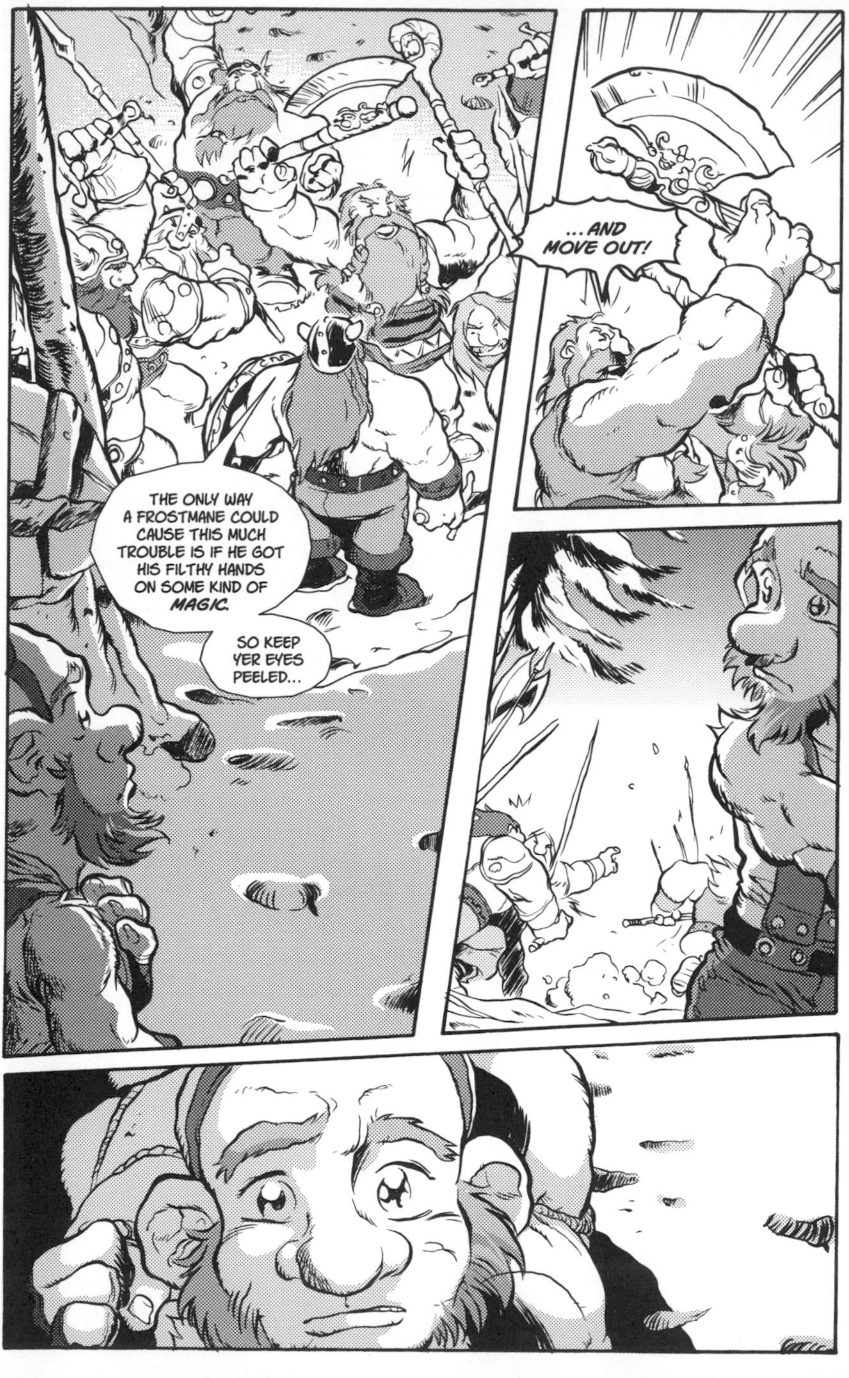
THE ONLY WAY A FROSTMANE COULD CAUSE THIS MUCH TROUBLE IS IF HE GOT HIS FILTHY HANDS ON SOME KIND OF *MAGIC*.
SO KEEP YER EYES PEELED...
...AND MOVE OUT!

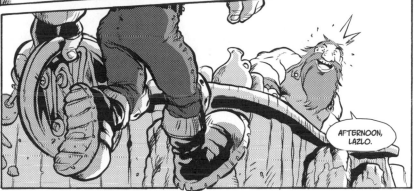

AFTERNOON, LAZLO.

MITE SURPRISED TO SEE YOU'RE NOT WITH THE HUNTING PARTY.

WELL...

...NO DISRESPECT... BUT COULDN'T I SAY THE SAME TO YOU?

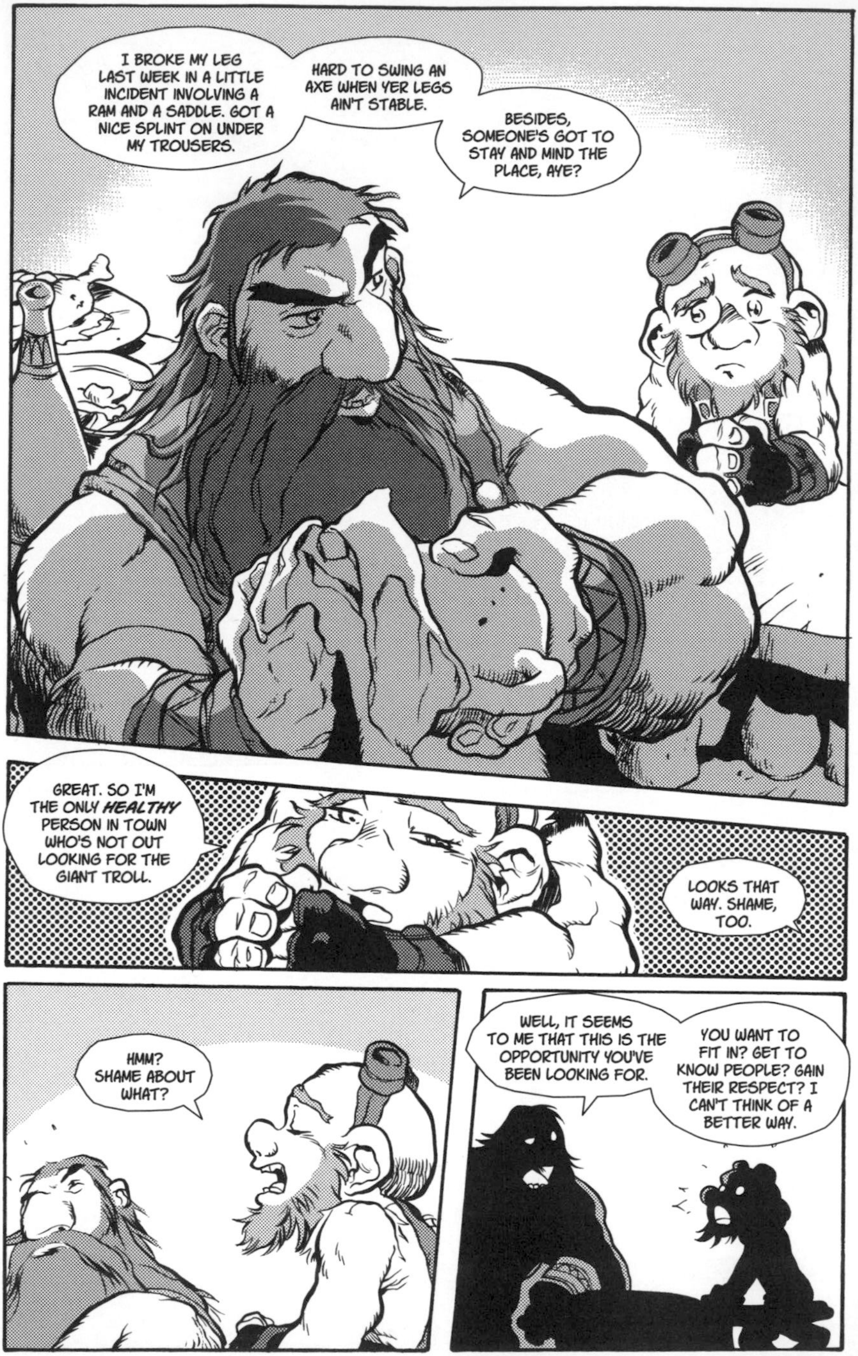
I BROKE MY LEG LAST WEEK IN A LITTLE INCIDENT INVOLVING A RAM AND A SADDLE. GOT A NICE SPLINT ON UNDER MY TROUSERS.
HARD TO SWING AN AXE WHEN YER LEGS AIN'T STABLE.
BESIDES, SOMEONE'S GOT TO STAY AND MIND THE PLACE, AYE?
GREAT. SO I'M THE ONLY ***HEALTHY*** PERSON IN TOWN WHO'S NOT OUT LOOKING FOR THE GIANT TROLL.
LOOKS THAT WAY. SHAME, TOO.
HMM? SHAME ABOUT WHAT?
WELL, IT SEEMS TO ME THAT THIS IS THE OPPORTUNITY YOU'VE BEEN LOOKING FOR.
YOU WANT TO FIT IN? GET TO KNOW PEOPLE? GAIN THEIR RESPECT? I CAN'T THINK OF A BETTER WAY.

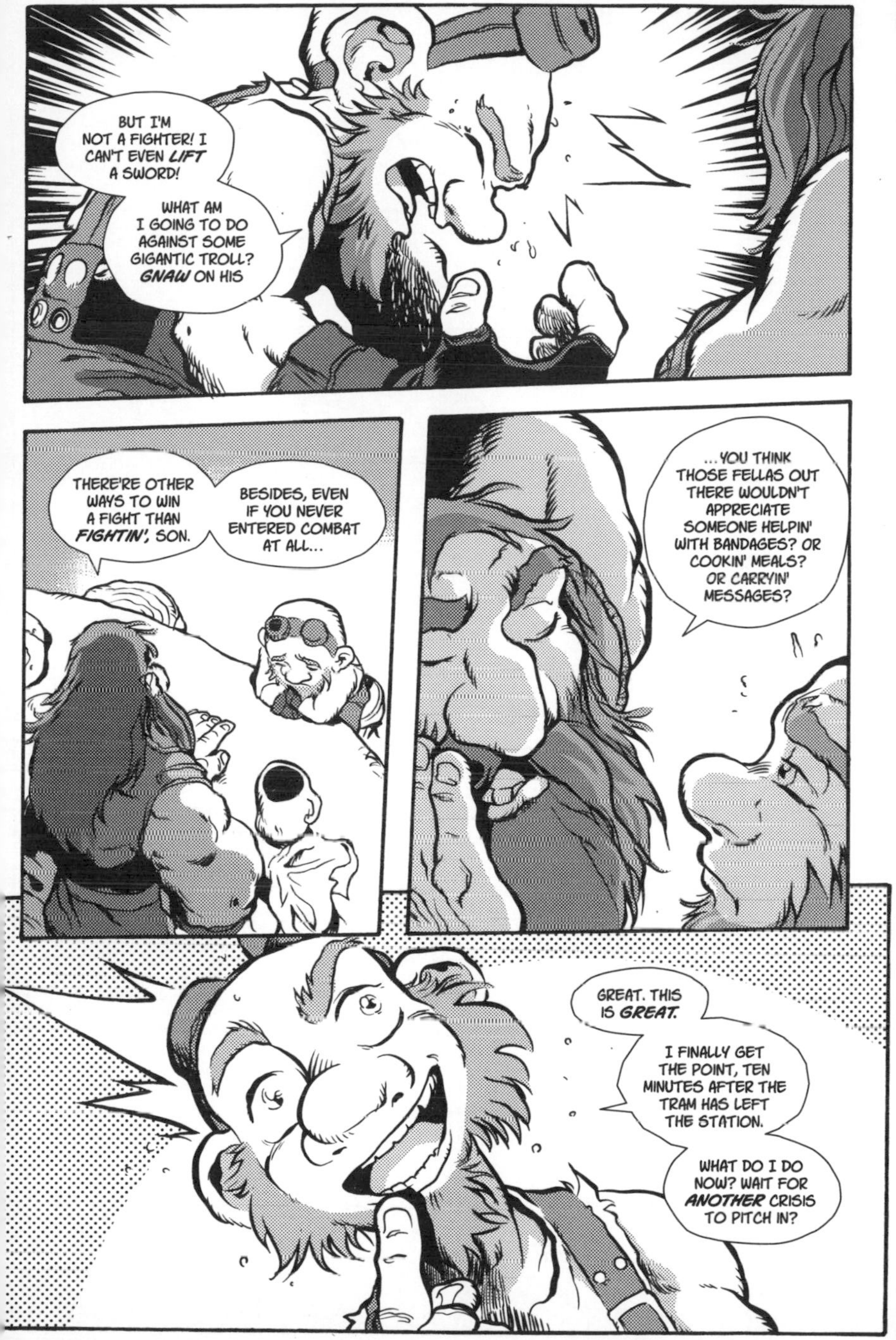
BUT I'M NOT A FIGHTER! I CAN'T EVEN *LIFT* A SWORD!
WHAT AM I GOING TO DO AGAINST SOME GIGANTIC TROLL? *GNAW* ON HIS
THERE'RE OTHER WAYS TO WIN A FIGHT THAN *FIGHTIN'*, SON.
BESIDES, EVEN IF YOU NEVER ENTERED COMBAT AT ALL...
...YOU THINK THOSE FELLAS OUT THERE WOULDN'T APPRECIATE SOMEONE HELPIN' WITH BANDAGES? OR COOKIN' MEALS? OR CARRYIN' MESSAGES?
GREAT. THIS IS *GREAT.*
I FINALLY GET THE POINT, TEN MINUTES AFTER THE TRAM HAS LEFT THE STATION.
WHAT DO I DO NOW? WAIT FOR *ANOTHER* CRISIS TO PITCH IN?

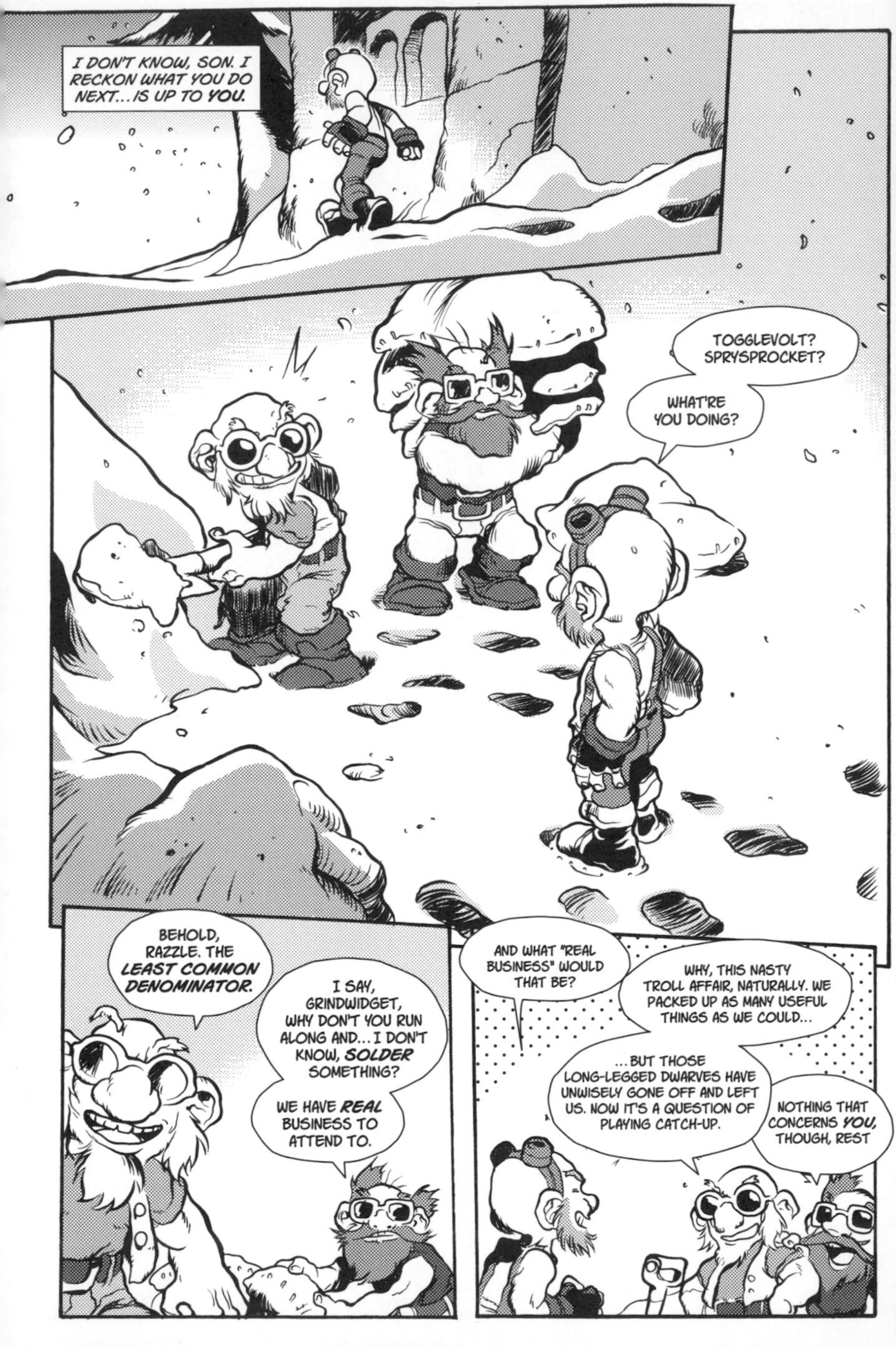

I DON'T KNOW, SON. I RECKON WHAT YOU DO NEXT... IS UP TO *YOU*.
TOGGLEVOLT? SPRYSPROCKET?
WHAT'RE YOU DOING?
BEHOLD, RAZZLE. THE ***LEAST COMMON DENOMINATOR***.
I SAY, GRINDWIDGET, WHY DON'T YOU RUN ALONG AND... I DON'T KNOW, ***SOLDER*** SOMETHING?
WE HAVE ***REAL*** BUSINESS TO ATTEND TO.
AND WHAT "REAL BUSINESS" WOULD THAT BE?
WHY, THIS NASTY TROLL AFFAIR, NATURALLY. WE PACKED UP AS MANY USEFUL THINGS AS WE COULD...
... BUT THOSE LONG-LEGGED DWARVES HAVE UNWISELY GONE OFF AND LEFT US. NOW IT'S A QUESTION OF PLAYING CATCH-UP.
NOTHING THAT CONCERNS ***YOU,*** THOUGH, REST

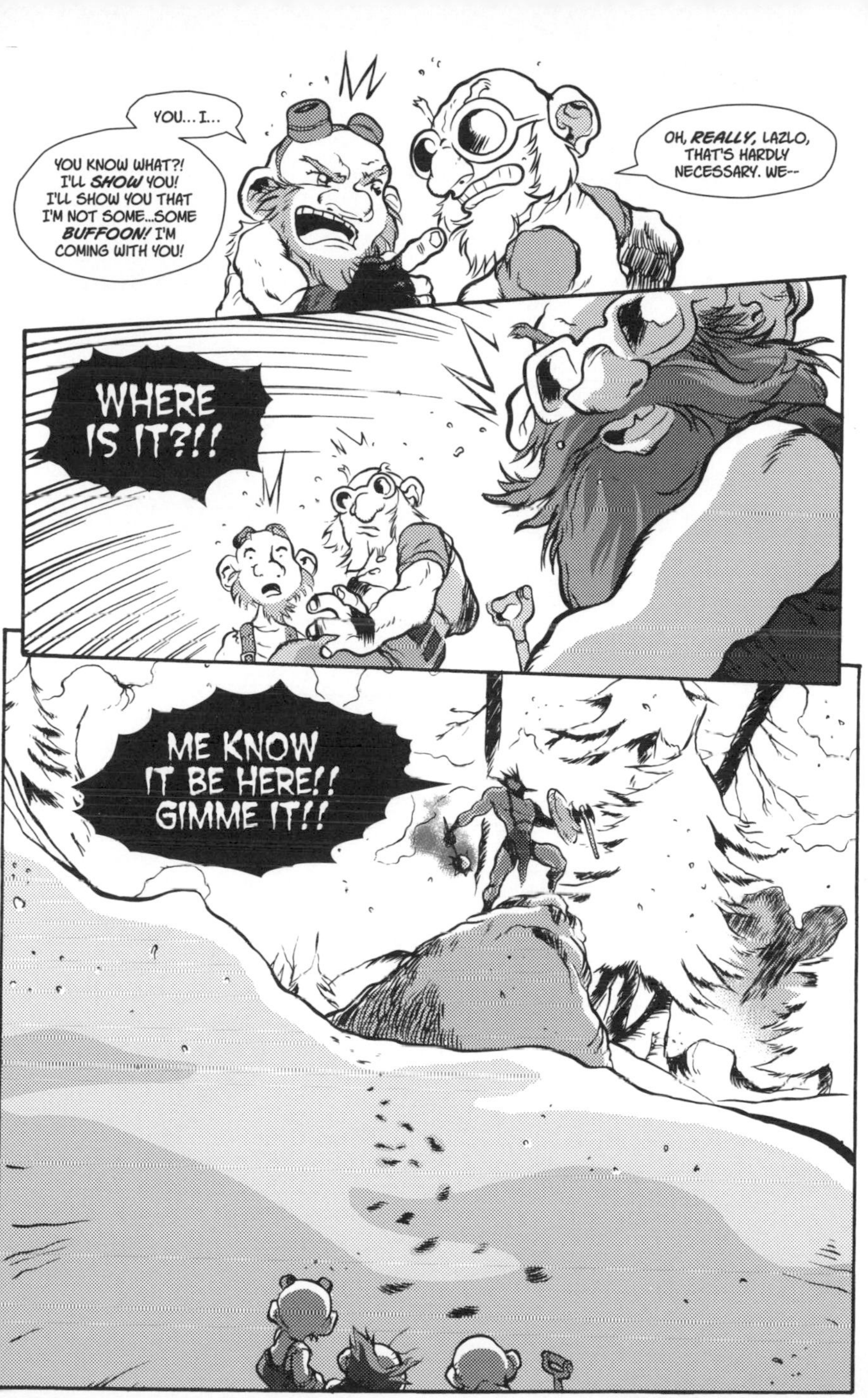
YOU... I...
YOU KNOW WHAT?! I'LL *SHOW* YOU! I'LL SHOW YOU THAT I'M NOT SOME...SOME *BUFFOON!* I'M COMING WITH YOU!
OH, *REALLY,* LAZLO, THAT'S HARDLY NECESSARY. WE--
WHERE IS IT?!!
ME KNOW IT BE HERE!! GIMME IT!!

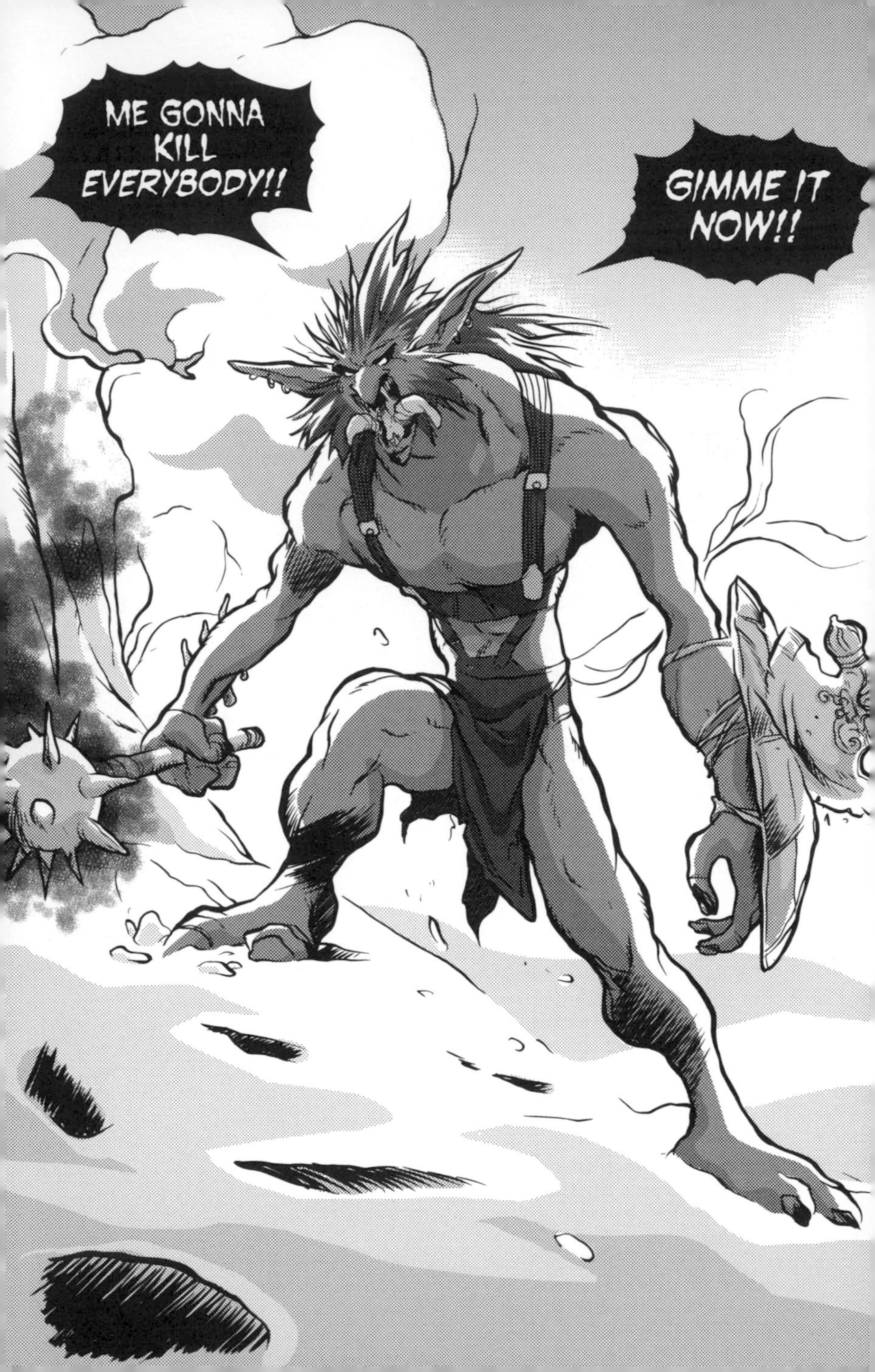
ME GONNA KILL EVERYBODY!!
GIMME IT NOW!!

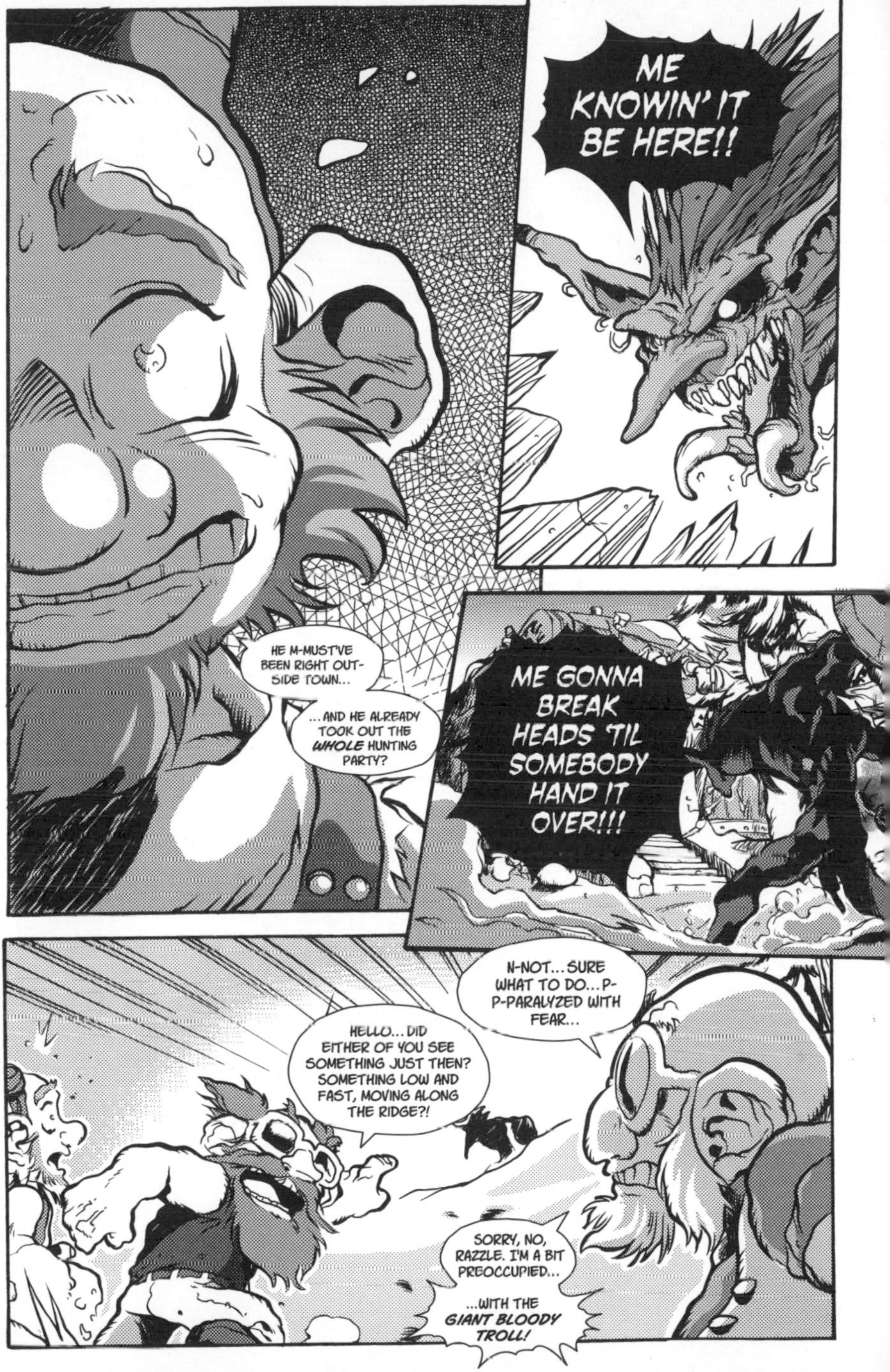
ME KNOWIN' IT BE HERE!!
HE M-MUST'VE BEEN RIGHT OUT-SIDE TOWN...
...AND HE ALREADY TOOK OUT THE *WHOLE* HUNTING PARTY?
ME GONNA BREAK HEADS 'TIL SOMEBODY HAND IT OVER!!!
HELLO... DID EITHER OF YOU SEE SOMETHING JUST THEN? SOMETHING LOW AND FAST, MOVING ALONG THE RIDGE?!
N-NOT... SURE WHAT TO DO... P-P-PARALYZED WITH FEAR...
SORRY, NO, RAZZLE. I'M A BIT PREOCCUPIED...
...WITH THE *GIANT BLOODY TROLL!*

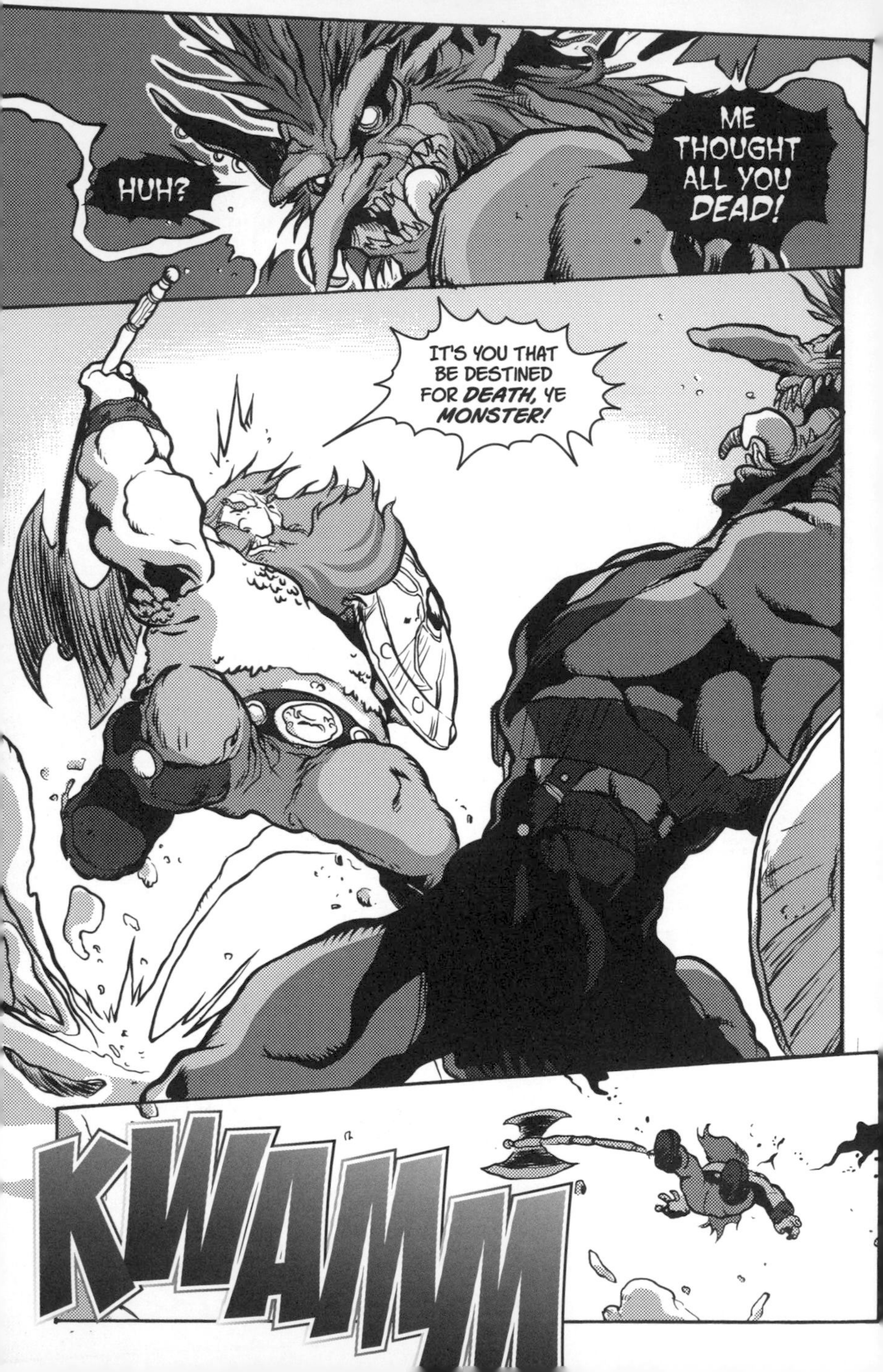
HUH?
ME THOUGHT ALL YOU DEAD!
IT'S YOU THAT BE DESTINED FOR DEATH, YE MONSTER!
KWAMM

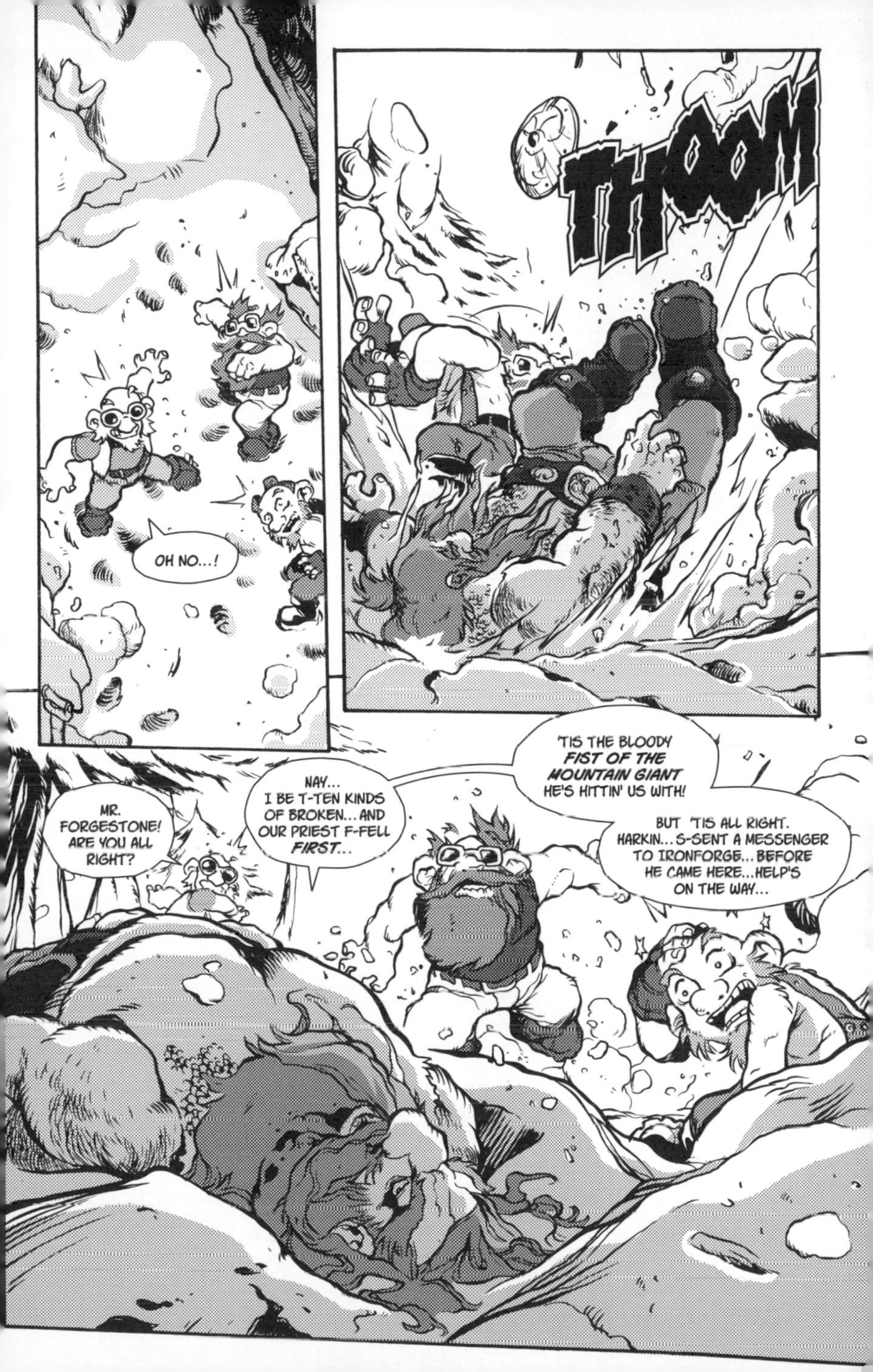

OH NO...!
THOOM
MR. FORGESTONE! ARE YOU ALL RIGHT?
NAY... I BE T-TEN KINDS OF BROKEN... AND OUR PRIEST F-FELL FIRST...
'TIS THE BLOODY FIST OF THE MOUNTAIN GIANT HE'S HITTIN' US WITH!
BUT 'TIS ALL RIGHT. HARKIN... S-SENT A MESSENGER TO IRONFORGE... BEFORE HE CAME HERE... HELP'S ON THE WAY...

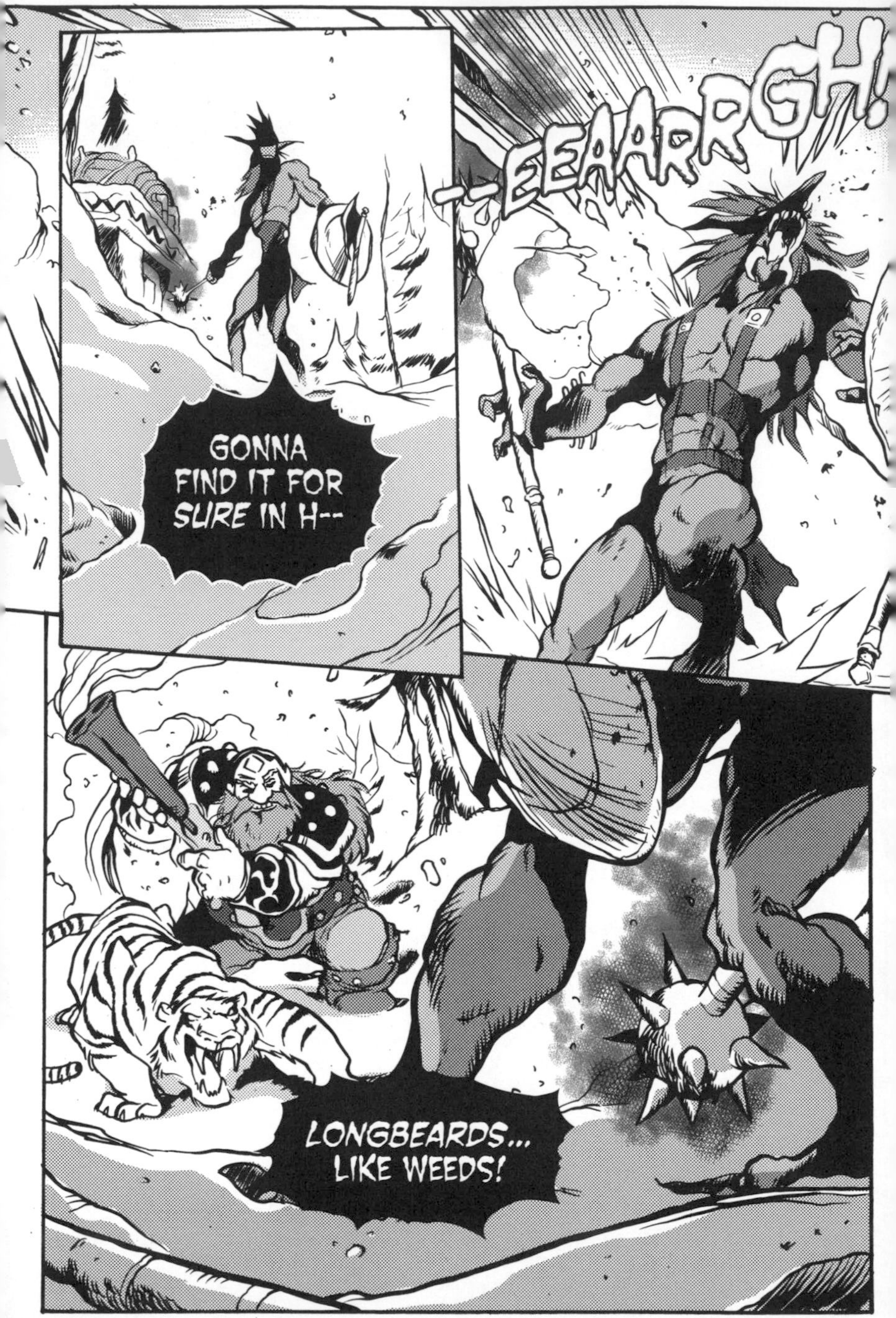
GONNA FIND IT FOR SURE IN H--
--EEAARRGH!
LONGBEARDS... LIKE WEEDS!

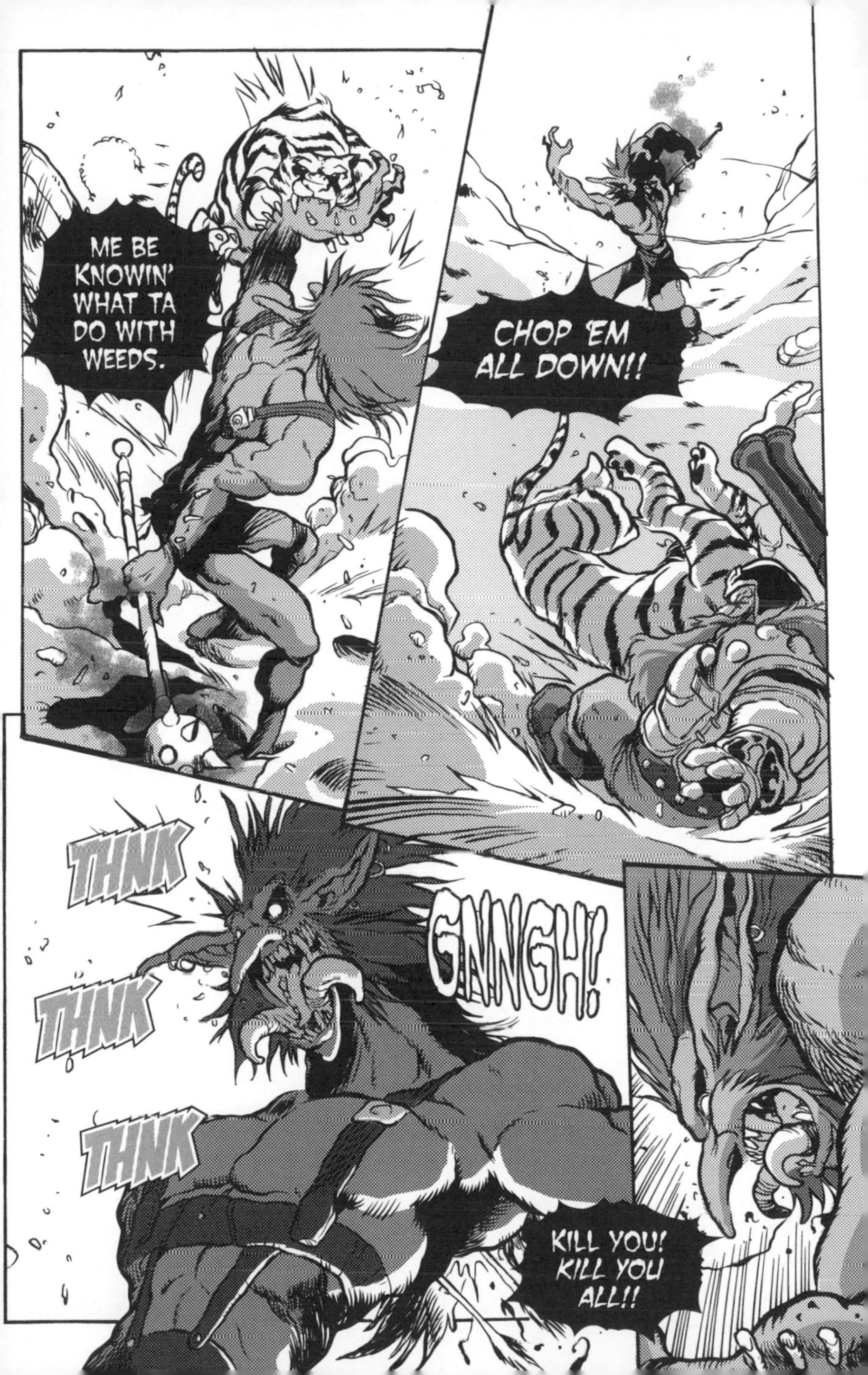
ME BE KNOWIN' WHAT TA DO WITH WEEDS.
CHOP 'EM ALL DOWN!!
THNK
THNK
THNK
GNNGH!
KILL YOU! KILL YOU ALL!!

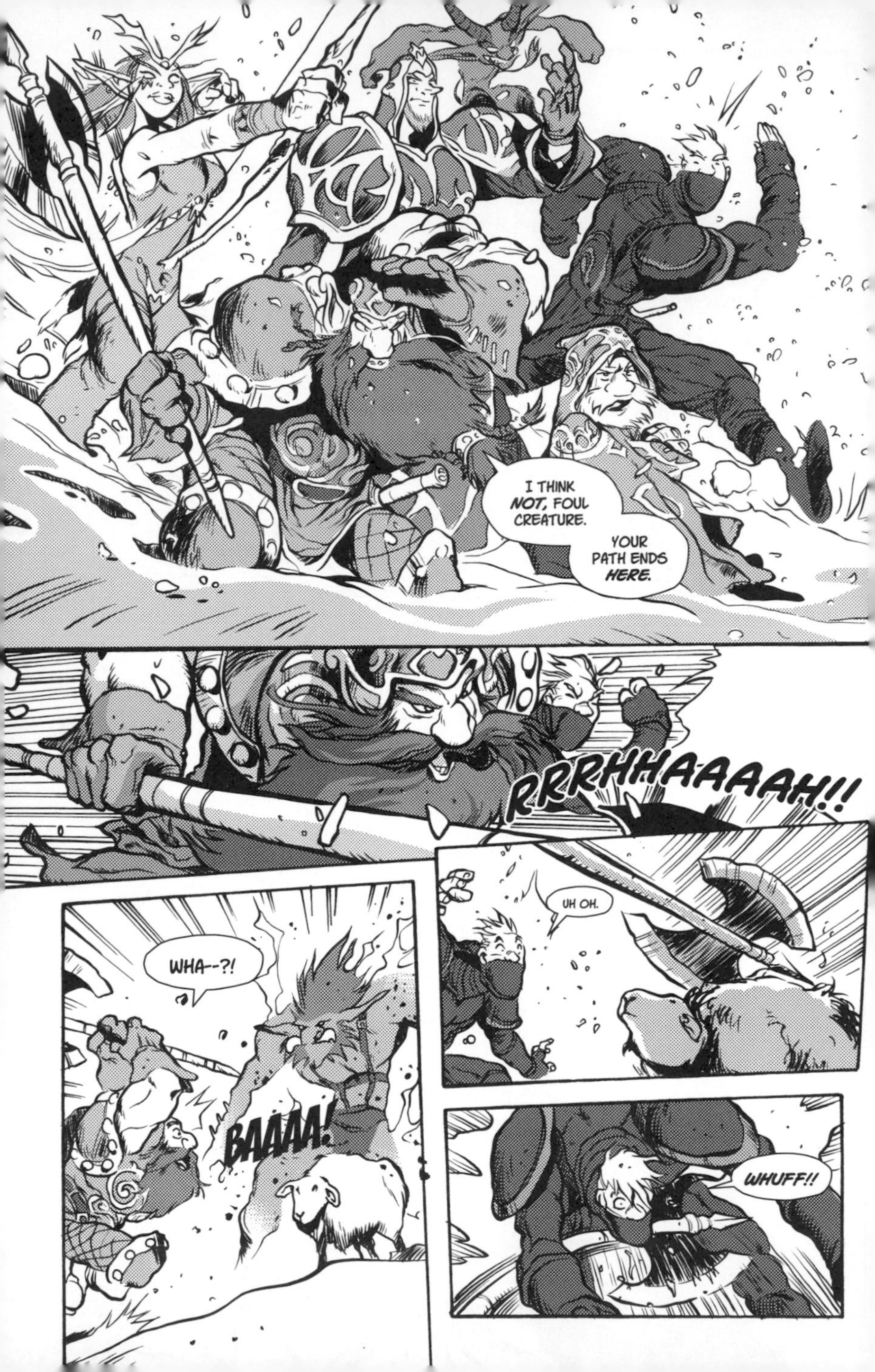
I THINK *NOT,* FOUL CREATURE.
YOUR PATH ENDS *HERE.*
RRRHHAAAAAH!!
WHA--?!
BAAAA!
UH OH.
WHUFF!!

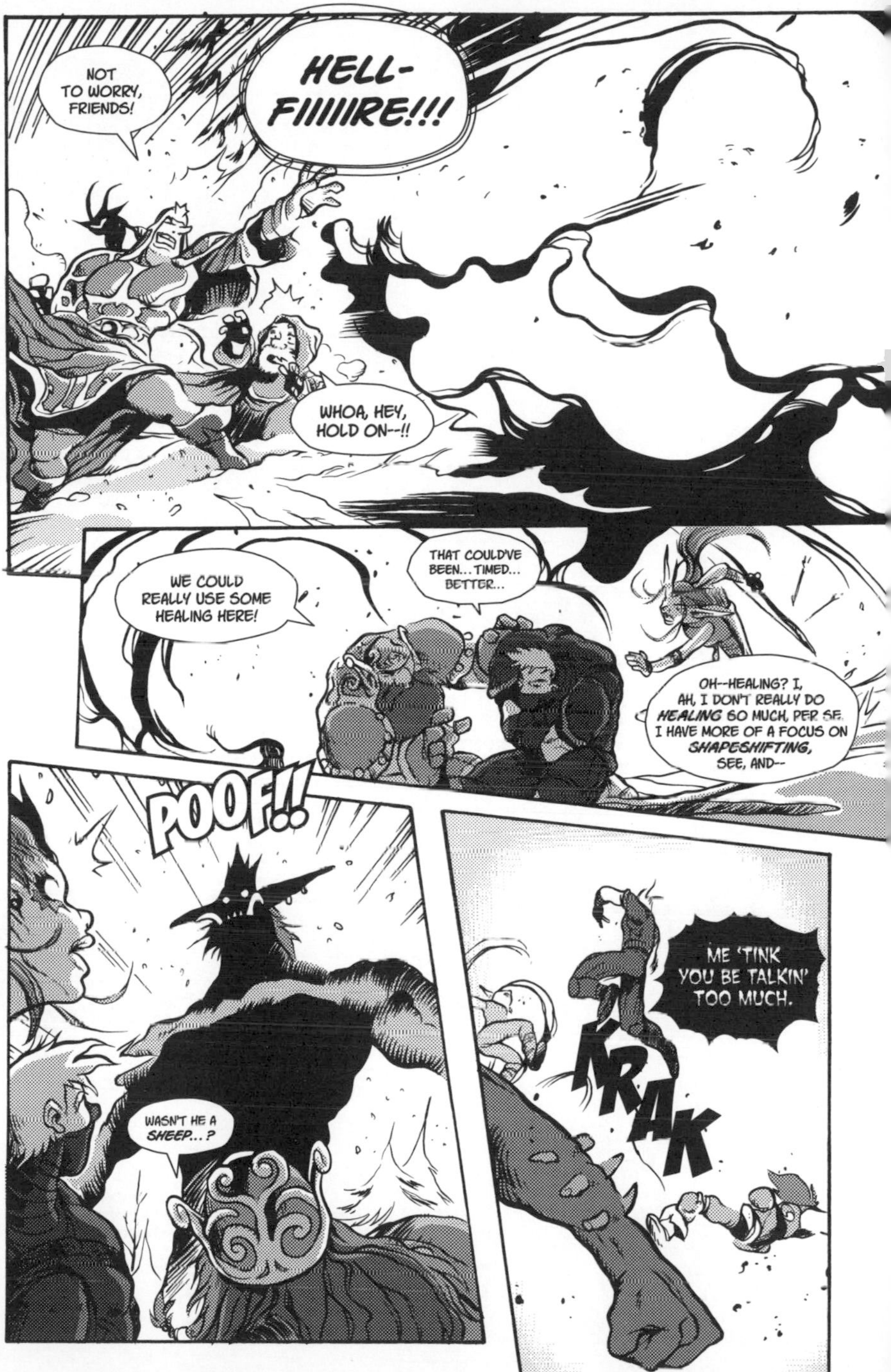
NOT TO WORRY, FRIENDS!
HELL-FIIIIRE!!!
WHOA, HEY, HOLD ON--!!
WE COULD REALLY USE SOME HEALING HERE!
THAT COULD'VE BEEN... TIMED... BETTER...
OH--HEALING? I, AH, I DON'T REALLY DO HEALING SO MUCH, PER SE. I HAVE MORE OF A FOCUS ON SHAPESHIFTING, SEE, AND--
POOF!!
WASN'T HE A SHEEP...?
ME 'TINK YOU BE TALKIN' TOO MUCH.
KRAK

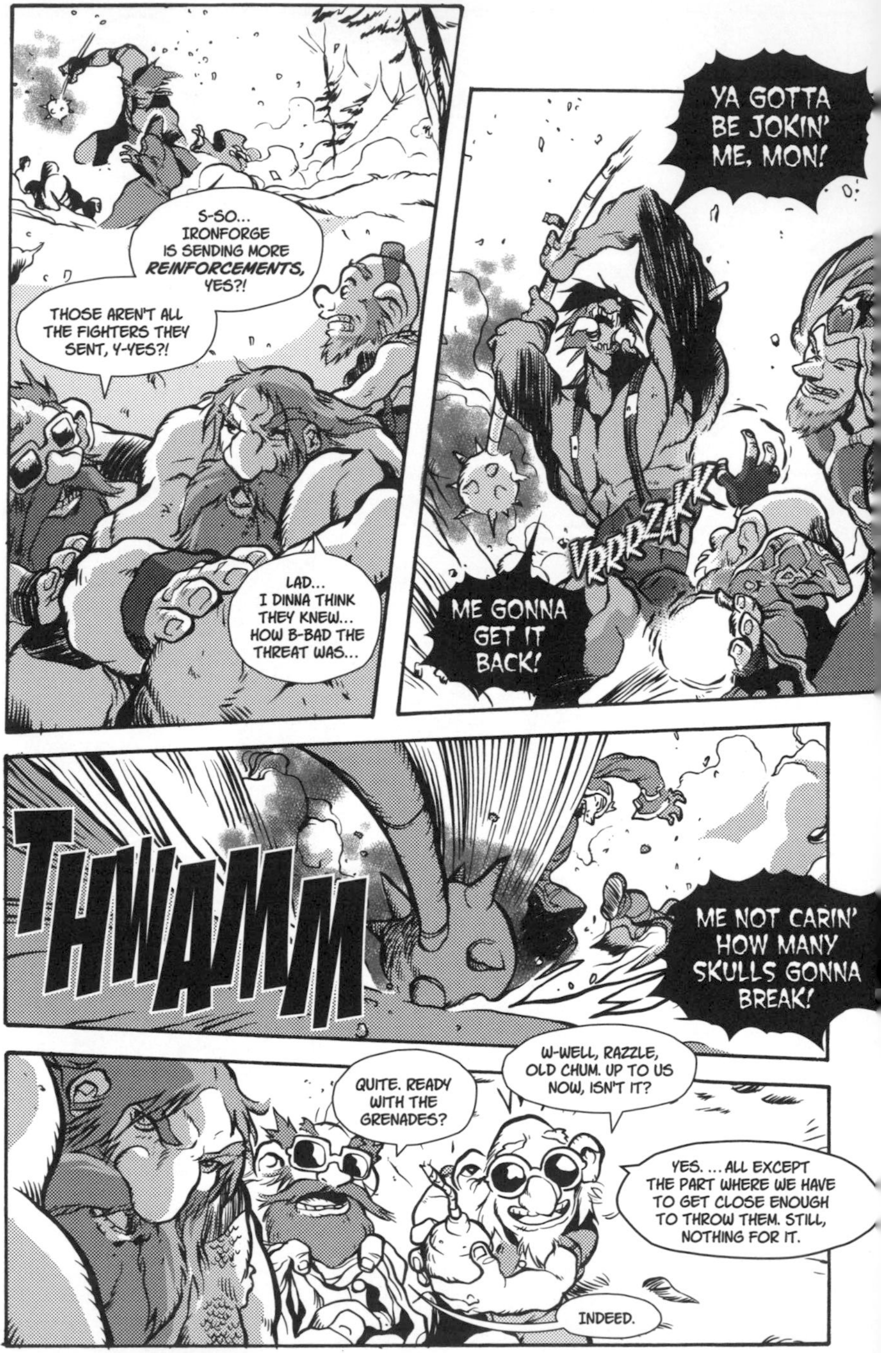
S-SO... IRONFORGE IS SENDING MORE REINFORCEMENTS, YES?!
THOSE AREN'T ALL THE FIGHTERS THEY SENT, Y-YES?!
LAD... I DINNA THINK THEY KNEW... HOW B-BAD THE THREAT WAS...
YA GOTTA BE JOKIN' ME, MON!
VRRRZAKK
ME GONNA GET IT BACK!
THWAMM
ME NOT CARIN' HOW MANY SKULLS GONNA BREAK!
QUITE. READY WITH THE GRENADES?
W-WELL, RAZZLE, OLD CHUM. UP TO US NOW, ISN'T IT?
YES. ...ALL EXCEPT THE PART WHERE WE HAVE TO GET CLOSE ENOUGH TO THROW THEM. STILL, NOTHING FOR IT.
INDEED.

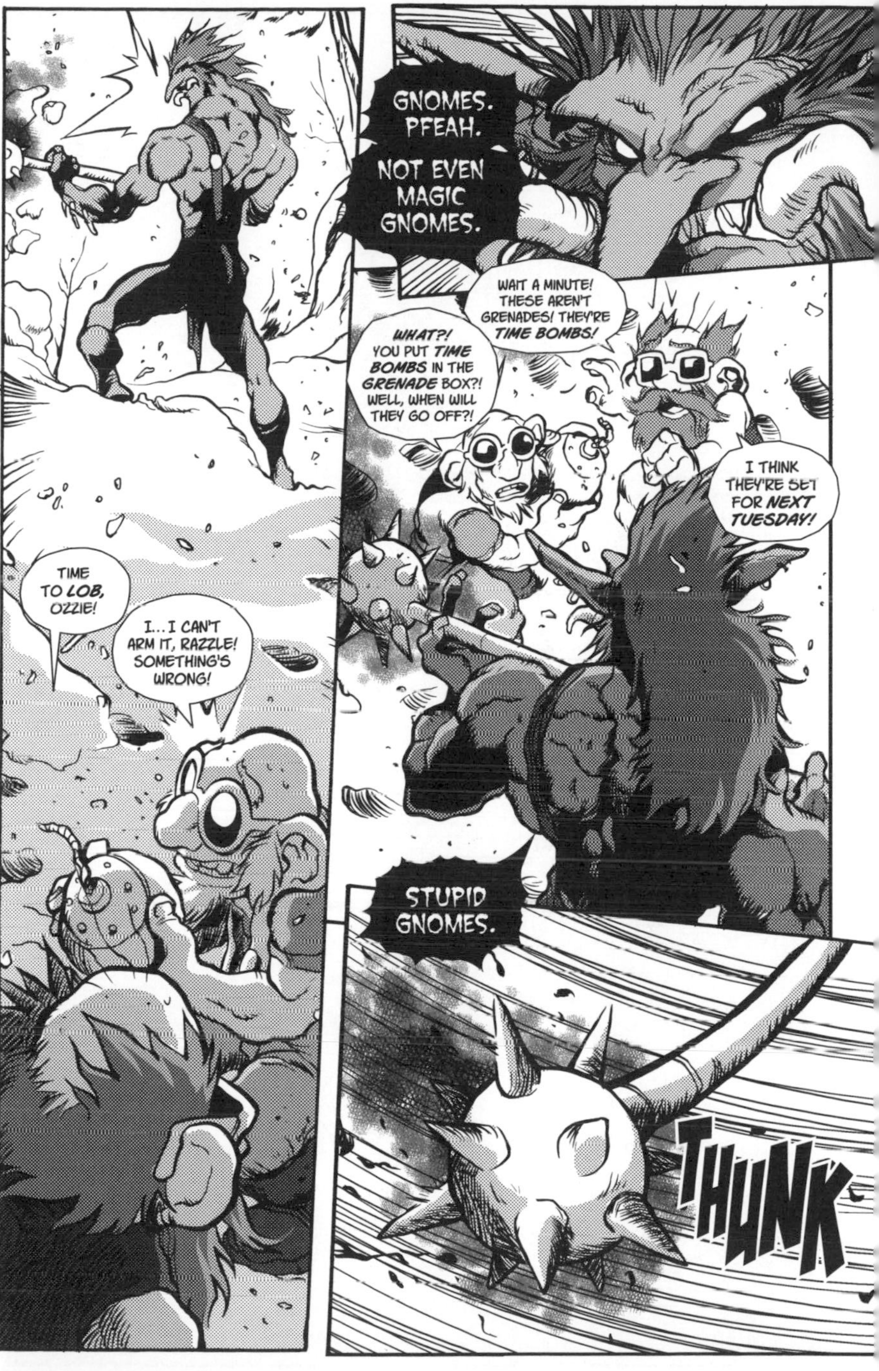
TIME TO LOB, OZZIE!
I... I CAN'T ARM IT, RAZZLE! SOMETHING'S WRONG!
GNOMES. PFEAH.
NOT EVEN MAGIC GNOMES.
WAIT A MINUTE! THESE AREN'T GRENADES! THEY'RE TIME BOMBS!
WHAT?! YOU PUT TIME BOMBS IN THE GRENADE BOX?! WELL, WHEN WILL THEY GO OFF?!
I THINK THEY'RE SET FOR NEXT TUESDAY!
STUPID GNOMES.
THUNK

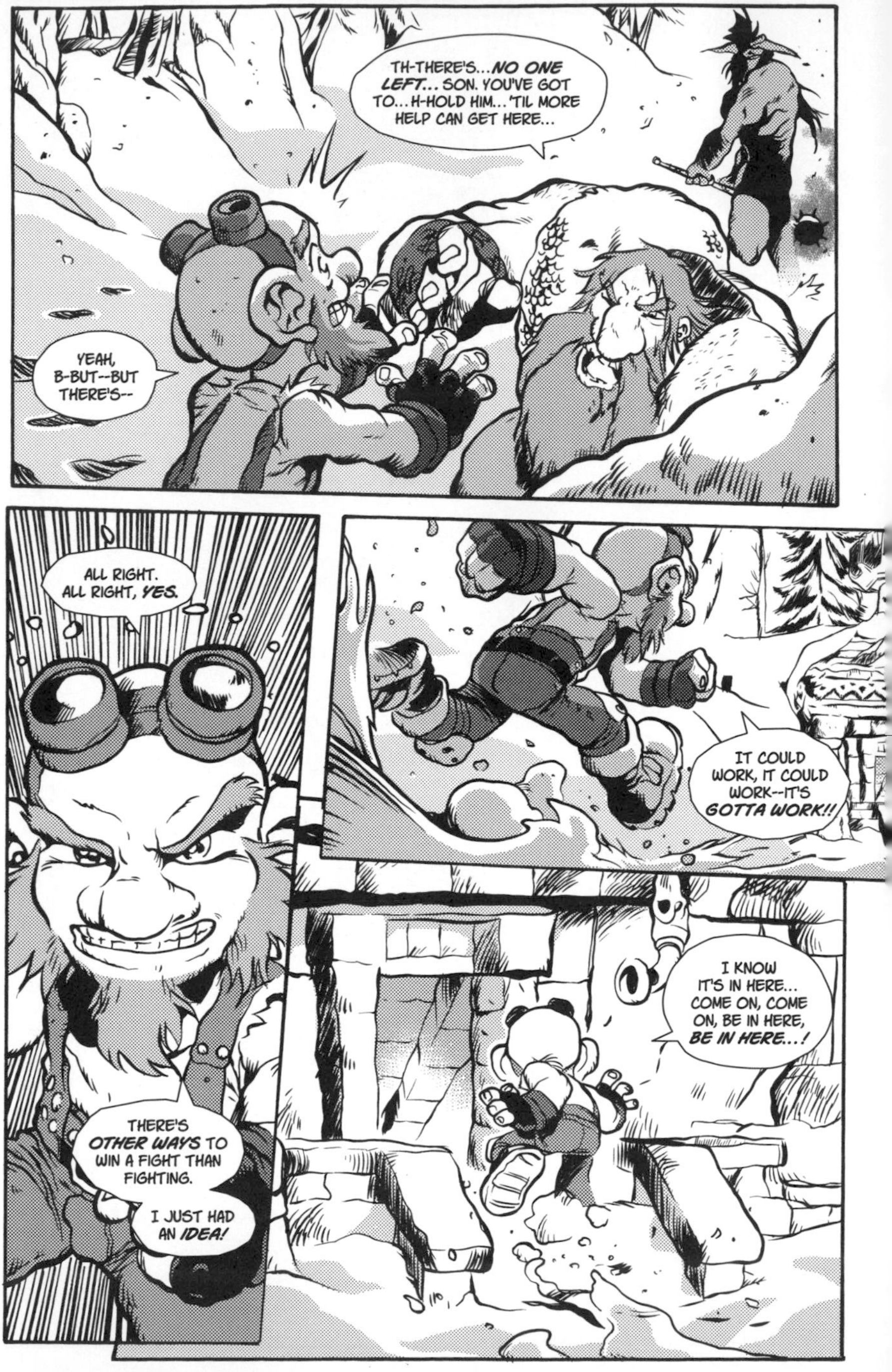
TH-THERE'S...NO ONE LEFT... SON. YOU'VE GOT TO...H-HOLD HIM...'TIL MORE HELP CAN GET HERE...
YEAH, B-BUT--BUT THERE'S--
ALL RIGHT. ALL RIGHT, YES.
THERE'S OTHER WAYS TO WIN A FIGHT THAN FIGHTING.
I JUST HAD AN IDEA!
IT COULD WORK, IT COULD WORK--IT'S GOTTA WORK!!
I KNOW IT'S IN HERE... COME ON, COME ON, BE IN HERE, BE IN HERE...!

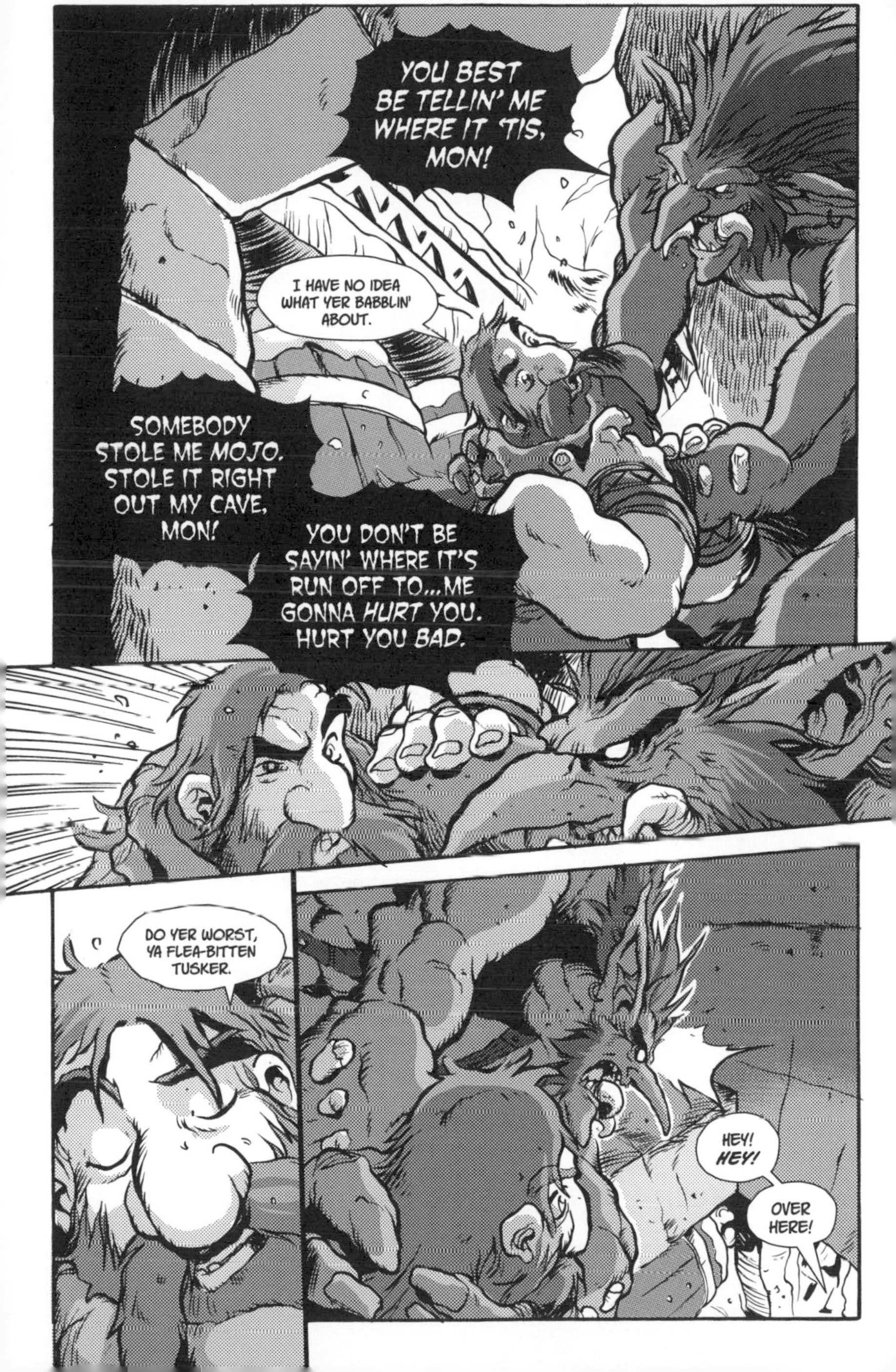
YOU BEST BE TELLIN' ME WHERE IT 'TIS, MON!
I HAVE NO IDEA WHAT YER BABBLIN' ABOUT.
SOMEBODY STOLE ME *MOJO*. STOLE IT RIGHT OUT MY CAVE, MON!
YOU DON'T BE SAYIN' WHERE IT'S RUN OFF TO... ME GONNA *HURT* YOU. HURT YOU *BAD*.
DO YER WORST, YA FLEA-BITTEN TUSKER.
HEY! **HEY!**
OVER HERE!

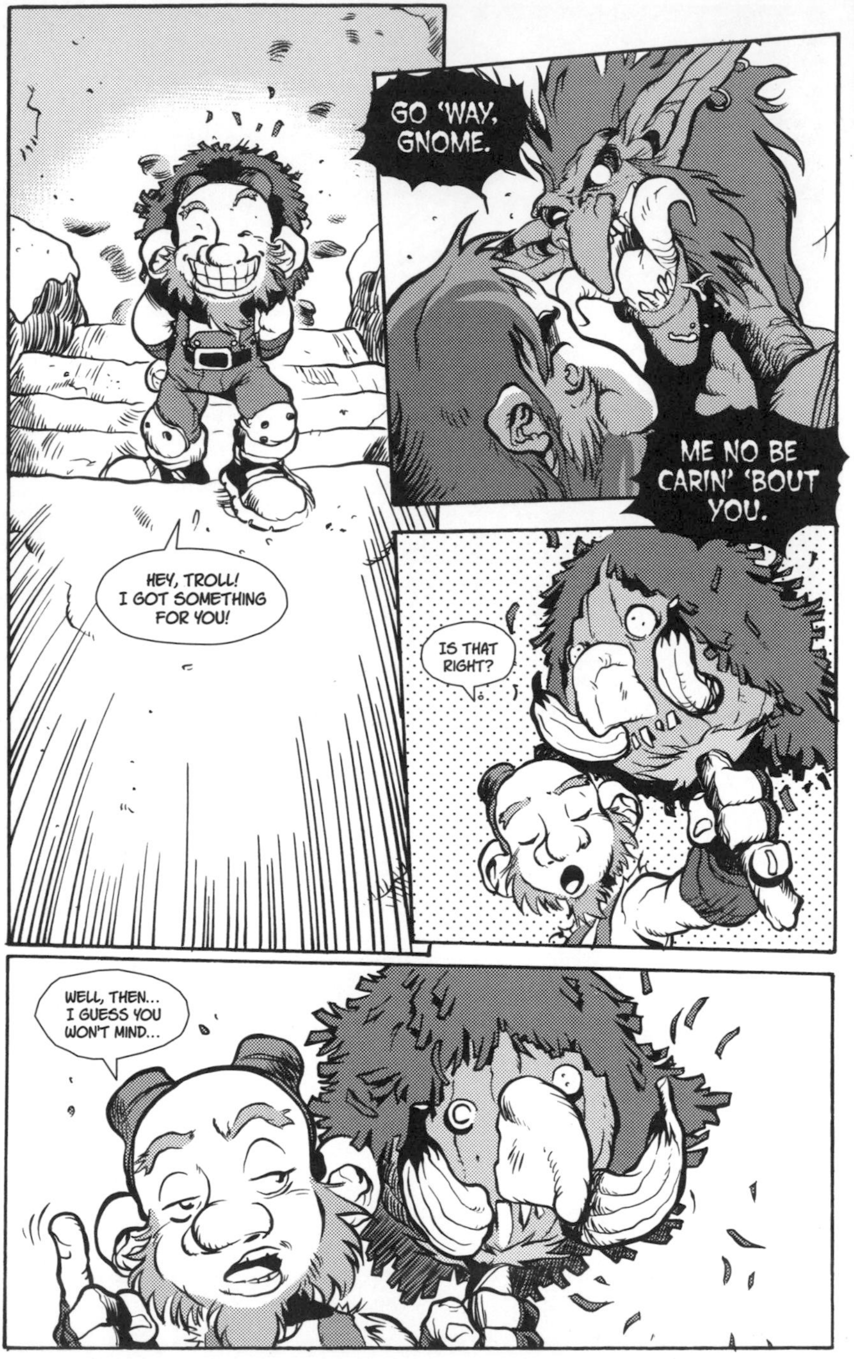
HEY, TROLL! I GOT SOMETHING FOR YOU!
GO 'WAY, GNOME.
ME NO BE CARIN' 'BOUT YOU.
IS THAT RIGHT?
WELL, THEN... I GUESS YOU WON'T MIND...

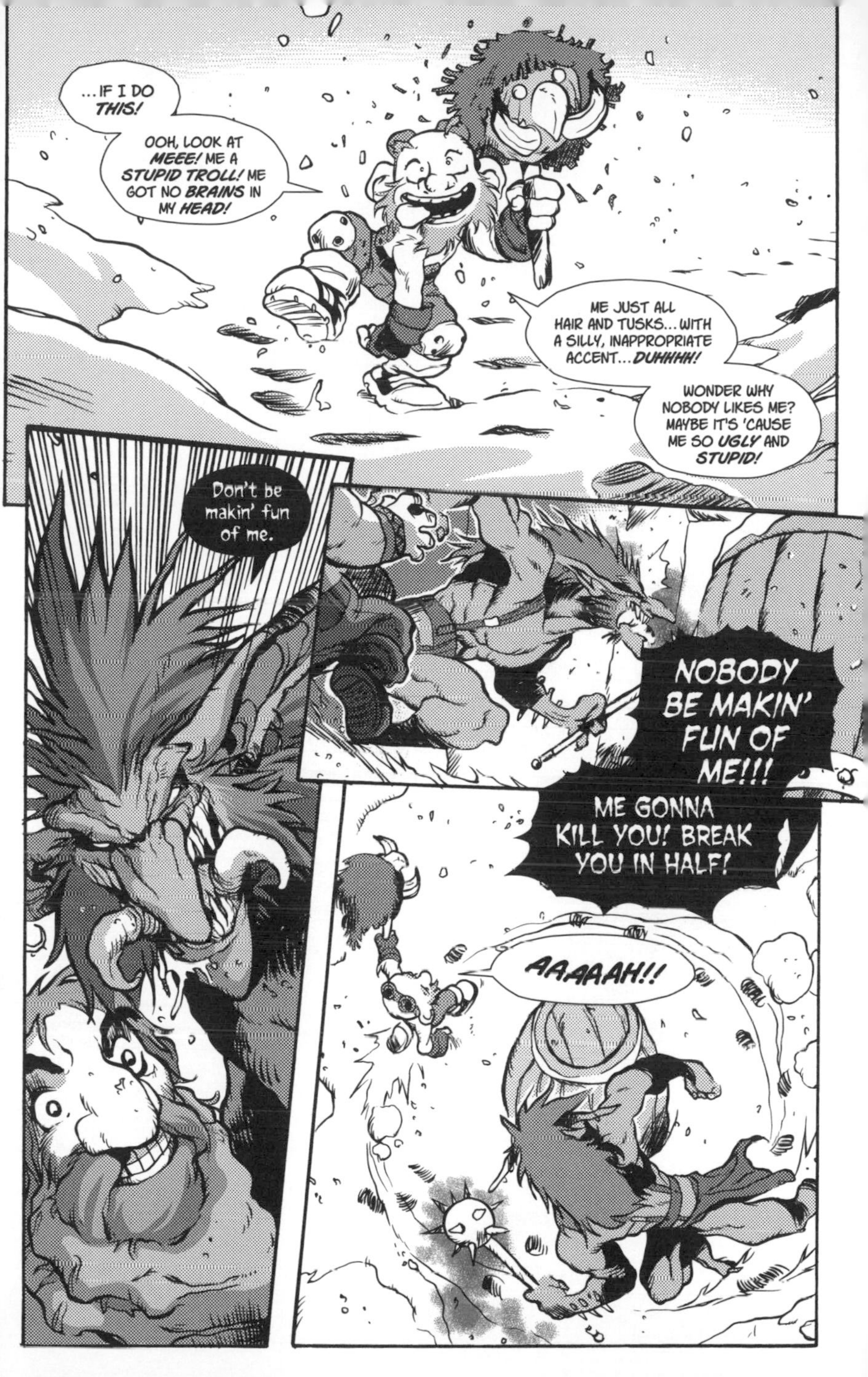
...IF I DO THIS!
OOH, LOOK AT MEEE! ME A STUPID TROLL! ME GOT NO BRAINS IN MY HEAD!
ME JUST ALL HAIR AND TUSKS... WITH A SILLY, INAPPROPRIATE ACCENT... DUHHHH!
WONDER WHY NOBODY LIKES ME? MAYBE IT'S 'CAUSE ME SO UGLY AND STUPID!
Don't be makin' fun of me.
NOBODY BE MAKIN' FUN OF ME!!!
ME GONNA KILL YOU! BREAK YOU IN HALF!
AAAAAH!!

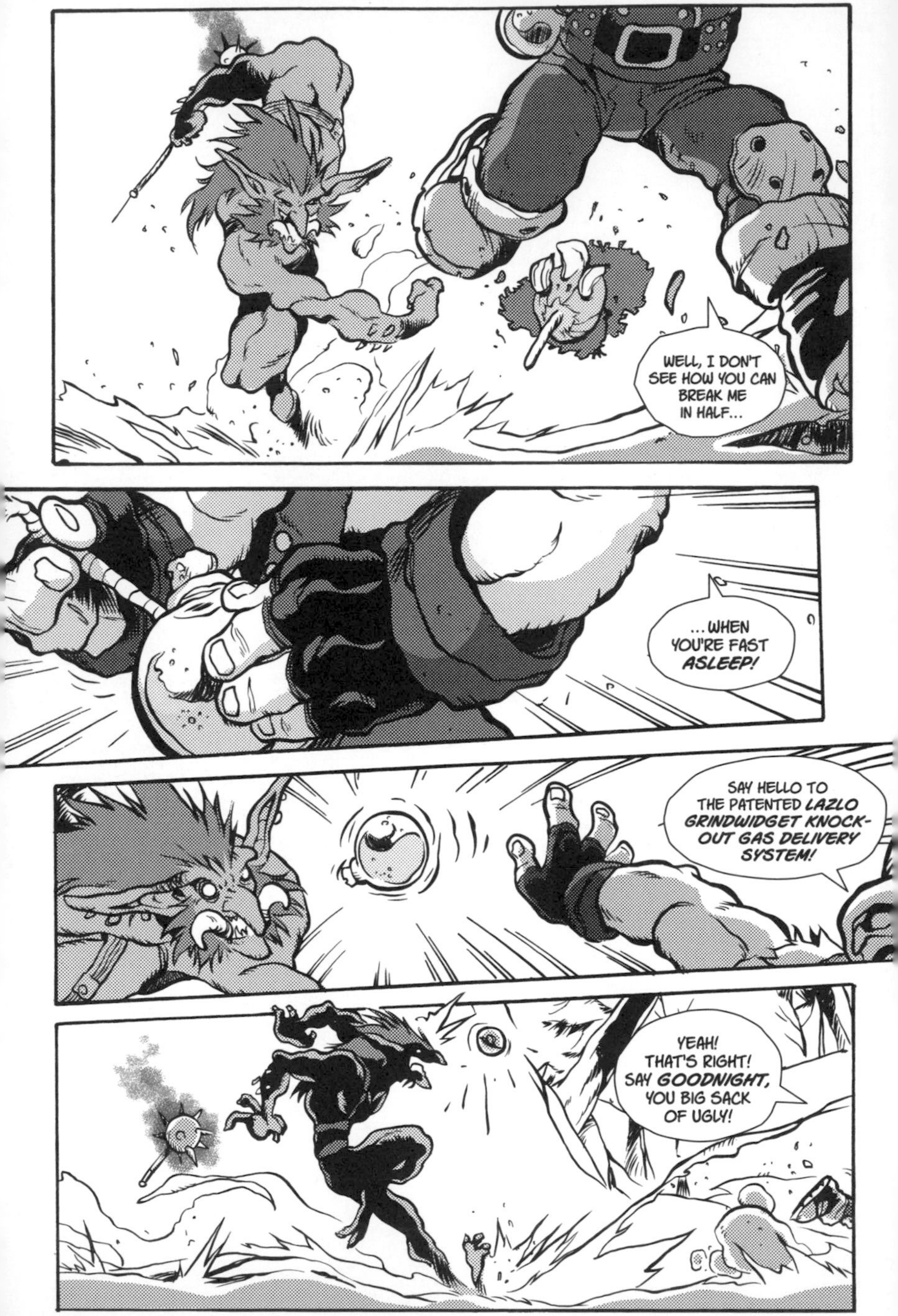
WELL, I DON'T SEE HOW YOU CAN BREAK ME IN HALF...
...WHEN YOU'RE FAST *ASLEEP!*
SAY HELLO TO THE PATENTED *LAZLO GRINDWIDGET KNOCK-OUT GAS DELIVERY SYSTEM!*
YEAH! THAT'S RIGHT! SAY *GOODNIGHT,* YOU BIG SACK OF UGLY!

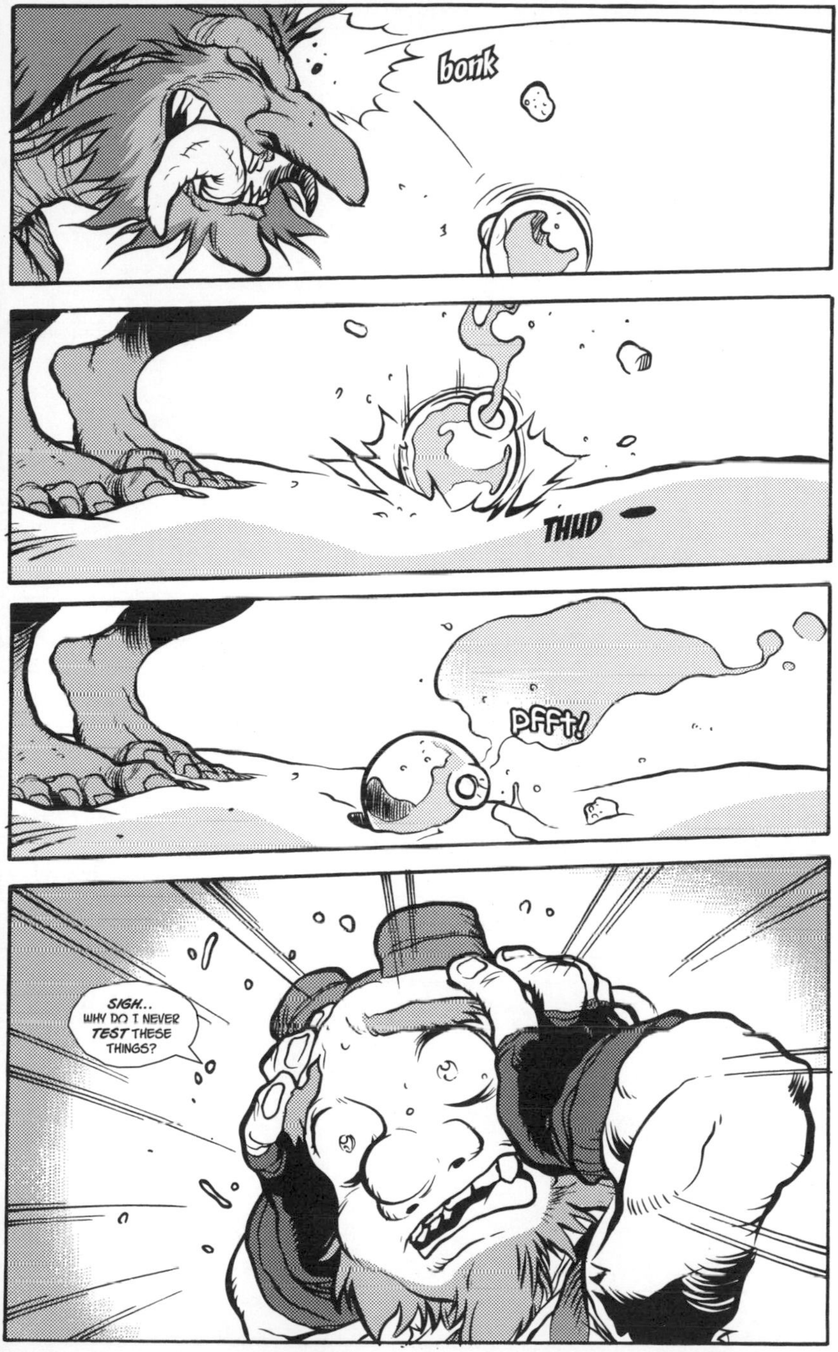
bonk
THUD
pFFt!
SIGH... WHY DO I NEVER TEST THESE THINGS?

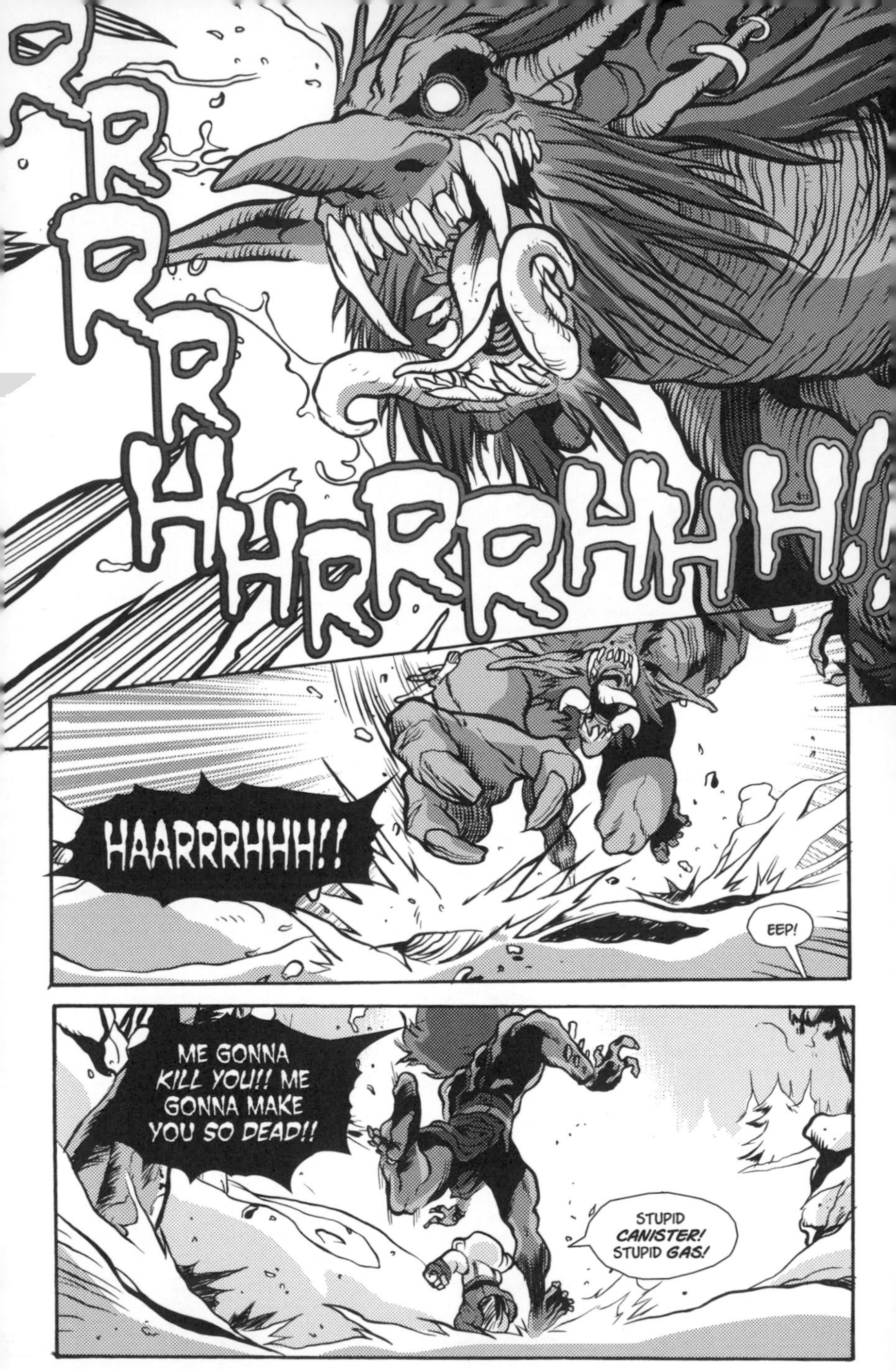
RRRHHRRRHHH!!
HAARRRHHH!!
EEP!
ME GONNA *KILL YOU!!* ME GONNA MAKE YOU SO *DEAD!!*
STUPID *CANISTER!* STUPID *GAS!*

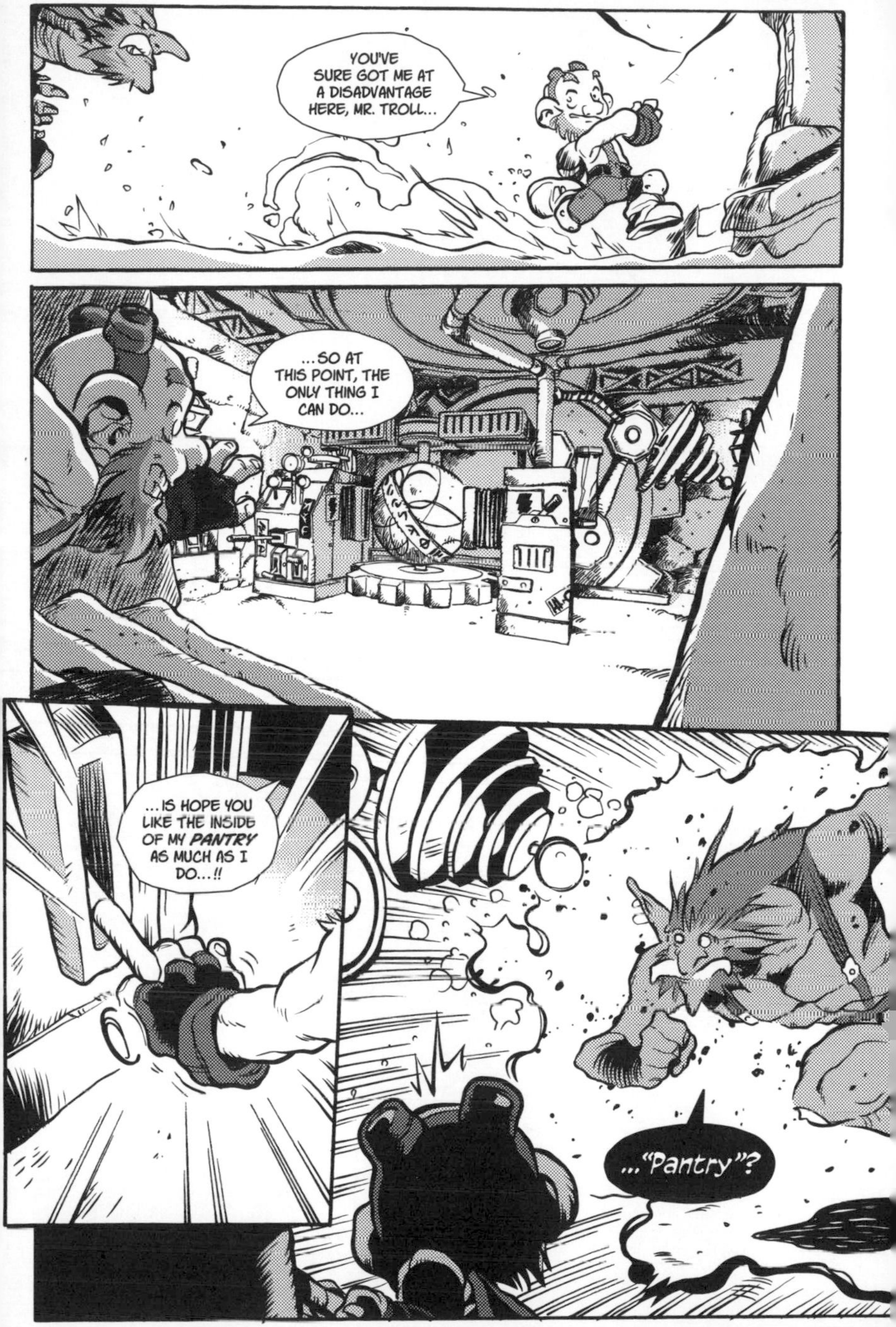
YOU'VE SURE GOT ME AT A DISADVANTAGE HERE, MR. TROLL...
...SO AT THIS POINT, THE ONLY THING I CAN DO...
...IS HOPE YOU LIKE THE INSIDE OF MY *PANTRY* AS MUCH AS I DO...!!
..."Pantry"?

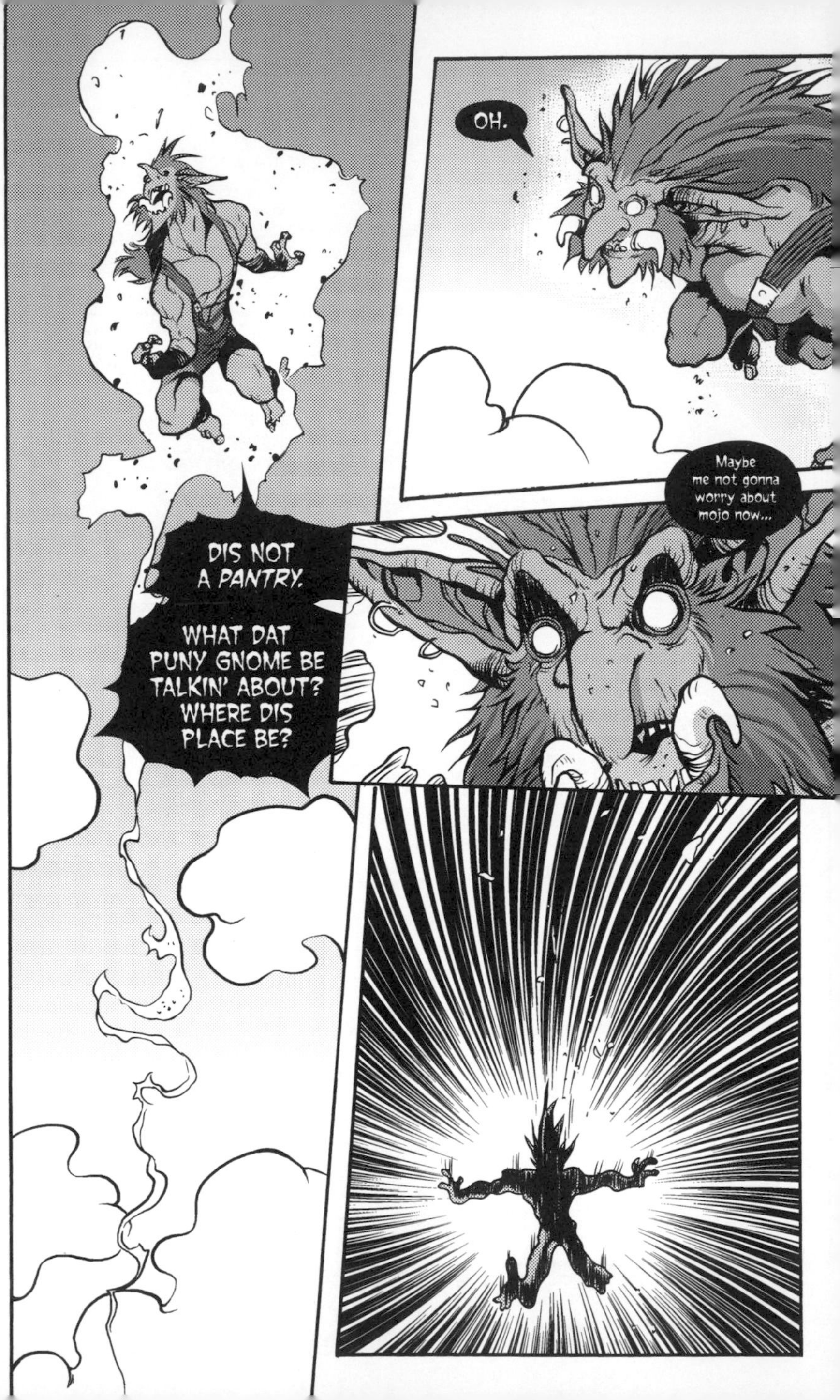
DIS NOT A PANTRY.
WHAT DAT PUNY GNOME BE TALKIN' ABOUT? WHERE DIS PLACE BE?
OH.
Maybe me not gonna worry about mojo now...

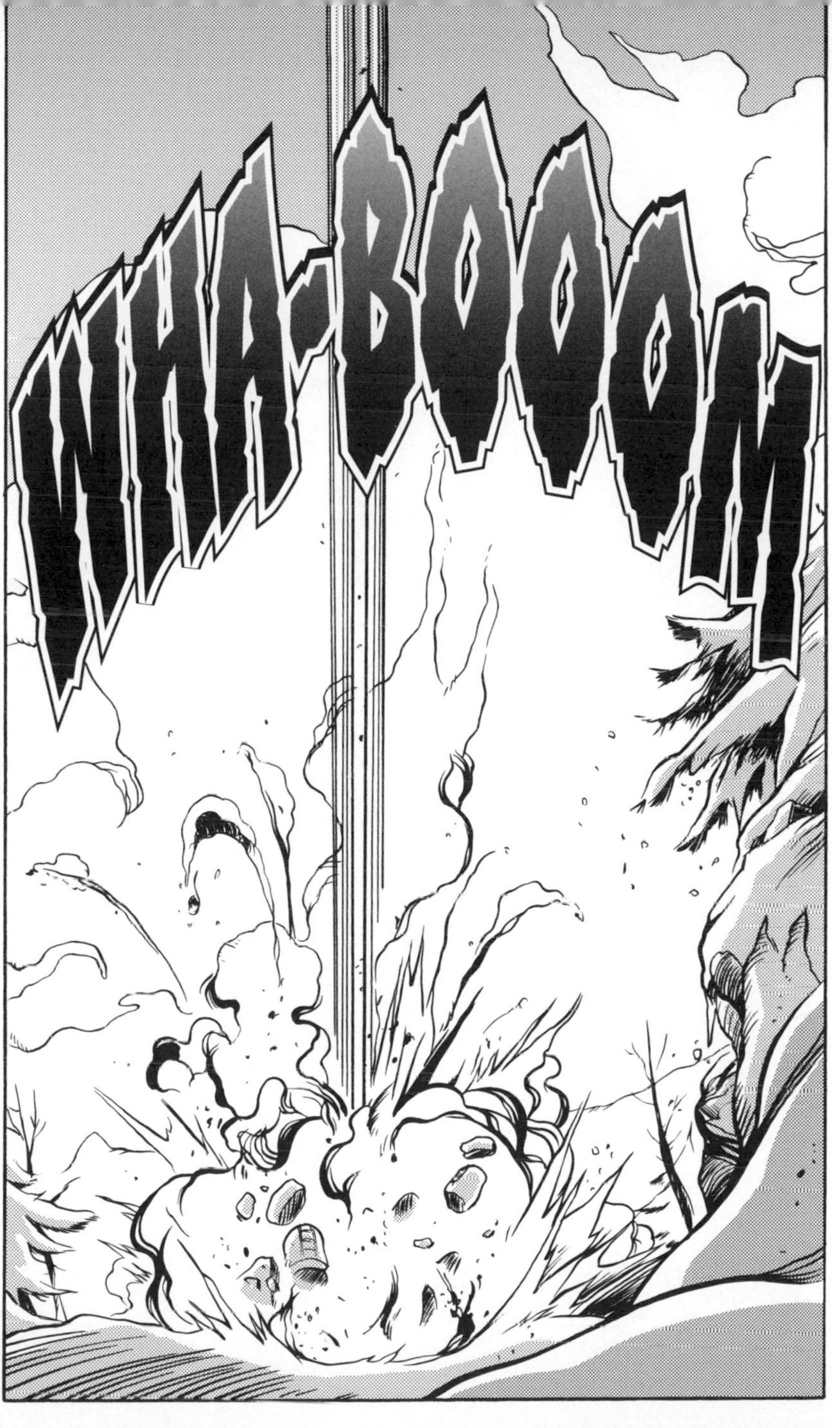
WHA-BOOOM

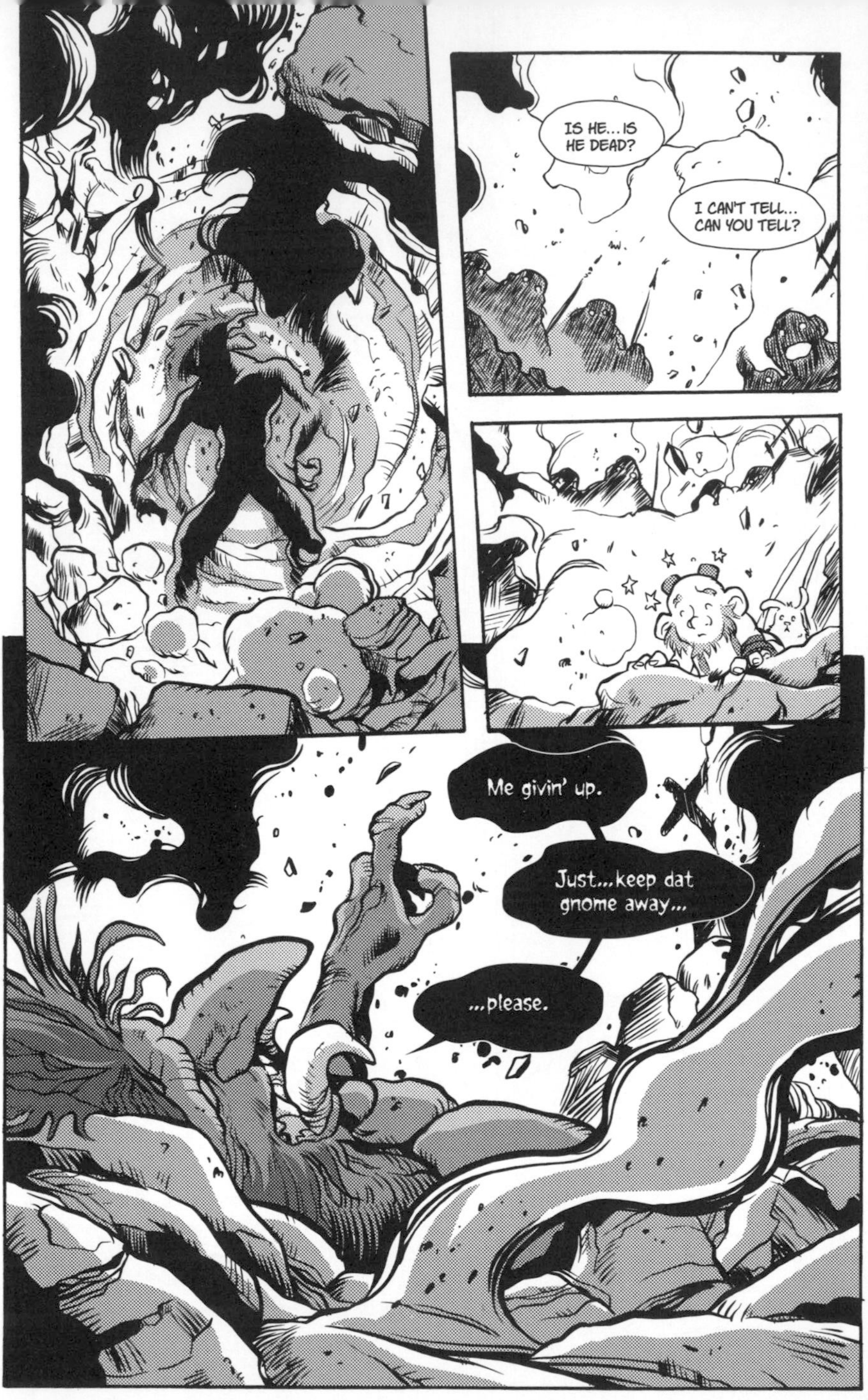
IS HE... IS HE DEAD?
I CAN'T TELL... CAN YOU TELL?
Me givin' up.
Just...keep dat gnome away...
...please.

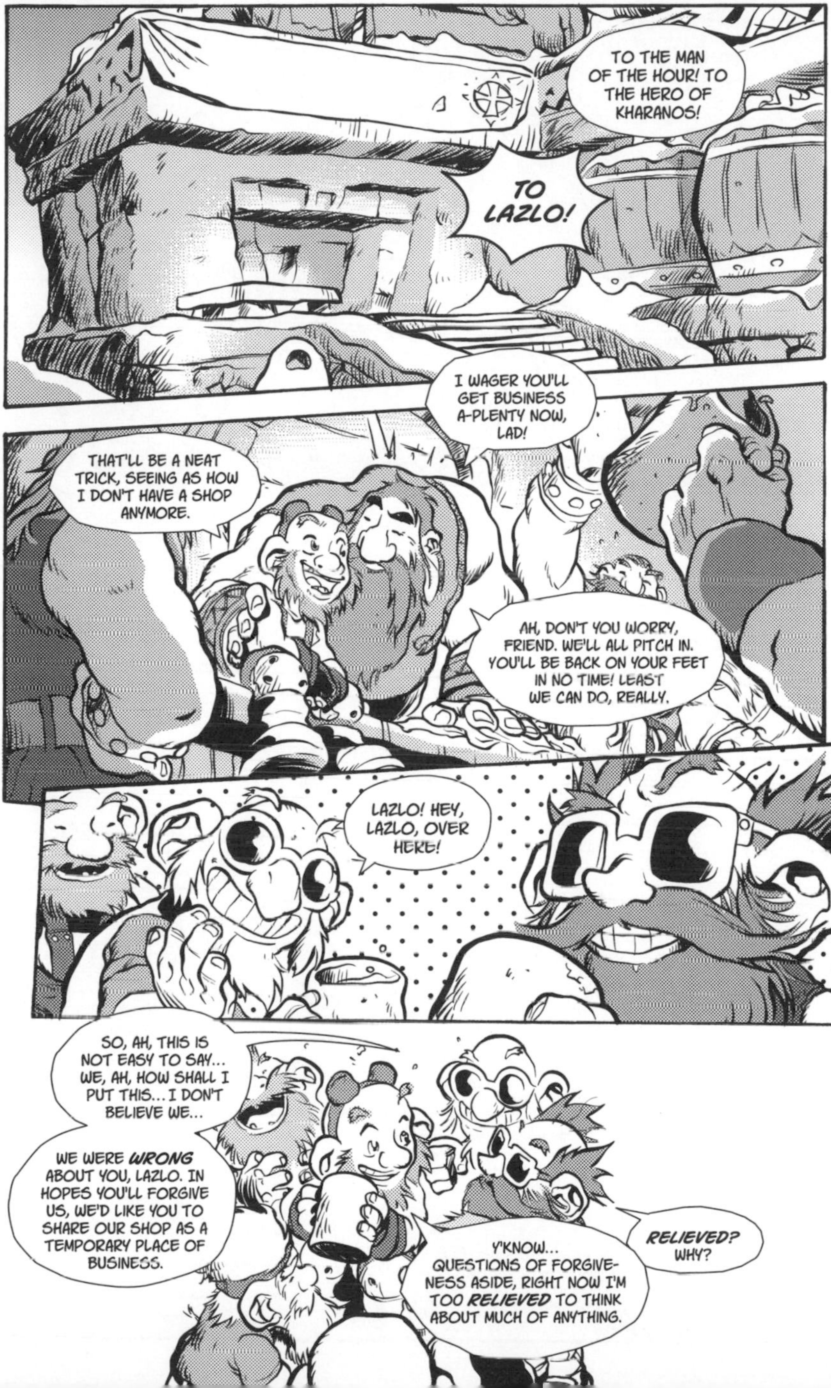
TO THE MAN OF THE HOUR! TO THE HERO OF KHARANOS!
TO LAZLO!
I WAGER YOU'LL GET BUSINESS A-PLENTY NOW, LAD!
THAT'LL BE A NEAT TRICK, SEEING AS HOW I DON'T HAVE A SHOP ANYMORE.
AH, DON'T YOU WORRY, FRIEND. WE'LL ALL PITCH IN. YOU'LL BE BACK ON YOUR FEET IN NO TIME! LEAST WE CAN DO, REALLY.
LAZLO! HEY, LAZLO, OVER HERE!
SO, AH, THIS IS NOT EASY TO SAY... WE, AH, HOW SHALL I PUT THIS... I DON'T BELIEVE WE...
WE WERE ***WRONG*** ABOUT YOU, LAZLO. IN HOPES YOU'LL FORGIVE US, WE'D LIKE YOU TO SHARE OUR SHOP AS A TEMPORARY PLACE OF BUSINESS.
Y'KNOW... QUESTIONS OF FORGIVENESS ASIDE, RIGHT NOW I'M TOO ***RELIEVED*** TO THINK ABOUT MUCH OF ANYTHING.
RELIEVED? WHY?

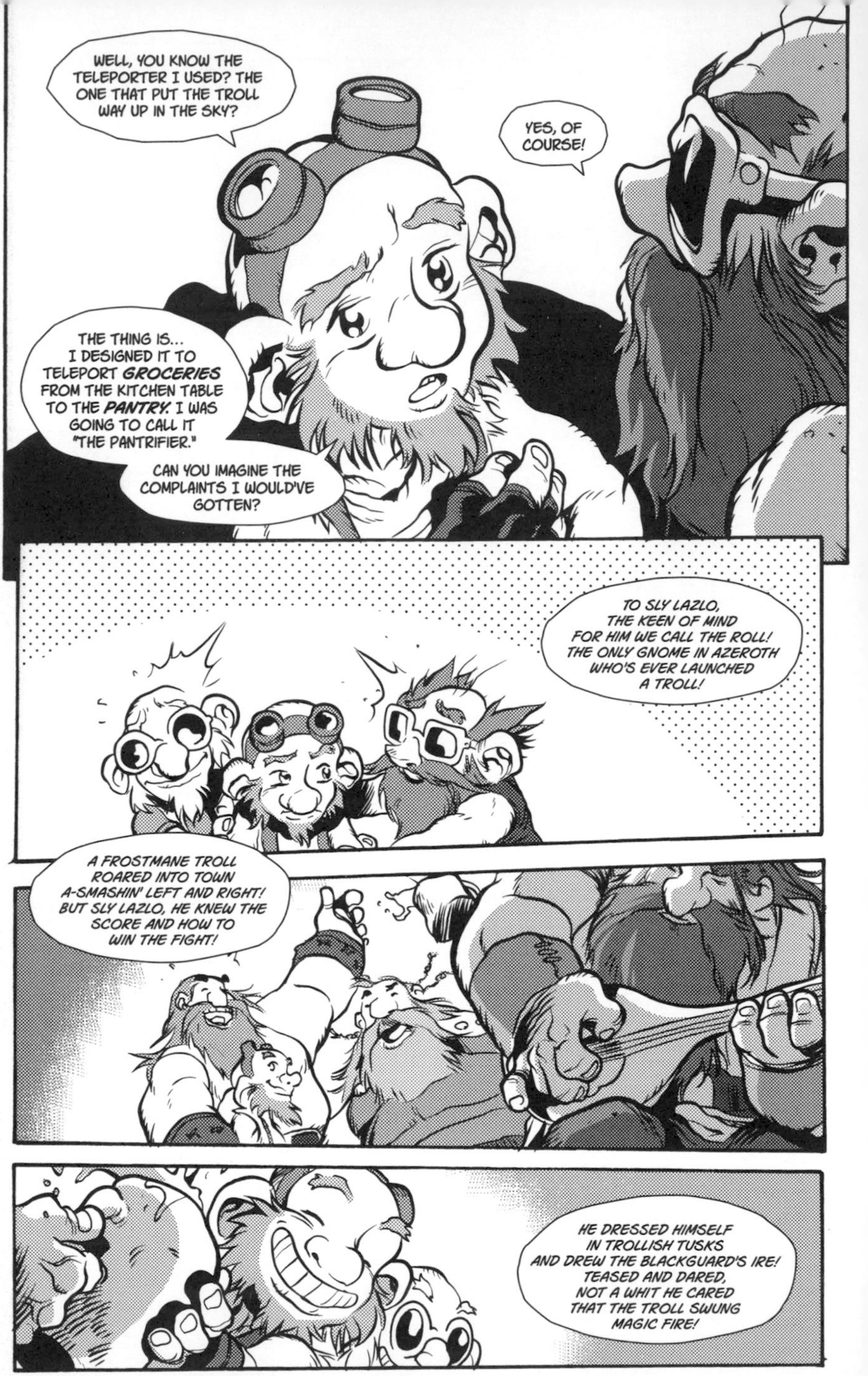
WELL, YOU KNOW THE TELEPORTER I USED? THE ONE THAT PUT THE TROLL WAY UP IN THE SKY?
YES, OF COURSE!
THE THING IS... I DESIGNED IT TO TELEPORT *GROCERIES* FROM THE KITCHEN TABLE TO THE *PANTRY.* I WAS GOING TO CALL IT "THE PANTRIFIER."
CAN YOU IMAGINE THE COMPLAINTS I WOULD'VE GOTTEN?
TO SLY LAZLO, THE KEEN OF MIND FOR HIM WE CALL THE ROLL! THE ONLY GNOME IN AZEROTH WHO'S EVER LAUNCHED A TROLL!
A FROSTMANE TROLL ROARED INTO TOWN A-SMASHIN' LEFT AND RIGHT! BUT SLY LAZLO, HE KNEW THE SCORE AND HOW TO WIN THE FIGHT!
HE DRESSED HIMSELF IN TROLLISH TUSKS AND DREW THE BLACKGUARD'S IRE! TEASED AND DARED, NOT A WHIT HE CARED THAT THE TROLL SWUNG MAGIC FIRE!

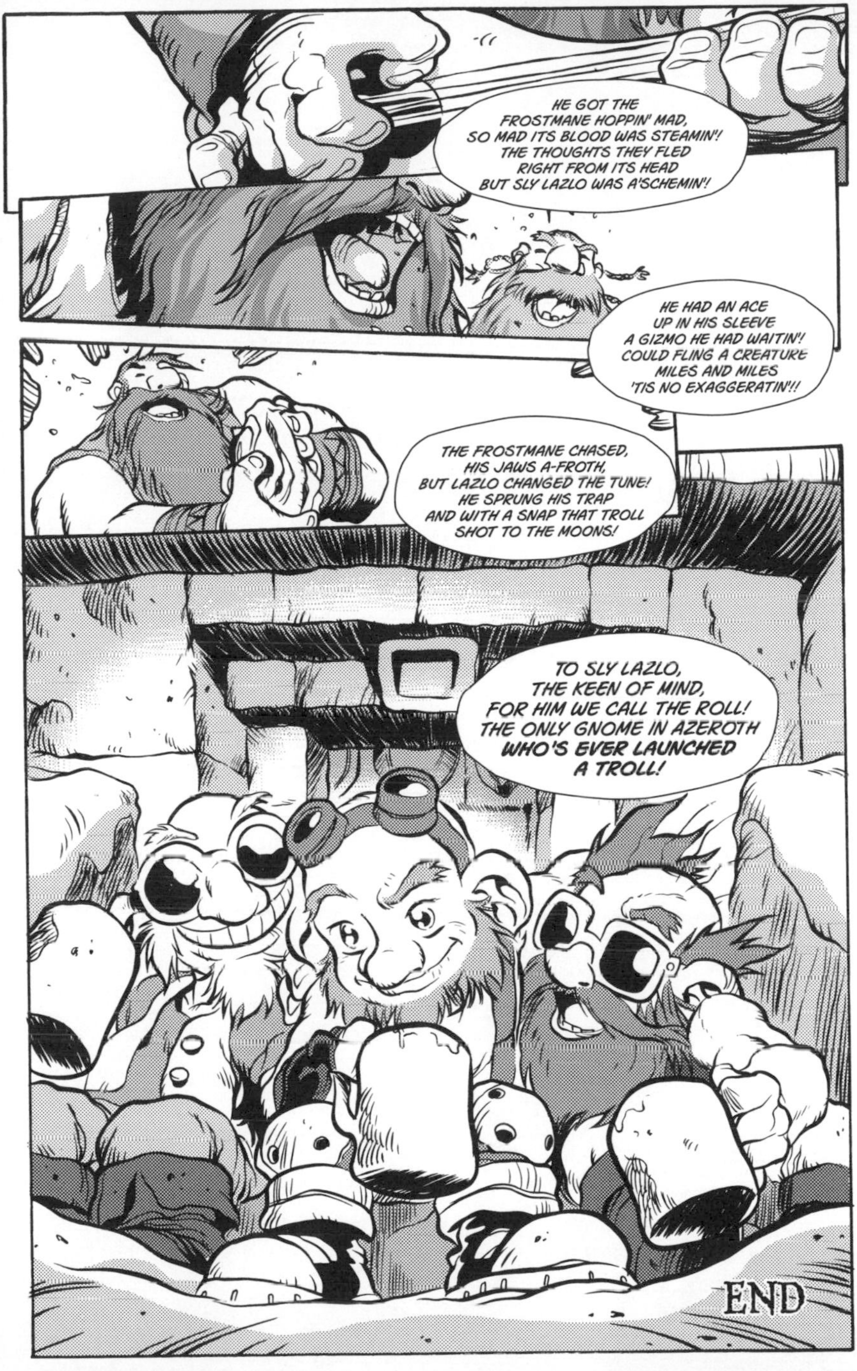
HE GOT THE FROSTMANE HOPPIN' MAD, SO MAD ITS BLOOD WAS STEAMIN'! THE THOUGHTS THEY FLED RIGHT FROM ITS HEAD BUT SLY LAZLO WAS A'SCHEMIN'!
HE HAD AN ACE UP IN HIS SLEEVE A GIZMO HE HAD WAITIN'! COULD FLING A CREATURE MILES AND MILES 'TIS NO EXAGGERATIN'!!
THE FROSTMANE CHASED, HIS JAWS A-FROTH, BUT LAZLO CHANGED THE TUNE! HE SPRUNG HIS TRAP AND WITH A SNAP THAT TROLL SHOT TO THE MOONS!
TO SLY LAZLO, THE KEEN OF MIND, FOR HIM WE CALL THE ROLL! THE ONLY GNOME IN AZEROTH WHO'S EVER LAUNCHED A TROLL!
END

WARCRAFT

LEGENDS
VOLUME ONE

AN HONEST TRADE

WRITTEN BY TROY LEWTER

PENCILS BY NAM KIM & STUDIOIL
STUDIOIL STAFF: AJ FORD 3, BEN HARVEY & SHIWAH WONG
LAYOUTS BY J.M
INKS BY MATT DALTON, KOSEN & ALISON ACTON
TONES BY CHOW HON LAM & MONICA KUBINA

EDITOR: TIM BEEDLE
ASSOCIATE EDITOR: SHANNON WATTERS
LETTERER: MICHAEL PAOLILLI

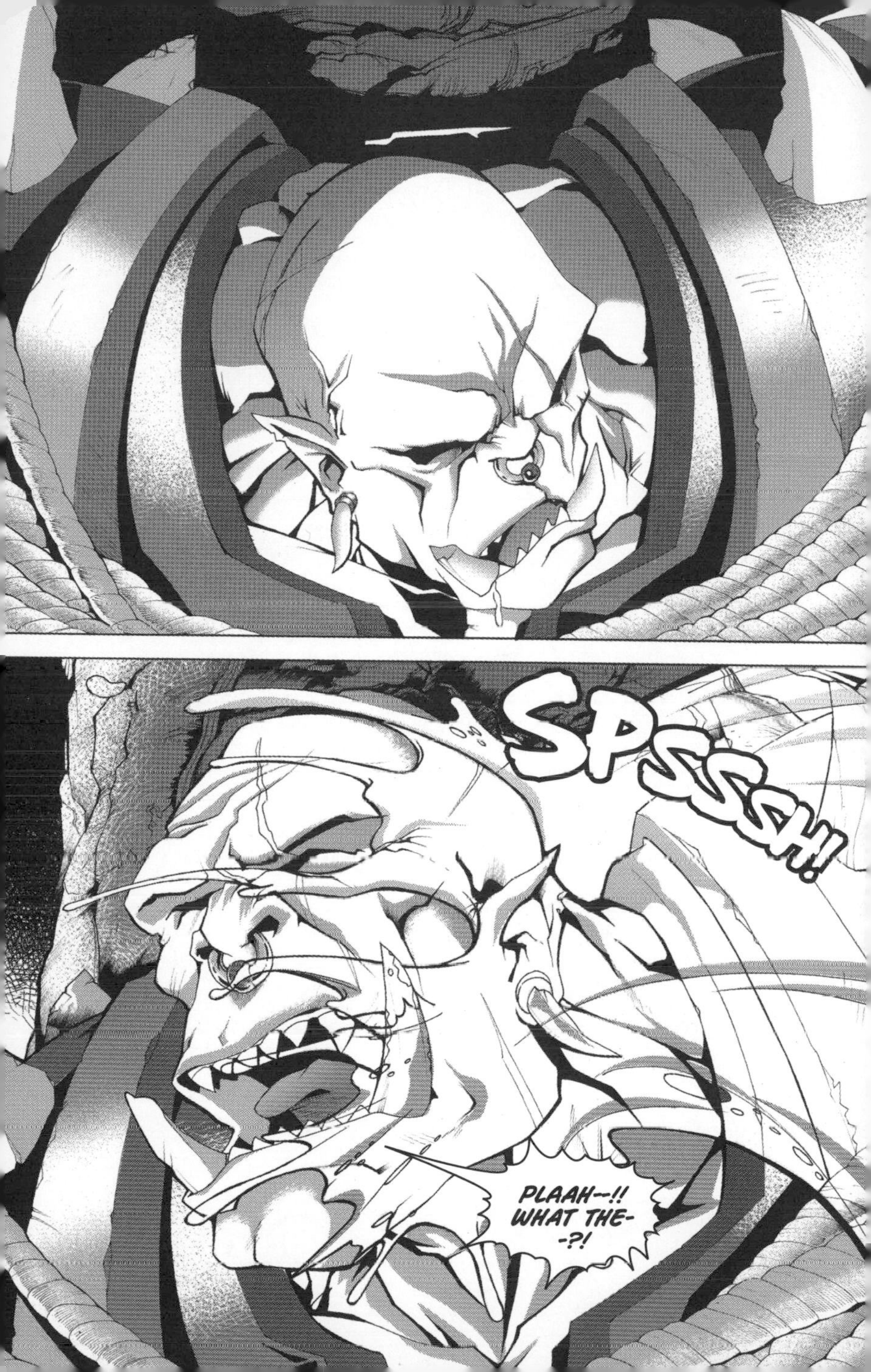
SPSSSH!
PLAAH--!! WHAT THE- -?!

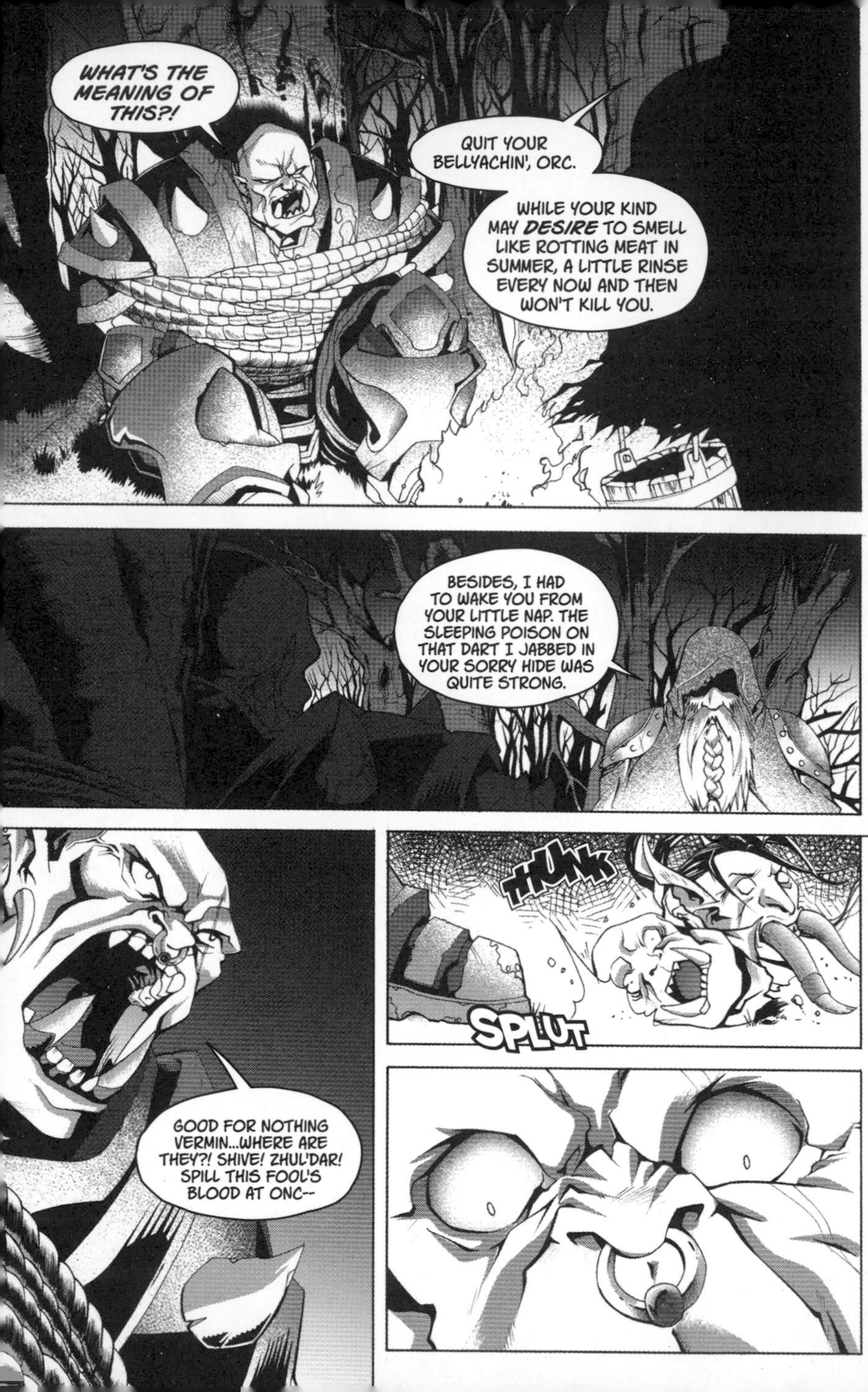
WHAT'S THE MEANING OF THIS?!
QUIT YOUR BELLYACHIN', ORC.
WHILE YOUR KIND MAY DESIRE TO SMELL LIKE ROTTING MEAT IN SUMMER, A LITTLE RINSE EVERY NOW AND THEN WON'T KILL YOU.
BESIDES, I HAD TO WAKE YOU FROM YOUR LITTLE NAP. THE SLEEPING POISON ON THAT DART I JABBED IN YOUR SORRY HIDE WAS QUITE STRONG.
GOOD FOR NOTHING VERMIN...WHERE ARE THEY?! SHIVE! ZHUL'DAR! SPILL THIS FOOL'S BLOOD AT ONC--
THUNK
SPLUT

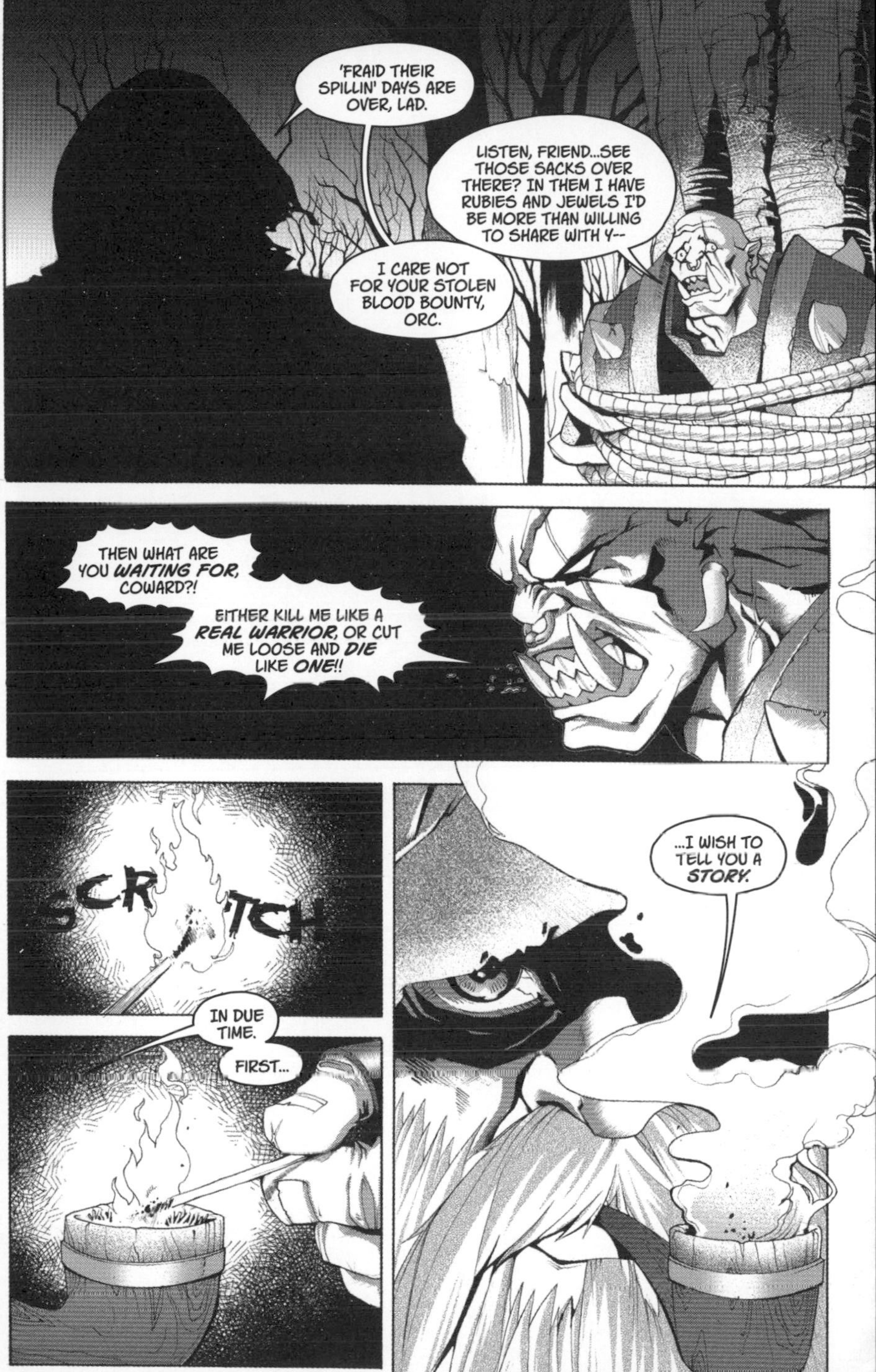
'FRAID THEIR SPILLIN' DAYS ARE OVER, LAD.
LISTEN, FRIEND...SEE THOSE SACKS OVER THERE? IN THEM I HAVE RUBIES AND JEWELS I'D BE MORE THAN WILLING TO SHARE WITH Y--
I CARE NOT FOR YOUR STOLEN BLOOD BOUNTY, ORC.
THEN WHAT ARE YOU WAITING FOR, COWARD?!
EITHER KILL ME LIKE A REAL WARRIOR, OR CUT ME LOOSE AND DIE LIKE ONE!!
SCRATCH
IN DUE TIME.
FIRST...
...I WISH TO TELL YOU A STORY.

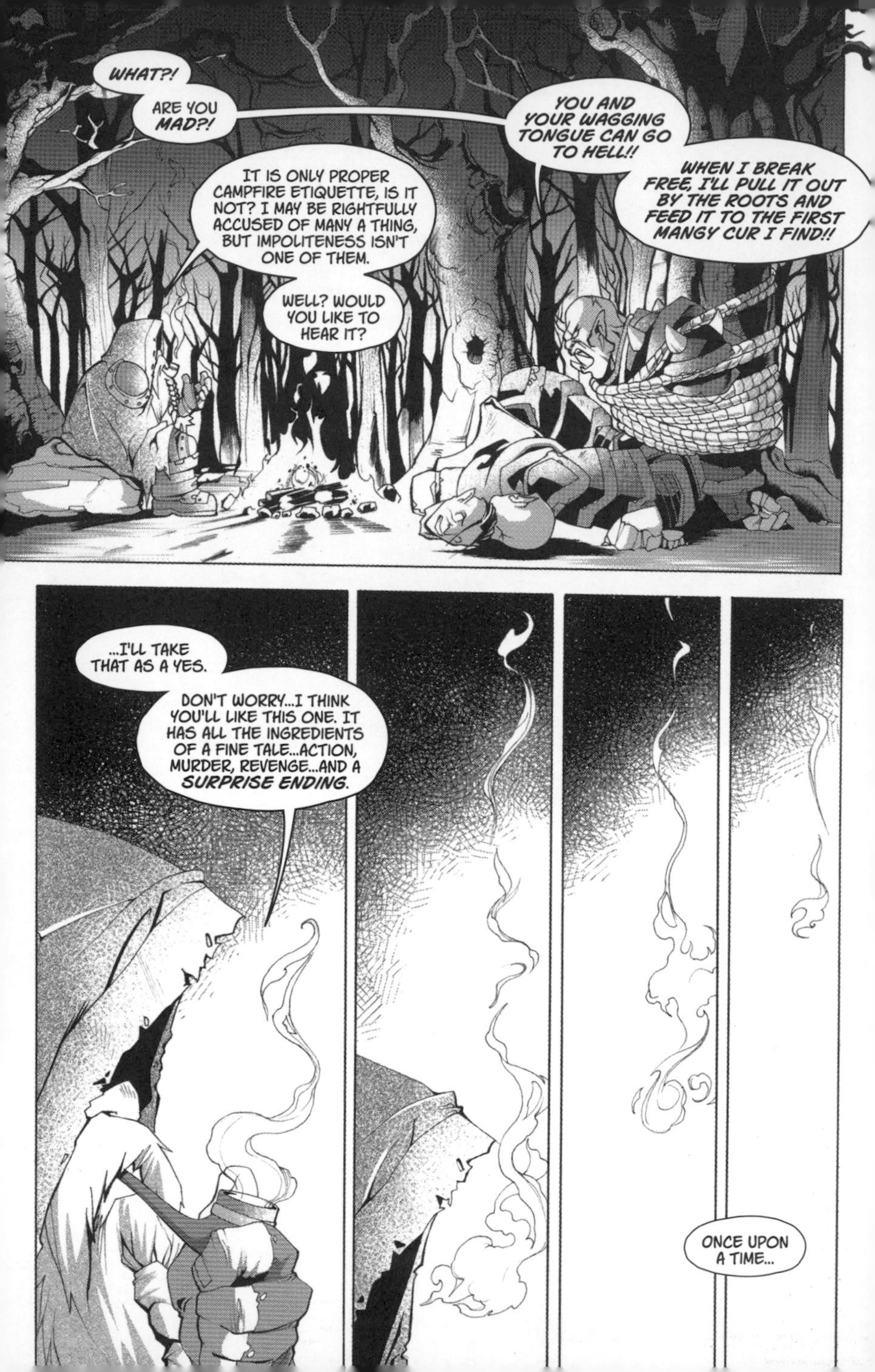
WHAT?!
ARE YOU MAD?!
YOU AND YOUR WAGGING TONGUE CAN GO TO HELL!!
WHEN I BREAK FREE, I'LL PULL IT OUT BY THE ROOTS AND FEED IT TO THE FIRST MANGY CUR I FIND!!
IT IS ONLY PROPER CAMPFIRE ETIQUETTE, IS IT NOT? I MAY BE RIGHTFULLY ACCUSED OF MANY A THING, BUT IMPOLITENESS ISN'T ONE OF THEM.
WELL? WOULD YOU LIKE TO HEAR IT?
...I'LL TAKE THAT AS A YES.
DON'T WORRY...I THINK YOU'LL LIKE THIS ONE. IT HAS ALL THE INGREDIENTS OF A FINE TALE...ACTION, MURDER, REVENGE...AND A SURPRISE ENDING.
ONCE UPON A TIME...

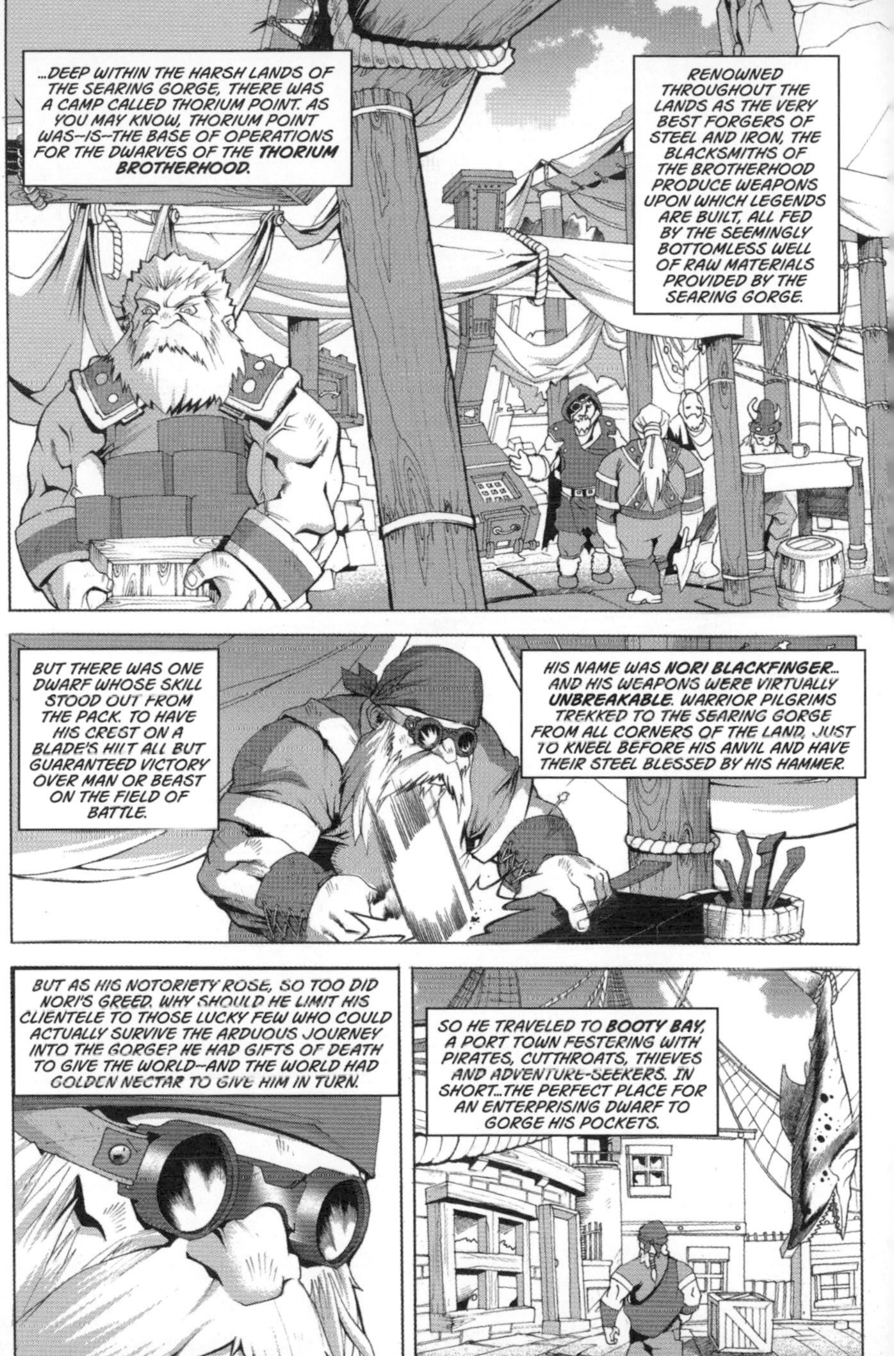
...DEEP WITHIN THE HARSH LANDS OF THE SEARING GORGE, THERE WAS A CAMP CALLED THORIUM POINT. AS YOU MAY KNOW, THORIUM POINT WAS--IS--THE BASE OF OPERATIONS FOR THE DWARVES OF THE **THORIUM BROTHERHOOD.**
RENOWNED THROUGHOUT THE LANDS AS THE VERY BEST FORGERS OF STEEL AND IRON, THE BLACKSMITHS OF THE BROTHERHOOD PRODUCE WEAPONS UPON WHICH LEGENDS ARE BUILT, ALL FED BY THE SEEMINGLY BOTTOMLESS WELL OF RAW MATERIALS PROVIDED BY THE SEARING GORGE.
BUT THERE WAS ONE DWARF WHOSE SKILL STOOD OUT FROM THE PACK. TO HAVE HIS CREST ON A BLADE'S HILT ALL BUT GUARANTEED VICTORY OVER MAN OR BEAST ON THE FIELD OF BATTLE.
HIS NAME WAS **NORI BLACKFINGER...** AND HIS WEAPONS WERE VIRTUALLY **UNBREAKABLE.** WARRIOR PILGRIMS TREKKED TO THE SEARING GORGE FROM ALL CORNERS OF THE LAND, JUST TO KNEEL BEFORE HIS ANVIL AND HAVE THEIR STEEL BLESSED BY HIS HAMMER.
BUT AS HIS NOTORIETY ROSE, SO TOO DID NORI'S GREED. WHY SHOULD HE LIMIT HIS CLIENTELE TO THOSE LUCKY FEW WHO COULD ACTUALLY SURVIVE THE ARDUOUS JOURNEY INTO THE GORGE? HE HAD GIFTS OF DEATH TO GIVE THE WORLD--AND THE WORLD HAD GOLDEN NECTAR TO GIVE HIM IN TURN.
SO HE TRAVELED TO **BOOTY BAY,** A PORT TOWN FESTERING WITH PIRATES, CUTTHROATS, THIEVES AND ADVENTURE-SEEKERS. IN SHORT...THE PERFECT PLACE FOR AN ENTERPRISING DWARF TO GORGE HIS POCKETS.

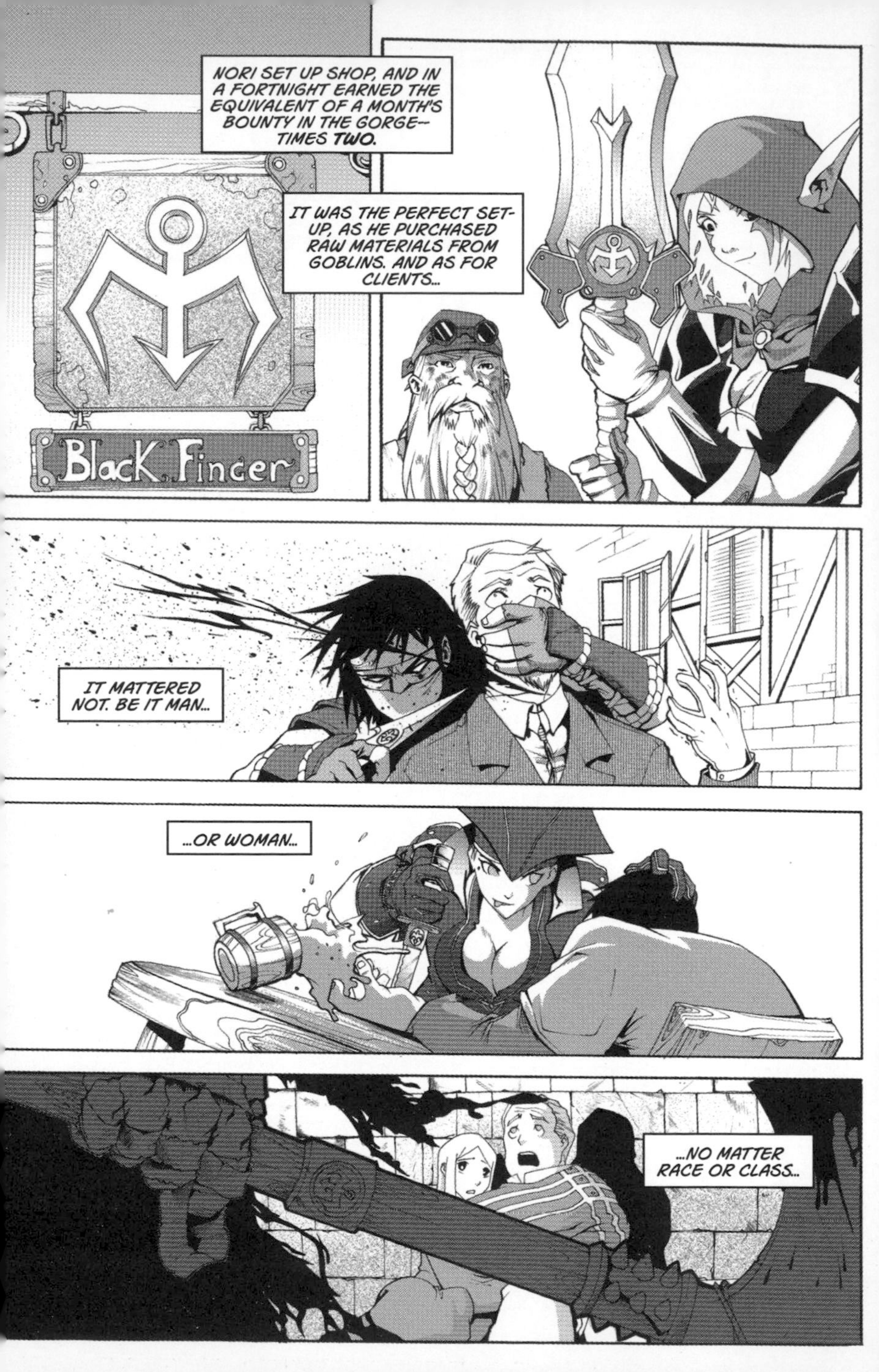

Black Finger
NORI SET UP SHOP, AND IN A FORTNIGHT EARNED THE EQUIVALENT OF A MONTH'S BOUNTY IN THE GORGE-- TIMES TWO.
IT WAS THE PERFECT SET-UP, AS HE PURCHASED RAW MATERIALS FROM GOBLINS. AND AS FOR CLIENTS...
IT MATTERED NOT. BE IT MAN...
...OR WOMAN...
...NO MATTER RACE OR CLASS...

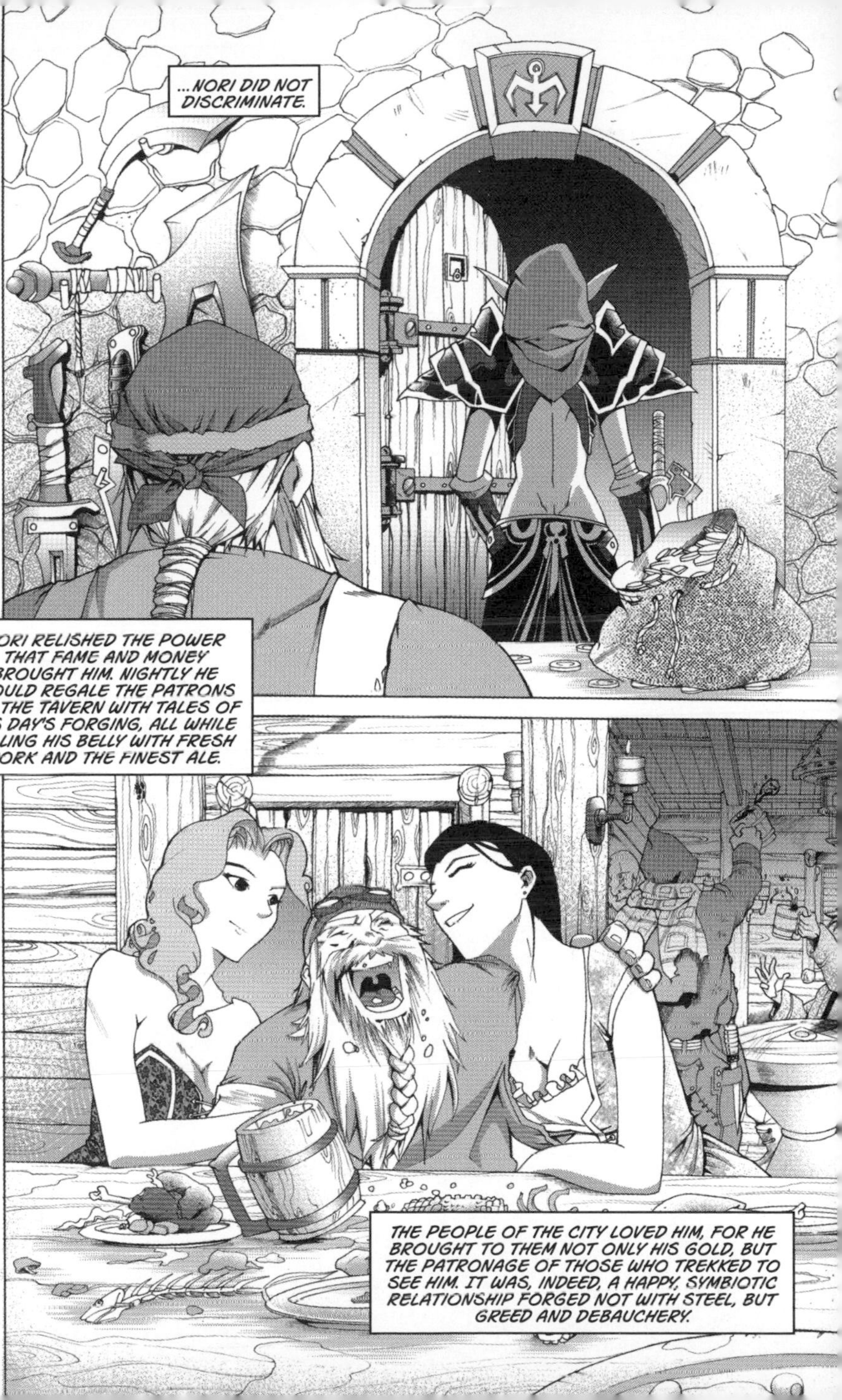
...NORI DID NOT DISCRIMINATE.
NORI RELISHED THE POWER THAT FAME AND MONEY BROUGHT HIM. NIGHTLY HE WOULD REGALE THE PATRONS OF THE TAVERN WITH TALES OF HIS DAY'S FORGING, ALL WHILE FILLING HIS BELLY WITH FRESH PORK AND THE FINEST ALE.
THE PEOPLE OF THE CITY LOVED HIM, FOR HE BROUGHT TO THEM NOT ONLY HIS GOLD, BUT THE PATRONAGE OF THOSE WHO TREKKED TO SEE HIM. IT WAS, INDEED, A HAPPY, SYMBIOTIC RELATIONSHIP FORGED NOT WITH STEEL, BUT GREED AND DEBAUCHERY.

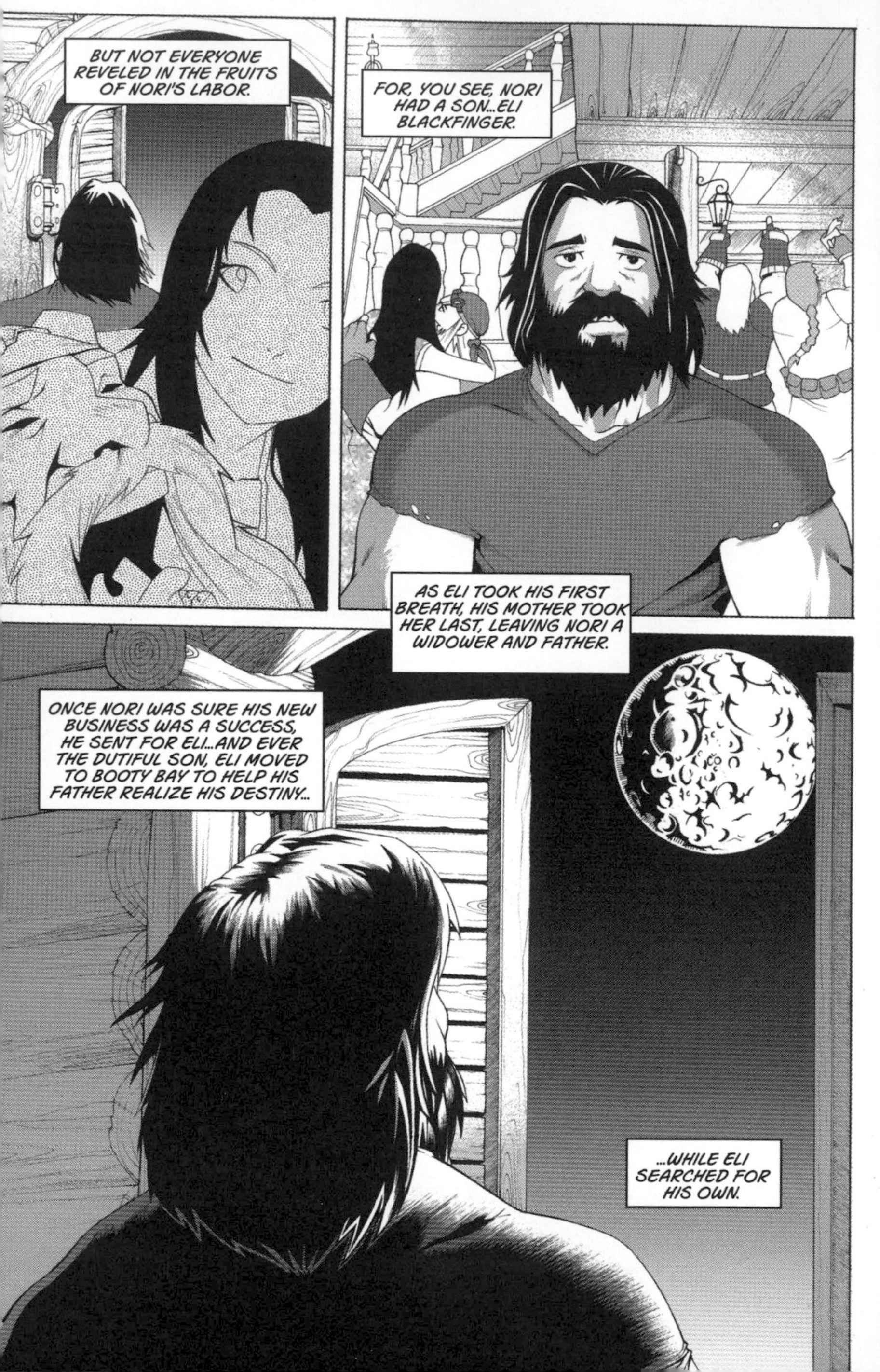
BUT NOT EVERYONE REVELED IN THE FRUITS OF NORI'S LABOR.
FOR, YOU SEE, NORI HAD A SON...ELI BLACKFINGER.
AS ELI TOOK HIS FIRST BREATH, HIS MOTHER TOOK HER LAST, LEAVING NORI A WIDOWER AND FATHER.
ONCE NORI WAS SURE HIS NEW BUSINESS WAS A SUCCESS, HE SENT FOR ELI...AND EVER THE DUTIFUL SON, ELI MOVED TO BOOTY BAY TO HELP HIS FATHER REALIZE HIS DESTINY...
...WHILE ELI SEARCHED FOR HIS OWN.

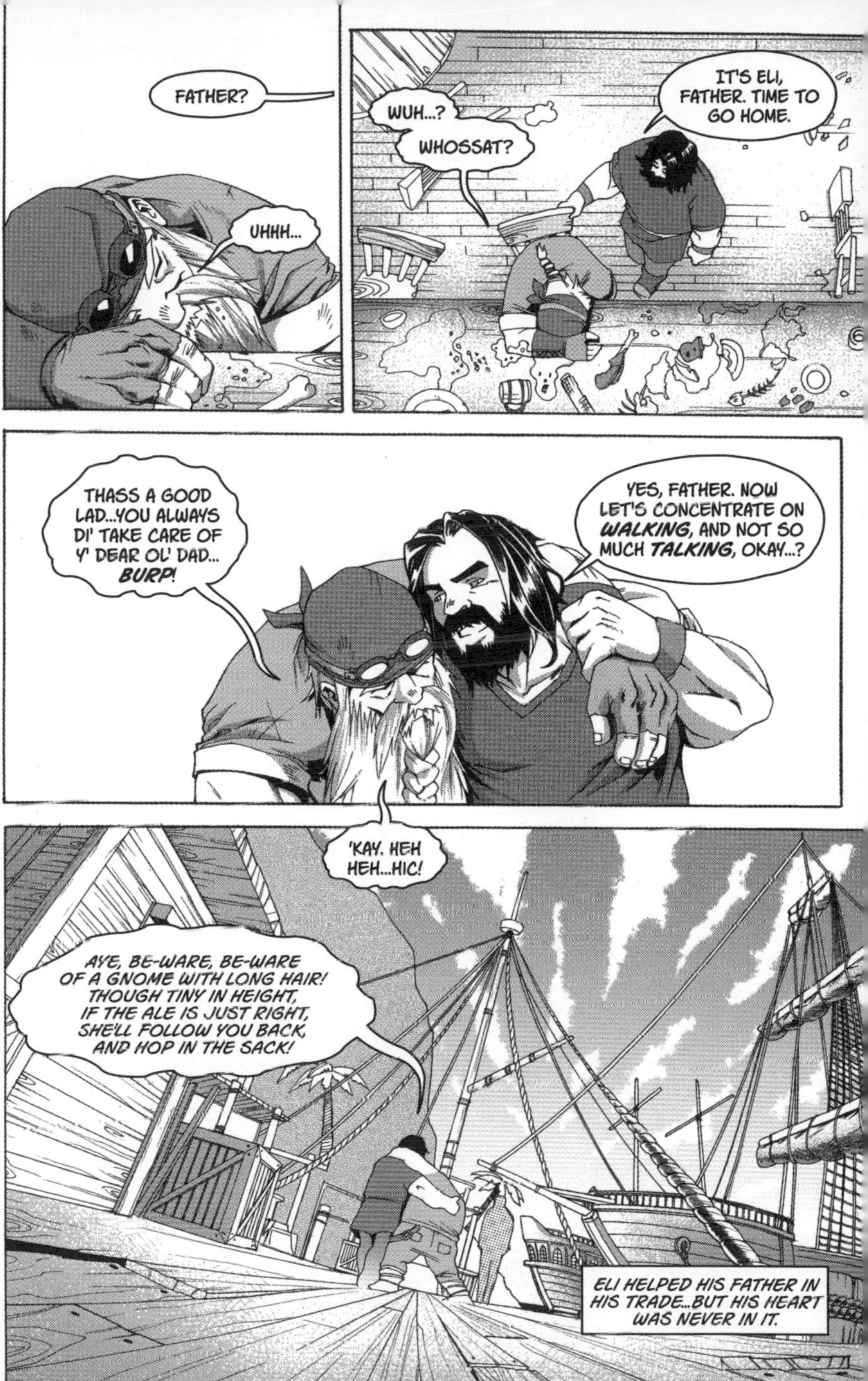
FATHER?
UHHH...
WUH...?
WHOSSAT?
IT'S ELI, FATHER. TIME TO GO HOME.
THASS A GOOD LAD...YOU ALWAYS DI' TAKE CARE OF Y' DEAR OL' DAD... BURP!
YES, FATHER. NOW LET'S CONCENTRATE ON WALKING, AND NOT SO MUCH TALKING, OKAY...?
'KAY. HEH HEH...HIC!
AYE, BE-WARE, BE-WARE OF A GNOME WITH LONG HAIR! THOUGH TINY IN HEIGHT, IF THE ALE IS JUST RIGHT, SHE'LL FOLLOW YOU BACK, AND HOP IN THE SACK!
ELI HELPED HIS FATHER IN HIS TRADE...BUT HIS HEART WAS NEVER IN IT.

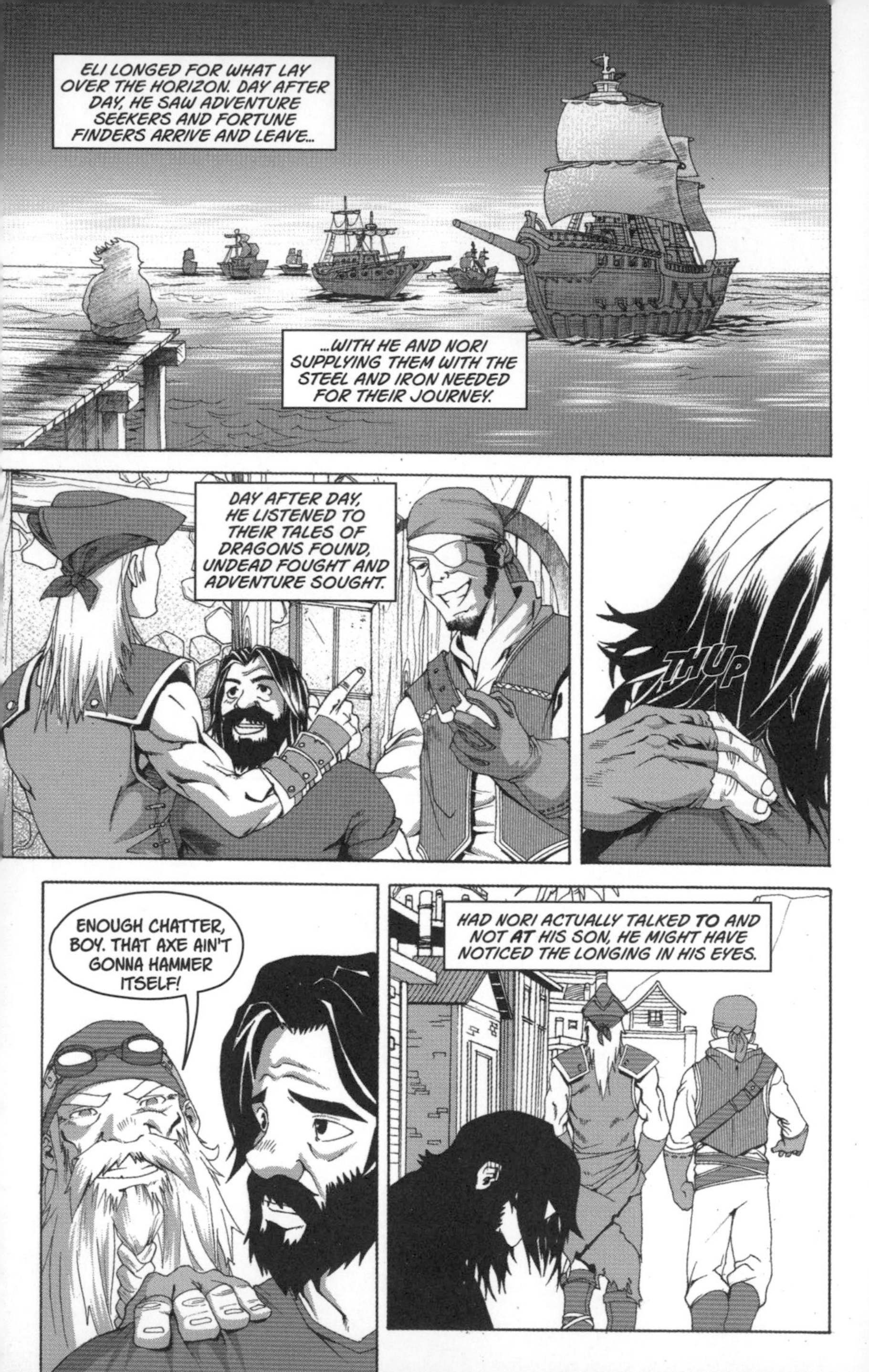
ELI LONGED FOR WHAT LAY OVER THE HORIZON. DAY AFTER DAY, HE SAW ADVENTURE SEEKERS AND FORTUNE FINDERS ARRIVE AND LEAVE...
...WITH HE AND NORI SUPPLYING THEM WITH THE STEEL AND IRON NEEDED FOR THEIR JOURNEY.
DAY AFTER DAY, HE LISTENED TO THEIR TALES OF DRAGONS FOUND, UNDEAD FOUGHT AND ADVENTURE SOUGHT.
THUP
ENOUGH CHATTER, BOY. THAT AXE AIN'T GONNA HAMMER ITSELF!
HAD NORI ACTUALLY TALKED TO AND NOT AT HIS SON, HE MIGHT HAVE NOTICED THE LONGING IN HIS EYES.

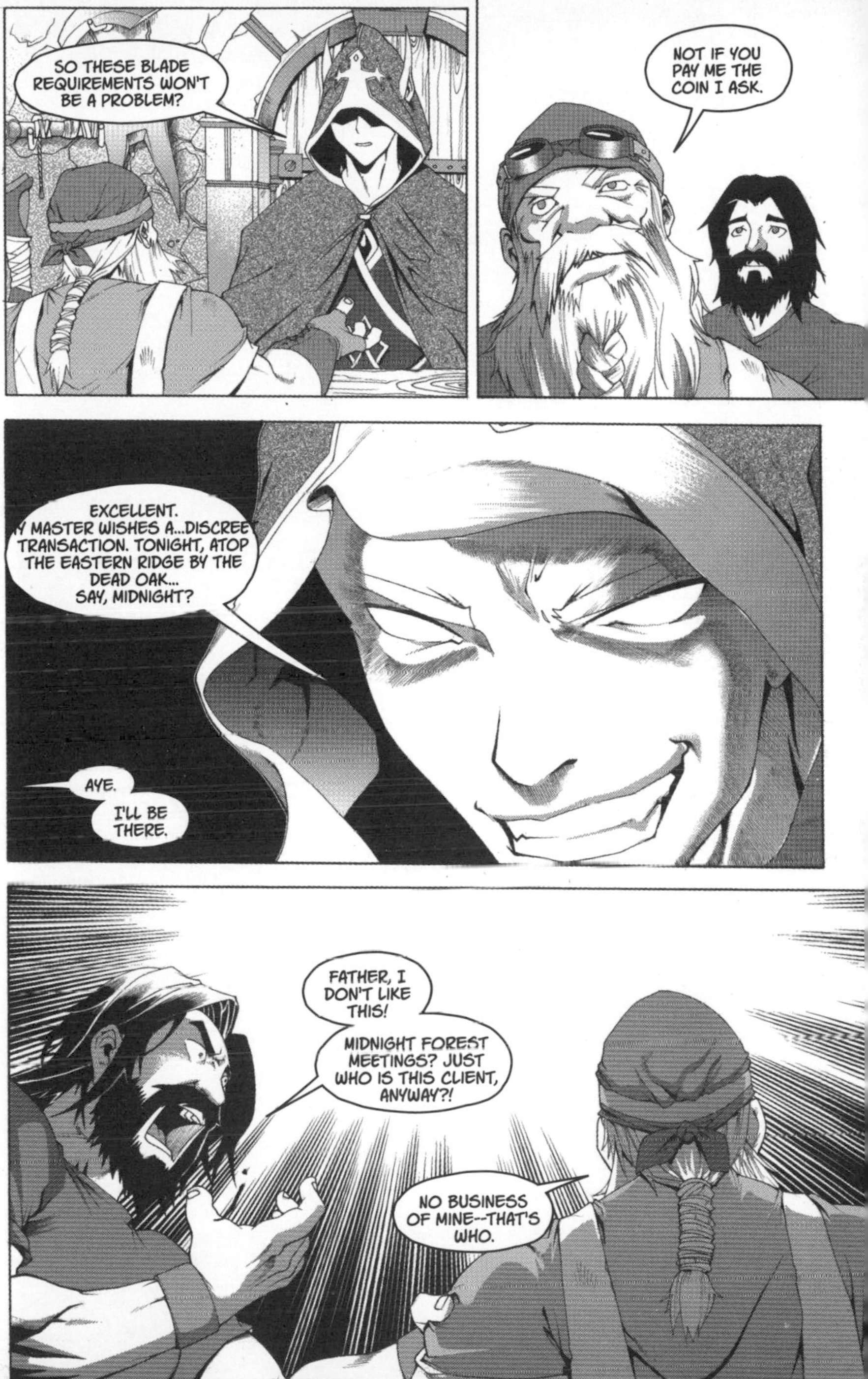
SO THESE BLADE REQUIREMENTS WON'T BE A PROBLEM?
NOT IF YOU PAY ME THE COIN I ASK.
EXCELLENT. Y MASTER WISHES A...DISCREE TRANSACTION. TONIGHT, ATOP THE EASTERN RIDGE BY THE DEAD OAK... SAY, MIDNIGHT?
AYE.
I'LL BE THERE.
FATHER, I DON'T LIKE THIS!
MIDNIGHT FOREST MEETINGS? JUST WHO IS THIS CLIENT, ANYWAY?!
NO BUSINESS OF MINE--THAT'S WHO.

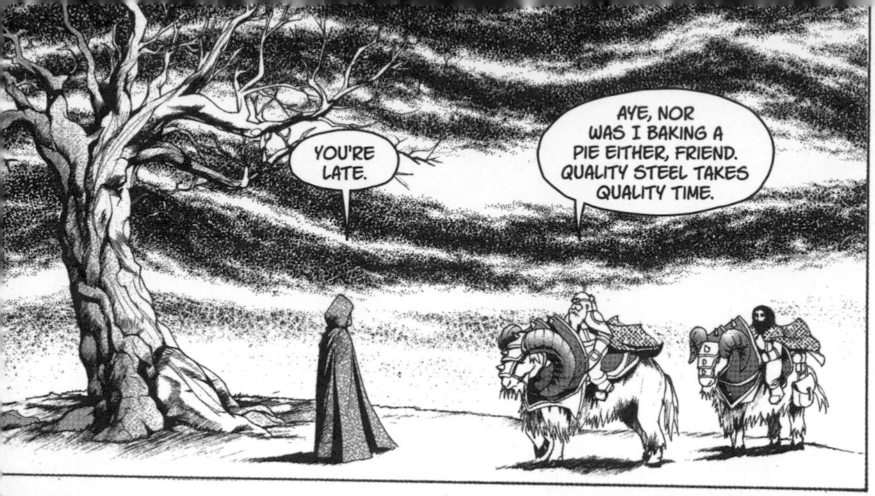
YOU'RE LATE.
AYE, NOR WAS I BAKING A PIE EITHER, FRIEND. QUALITY STEEL TAKES QUALITY TIME.
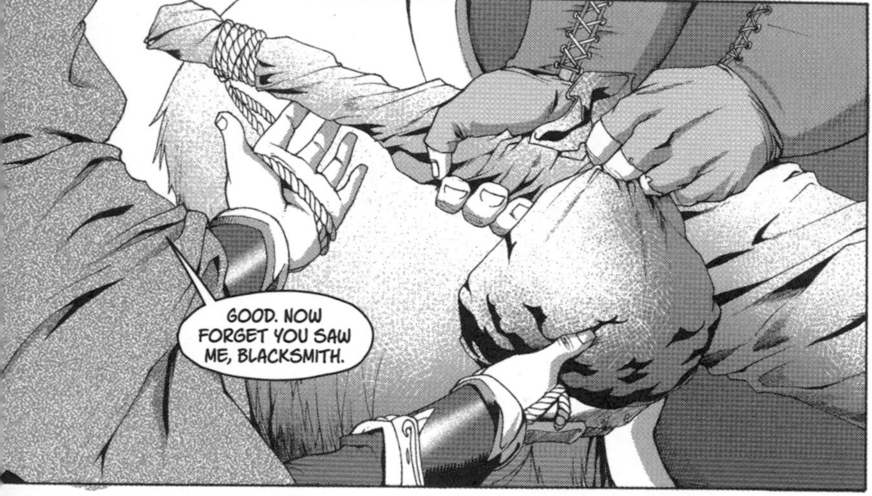
GOOD. NOW FORGET YOU SAW ME, BLACKSMITH.
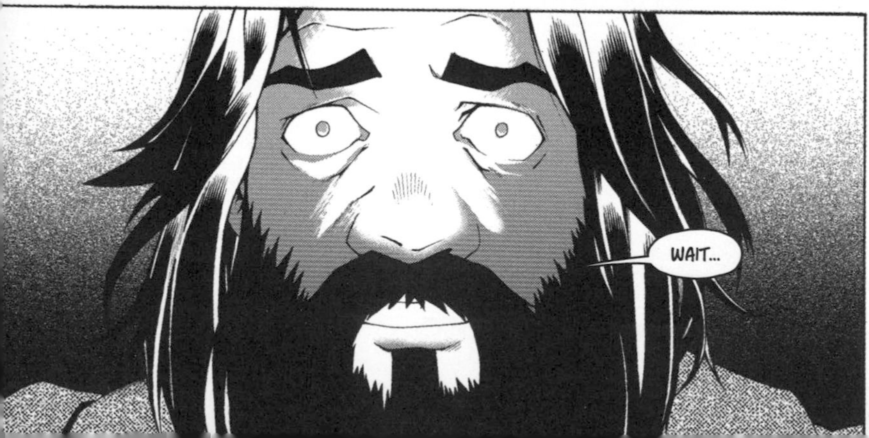
WAIT...

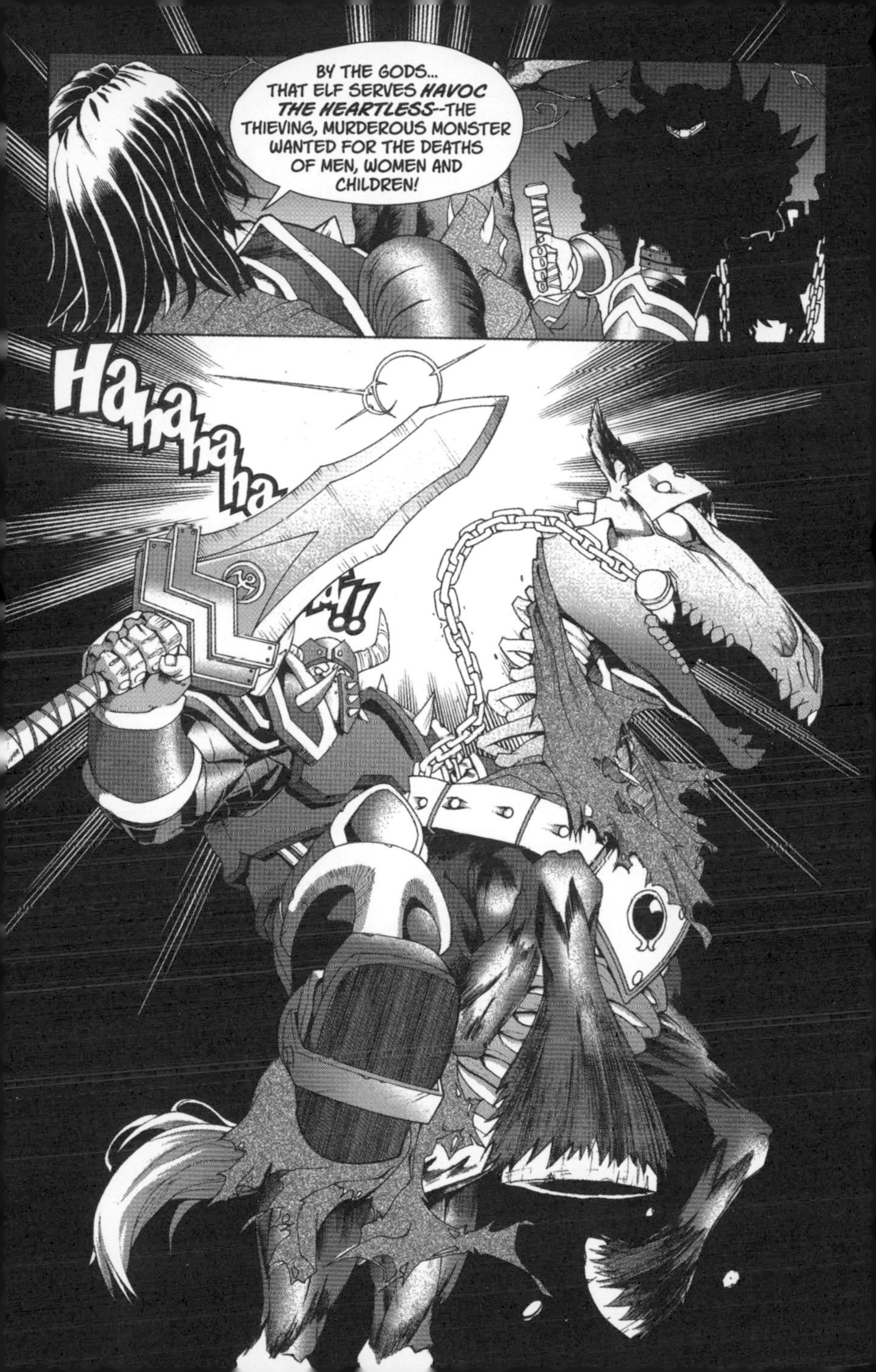
BY THE GODS... THAT ELF SERVES *HAVOC THE HEARTLESS*--THE THIEVING, MURDEROUS MONSTER WANTED FOR THE DEATHS OF MEN, WOMEN AND CHILDREN!
Hahahahaha

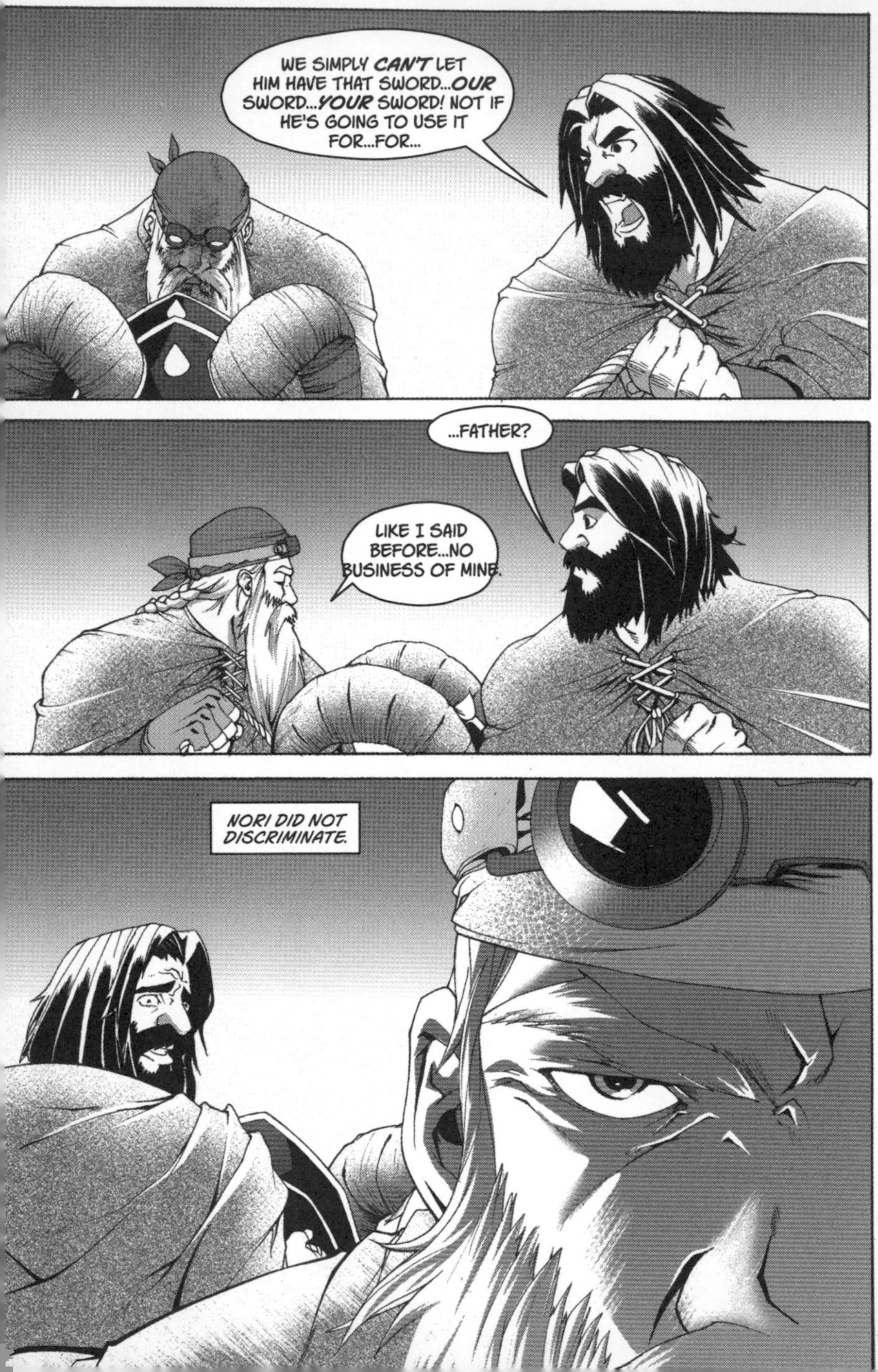
WE SIMPLY CAN'T LET HIM HAVE THAT SWORD...OUR SWORD...YOUR SWORD! NOT IF HE'S GOING TO USE IT FOR...FOR...
LIKE I SAID BEFORE...NO BUSINESS OF MINE.
...FATHER?
NORI DID NOT DISCRIMINATE.

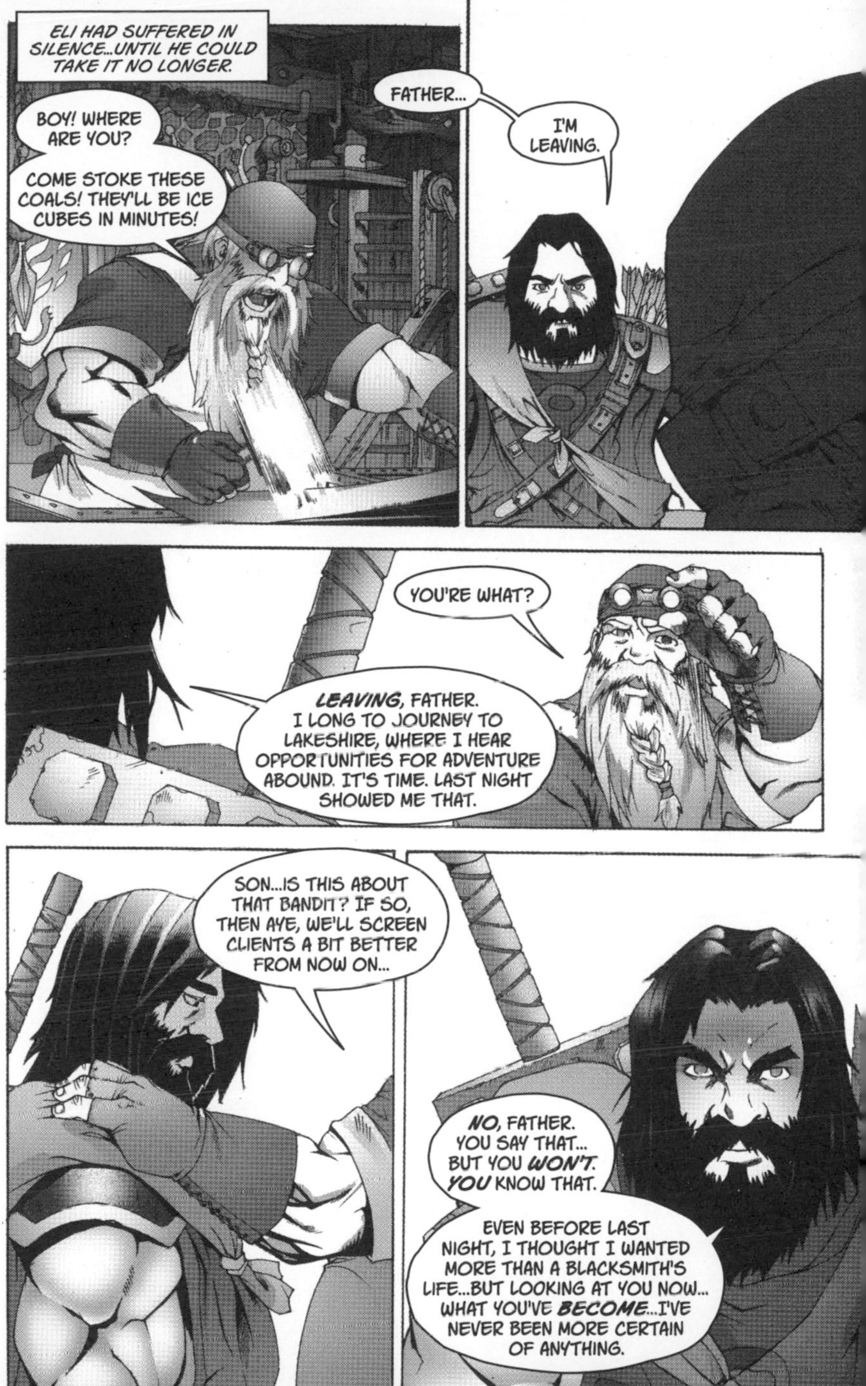
ELI HAD SUFFERED IN SILENCE...UNTIL HE COULD TAKE IT NO LONGER.
BOY! WHERE ARE YOU?
COME STOKE THESE COALS! THEY'LL BE ICE CUBES IN MINUTES!
FATHER...
I'M LEAVING.
YOU'RE WHAT?
LEAVING, FATHER. I LONG TO JOURNEY TO LAKESHIRE, WHERE I HEAR OPPORTUNITIES FOR ADVENTURE ABOUND. IT'S TIME. LAST NIGHT SHOWED ME THAT.
SON...IS THIS ABOUT THAT BANDIT? IF SO, THEN AYE, WE'LL SCREEN CLIENTS A BIT BETTER FROM NOW ON...
NO, FATHER. YOU SAY THAT... BUT YOU WON'T. YOU KNOW THAT.
EVEN BEFORE LAST NIGHT, I THOUGHT I WANTED MORE THAN A BLACKSMITH'S LIFE...BUT LOOKING AT YOU NOW... WHAT YOU'VE BECOME...I'VE NEVER BEEN MORE CERTAIN OF ANYTHING.

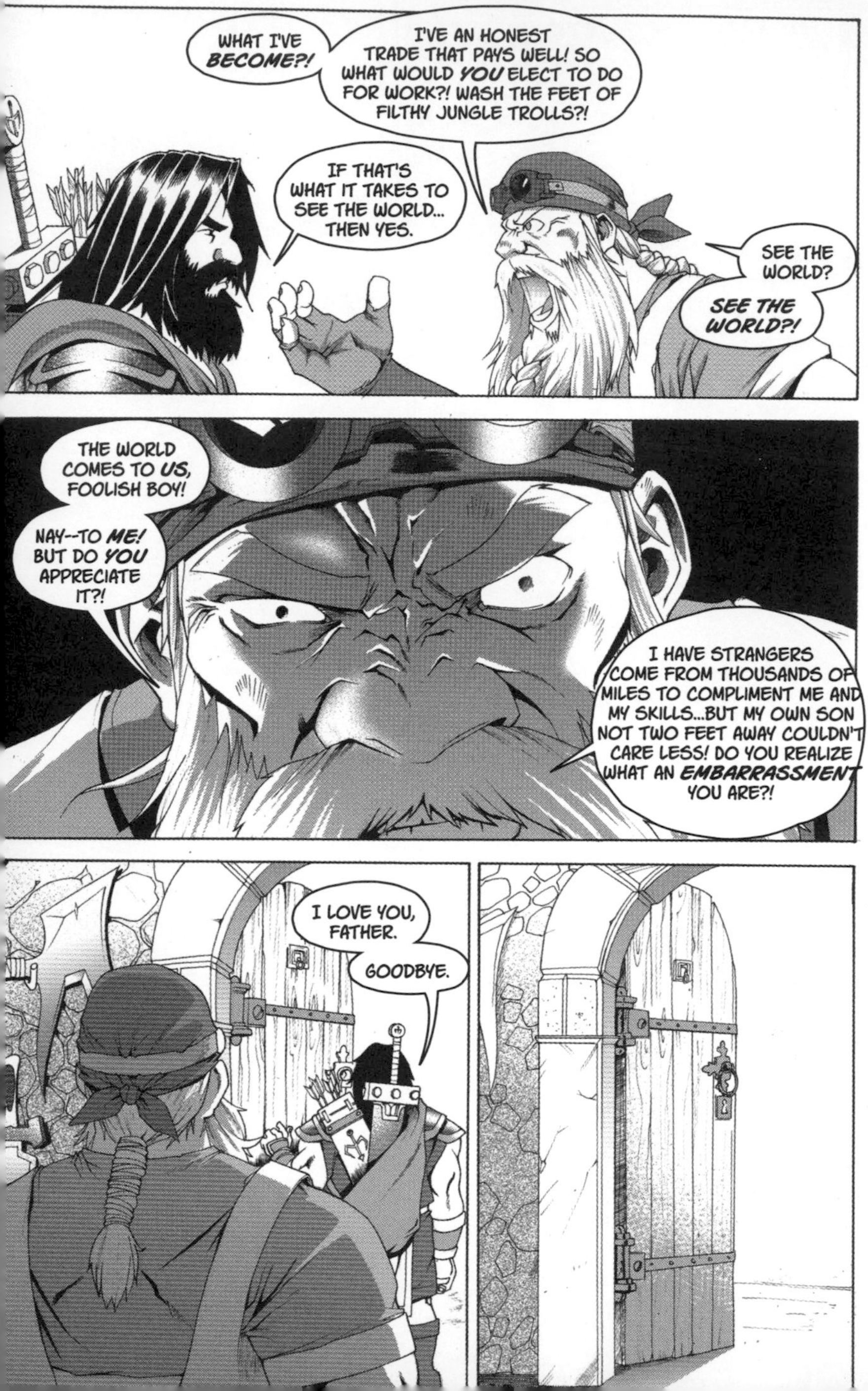
WHAT I'VE BECOME?!
I'VE AN HONEST TRADE THAT PAYS WELL! SO WHAT WOULD YOU ELECT TO DO FOR WORK?! WASH THE FEET OF FILTHY JUNGLE TROLLS?!
IF THAT'S WHAT IT TAKES TO SEE THE WORLD... THEN YES.
SEE THE WORLD?
SEE THE WORLD?!
THE WORLD COMES TO US, FOOLISH BOY!
NAY--TO ME! BUT DO YOU APPRECIATE IT?!
I HAVE STRANGERS COME FROM THOUSANDS OF MILES TO COMPLIMENT ME AND MY SKILLS...BUT MY OWN SON NOT TWO FEET AWAY COULDN'T CARE LESS! DO YOU REALIZE WHAT AN EMBARRASSMENT YOU ARE?!
I LOVE YOU, FATHER.
GOODBYE.

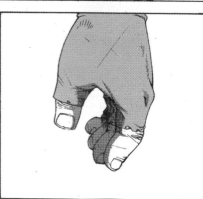

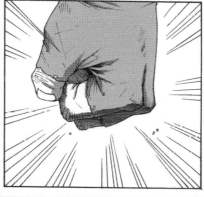

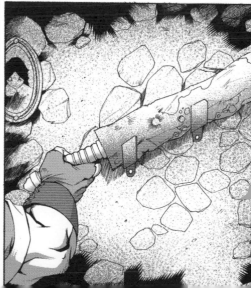

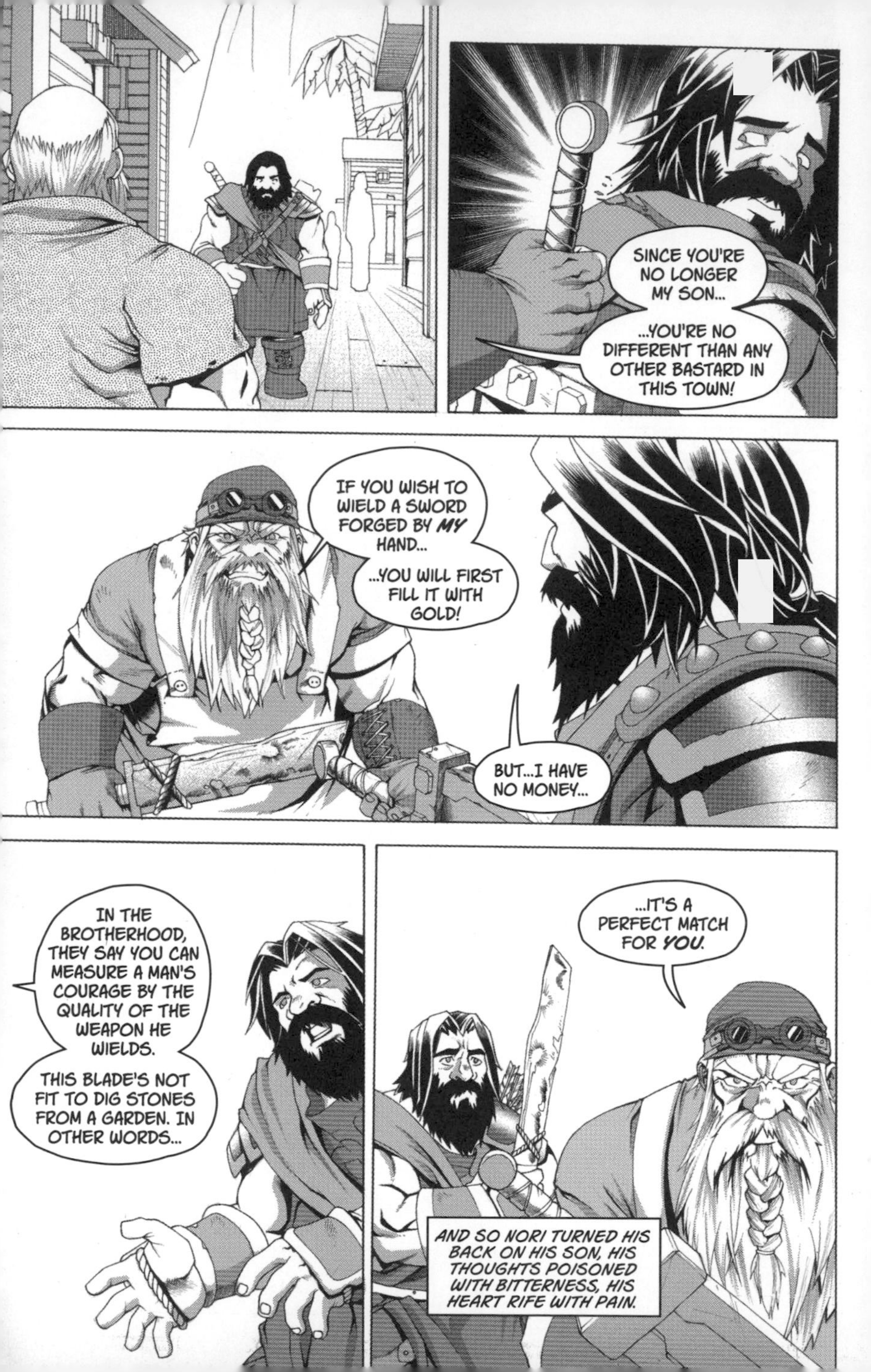
SINCE YOU'RE NO LONGER MY SON...
...YOU'RE NO DIFFERENT THAN ANY OTHER BASTARD IN THIS TOWN!
IF YOU WISH TO WIELD A SWORD FORGED BY *MY* HAND...
...YOU WILL FIRST FILL IT WITH GOLD!
BUT...I HAVE NO MONEY...
IN THE BROTHERHOOD, THEY SAY YOU CAN MEASURE A MAN'S COURAGE BY THE QUALITY OF THE WEAPON HE WIELDS.
THIS BLADE'S NOT FIT TO DIG STONES FROM A GARDEN. IN OTHER WORDS...
...IT'S A PERFECT MATCH FOR *YOU*.
AND SO NORI TURNED HIS BACK ON HIS SON, HIS THOUGHTS POISONED WITH BITTERNESS, HIS HEART RIFE WITH PAIN.

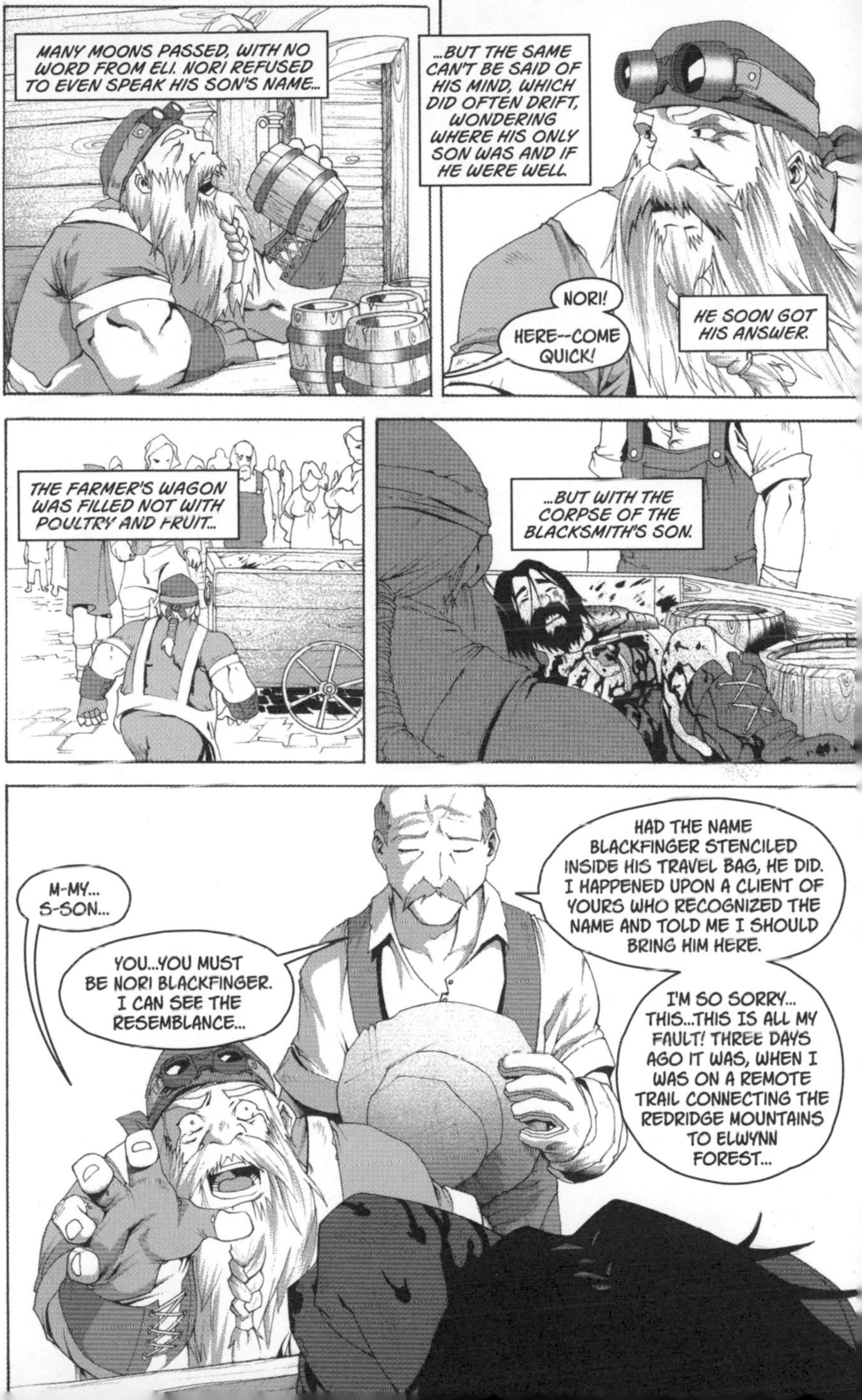
MANY MOONS PASSED, WITH NO WORD FROM ELI. NORI REFUSED TO EVEN SPEAK HIS SON'S NAME...
...BUT THE SAME CAN'T BE SAID OF HIS MIND, WHICH DID OFTEN DRIFT, WONDERING WHERE HIS ONLY SON WAS AND IF HE WERE WELL.
NORI!
HERE--COME QUICK!
HE SOON GOT HIS ANSWER.
THE FARMER'S WAGON WAS FILLED NOT WITH POULTRY AND FRUIT...
...BUT WITH THE CORPSE OF THE BLACKSMITH'S SON.
M-MY... S-SON...
YOU...YOU MUST BE NORI BLACKFINGER. I CAN SEE THE RESEMBLANCE...
HAD THE NAME BLACKFINGER STENCILED INSIDE HIS TRAVEL BAG, HE DID. I HAPPENED UPON A CLIENT OF YOURS WHO RECOGNIZED THE NAME AND TOLD ME I SHOULD BRING HIM HERE.
I'M SO SORRY... THIS...THIS IS ALL MY FAULT! THREE DAYS AGO IT WAS, WHEN I WAS ON A REMOTE TRAIL CONNECTING THE REDRIDGE MOUNTAINS TO ELWYNN FOREST...

I WAS ON MY WAY BACK FROM SELLING MY GRAIN AND PRODUCE AT STORMWIND, AND THIS ROUTE PROMISED TO CUT MY JOURNEY IN HALF.

CURSE ME, I SHOULD HAVE KNOWN BETTER! RUMORS OF BANDITS IN WAIT THERE WERE WHISPERED TOO OFTEN TO BE UNTRUTHS.

THEY CAME OUT OF NOWHERE...

WE'LL BE TAKING THE GOLD, OLD

I TRIED TO FIGHT THEM OFF...

...BUT I WAS NO MATCH.

THEY WERE LED BY NONE OTHER THAN THAT FIENDISH MURDERER—HAVOC!

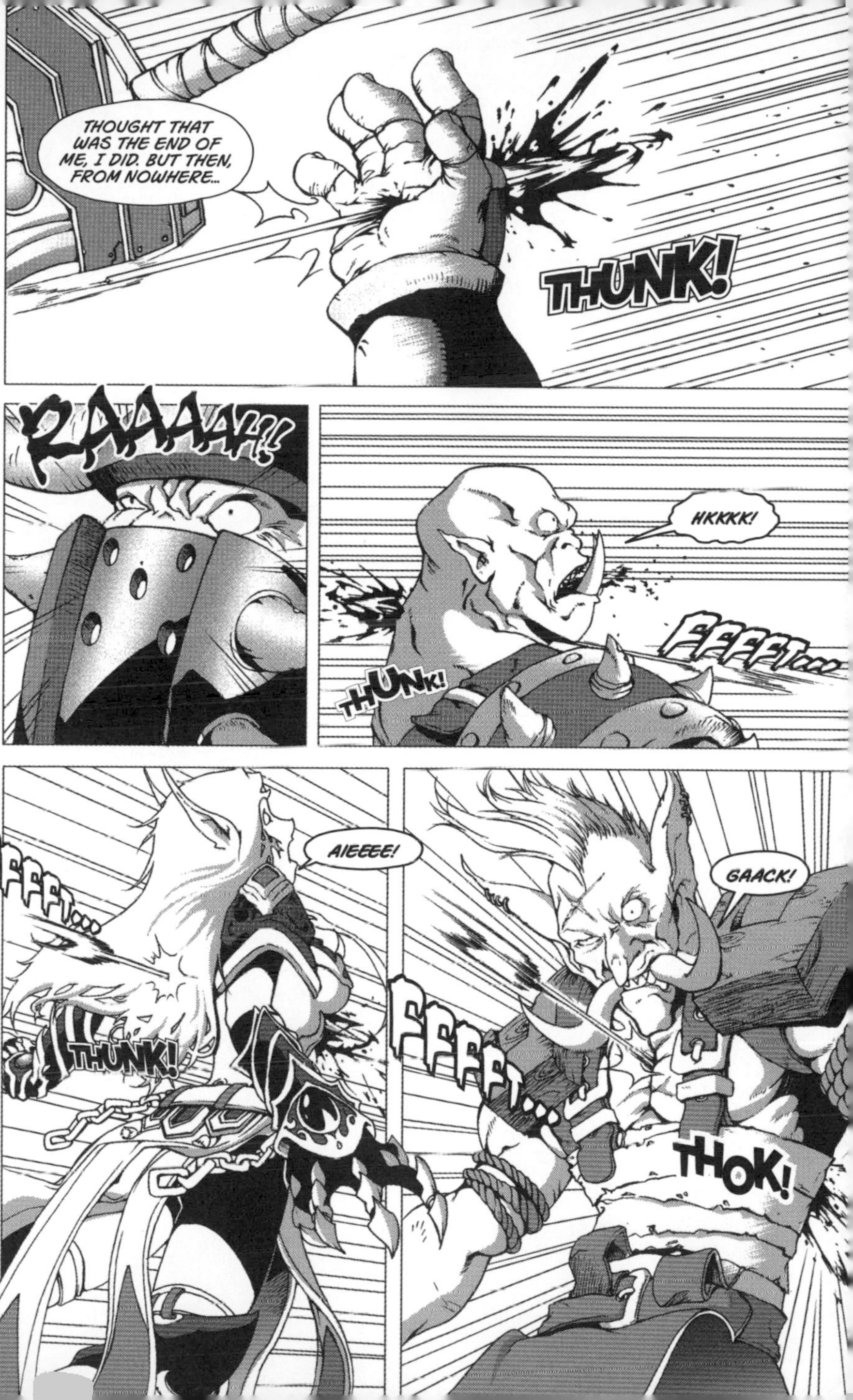
THOUGHT THAT WAS THE END OF ME, I DID. BUT THEN, FROM NOWHERE...
THUNK!
RAAAAH!!
HKKKK!
FFFFT...
THUNK!
FFFFT...
AIEEEE!
THUNK!
GAACK!
FFFFT...
THOK!

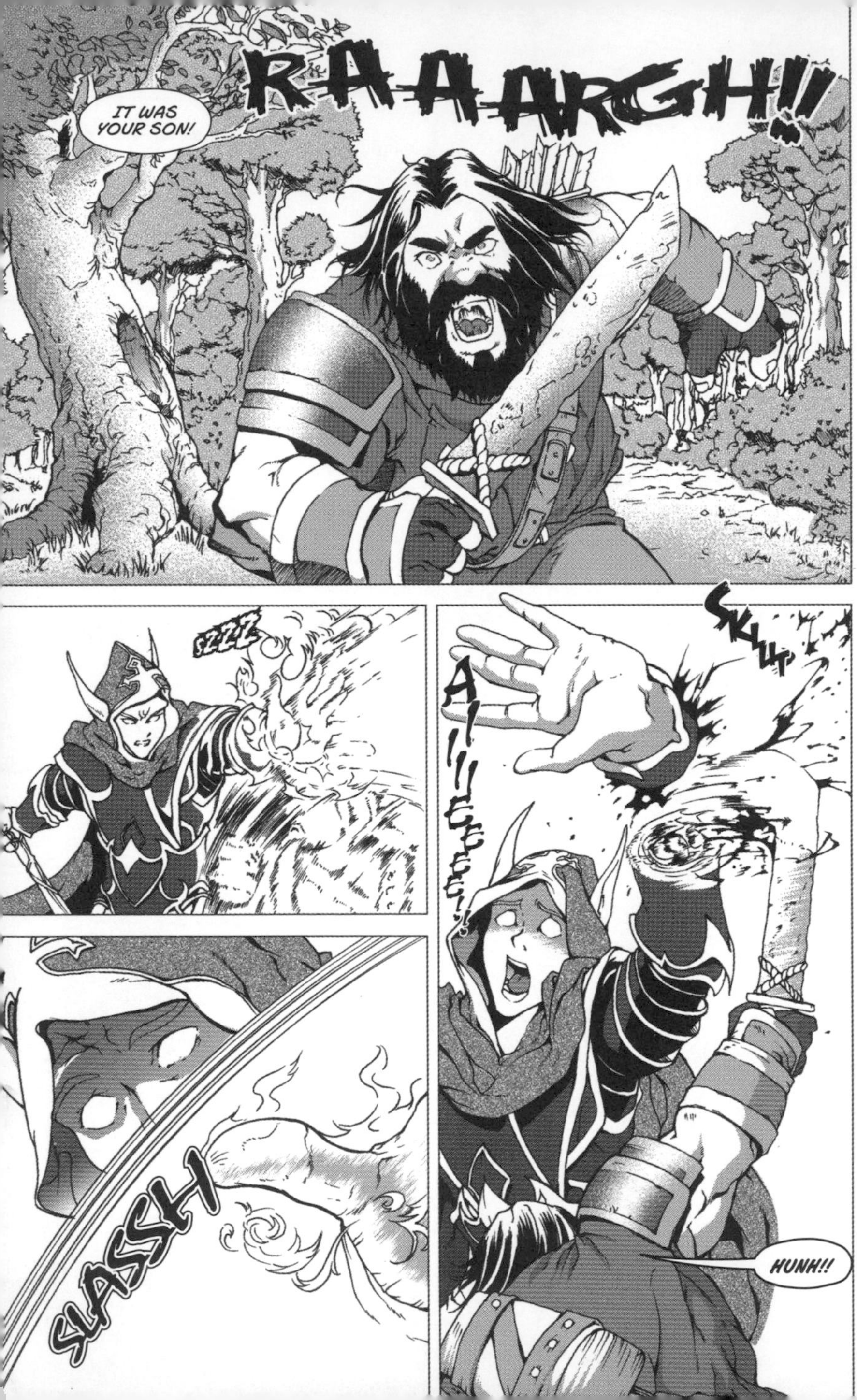
IT WAS YOUR SON!
RAAAARGH!!
SZZZ
SLASH
SKLUP
AIIIEEEE!!
HUNH!!

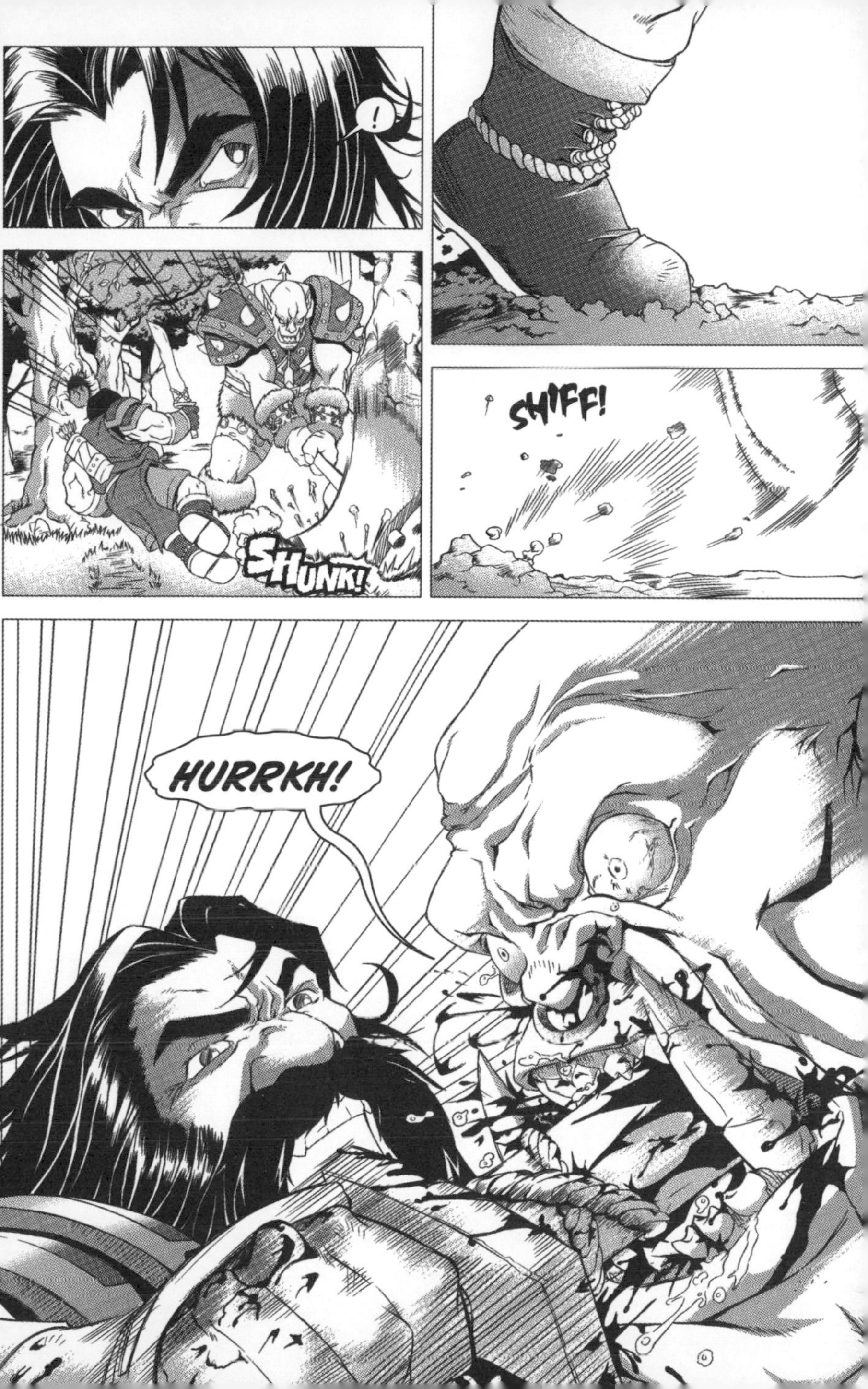
!
SHUNK!
SHIFF!
HURRKH!

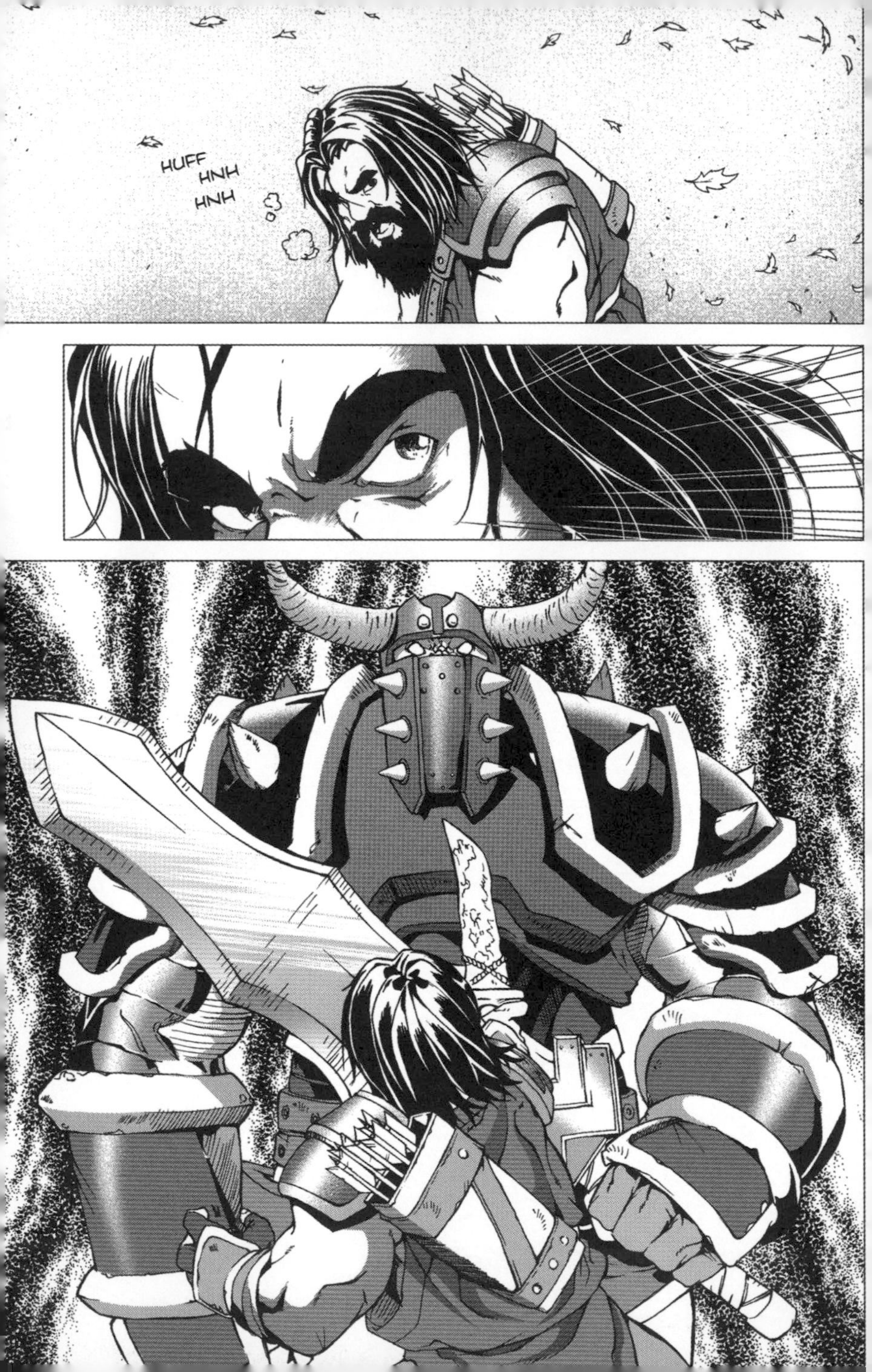
HUFF
HNH
HNH

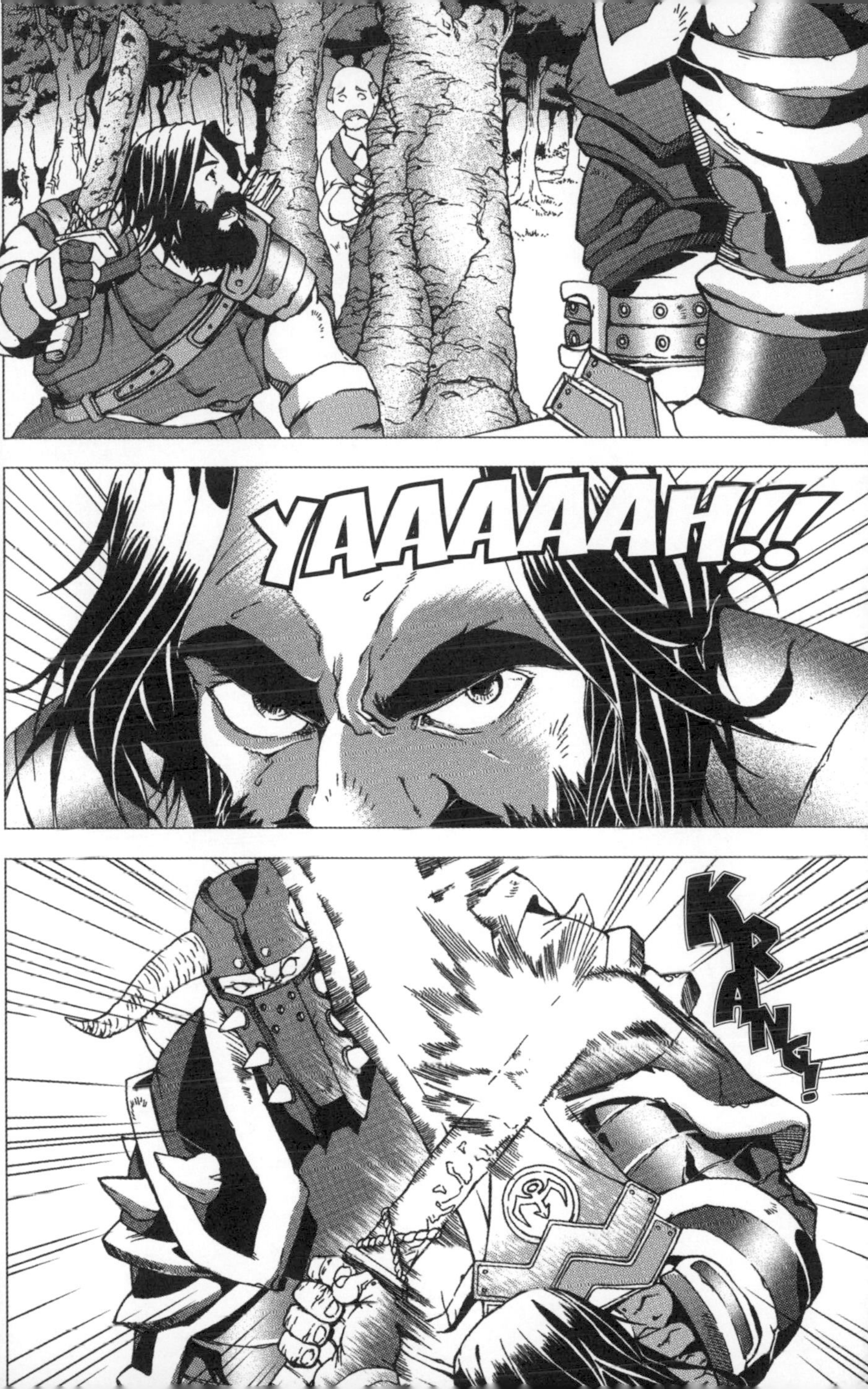
YAAAAAAH!!
KRANG!

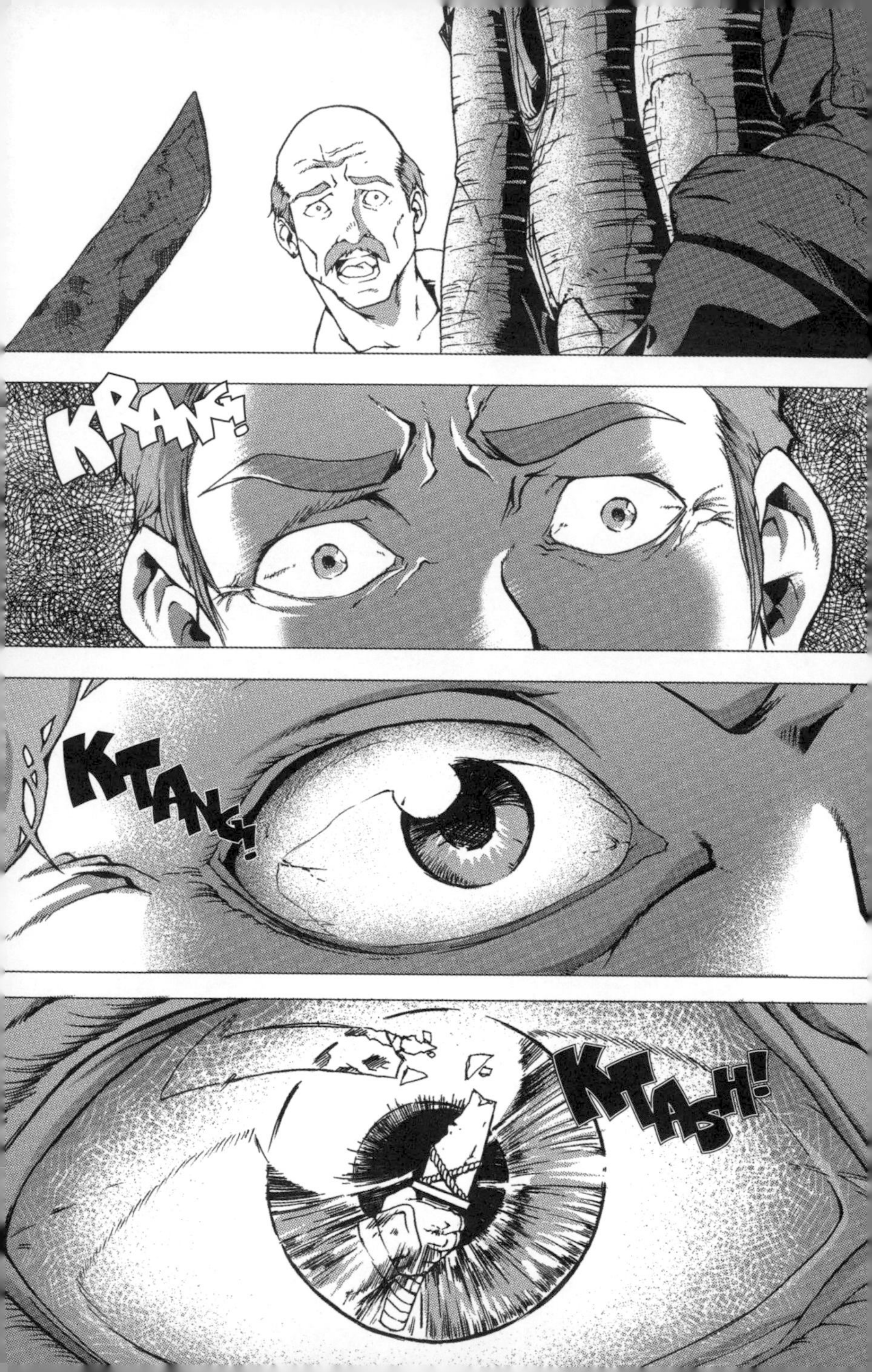
KRANG!
KTANG!
KTASH!

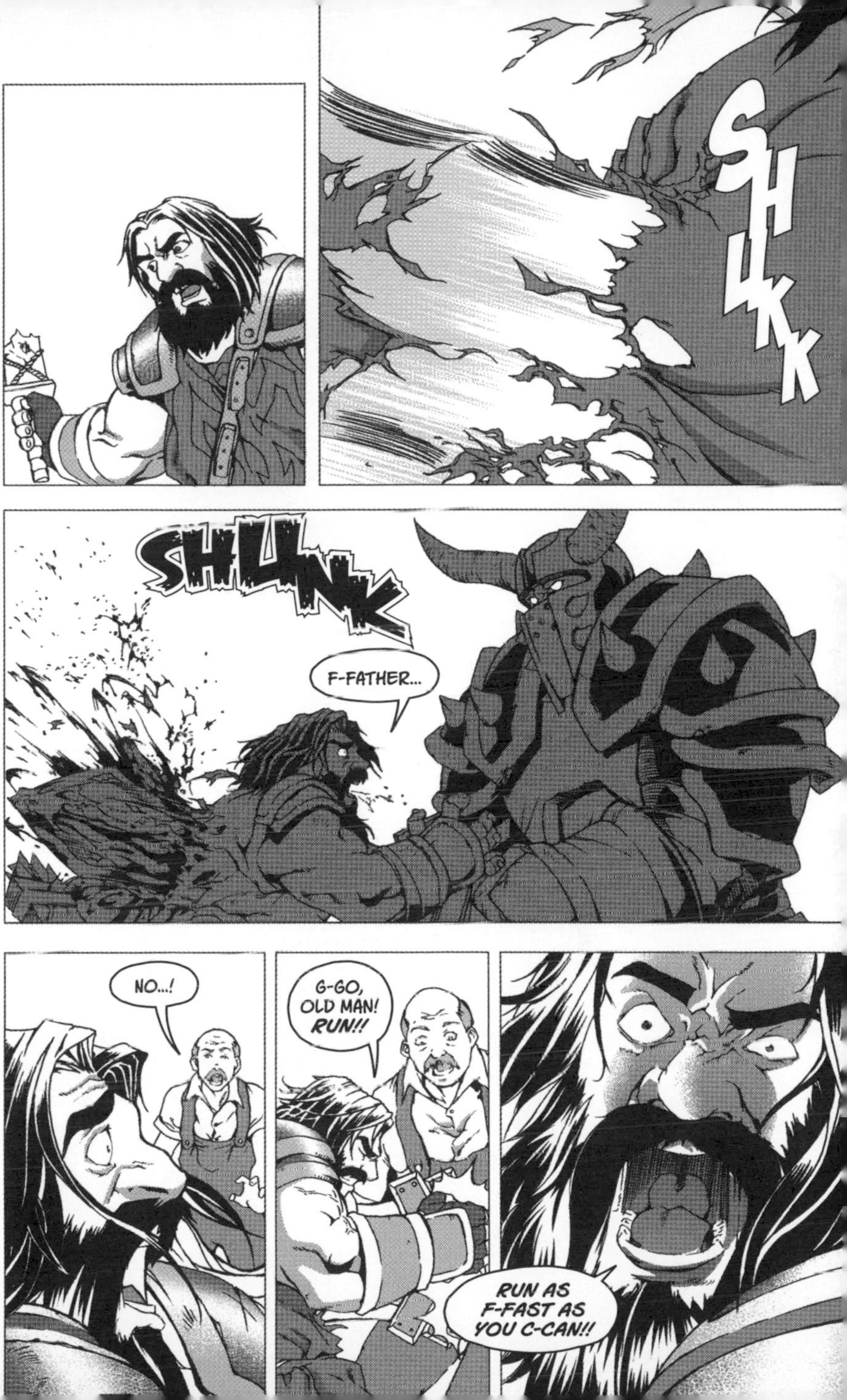
SHUKK
SHUNK
F-FATHER...
NO...!
G-GO, OLD MAN! RUN!!
RUN AS F-FAST AS YOU C-CAN!!

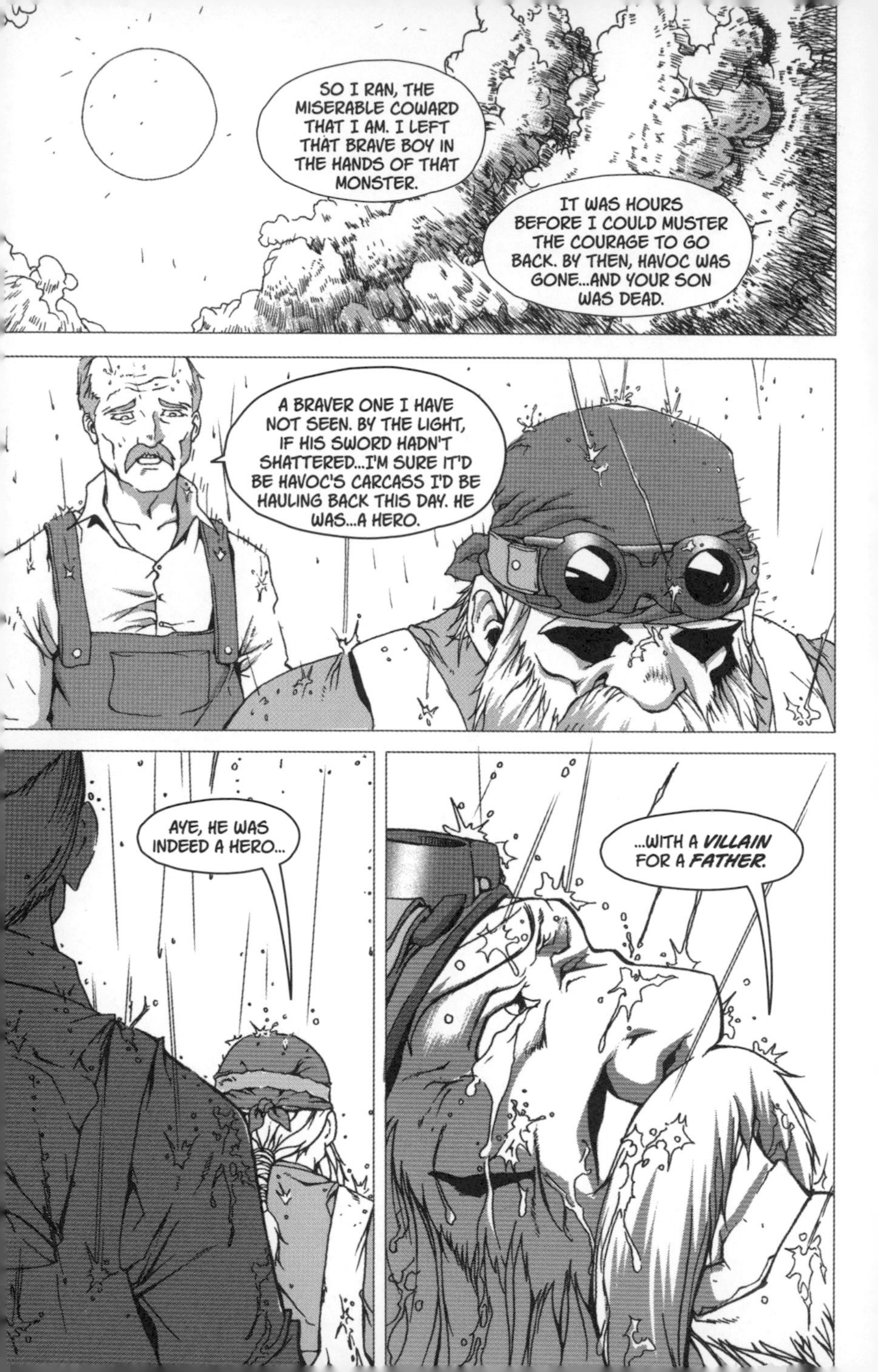

SO I RAN, THE MISERABLE COWARD THAT I AM. I LEFT THAT BRAVE BOY IN THE HANDS OF THAT MONSTER.
IT WAS HOURS BEFORE I COULD MUSTER THE COURAGE TO GO BACK. BY THEN, HAVOC WAS GONE...AND YOUR SON WAS DEAD.
A BRAVER ONE I HAVE NOT SEEN. BY THE LIGHT, IF HIS SWORD HADN'T SHATTERED...I'M SURE IT'D BE HAVOC'S CARCASS I'D BE HAULING BACK THIS DAY. HE WAS...A HERO.
AYE, HE WAS INDEED A HERO...
...WITH A *VILLAIN* FOR A *FATHER.*

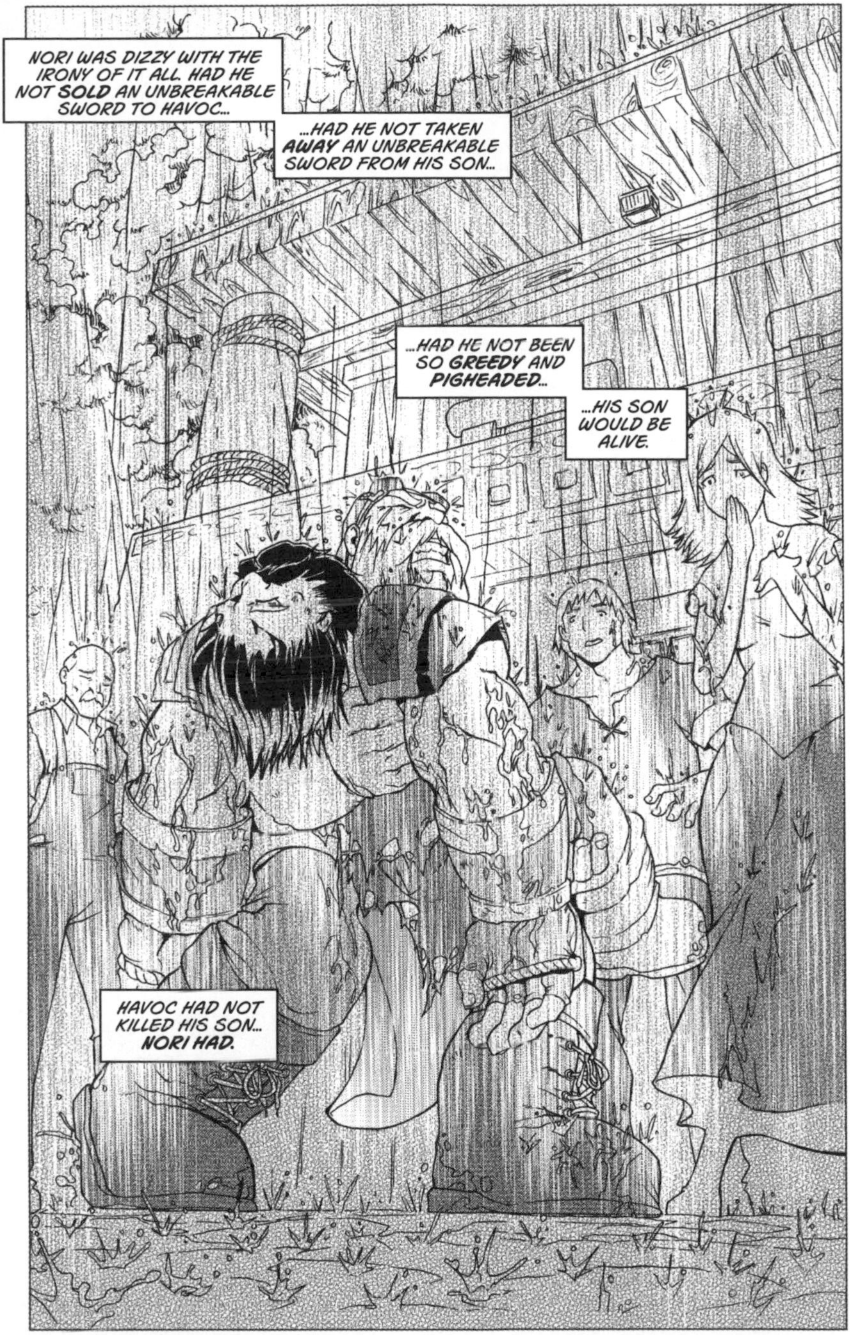
NORI WAS DIZZY WITH THE IRONY OF IT ALL. HAD HE NOT SOLD AN UNBREAKABLE SWORD TO HAVOC...
...HAD HE NOT TAKEN AWAY AN UNBREAKABLE SWORD FROM HIS SON...
...HAD HE NOT BEEN SO GREEDY AND PIGHEADED...
...HIS SON WOULD BE ALIVE.
HAVOC HAD NOT KILLED HIS SON... NORI HAD.

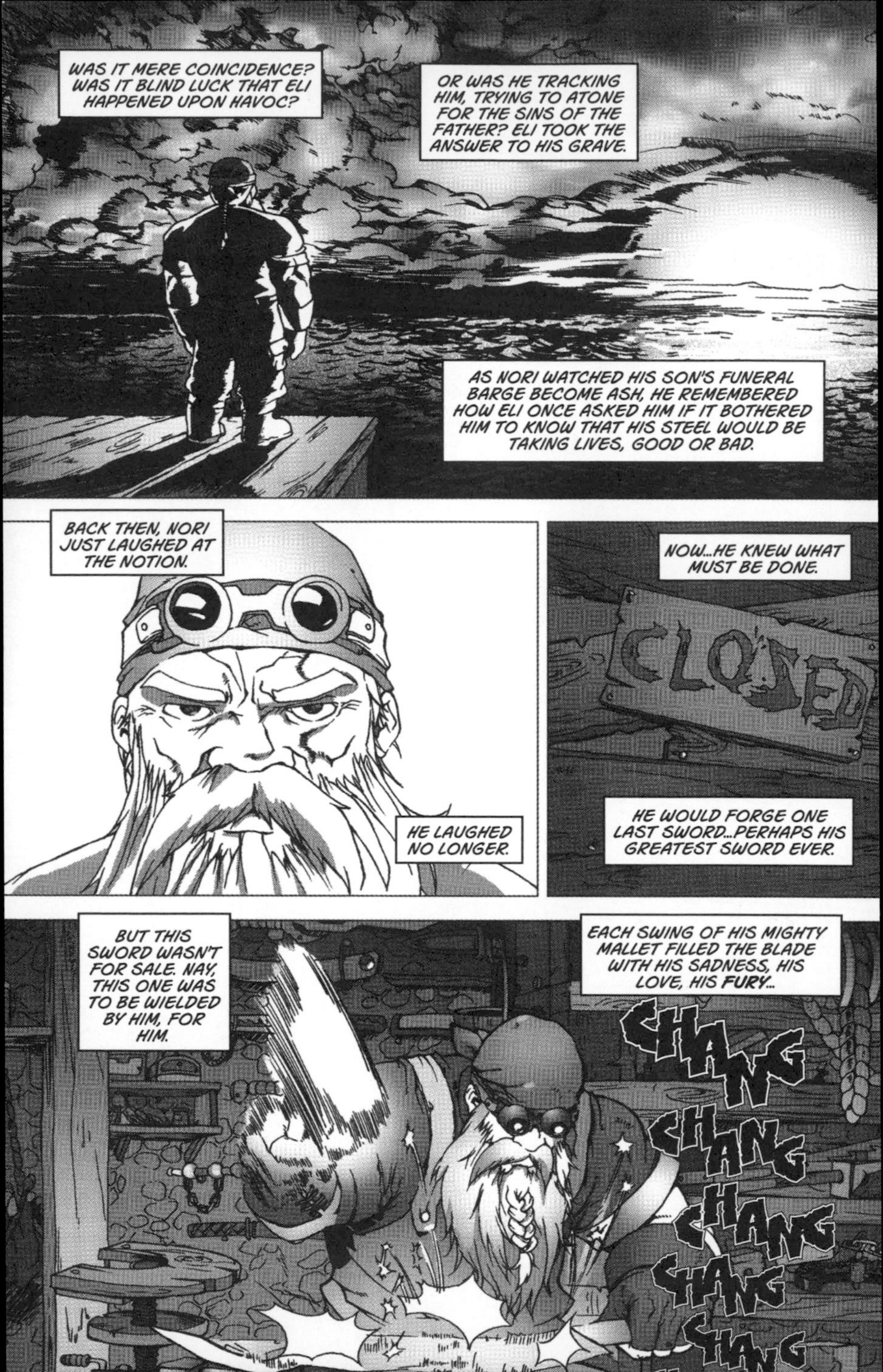
WAS IT MERE COINCIDENCE? WAS IT BLIND LUCK THAT ELI HAPPENED UPON HAVOC?
OR WAS HE TRACKING HIM, TRYING TO ATONE FOR THE SINS OF THE FATHER? ELI TOOK THE ANSWER TO HIS GRAVE.
AS NORI WATCHED HIS SON'S FUNERAL BARGE BECOME ASH, HE REMEMBERED HOW ELI ONCE ASKED HIM IF IT BOTHERED HIM TO KNOW THAT HIS STEEL WOULD BE TAKING LIVES, GOOD OR BAD.
BACK THEN, NORI JUST LAUGHED AT THE NOTION.
HE LAUGHED NO LONGER.
NOW...HE KNEW WHAT MUST BE DONE.
CLOSED
HE WOULD FORGE ONE LAST SWORD...PERHAPS HIS GREATEST SWORD EVER.
BUT THIS SWORD WASN'T FOR SALE. NAY, THIS ONE WAS TO BE WIELDED BY HIM, FOR HIM.
EACH SWING OF HIS MIGHTY MALLET FILLED THE BLADE WITH HIS SADNESS, HIS LOVE, HIS FURY...
CHANG
CHANG
CHANG
CHANG
CHANG

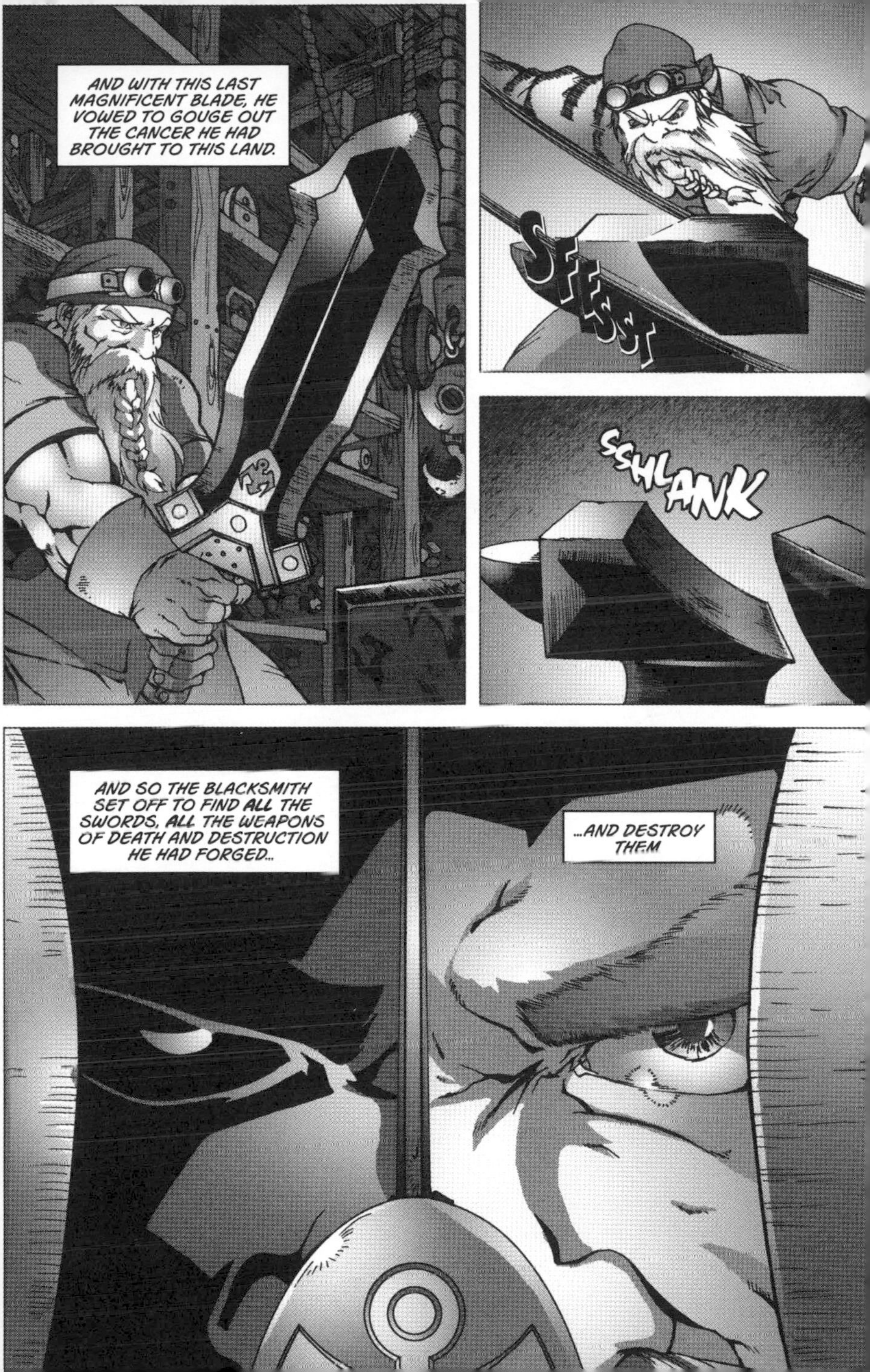
AND WITH THIS LAST MAGNIFICENT BLADE, HE VOWED TO GOUGE OUT THE CANCER HE HAD BROUGHT TO THIS LAND.
SFESST
SSHLANK
AND SO THE BLACKSMITH SET OFF TO FIND ALL THE SWORDS, ALL THE WEAPONS OF DEATH AND DESTRUCTION HE HAD FORGED...
...AND DESTROY THEM

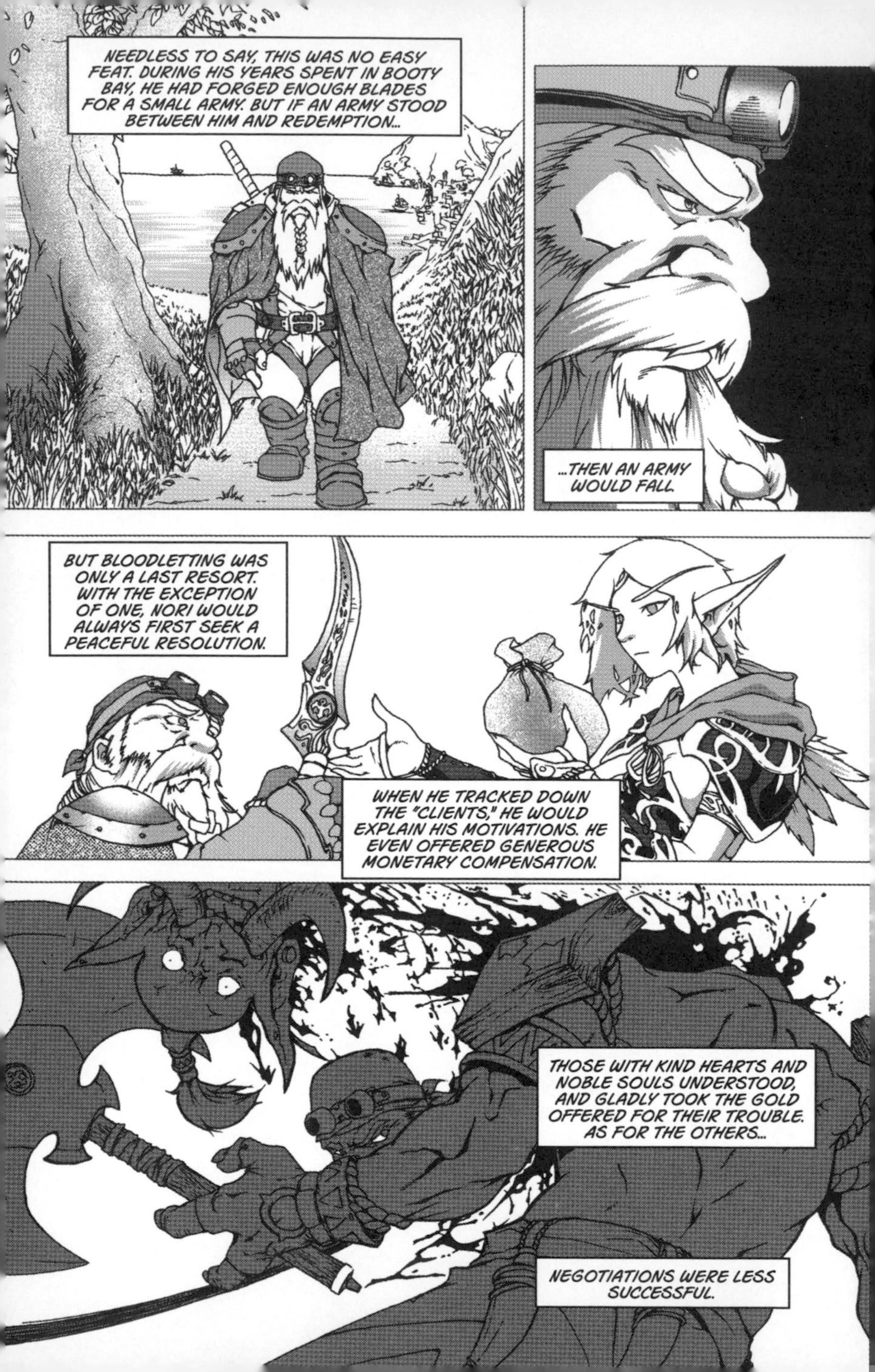
NEEDLESS TO SAY, THIS WAS NO EASY FEAT. DURING HIS YEARS SPENT IN BOOTY BAY, HE HAD FORGED ENOUGH BLADES FOR A SMALL ARMY. BUT IF AN ARMY STOOD BETWEEN HIM AND REDEMPTION...
...THEN AN ARMY WOULD FALL.
BUT BLOODLETTING WAS ONLY A LAST RESORT. WITH THE EXCEPTION OF ONE, NORI WOULD ALWAYS FIRST SEEK A PEACEFUL RESOLUTION.
WHEN HE TRACKED DOWN THE "CLIENTS," HE WOULD EXPLAIN HIS MOTIVATIONS. HE EVEN OFFERED GENEROUS MONETARY COMPENSATION.
THOSE WITH KIND HEARTS AND NOBLE SOULS UNDERSTOOD, AND GLADLY TOOK THE GOLD OFFERED FOR THEIR TROUBLE. AS FOR THE OTHERS...
NEGOTIATIONS WERE LESS SUCCESSFUL.

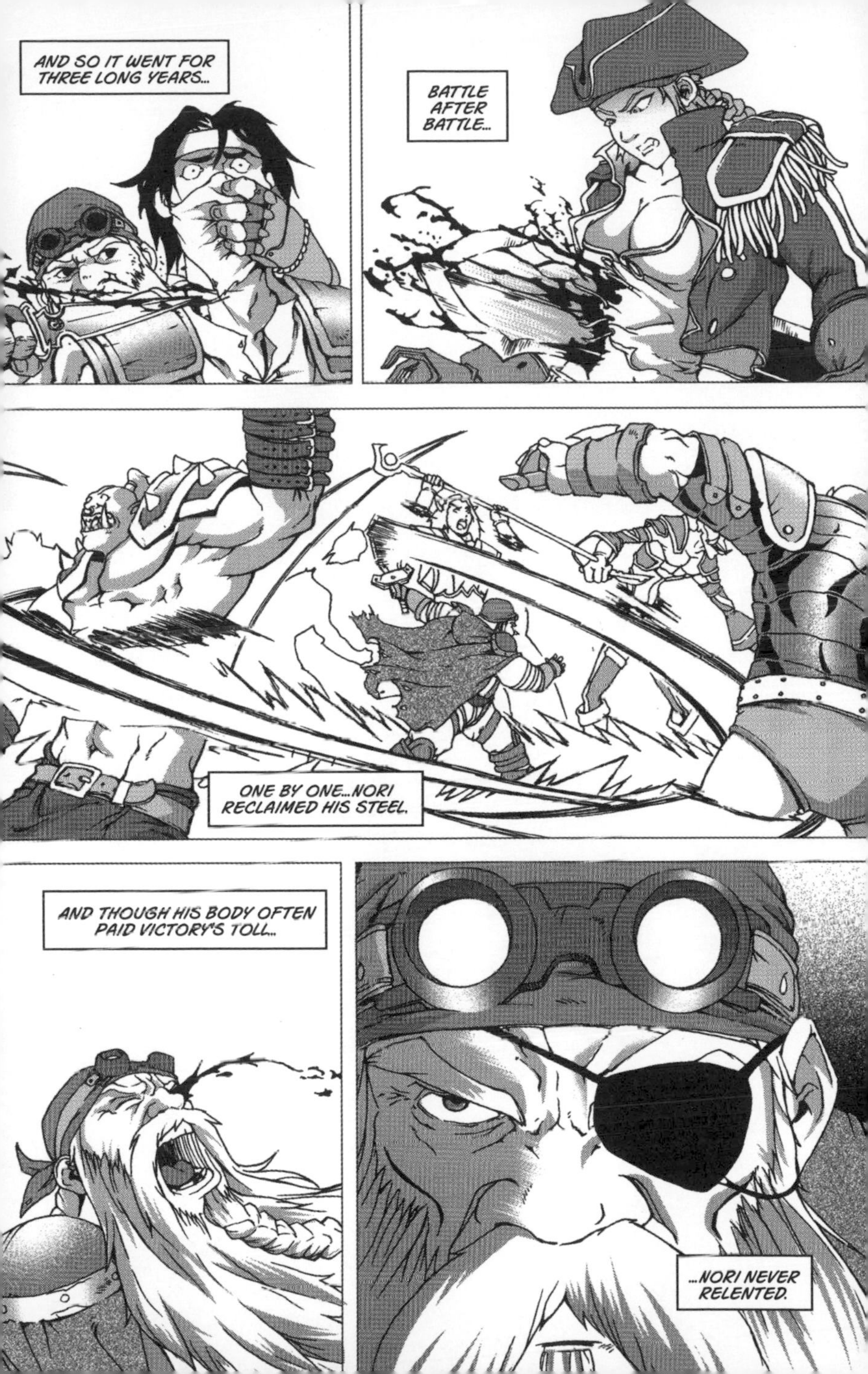
AND SO IT WENT FOR THREE LONG YEARS...
BATTLE AFTER BATTLE...
ONE BY ONE...NORI RECLAIMED HIS STEEL.
AND THOUGH HIS BODY OFTEN PAID VICTORY'S TOLL...
...NORI NEVER RELENTED.

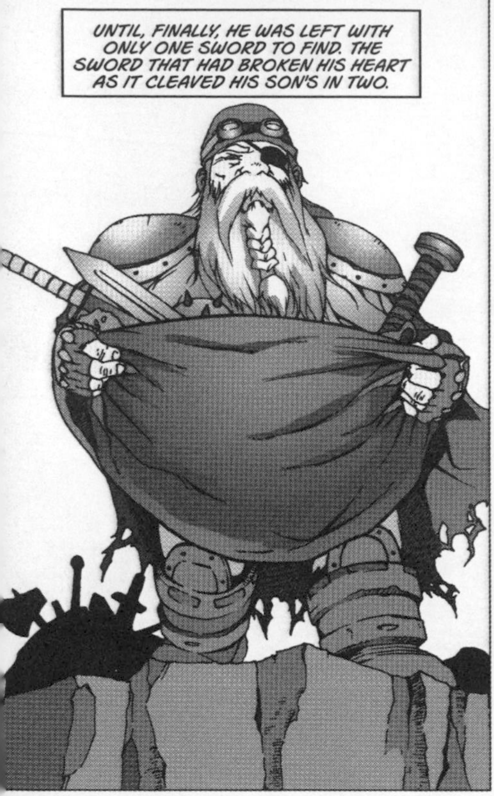
UNTIL, FINALLY, HE WAS LEFT WITH ONLY ONE SWORD TO FIND. THE SWORD THAT HAD BROKEN HIS HEART AS IT CLEAVED HIS SON'S IN TWO.

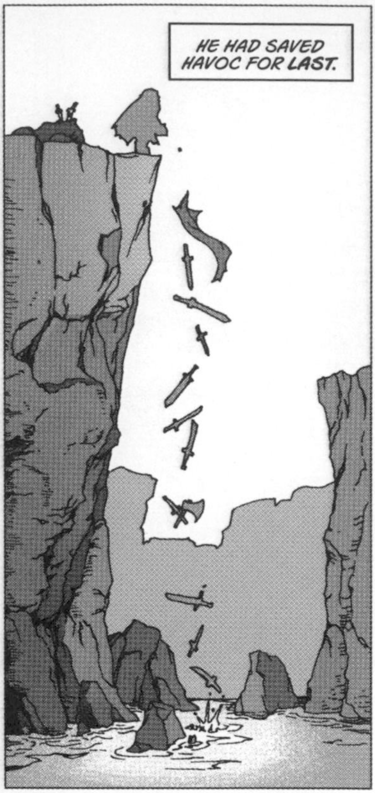
HE HAD SAVED HAVOC FOR **LAST.**

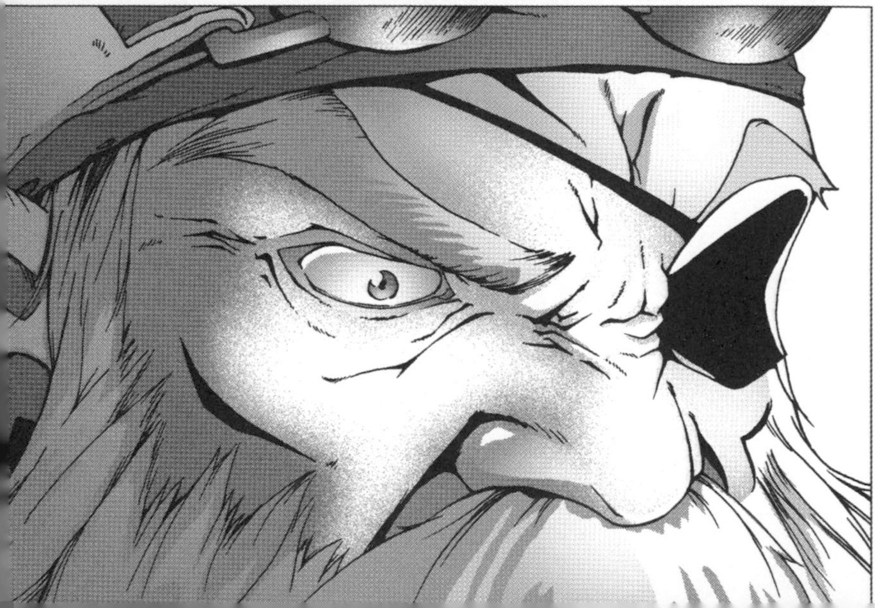

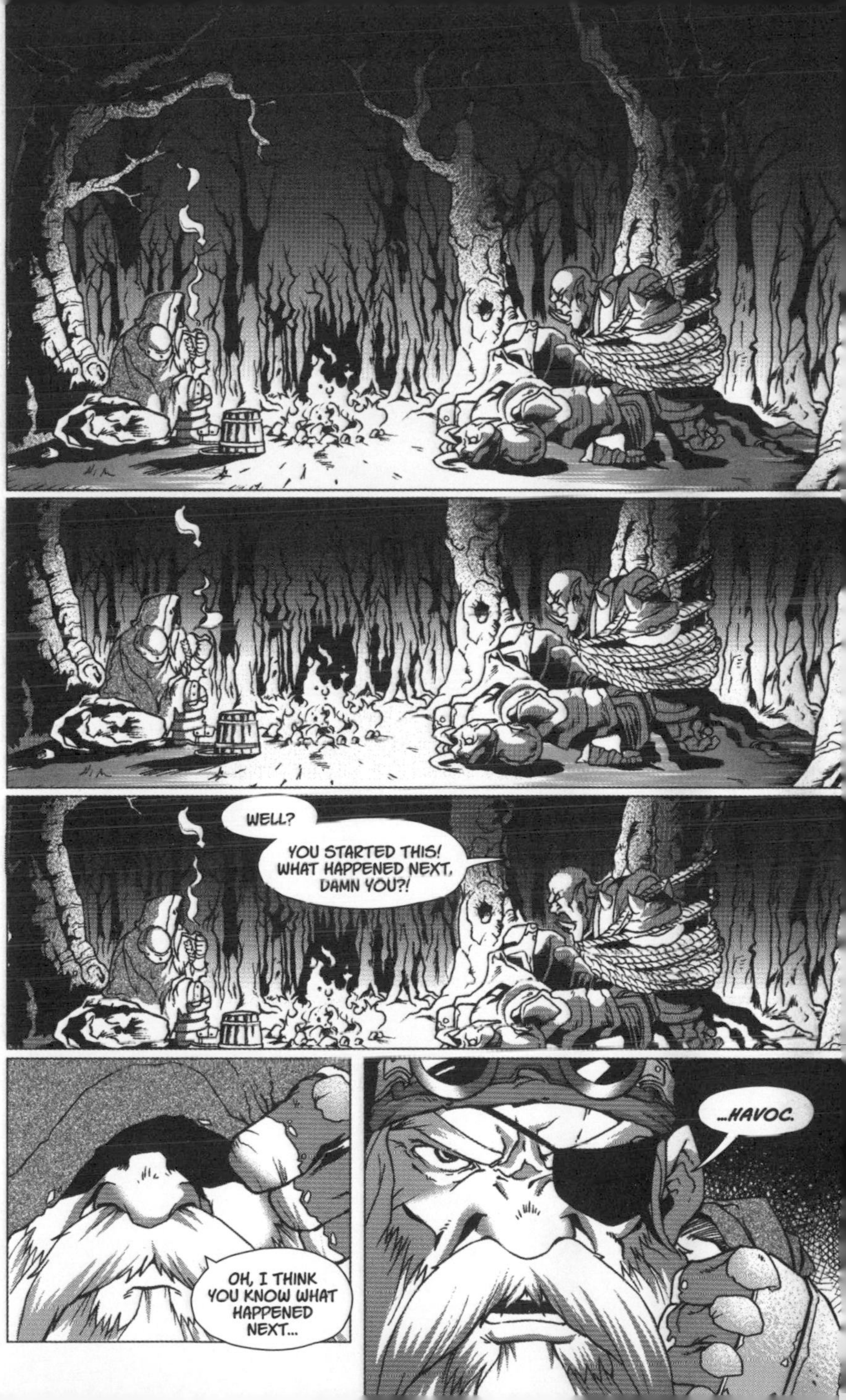
WELL?
YOU STARTED THIS! WHAT HAPPENED NEXT, DAMN YOU?!
OH, I THINK YOU KNOW WHAT HAPPENED NEXT...
...HAVOC.

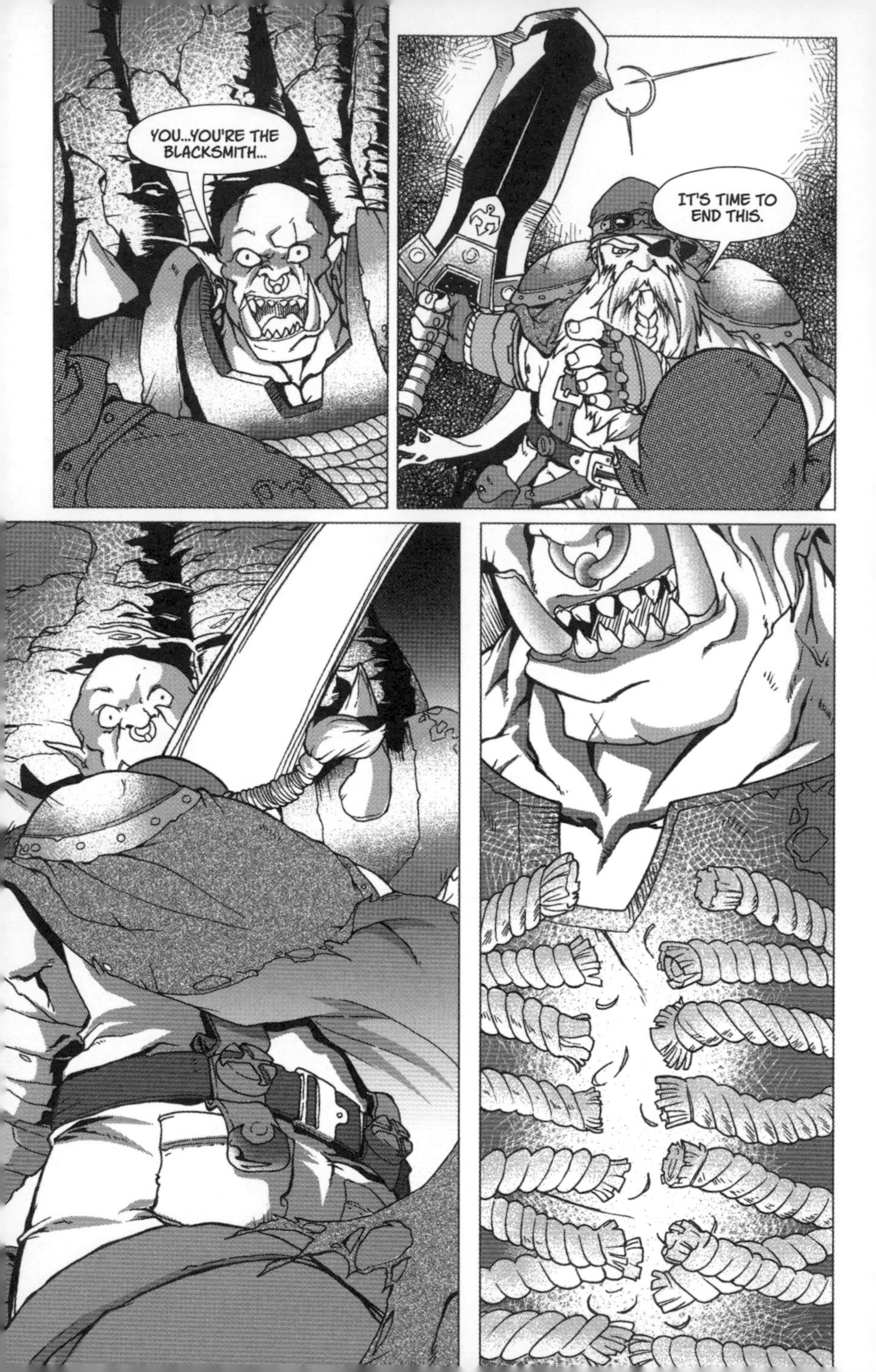
YOU...YOU'RE THE BLACKSMITH...
IT'S TIME TO END THIS.

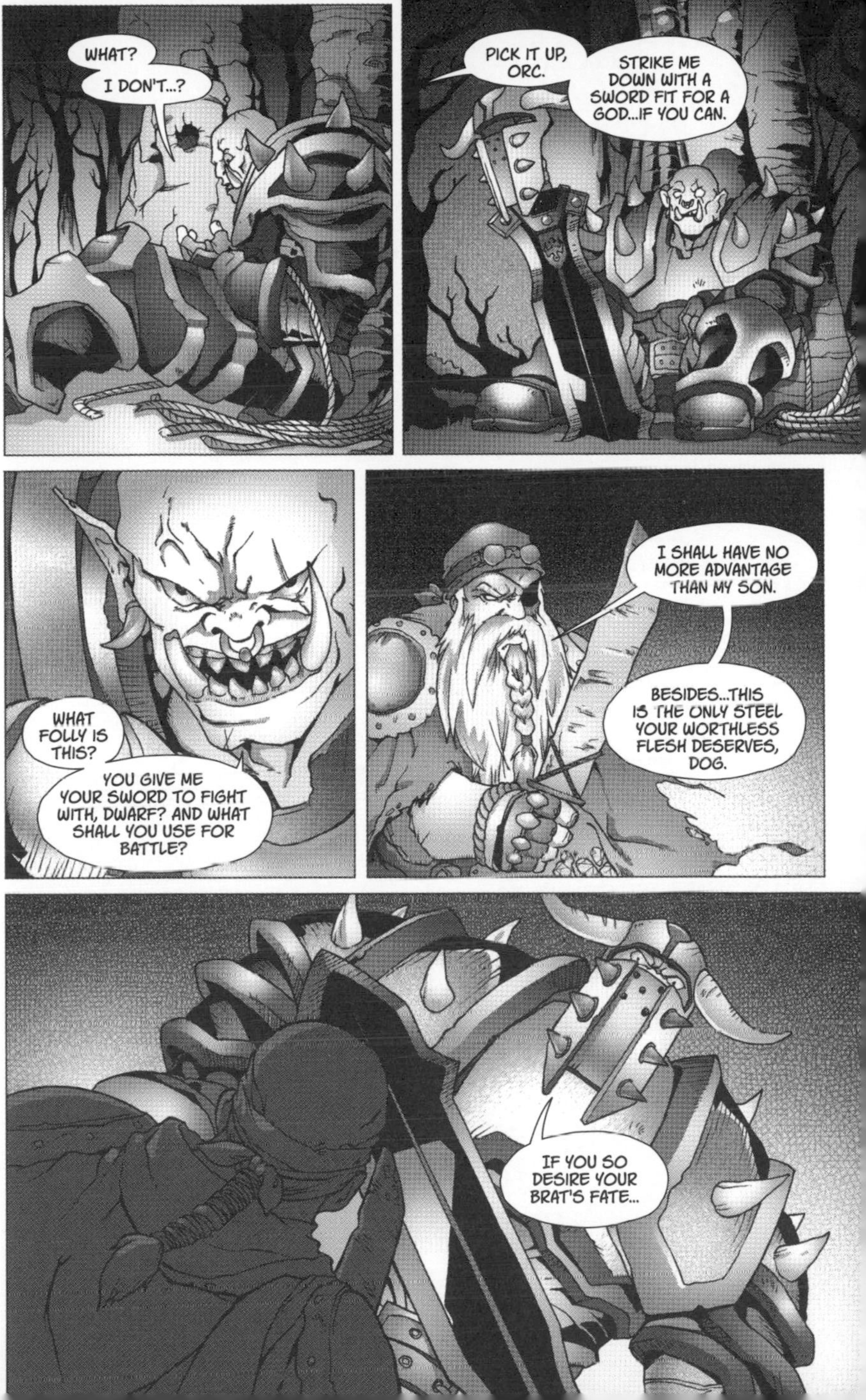
WHAT?
I DON'T...?
PICK IT UP, ORC.
STRIKE ME DOWN WITH A SWORD FIT FOR A GOD...IF YOU CAN.
WHAT FOLLY IS THIS?
YOU GIVE ME YOUR SWORD TO FIGHT WITH, DWARF? AND WHAT SHALL YOU USE FOR BATTLE?
I SHALL HAVE NO MORE ADVANTAGE THAN MY SON.
BESIDES...THIS IS THE ONLY STEEL YOUR WORTHLESS FLESH DESERVES, DOG.
IF YOU SO DESIRE YOUR BRAT'S FATE...

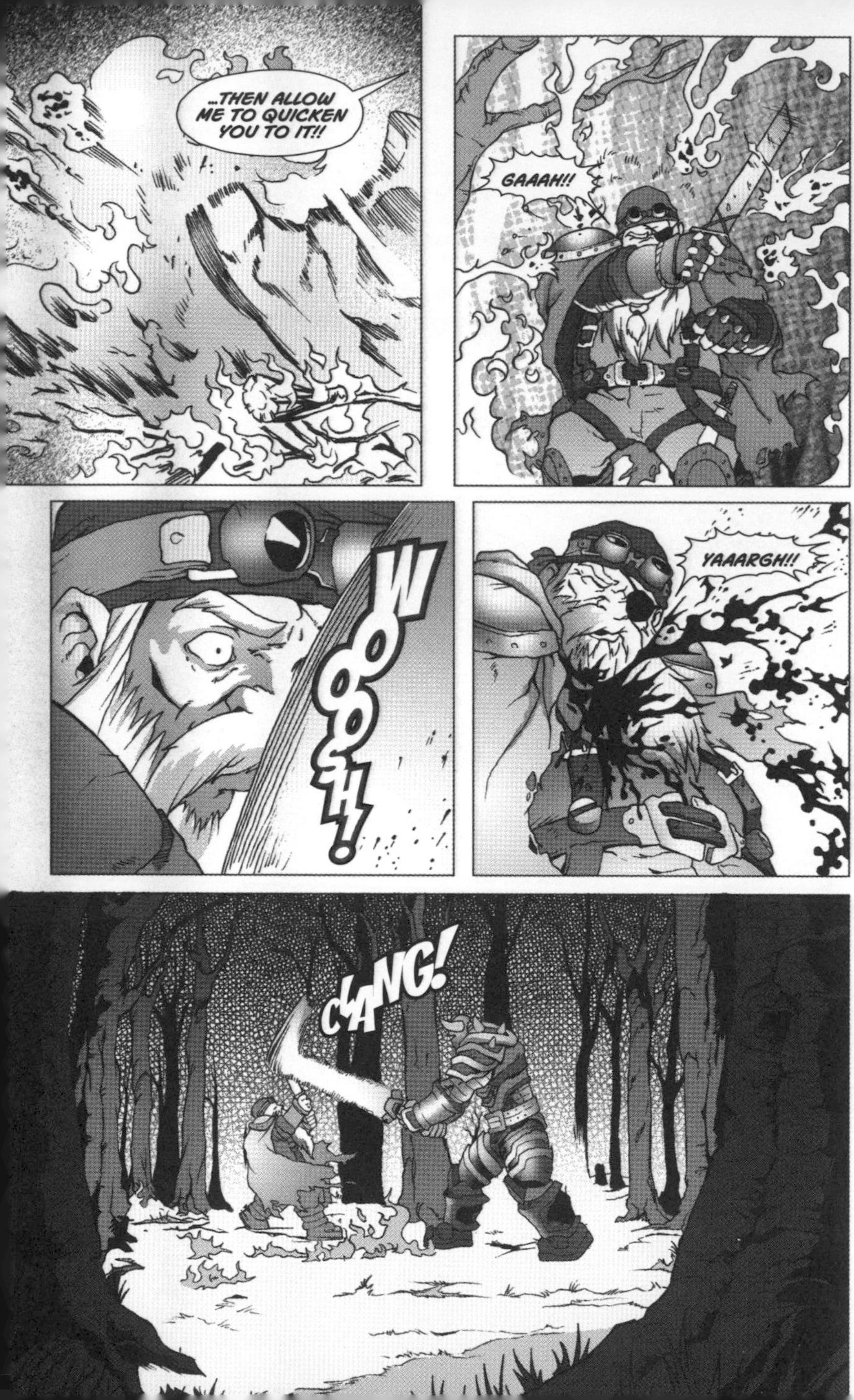
...THEN ALLOW ME TO QUICKEN YOU TO IT!!
GAAAH!!
WOOOOSH!
YAAARGH!!
CLANG!

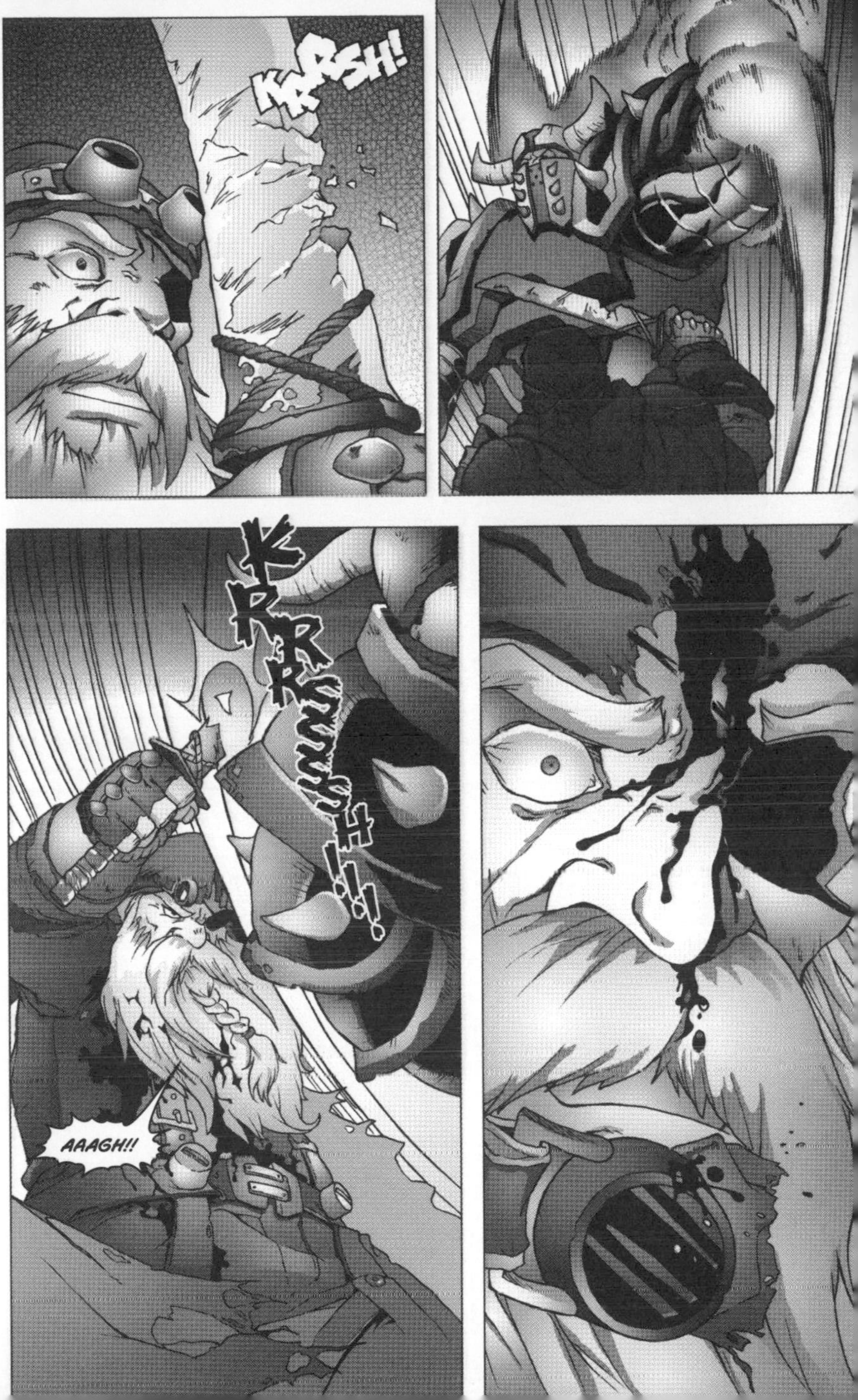
KRRSH!
KRRRSSSH!!!
AAAGH!!

YOU'VE BEEN TRACKING ME ALL THIS TIME, DREAMING OF THIS MOMENT...AND *THIS* IS THE BEST YOU CAN MUSTER?

PATHETIC.

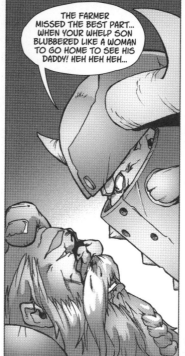

THE FARMER MISSED THE BEST PART... WHEN YOUR WHELP SON BLUBBERED LIKE A WOMAN TO GO HOME TO SEE HIS DADDY! HEH HEH HEH...

UNH?!

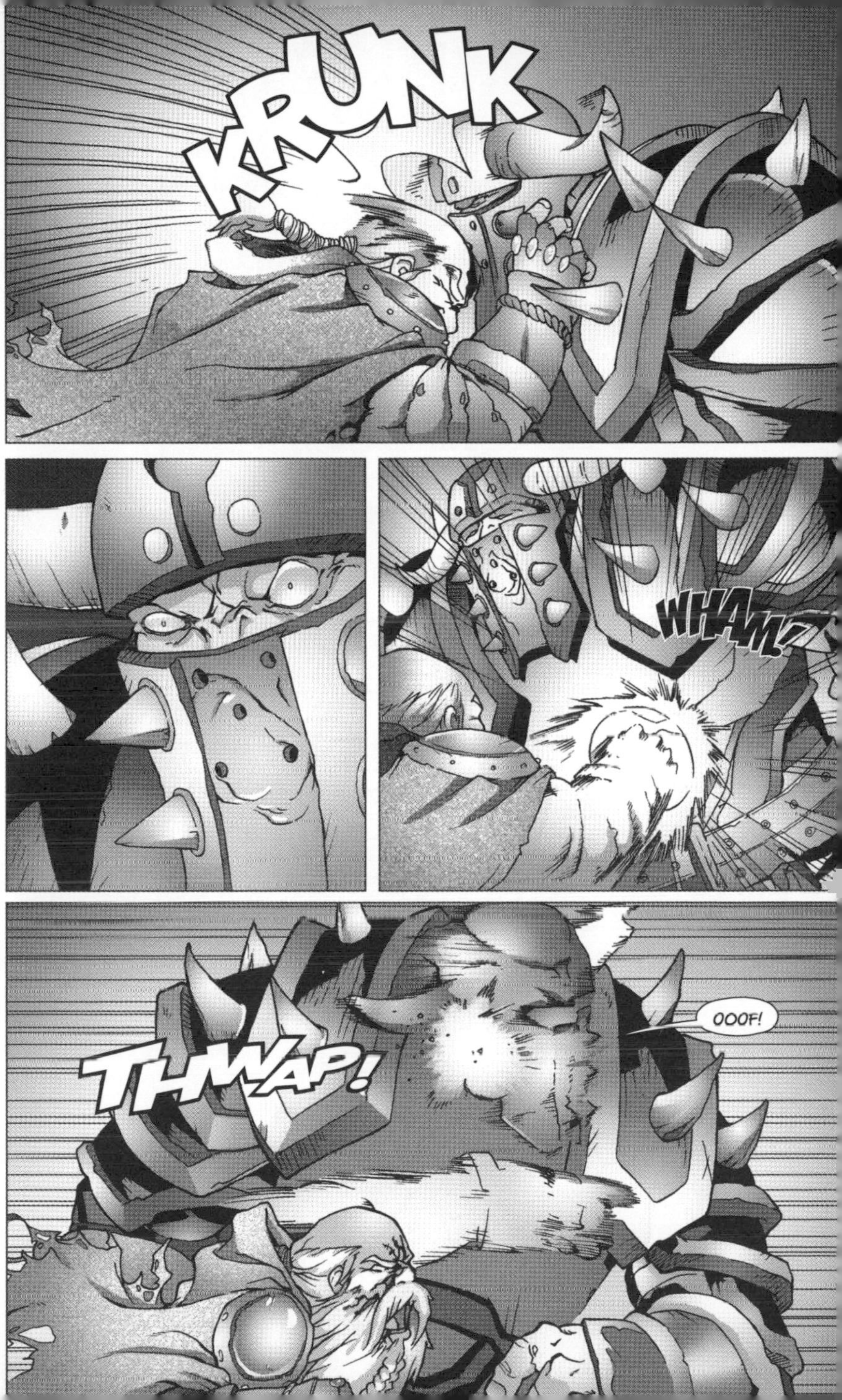
KRUNK
WHAM!
THWAP!
OOOF!

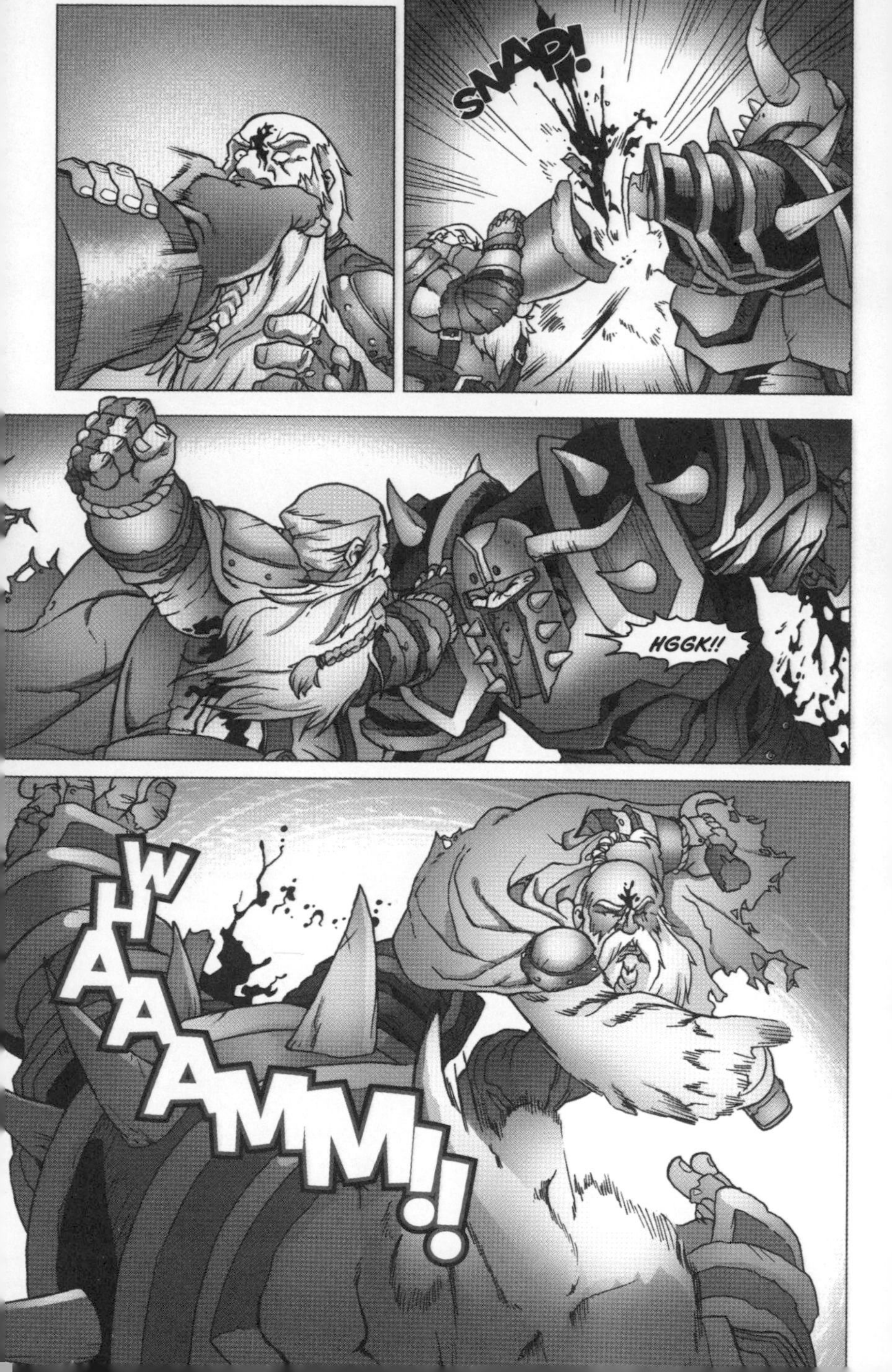
SNAP!
HGGK!!
WHAAAMMM!!

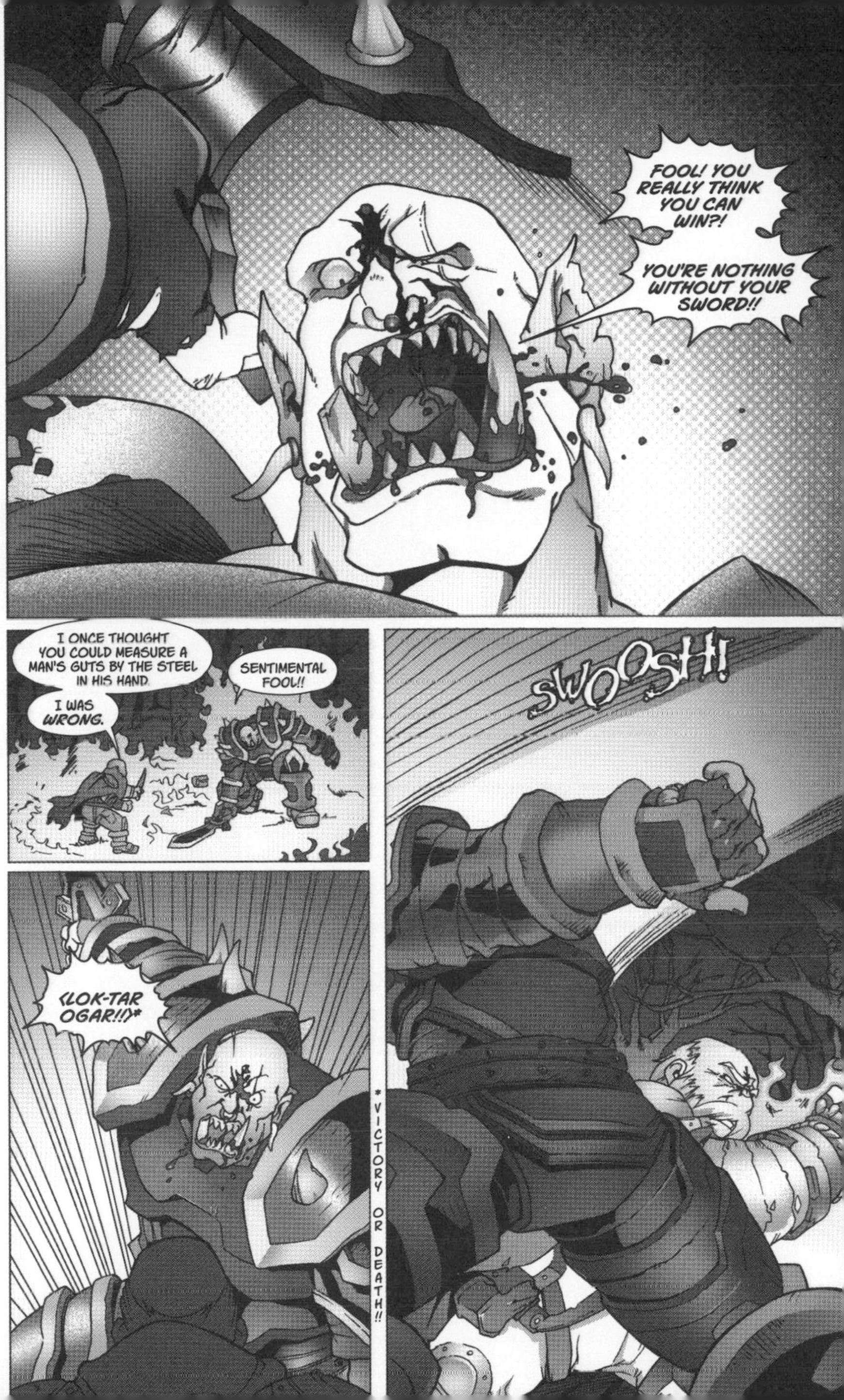
FOOL! YOU REALLY THINK YOU CAN WIN?!
YOU'RE NOTHING WITHOUT YOUR SWORD!!
I ONCE THOUGHT YOU COULD MEASURE A MAN'S GUTS BY THE STEEL IN HIS HAND.
I WAS WRONG.
SENTIMENTAL FOOL!!
<LOK-TAR OGAR!!>*
* VICTORY OR DEATH!!
SWOOSH!

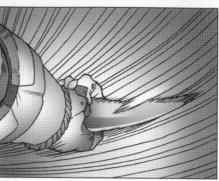

SHH-THUNK!

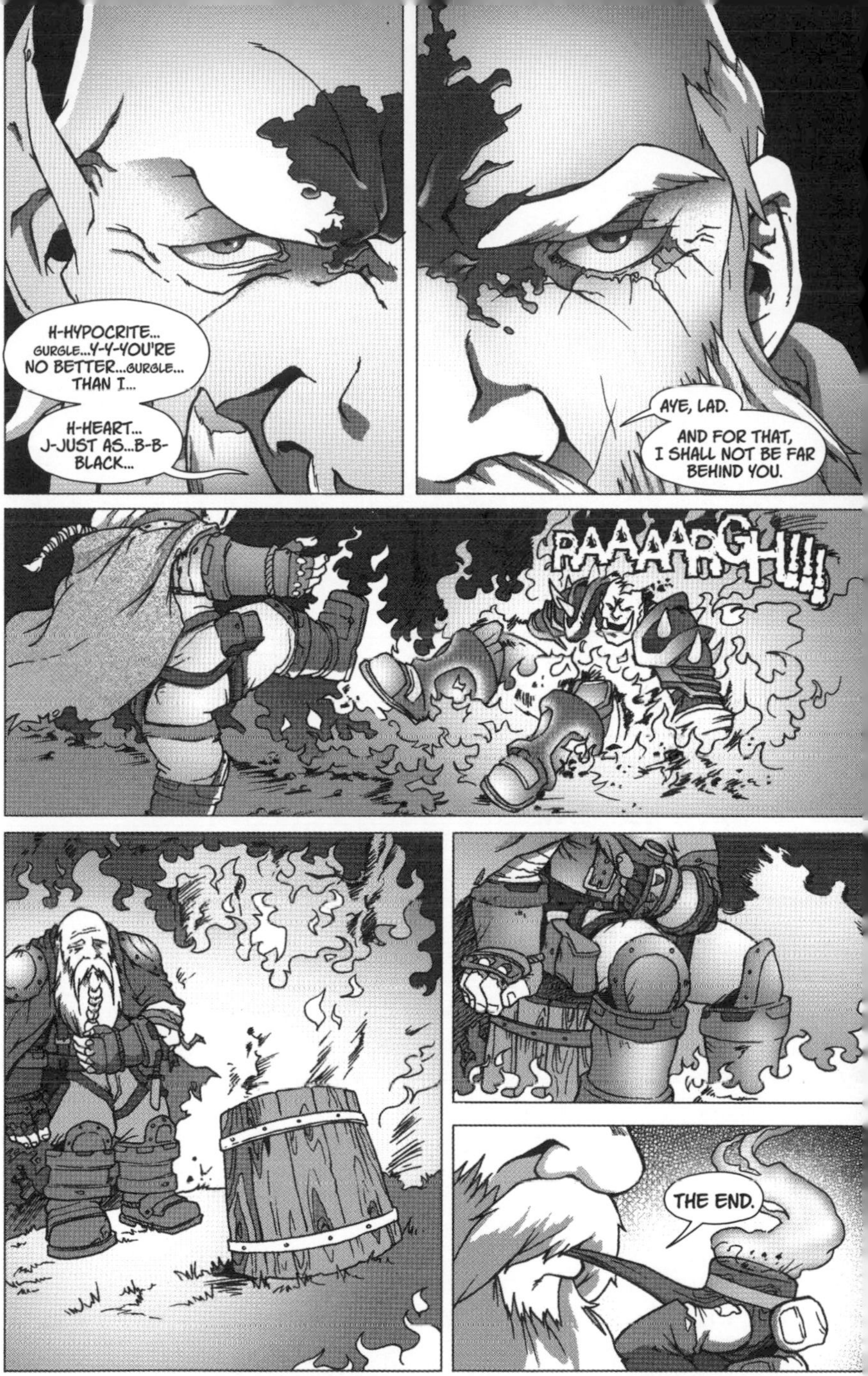
H-HYPOCRITE... GURGLE...Y-Y-YOU'RE NO BETTER...GURGLE... THAN I...
H-HEART... J-JUST AS...B-B-BLACK...
AYE, LAD.
AND FOR THAT, I SHALL NOT BE FAR BEHIND YOU.
RAAAARGH!!!
THE END.

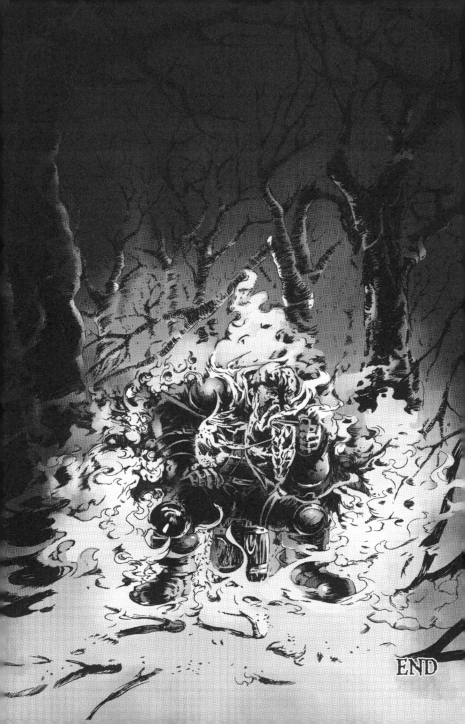

END